A CHARACTER OF THE TRIMMER

SIR GEORGE SAVILE
MARQUIS OF HALIFAX

After the portrait in the possession of His Grace the Duke of Devonshire

A *CHARACTER* OF THE TRIMMER

Being a Short Life *of the* First Marquis *of* Halifax

BY

H. C. FOXCROFT

CAMBRIDGE

At The University Press

1946

CAMBRIDGE
UNIVERSITY PRESS

University Printing House, Cambridge CB2 8BS, United Kingdom

Cambridge University Press is part of the University of Cambridge.

It furthers the University's mission by disseminating knowledge in the pursuit of education, learning and research at the highest international levels of excellence.

www.cambridge.org
Information on this title: www.cambridge.org/9781107455641

First published 1946
First paperback edition 2014

A catalogue record for this publication is available from the British Library

ISBN 978-1-107-45564-1 Paperback

FRATRI DILECTO

J. T. F.

MDCCCLXXIX—MDCCCCX

IN STUDIIS HISTORICIS VERSATO

MUNERIBUS OFFICII SUI PRAECLARE FUNCTO

APUD NILI RIPAS

MELIORA NI FATA VETUISSENT POLLICITO

QUI NATU ME MINOR

MAJOR EHEU MORTE SUA

DESIDERIUM AMICIS RELIQUIT INEXPLEBILE

HOC OPUS SENECTUTIS MEAE

TANDEM TRIBUI.

Contents

Preface

The origin of the present work seems to demand some preliminary explanation.

In the year 1897 there appeared a *Life and Works of the first Marquis of Halifax*—the earliest and, up to now, sole attempt of this nature—by the present author. Though the work of a then young and quite inexperienced writer, it had the good fortune to attract and retain the attention of experts in the period in question. Its length, however, and a multiplicity—it may be feared a superfluity—of footnotes acted as an almost complete deterrent to the general reader. It has long been the wish of its author to produce a less ponderous biography, which might arouse a wider interest in the personality and career of this great Englishman.

As the present work is in the main a condensation of the original *Life*, it has been found possible to dispense altogether with references, save where fresh evidence is concerned; and such references have been relegated to the end of the volume.

For the benefit of readers who are not acquainted with the original work, it is here only necessary to state, in a few words, that the personal papers of the first Marquis passed into the hands of his granddaughters, co-heiresses of his son, the second and last Marquis. These included as their most important item two copies of a MS. containing Memoirs of his own Life, by the Marquis himself. Of these one copy is believed to have been burnt by his old friend, Lord Nottingham, the father-in-law of the second Marquis. The second was, it is said, destroyed in the eighteenth century, by one of his granddaughters, at the instance of the poet Pope, who considered them too critical of his own (the Roman Catholic) Church.

The remaining papers eventually passed by marriage into the custody of two great families, Devonshire and Spenser; whose representatives in 1897 most courteously and generously placed them at the disposal of the present writer. Permission to use the

Coventry papers at Longleat was, in like manner, granted by the then Marquis of Bath.

In the present instance the writer is greatly indebted to Mr de Beer, who most kindly provided a complete list of the more recent works on the period, invaluable to one whose seventeenth-century researches have been unavoidably pretermitted since 1907. Sincere thanks are also due to His Grace the Duke of Devonshire for permission to include a reproduction of the fine portrait of Lord Halifax, now in his possession.

The judgements expressed in this work are not always those of 1897, some having been naturally matured and modified by the lessons of practical experience in the political field.

H. C. F.

LIFE OF HALIFAX

CHAPTER I

BIRTH, ANCESTRY, & CHILDHOOD

OUR first introduction to the subject of this memoir is of a somewhat ironic character. For it is Lord Wentworth—the 'Strafford' of History—who, in a letter of admonition addressed to a ward his nephew, appends this perfunctory postscript: 'Pray you present my service to my niece, and God give her long comfort of the son, Charles Price tells me, God hath sent her.' Thus does the most 'thorough' of English statesmen introduce to us the future 'Trimmer'.

The son and heir so cursorily presented to us had been born on 11 November 1633, a scion of one of the most outstanding among the great Yorkshire families. Some authorities would trace its origin to one 'Sheville', who figures on the Roll of Battle Abbey; while, on the other hand, the great Roman House of the Savelli was ready to 'cry cousinship', a claim in which our Lord Halifax was to show some interest.

But the greater Yorkshire antiquaries look to the borders of Anjou, and suppose its progenitors to have come over with Geoffrey Plantagenet. Certain it is, that during the thirteenth century we find the clan already settled in that south-west corner of the West Riding where most of the offshoot subsequently flourished.

There wealthy marriages, and the successive dying out of elder or co-related lines—one of these, that of Eland of Eland, by a horrible and criminous catastrophe—concentrated an agglomeration of rich manors in the hands of the Saviles of Thornhill; who, by the sixteenth century, had become a power in the north. They had inter-married with the reigning House of Tudor; and what was of greater local moment, with the powerful Talbots of Hallamshire, who then ruled, like petty kings, among the sturdy cutlers of Sheffield.

This line, in its turn, dies out; and a Sir George Savile of Lupset, the first baronet (of Nova Scotia), succeeds to its accumulated possessions. He forms fresh ties with the Talbot family; and his wife, a Lady Mary, brings as her dowry the reversion of another great property, namely, the estate of Rufford Abbey in Sherwood, conferred on the Earls of Shrewsbury at the Dissolution.

Such was the ancestry of the Savile whose career we are about to follow; and on whose outlook the family antecedents exercised no small influence. For in him we shall find pride of race, and racial ambition, striving at rather fantastic odds with the logical conceptions of a sceptical intellect.

It was a second Sir George, son of the first baronet, who married (as his second wife) the daughter of a neighbouring baronet; and what was of more importance, the sister of Thomas Wentworth, then a boy of thirteen.

Sir George survived his marriage only seven years; but he must have possessed outstanding qualities, since he had already inspired in his youthful brother-in-law the most passionate devotion. That this affection was reciprocated we learn from the fact that Savile left his two little sons under the care, not only of his former Oxford tutor, by that time Archbishop of Canterbury, but also under that of the young Sir Thomas Wentworth; who had just succeeded, at the age of twenty-one, to an estate of £6000 a year, and the charge of eleven brothers and sisters.

His boundless energy, none the less, found time and means for accomplishing this new task. In the Savile Chapel at Thornhill he raised a magnificent monument to his brother-in-law's memory. He took into his already large household his sister, and his sister's sons, and made their interests his own. 'He spent', writes his confidant, Sir George Radcliffe, 'eight years time besides his pains and money, in soliciting the businesses and suits of his nephews'; which, being extremely involved, obliged him 'to go every term to London about that alone'. These interests, complicated as they were by widespread family dissensions, eventually affected Wentworth's relations with the then omnipotent favourite Buckingham, and drove him into opposition to the Court.

The elder of his two charges, who succeeded to the baronetcy, died in 1626, while at the University; about which date, Wentworth's opposition to the Court had led to his imprisonment in the Fleet. But by 1628 the Court had secured his support, and he had thus become a Privy Councillor, receiving at the same time a peerage, and the vast responsibilities accruing to the Presidency of the North.

The second son succeeded to the title and estates, and had only reached the age of seventeen when he received a fresh proof of his uncle's solicitude. For it was to Wentworth's suggestion and influence that he owed his marriage with Anne, eldest daughter of Thomas, first Lord Coventry, Keeper of the Great Seal, which took place at Thornhill, 29 December 1629; and of which, as we have seen, the George Savile in whom we are interested was the first-born son.

In a room familiar to the present writer from childhood, two portraits once hung face to face. There the dark brooding countenance of 'Black Tom' (his deferential secretary in the background) confronted the suave decorous presentment of the sedate Lord Keeper, his hand on the purse of the Seal. From these men, so dissimilar in character and fortune, the subject of this biography may well have derived complementary qualities. If personal pride and personal courage, if self-reliance and brilliance of intellect were special characteristics of the Wentworth strain, in him they were tempered by the prudence and caution which distinguished Lord Coventry, an excellent, though scarcely brilliant, man.

The Lord Keeper and the Lord President, however, soon found in this family connection the bond of a common interest. It is Coventry who breaks to Wentworth the news of the death of a 'little kinswoman' Mary, the first child of the young couple. Coventry it is who expresses a hope that the suitor of a younger daughter may 'in mind as well as in... body resemble my son Savile, whose match your Lordship first moved and begun'; while the Lord President confesses he loves his nephew like a son, 'as much in remembrance of his father (a person in truth of as much virtue and nobleness as ever I knew) as of my sister'.

The young bride herself had formed one of a remarkable family group. A sister was to become the reputed author of a once famous work: *The Whole Duty of Man*. Two of her brothers, William and Henry, while leaving their own lesser mark on the history of their time, were to play significant parts in the career of their more celebrated nephew, and the new Lady Savile herself was to evince during the dark days of the impending civil wars an energy, an ability and an heroic self-devotion of no mean order.

Meanwhile, the character of her young husband—a father at the age of nineteen—had developed early; for, in the letter from which we have already quoted, the counsels of his guardian uncle suggest a disposition peculiarly impetuous and daring, not to mention a strong vein of sarcasm, which he very certainly transmitted to his son. But his uncle's affection was not impaired, although his spirit and daring soon brought the young Yorkshireman into collision with the Vice-President and Council of the North—the representatives of his formidable uncle. Even when the irritated Vice-President complains that at this rate the Council of the North may soon sit down and let Sir William govern, the Lord President writes to his refractory young kinsman rather in sorrow than in anger. His warnings are indeed forcible; yet he concludes that, none the less, 'I must in all things prefer my nephew Savile before all other men or subjects in the north of England'. His remonstrances were vain; and even when (with a confidence pathetically misplaced) he warns his imperious nephew that, secure in his own truth and the justice of 'my Master', he can afford to ignore 'such assaults', the young man remains obdurate.

The death of the Lord Keeper, which, about this time, deprived the Court of the one statesman who commanded popular confidence, will also have deprived his obstreperous son-in-law of a monitor who might have exerted a restraining influence. For during the Short Parliament—in which his speech on ship-money seems to have been particularly telling—and again at the beginning of the Long Parliament, young Sir William Savile vigorously supported the popular cause, narrowly escaping imprisonment.

The attainder and execution of his uncle, however, seem to have completely reversed his sympathies; and thenceforth he became an ardent and active adherent of the Royal cause.

The tragedy of his great-uncle may well have been the first public event which left its mark on the mind of the child George, then between seven and eight years old; but from him it eventually drew a different conclusion. For chance has preserved for us the bitter verdict of his later days on the conduct of the King himself.

Sir William had promptly taken his stand beneath the Royal banner at Nottingham. His household—which now included a young brother-in-law, Ashley Cooper, the brilliant, precocious lad of twenty who was destined to become, as Lord Shaftesbury, first the political associate, and then the most notable opponent of Sir William's famous son—had removed from the threatened area of Rufford first to Thornhill, then to Durham, and then to Shropshire.

One result of this move was that on 15 February 1642/3 the boy George, then aged nine, and a brother William, who was to die young, were entered at Shrewsbury Grammar School, then under the tutelage of Thomas Challoner, a strong Royalist; the town itself and even a part of the school building being at the time occupied by the Royalist forces.

Meanwhile, Sir William himself was playing a brief but distinguished part in the Yorkshire campaign. In May 1643 he was appointed Governor of Sheffield, to which place he seems to have removed part of his family, the two schoolboys, we must suppose, excepted; but he himself was soon called away to Pontefract. A rumour that he had lost favour with the King was contradicted by a holograph letter from His Majesty; and still more emphatically by his appointment, towards the end of the year, to the Governorship of York. Before, however, he could be joined there by any of his family, the new Governor had died at his last post. By 25 January 1643/4, Sir William Savile, at the age of thirty-one, had breathed his last: and on 15 February he was buried with his fathers in Thornhill Church.

CHAPTER II

YOUTH

BEFORE his death Sir William Savile is known to have expressed great and well-founded anxiety for the safety of Sheffield Castle. We can therefore hardly suppose that his young son had been removed thither from the comparative safety of Shrewsbury. In fact, soon after the disastrous conflict of Marston Moor Major-General Crawford had received orders to reduce that stronghold. The defiant response which was returned to the formal summons to surrender was ascribed by him to the high spirit of Lady Savile, her situation notwithstanding; for she awaited the birth of a posthumous child. The besiegers then opened fire; but it was only after a fortnight's siege, and against the vigorous and repeated remonstrances of the gallant lady, that the garrison, moved by her peril rather than by her appeals, forced a parley upon its commanding officers, 14 August 1644. The terms of surrender were highly favourable; the garrison marched out with all the honours of war, while Lady Savile was accorded a safe and honourable retirement to Thornhill or elsewhere, with all her household and family. This last probably included two young daughters both of whom lived to marry, but died young; and also her youngest son Henry, then but two years old. A posthumous son, born the day after the surrender and christened Talbot, did not survive to manhood.

Meanwhile, the affairs of her eldest son, the young Sir George, were receiving attentions from the enemy with which his friends could very well have dispensed.

The family estates had been duly settled upon him, and his father's bequest by will included only his armour and weapons 'with the furniture thereto belonging'. Settlements notwithstanding, however, Sir William Savile had not been four months in his grave ere an Ordinance bestowing on Lord Wharton the wardship of Sir William's son and heir had been read in the House of Commons; which did not, however, become law till after the decisive battle of Naseby. This measure specifically devolved on Lord Wharton the guardianship of the child, the care of his education, and a yearly allowance out of the profits of the estate. These were vested in trustees who, it appears, were instructed to pay

Lord Wharton, by instalments, a total of £4000 out of the rents, 'for the supplying of his Lordship's pressing wants'. He seems to have actually obtained an immediate advance of £2000, which the young Sir George, after the Restoration, in vain attempted to recover.

So far as the personal guardianship was concerned, however, it is doubtful whether Lord Wharton ever succeeded, even temporarily, in enforcing his claims. Lady Savile was a woman of resource, as well as of determination. Whether she had removed her son from Shrewsbury upon the fall of Sheffield we do not know; but at any rate the two boys cannot have remained there after 22 February 1644/5, when, Shrewsbury having been captured by the Parliamentarians, a Puritan replaced Challoner. But it is certain that on 26 November 1646 Lady Savile obtained from the King, while in the Scots' quarters at Newcastle, an engagement under the sign-manual confirming to her with proper legal formality a grant 'already heretofore' made to her of the wardship and marriage of her son Sir George Savile.

That Lady Savile should under these circumstances have preferred a foreign education for her son was only a plausible conjecture in 1897, but it has been recently substantiated by the researches of Miss Phare.[1] We now know that on 4 December 1647, when just fourteen, he was at Angers, then a University town, with his young uncle, William Coventry, who was seven years his senior; and who, though barely of age, must have already served in the Royal forces, and even commanded a company.

How long either remained at Angers we do not know. But about two years later, October 1649, we find Savile at Leghorn, a month later at Naples, and at both places apparently under the charge of a tutor whose name seems to have been Davidson. By the beginning of 1650 (n.s.) when Savile was just sixteen, we find them at Rome; since on 24 January 1649/50 Cardinal Savelli, we are told, 'made very much' of the lad, 'called him cousin and showed him how it was so'.

In the following August 1650 he is again found with his tutor in France, was apparently there still on 16 February 1650/1, and perhaps may not have returned to England till just the time for his coming of age, November 1654.

It is clear, therefore, that George Savile never experienced, save for a few transient periods, the average English education of his time and class. He was never at an English University. His stay at Shrewsbury had been short; subsequent intervals at home, under a tutor, must have been brief and broken. Between the ages of, say, fourteen to twenty-one, he had lived alternately in France and Italy. What impression will this have left on his mind, character, and literary tastes?

He will no doubt have suffered, as all men must do, from the effects of an irregular education. One does not imagine him a man of wide reading. On the other hand, this vagabond youth had no doubt its advantages. It will have saved him from a purely insular standpoint, and induced a precocious development of talent and outlook: with a premature knowledge of the world, derived not so much from books and theories, as from men and events.

The influence of his French and Italian sojourns does not seem to have been one of attraction. Italy is never mentioned in any of his extant speeches or writings; and if contact with Roman Catholicism at its centre had any effect on him, it was evidently one of repulsion.

Of France—of French aims, French ideas, French policy, French ambitions—he was through life the bitter and consistent foe. But his views can hardly have been formed by his own youthful experiences; for the France of his youth was by no means the grandiose, pseudo-classical, despotic, aggressive France of his mature aversions. It was the disturbed, impotent and faction-ridden France of Mazarin and the Fronde.

We may therefore conclude that the main effect of his early expatriation was the intensification of that passionate patriotism which he has himself likened to idolatry.

From a literary point of view we may perhaps derive from his early initiation into the graces of French style that 'something' brilliant, pointed, and epigrammatic, which differentiates the writings of this most English of statesmen from others of his day and generation. But this he did not owe to the literary fashions of the 'siècle Louis Quatorze'. Its great writers had not, in his youth, risen above the horizon; and no Academy had yet laid down laws for all literary contemporaries. Montaigne alone, whose fame had almost reached its centenary, rose before him as an example.

What effect, then, may we suppose to have resulted from his probably complete unfamiliarity—during this comparatively long period—with English literature?

One curious result is possible; he may have been thrown back upon the study of the English Bible. That volume, at least, his devout mother will have pressed upon him, however hurried may have been his departure from England. From that book, almost exclusively, his quotations are drawn; and from it he may have unconsciously derived his almost invariable retention of the beautiful termination 'eth' in the third person singular, then rapidly growing archaic, and the loss of which, half a century later, Addison was so feelingly to deplore.

His return home, we have already suggested, coincided with the attainment of his majority. His mother's exertions on behalf of his estates seem to have been successful; and the young Sir George found himself a rich man, when poverty was almost the distinguishing mark of the Cavalier. This wealth he, through life, increased by prudent financial management.

Before the existence of Government loans, opportunities for investment of capital were very scanty. Mortgage transactions and the traffic in annuities were the only recognized resource of careful investors. Sir George from the first, apparently on the advice of his mother, dealt largely in these financial commodities, in which matters, it would seem, his generosity equalled his prudence.

During his absence abroad his mother's services to the Royal cause had been outstanding. She is frequently eulogized in the writings of Dr Barwick, himself a kind of historical 'Dr Rochecliffe'. The daring surprise at Pontefract Castle was ascribed to her inventive genius. This was followed by the recapture of Thornhill, the old Savile seat: an indifferent moated residence, so it was said; but this was, almost immediately after, accidently destroyed by fire. Other exploits ascribed to her instigation were the kidnapping of a Parliamentary General, and the extraction of a Royalist leader from prison at the very 'foot of the gallows'.

Since the destruction of Thornhill, Rufford Abbey in Sherwood had become the principal seat of the family. This fine old mansion, which has so recently passed out of Savile hands, had been originally a foundation of the Cistercian order; and had, as we have seen, together with its enormous possessions, descended to the Saviles from the original Talbot grantees. That family had transformed the conventual building into a handsome dwelling-house, famed for its magnificent Elizabethan banqueting hall.

Lying 'sequestered' in the forest, it was 'very pleasant and commodious' for hunting; and had often entertained King James and King Charles, his son, for that purpose while on their way to

Scotland. Here the young Sir George, whose mother appears to have remarried soon after his coming of age, now settled down to lead the life of an opulent country gentleman of the time. He had his town house (at the corner of Queen Street) in the then fashionable quarter of Lincoln's Inn Fields, which was known as 'Carlyle' or 'Savil' House.

Meanwhile, it was natural that the son of so redoubted a mother should soon fall under political suspicion.

Not a year after his attaining his majority a wave of unrest spread among Royalist circles in the north. It was not sponsored by the more responsible leaders, or countenanced by the great bulk of the rank and file. A meeting, however, on Marston Moor, seems to have been headed by Lord Rochester, but it soon dispersed. Rumour next reported a party of about 200, said to have assembled at Rufford Abbey. Sir George himself was in London; but his former tutor, Mr Davidson, was among the company, and William Coventry was said to have arrived post haste—probably, if we accept Clarendon's view of him, with deterrent intentions. Anyhow, the meeting, on a suspicion of treachery, broke up in alarm.

Apparently through traitorous servants, information had actually reached the authorities; and the matter had been held of sufficient importance to warrant a letter of inquiry from Cromwell himself; but it is now impossible to ascertain the actual facts, since little reliance can be placed on rambling depositions made two years later by the servant informers. Only a few arrests were made at the time, and Mr Coventry was only detained till Savile should have appeared before Cromwell. One would like to know whether so dramatic a confrontation ever really took place.

Savile, at any rate, felt himself free to give 'hostages to fortune'. On 29 December 1656 at the age of twenty-three—after an abortive treaty with the exiled House of Butler—Sir George married into another Royalist family. His bride, who brought him £10,000, was Dorothy, only daughter of Henry Spencer, first Earl of Sunderland, a gallant and accomplished young man who had fallen, thirteen years before, in the Royalist ranks at Newbury.

Her brother, Robert, second Earl, was a good deal younger than his new brother-in-law, and twenty years were to elapse before his tortuous public career impinged on that of her husband.

But his mother, Dorothy Lady Sunderland—the 'Sacharissa' of Waller's youth, and sister to Algernon and Henry Sidney—one of the most virtuous, beautiful, and charming women of that century, conceived for her young son-in-law a strong affection, which was to survive the death of her daughter, and Savile's remarriage.

Concerning the young wife herself we know very little. Allusions in the letters of her merry brother-in-law, Henry Savile, who went up to Oxford the year after her marriage, suggest that she was lively and agreeable, but throw no light on her relations with her husband.

CHAPTER III

THE RESTORATION. SAVILE ENTERS POLITICS. ASCENDANCY OF CLARENDON

WHETHER Sir George shared in the complicated intrigues which preceded the Restoration we do not know. Chancellor Hyde had certainly, before the end of 1659, secured a letter to the young Yorkshireman from the hand of Charles himself. It is equally certain that in the 'Convention Parliament', which actually restored the King, Sir George Savile shared, with Mr William Lowther, the representation of Pontefract; but nothing further is heard of him before it dissolved on 24 December. We only know that in the following Parliament, which met 16 May 1661, and remained in being for nearly eighteen years, his place was taken by another important Yorkshireman, and that he never again took his seat in the House of Commons.

Meanwhile, his family responsibilities were increasing. His eldest son, named after himself, had died within the year; but another, born at Rufford in 1661, was christened Henry, after the young baronet's only remaining brother; who thus, for the second time, ceased to be his heir-presumptive. The young uncle, who acknowledges the compliment in a good-natured letter, suggestive of previous (and no doubt entirely well-deserved) elder brotherly admonitions, will, however, demand a good deal of our attention throughout this history. For Harry Savile was emphatically the charming, amiable scapegrace who tries to the utmost the patience of his friends, and never forfeits their affection. Sweet-tempered, indolent, witty, fond of pleasure, careless of consequences, his letters reveal to us the best of good fellows, the most delightful correspondent of his age. His debts, his follies, his escapades, and, after he had obtained a small appointment at Court, his periodic intervals of disgrace, were a constant source of anxiety to the family at large; while once at least he was compelled to take refuge from obloquy and his creditors in his beloved Paris. But whether imploring in a highly penitent and lugubrious strain the good offices of a favourite uncle, or insinuating with delicious effrontery that a fatted buck would appropriately grace the return of a prodigal nephew—whether dilating with amusing solemnity upon entirely futile projects of study and retirement, or ingenuously betraying a renewed and vivid interest in life and frivolity—the good-natured ne'er-do-well failed not to repay, with a warm and almost passionate loyalty, the unvarying kindness of his elder brother. For politics, save as they affected the passing and precarious interests of Mr Henry Savile, that young gentleman, in his earlier days, cared extremely little. It was not till he had expiated the follies of a very protracted youth that he was to develop, as English representative at Versailles, both energy and patriotism; with an honourable (and perhaps somewhat honorary) attachment to the Protestant religion which, under James II, was to cost him a place.

The loss of Sir George's eldest son was soon succeeded by another family blow; his mother did not long survive the birth of her second grandson. Grief, we are told, at the orgy of riot and profanity which had from the first disgraced the restored Court, had hastened her end. She had fallen an easy prey to a melancholy disorder, and in the summer of 1662, at Wimpole, the seat of a second husband, Sir John Chicheley, she had 'rendered her great and innocent soul to God'.[2]

Meanwhile, her son was becoming a person of importance both in town and country. He was much in London, and was soon regarded as a likely aspirant for a seat in the House of Lords. His wealth, his vast possessions,[3] his 'orderly and splendid way of living', naturally drew men's attention. A fine face and figure, as represented in the beautiful early portrait which we are kindly allowed to reproduce, must, despite the long and 'ugly' nose at which its owner jested, have proved very attractive; while his intellectual superiority and brilliant conversational powers gave him a more real and personal distinction. 'Came to visit me', writes Evelyn 27 September 1662, 'Sir George Savile....Sir George was a witty gentleman, if not a little too prompt and daring.'

In his own county meanwhile—for, though accident had settled him on his Nottinghamshire estates, he was by birth and interests essentially a Yorkshireman—he was becoming an acknowledged leader among the younger generation of the great Cavalier houses. These young gallants scintillated round the person of the Lord Lieutenant of the West Riding, the splendid and notorious Duke of Buckingham, by marriage the owner of vast Yorkshire estates. Under him Savile became Deputy Lieutenant, a Commissioner for the Execution of the Corporation Acts, and Colonel of the West Riding Militia (which was called into action by the abortive Puritan rising of Farley Wood). But the relations between the two men seem soon to have passed the business stage, and the keen and vigorous wit of Savile no doubt exerted its fascination over the no less brilliant, if unstable, intelligence of the vivacious Duke.

Their intercourse, however, reacted unfavourably on Savile's private reputation. The Duke, indeed, had not, so far, attained to the degree of profligacy which was to make his name a byword; and it seemed not impossible that, the heats of youth once over, he might rise to heights of real statesmanship. But the society which surrounded him can never have been characterized by sobriety. Against Sir George himself, a man of simple and almost severe tastes, and possibly of a delicate constitution, the charge of personal licence seems never to have been adduced by contemporaries. But the Buckingham symposia will no doubt have stimulated the irreverent sarcasm and the heterodox speculations by which he earned for himself (as had his predecessor Montaigne) a reputation for Atheism. 'He was', says Burnet, 'a man of a great and ready wit; full of life and very [amusing], much turned to satire. He let his wit run much on matters of religion, so that he passed for a bold and determined atheist.'

What his opinions may have been in very early life we do not know; he has himself observed that religious unbelief, or at least religious indifference, 'is too natural in the beginnings of life to be heavily censured'. But in later days, at any rate, he vehemently repelled the accusation. 'He always protested to me', says Burnet, 'that he was no atheist, and said he believed there was not one in the world.'

It is abundantly clear that Savile joined to a strong taste for religious speculation, and an acute sceptical intellect, a scorn for religious shibboleths, a contempt for cant and bigotry, a keen eye for the failings of the clergy, and a sarcastically unbridled tongue. Reserved in matters of business, guarded in correspondence, the prudence of Savile failed him completely in conversation and debate. Through life he was incapable of suppressing an epigram, however pungent or profane; and his most extravagant paradoxes were no doubt often accepted by the literal-minded as the expression of matured conviction.

It is equally clear that he was never orthodox in creed, even according to the widest limits of contemporary Latitudinarianism. He himself confessed (according to Burnet) 'he could not swallow down everything that divines imposed on the world; he was a Christian in submission; he believed as much as he could, and he hoped God would not lay it to his charge that he could not digest iron...nor take unto his belief things that must burst him; if he had any scruples they were not sought for...by him; for he never read an atheistical book'. But it is clear, on the other hand, that he was far from being irreligious; and the very curious reminiscences of a private chaplain, to which we shall refer later on, show that he held firmly a somewhat rationalistic form of Christianity; probably—in revulsion from Athanasian complexities—verging on Unitarianism.

Ecclesiastically he was always unalterably opposed to Roman pretensions; critical of the High Church school, to which his devout mother had belonged; and anxious to improve relations between the Anglican Church and the Protestant dissenters.

In politics, meanwhile, his connection with Buckingham naturally drew him towards the anti-Clarendon opposition. Of this, Buckingham, after he had been refused, at Clarendon's instigation, the Presidency of the North, had become the mainspring; while Savile himself must have been further influenced by his close and intimate relations with his uncle, William Coventry.

Between Coventry and the Chancellor antagonism had existed even from the days of the Protectorate, during which Clarendon had resented the younger man's aloofness from political activity. He had equally resented his prompt appearance at Breda, once the Restoration had become inevitable. For this opportune arrival had coincided with a vacancy in the post of secretary to the heir-presumptive which Coventry had succeeded in securing. It was a position of great importance, and rendered doubly so by the immediate appointment of the Duke to the position of Lord High Admiral, and Coventry's own appointment as Commissioner of the Navy.

His ability is unquestioned. 'He was', says Burnet, 'a man of great notions and eminent virtues; capable of bearing the Chief Ministry as he was once thought very near it.' Even more striking is the testimony of Clarendon, in a passage wherein the writer's sense of justice and hearty dislike of Coventry very obviously contend. For he admits that 'his parts were very good, if he had not thought them better than any other man's. And he had diligence and industry which men of good parts are too often without which made him to have at least credit and power...with the

Duke' of York. Moreover, as Clarendon honestly allows, 'he was without those vices which were too much in request and which make men most unfit for business'. The old statesman none the less proceeds to charge him with self-sufficiency, love of criticism, combativeness, pride, insolence, boundless ambition, and a want of principles in religion or State which rendered him of one mind to-day and another to-morrow. Sir William, in fact, like the more famous nephew whom he probably excelled in administrative ability, though his inferior in originality of mind, imaginative insight, and intellectual ability, was, in practice, a 'Trimmer'; and so might an aggrieved opponent have described the Lord Halifax of after years.

Coventry by no means confined his energies to official routine and reform. He had sat for Yarmouth since the beginning of the existing Parliament with the reputation of an able man and a good speaker, and it was here that the antagonism between him and the Chancellor reached its height. He was understood to represent the Duke's interest in the Lower House, and was regarded as inspiring a 'youth movement' there, as resentful of the Chancellor's long tenure of office, as of his political attitude, which it considered out of date. In fact, it soon became evident that Coventry aspired, in modern parlance, to 'lead the House'.

Clarendon, meanwhile, with his imperious jealousy of the younger generation—a jealousy almost pardonable in one who, while the sole representative of statesmanship in the exiled Court, had been so long and so often a target for unscrupulous intrigues—endeavoured to repress the audacious newcomer; and only succeeded in adding to the phalanx of rising and mutinous talent.

When, moreover, in March 1664/5 a naval war, very popular at first on account of trade rivalry, broke out between Great Britain and the Dutch Netherlands, the importance of Coventry's position was correspondingly intensified, and he soon received the honour of knighthood, and a seat in the Privy Council.

The ravages of the Great Plague were compelling the Court to disperse itself into the provinces, and the Duke of York and his Duchess—influenced, says Clarendon, by Coventry—resolved to spend the summer at York. The local magnates hastened to present their duty, and conspicuous among them was, of course, Coventry's nephew, Sir George. He entertained the Duke with great splendour at Rufford, and in return Coventry procured for him, from the Duke, the promise of a peerage.

The obvious fondness of Halifax for those hereditary distinctions, for which, in speculative discussion, he affected a stoical contempt, was the fruitful topic for sarcasm among his contemporaries. For in familiar discourse he was wont to argue (so 'Saviliana' informs us) that 'Titles and honours...being hereditary in Europe did take off a great deal of their worth. That if men must raise their own dignity, they would first endeavour to raise their own virtue'; and '...Noblemen would all be men of honour, indeed, if none but for honourable actions were made noble'.

The simple-minded reporter recalls such rhapsodies—which were perhaps merely advanced for the sake of argument—without a sense of incongruity; but in Burnet, Halifax found a more acute critic. 'When', says the Doctor, 'he talked to me as a philosopher of his contempt of the world, I asked him what he meant by getting so many new titles, which I called the hanging himself about with bells and tinsel. He had no other excuse for it but this, that since the world were such fools as to value these matters a man must be a fool for company; he considered them but as rattles; yet rattles please children; so these might be of use to his family. His heart was much set on raising his family.' This last shrewd touch, one feels, in part explains the paradox. As head of one of the oldest among the great Yorkshire clans, Halifax was unable to repress an inherent passion for its aggrandizement, which from a philosophic point of view he could not easily justify.

But while such explanation is needed for later steps in rank which were often injurious to his political reputation and interests, his original desire for a peerage had a reasonable and practical motive. He had not—why, we do not know—succeeded in securing for a second term a seat in the Lower House; and as in those days nothing save death, a dissolution of Parliament, or elevation to the Upper House, could sever the ties between Members and constituencies, vacancies were very rare. The second Parliament of Charles II lasted eighteen years, during which time Halifax, but for his peerage, might have been altogether excluded from the political arena.

Parliament, in consequence of the Plague, met that year at Oxford. There the Duke lost no time in consulting the Chancellor —by that date his acknowledged father-in-law—concerning the promised promotion, and explained that both he and his wife were committed in the matter. He allowed that the King had recently taken a resolution, on the Duke's own advice, to make no more

Peers; but urged 'That Sir George had one of the best fortunes of any man in England, and lived the most like a great man; that he had been very civil to him and his wife, and treated them at his house in a very splendid manner', and that a repulse, in fine, would be very injurious to himself.

Such an appeal on behalf of Coventry's nephew, and the political ally of Buckingham, was naturally displeasing to Clarendon, and he showed the Duke his displeasure. He deprecated in general any departure from a rule so recently established, and objected in particular to the proposed candidate for honours.

'Sir George Savile', he said, 'was a man of a very ill reputation amongst men of piety and religion and was looked upon as void of all sense of religion even to the doubting, if not denying, that there is a God, and that he was not reserved in any company to publish his opinions;...it would neither be for his highness' honour to propose it, nor for the King's to grant it, at a time when all licence in discourse and in actions was spread over the kingdom to the heartbreaking of very many good men.'

The Duke, however, continued to persist; but Charles on his part clearly recognized the inconvenience of such a precedent; and the favour was definitely refused.

The Duke showed considerable mortification, resented Clarendon's interference, told Coventry all that had happened, and 'in his passion' betrayed to him the gist of Clarendon's censures; which were, of course, duly reported to Sir George. Finally, he took unto his bedchamber a younger brother of Sir George whom he had only seen in the north, our young friend Harry, in fact. He being, in the words of Clarendon, 'a young man of wit and incredible presumption', omitted no occasion to vent his malice against the Chancellor, 'with a licence that in former times would have been very penal *though it had concerned a person of a much inferior quality in the State*'. It is difficult to avoid a smile at this picture of lively Impudence at the heels of injured and impotent Dignity.

The Great Plague meanwhile was producing another incidental result which curiously modifies, for posterity, the aspersions cast on Sir George by the Chancellor.

Two years before the Plague, Sir George had appointed as his Chaplain, and presented to the living of Eyam—a small parish on his Derbyshire estate just vacated for Nonconformity—a young Cambridge graduate, William Mompesson. A year later, on the outbreak of the Plague, infection reached Eyam in bales of merchandise. The courage with which Mompesson induced his unhappy parishioners to draw a voluntary cordon round their village, and the self-sacrifice with which he, his wife, and his predecessor, devoted themselves to the service of the death-stricken community have immortalized Mompesson's name. The Plague raged unceasingly for a year; his wife died, and, in expectation of his own death, he wrote a pathetic, if stilted, letter to his patron. He thanks him for his 'noble favours', professes his own 'love and honour' for his benefactor, and commends to his care and executorship his 'distressed orphans'. He urges upon him and his family the blessings of a Christian life, and trusts he will select a 'humble, pious' man as his successor; for whom 'could I see your face' before death he would leave advice as to his treatment of the parishioners. Finally, he requests his prayers and those of his neighbours. Strange appeals to the atheist of Clarendon's detestation!

Mompesson, however, did not die. Three years later his patron appointed him to the living of Eakring, a few miles from Rufford. There the fear of possible contagion, even at so great a distance of time, rendering his new parishioners averse to receive him, Savile allowed him a residence within the precincts of Rufford Park. At Eakring he eventually died, fourteen years after the death of his patron, having refused the Deanery of Lincoln in favour of a friend.

The respect owed to his courage and his virtues seems to have been qualified, in the case of Halifax, by a certain impatience of his foibles, and notably of the adulation whereof Savile himself was the object. For it is certain that Mompesson was the Chaplain who once, in his presence, prayed for Halifax as his 'Lord and Patron'. Whereupon, it is said, Halifax was 'very angry; and asked him if he could not be content to play the fool, but he must let the world know whose fool he was'.

Yet Mompesson's devotion survived the most robust rebuffs, since it is to him we must ascribe the anonymous manuscript 'Saviliana' already mentioned. This was evidently written after Savile's death as a preface to the posthumous *Miscellanies* of 1700, in which collection, however, it was never included. Rediscovered by the present writer among the Spencer archives, it constitutes, despite its exaggerated eulogies, a most valuable addition to our knowledge of Halifax himself. It settled, for instance, and for all time, the long-standing controversy as to the authorship of *The Character of a Trimmer*.

From this necessary excursus we must now, however, return to the year 1666, and the progress of the Dutch War. The inconclusive course of our naval operations was intensifying Ministerial feuds and official recrimination; and through his intimacy with Coventry, Savile was drawn into the vortex, of which the Navy Office was the centre. That Office suffered severely from financial stringency, which was a perennial feature of the restored Government; and was, moreover, divided on the question of command. For political reasons, the efficient commanders who, under the fostering care of Cromwell, had risen from the ranks, were being replaced, with disastrous results, by ignorant young courtiers, devoted to pleasure and impatient of restraint; while Coventry struggled in vain to reform a system he was powerless to control. From him Sir George no doubt derived the strong interest he always evinced in matters naval. Some experimental knowledge of seamanship (so, in later life, he maintained) should be as essential a part of an English gentleman's education as a course of military service to a French grandee; and to the question of command we shall soon find him devoting one of his most interesting essays.

Meanwhile, it was no doubt through Coventry's introduction that he was extending his acquaintance among the more rising diplomats; especially with Mr Temple, an accomplished young Irishman who was to become famous as Sir William Temple; and who, after a preliminary secret mission as envoy to the Bishop of Munster, had just been appointed Resident at the Court of Brussels. Three months later, France, under her ambitious young monarch Louis XIV, had suddenly joined forces with the Dutch; and it is a letter to Temple written a few days later (15 February 1666) which first brings us into personal contact with Sir George himself. It runs as follows:

5 *February* 1666 (N.S.)

Sir, It is a sin against the Public, and a trespass upon you, at this time to clog you with such an idle correspondence as mine; but I find I consider my own interests before yours; being not able to make you an expression of my kindness at so dear a rate as the denying myself the satisfaction of hearing from you. And therefore I take hold of your offer, and beg you would sometimes bestow a letter upon me; which shall be as welcome for telling me you are well, as it can be for the best news it bringeth in relation to the public; for which if I can be concerned next to what I am for my best friends, it is the utmost I will pretend to in that matter. I find his Majesty of France will be an angry enemy. He doth not declare War like an *honnête homme*; and therefore I hope he will not pursue it like a wise one.

I do not despair, but that the English who use to go into France for their breeding, may have the honor [for] once to teach them better manners. The League with Spain is a good circumstance to make us able to do it. It is so seasonably and well done, that I will suppose you had a Hand in it. In the meantime we have great alarms the Monsieur will invade us which makes everybody prepare for their entertainment, and I hope they will neither find us so little ready, or so divided as perhaps they expect.

I will not make this longer when I have assured you I am

Sir,

Your most faithful humble

Servant,

GEORGE SAVILE

It is an interesting coincidence that the first letter of Savile hitherto recovered should raise the issue which provides the key to his whole subsequent career. 'The greatness of France', wrote Methuen to Halifax, nearly thirty years later, 'as I have heard your Lordship observe hath made all old politics useless.'

Long after this date, in his *Character of a Trimmer*, Halifax may have exaggerated the part played by France (at the epoch we are considering) in the intensification of Anglo-Dutch animosities. But from the first he showed as singular a sagacity in recognizing the common interests which underlay these our surface differences, as in estimating the dangers to European peace and English liberties involved in the aggressive despotism of the new French regime. For Louis XIV, with his motto 'l'État c'est moi', his territorial ambition, his claim to a hegemony of western Europe, his thirst for American and even Asiatic Empire, was indeed a prevision of the yet more extravagant tyrannies of yesterday and to-day. His aims were the aims of a Napoleon, or a Hitler; and his 'totalitarian' hatred of the Protestant, rivals Hitler's hatred for the Jew.

The same theme is developed in a second letter to Temple dated 4 April 1666. He writes:

You make me sensible of the inconvenience of living out of the world, now . . . that I find it impossible for me to write three lines of sense in exchange for your letters that are so full of everything which can make them welcome. I am so ashamed you should converse with a dead man, that I almost wish the French landed upon our coast, thinking it better to write you a sad story than none. How soon I may be furnished with something of this kind dependeth upon our Success at Sea, and the faith of your Bishop [of Munster], which may well be shaken if you do not support it with your Bills of Exchange; He is likely to be so over-matched this next Campagne, that I doubt he will be tempted to break faith with Hereticks rather than be a Martyr in our Calendar. I should be glad to hear Spain would come into our Scales to help us to weigh down our Enemies; but I fear their ill luck in the late War, hath not left them spirit enough to fall out with the French, though their Interest provoketh them to it. Besides the crown is in a cradle; and a Spanish Council I imagine to be as slow an assembly as a House of Commons. So that we must rely upon the Oak and courage of England to do our business, there being small appearance of anything to help us from abroad....

By June, indeed, the rumours of a French or Dutch invasion had become so importunate, that the Government hurriedly issued commissions to persons of consideration, empowering them to raise troops of horse, to be subsequently incorporated into regiments. One of these was directed to Sir George, who on 5 July wrote as follows from Pontefract to his friend and neighbour Sir Philip Monckton: 'I desired my lord Duke to propose that to you for which I wanted confidence...nobody is abler to do the King service, if there should be occasion to use officers as well as to list them. I do intend, if nothing happens to divert me from it, to be to-morrow night at York....In the mean time I hope you will be picking up men that are tolerably horsed, which I find will be the greatest difficulty.' He has selected a cornet who is trying to enlist men in Nottinghamshire and has chosen a quartermaster and two corporals, leaving the third for his lieutenant to propose. The Duke, he understands, will furnish Savile himself with pistols and holsters.

In York, Savile stayed about two months. He corresponded with his brother about getting equipment; and we are amused to find the good-natured spendthrift's determination that his brother, proverbially indifferent to dress, shall be 'modish for once'. 'A handsome belt', he remarks with malicious satisfaction, 'will cost eight pounds, and if you have a sword for six more you will be a happy man.' Buckingham was also quartered at York, and Savile acted as his second in a duel wherein the Duke is said to have shown much pusillanimity.

This scare of invasion soon passed; Savile's troop was disbanded in September and we find his brother rallying him, in his usual liveliness, on his approaching descent 'from a great captain to a country knight'. Only a week later, however, in letters of which the light and reckless tone belies an undercurrent of real bitterness, Henry announces his own intention of joining the fleet, with the avowed object of meeting his death. The cause of this sudden (and entirely transient) despondency[4] was not revealed even to his brother; but a second letter, despatched from the fleet, expresses the most sincere and passionate gratitude for the affectionate solicitude of Sir George.

Though the danger of an actual descent seemed for the moment postponed, a general sense of uneasiness pervaded all classes. The conduct of the war, it was felt, had been in the highest degree unsatisfactory, and the dissatisfaction demanded an outlet. When, therefore, on 21 September Parliament met, the 'Country' gentlemen, as distinguished from dependents of the Crown, had come up in no good humour. They began to regard themselves and to be regarded by others as a body whose interests were opposed to those of the Court. Touched both in pride and in pocket by the waste of public money, they were embittered by the ill success of the war; while the profligacy of Whitehall stirred into sullen discontent a remaining leaven of Puritan asceticism. This 'Faction', as it was called, in the Lower House, acted in alliance—an informal alliance it is true—with the heirs of the old 'Presbyterian' tradition in the Upper House.

The animosity of these mutineers naturally centred itself upon Clarendon, the ostensible head of the Government; and was therefore reinforced, and in a manner directed, by the Chancellor's enemy and rival, the Duke of Buckingham. It is, indeed, impossible to credit the Duke with motives more exalted than jealousy of the Minister, resentment against his master, and the fitful ambition which occasionally animated his really considerable abilities. But as Clarendon has already reminded us, men's eyes were still blinded by his patriotic professions, his 'quality and condescension' and his fascinating manners.

Thus encouraged, the country gentlemen did not spare their censures; and, easily recognizing the David of this new political Adullam, the Government retorted. The Session had barely closed ere the Duke was summarily dismissed from all his offices, the Yorkshire Lieutenancy included. Moreover, a warrant was issued for his arrest, on an absurd charge of treasonable conspiracy with an astrologer, one Heydon; whom, by the way, he had first met in the society of Savile, when both had made the charlatan a laughing stock. Buckingham absconded; while Savile and others resigned the commissions they had held under him, thus definitely committing themselves to the party of discontent.

Some measure of conciliation, however, now appeared advisable; so Sir William Coventry and Ashley were appointed to seats on a new Treasury Board, a step which created general satisfaction. The new Commission buckled with a will to the gigantic task of financial reform, but it was too late. Crippled by enormous debts, his country exhausted, his sailors mutinous for want of pay, Charles II saw the necessity of a negotiated peace.

In anticipation of its conclusion the English Government resolved, on economic grounds, against commissioning the fleet. Responsibility for this fatal step was angrily debated; in all probability it was a counsel of necessity, which none approved, but in which all were forced to concur.

Of this error De Witt took immediate advantage. By 3 June the Dutch fleet swept the Channel; by 10 June Sheerness was taken. How manfully Coventry and Pepys worked, despatching fireships, etc., but to what little purpose—how terrible was the retribution which had so suddenly fallen on a corrupt and shiftless administration—the terror, the confusion, the insubordination of that appalling conjuncture—these are all writ down for us in the graphic pages of Pepys.

Sir George appears to have gone down to the seat of action, probably as a volunteer in the General's train. He seems to have been at first inclined to minimize the peril, being satisfied it was only (in the words of a correspondent) 'a little brag of the Dutch'. But the crowning disaster still impended, and Sir George was himself at Chatham when on 13 June the Dutch, having broken the boom, burnt the vessels there. 'A Parliament!' was the universal cry, and Sir George was among the most urgent. The Government once more appealed to the patriotism of volunteers, and Savile's former Commission having been renewed, he again applied, in a letter dated 13 June, to Sir Philip Monckton. He writes:

> I do not doubt but you will hear the confusion we are in here since the burning of our ships by the Dutch at Chatham. I was a melancholy spectator of that business, so that I could tell you the particulars, if it were not so unpleasant to me to repeat them, as it would be to you to read them. It is feared they may attempt the firing of the ships we have left upon the river, and the possibility, they being masters of the sea, may suddenly invade us, maketh the King resolve to raise a great many horse, and hath made me a captain again, which though I should have avoided at

> another time [he evidently glances here at the disgrace of Buckingham] yet in this emergency I lay aside all other considerations, as I believe you will do.... You shall know the precise day of the rendezvous and where we are to have arms; [that is] if we should be invaded, and that we are engaged in a formed war.

A few days later he writes again, this time from Rufford, expressing his thanks for a satisfactory reply:

> I cannot enough commend your zeal for your country. I wish those that have brought us to this condition would yet take such measures as might help us out of it. If you and I do our parts in our little sphere, it will be a satisfaction to us, though it should not preserve us. I hear nothing since I came down, so that I conclude the enemy hath attempted nothing upon the Thames. Whether we shall be invaded or no, seemeth to be in the power of the French and Dutch; now that they have taken the sea from us, it is good to provide against the worst.

Among the many and pressing problems which presented themselves, that of the qualifications for command seems to have specially obsessed him; and when, towards the close of 1667, a correspondent inquired whether he had any 'expedients' to offer in relation to the existing crisis, we have little doubt that he sketched, in a letter or essay, *A Rough Draft of a New Model at Sea.* This, presumably in an enlarged version, appeared in print, but anonymously, a year before his death, when the Service, under William III, was confronted by similar problems.

That this published pamphlet had been conceived, if in a less extended form, many years before, and had been imperfectly revised for the publication of 1694, is proved by the fact that in it the writer describes himself as a man outside the Parliamentary arena. This could never have been applicable to Savile after 13 June 1667/8, when he was to receive his peerage.

The present writer claims no affinity with that school of thought, whose 'higher' criticism decides textual dilemmas by appeal to the inner consciousness of the critic. But in such a case as this conjecture, while it remains conjecture, may be pardonable. We will then conjecture that the original letter or essay was a very brief affair, including perhaps merely a statement of the problem, and the very characteristic solution. If so the elaborate and rather cynical excursus on the comparative values of Absolutism, Republicanism and Constitutionalism, which contains some of his most mature and brilliant aphorisms, may have been added in 1694. We will therefore confine ourselves in this present connection to the presumably earlier passages.

I will make no Introduction [so he began] to the following discourse than that as the importance of our being strong at sea was ever very great, so now in our present circumstances it is grown to be much greater; because as formerly our force in shipping contributed greatly to our trade and safety, so now it is become indispensably necessary to our very being. It may be said now to England 'Martha, Martha, thou art busy about many things, but one thing is necessary.' To the question 'What shall we do to be saved in this world' there is no answer but this, 'Look to your Moat'. The first Article of an Englishman's political creed must be that he believes in the sea, etc.; without that there need be no General Council to pronounce him incapable of salvation, etc.

In fine, he winds up the controversy concerning the 'tarpaulins' (Jack Tars) and the 'gentlemen' by suggesting that while from a political point of view it is desirable that neither the tarpaulins nor the gentlemen should monopolize command, no gentlemen ought to obtain a commission till 'so trained up by a continued habit of living at sea that they may have a right of being admitted free denizens of Wapping...'. Under which circumstances, he adds, 'a gentleman will necessarily command more respect than the mere seaman', etc.

But while Savile thus sketched out a future policy for Parliament, the friends of Clarendon were said to be opposing the Summons so ardently desired by the Chancellor's opponents. The Exchequer, however, could not furnish pay for the forces, and about the end of June Parliamentary writs were therefore issued for 25 July.

Scarcely was the proclamation out ere Buckingham surrendered to the warrant against him. He had little difficulty in clearing himself of a rather ridiculous charge, and was released on 17 July.

Three days later Sir George wrote from Rufford to his Yorkshire friend, Sir Thomas Osborne, who was to become later, under many successive titles, one of his bitterest adversaries. 'The letters this post speak more doubtfully of a peace, so I presume the Parliament must [really] meet; my lord of Buckingham hath kissed the King's hand.' He excuses himself for not waiting on his correspondent; 'the coming to you now would be a greater rudeness than staying away; the measles being among my children, which maketh me conclude I must be an unwelcome guest and a dangerous one, where there are so many little ones, besides the special concern I am to have for my god-daughter's pretty face, which I would not have spoiled though but for a week.'

Parliament in effect met, but was prorogued, after four days' sitting. The Members naturally resented so useless an inconvenience and expense; the next Session, it was felt, would be very stormy; and Clarendon was designated on all hands—his son-in-law, the Duke of York, being almost the only exception—as the appropriate Jonah. On 31 August he, at the King's command, resigned the Great Seal, and forty-eight hours later Sir William Coventry, as one of his most ardent opponents, felt it incumbent on him to sever his connection with Clarendon's son-in-law, the Duke of York, and therefore with the Navy.

Meanwhile, however, Clarendon's disgrace effectively transferred power into the hands of his adversaries, who certainly at the moment represented popular sympathies. Among these the Duke of Buckingham and William Coventry were predominant. Both, as Henry Savile hastened to assure his brother, were particularly concerned for the interests of Sir George Savile, and especially for his long-desired elevation to a seat in the House of Lords. Indeed, Harry was 'positively' convinced this would be done before Parliament met. In the event, however, it did not take place till three months later, and then under peculiar circumstances. What were these? Let us see.

A Commission for inquiring into Naval expenditure, which had been strongly advocated during the preceding Session and which had received the Royal Assent on 19 November, contained the curious proviso that no Member of Parliament (i.e. we presume of the *Lower* House) should sit on the Commission. Among the Commissioners selected Sir George Savile stands conspicuous; and hardly had Parliament risen when the King, with a rather obvious intention of propitiating the Commissioner, conferred on the young baronet the long-coveted distinction of a peerage. 'This', says Pepys, 'I believe will displease the Parliament.'

The letters patent, however, emphasize the antiquity of the Savile family, and its services to the late King 'of pious memory' as well as to the reigning monarch. They were issued 13 January 1667/8; and on 23 January Sir George was summoned for the ensuing Session as 'Baron Savile of Eland and Viscount Halifax'; titles carefully selected with reference to the history of his family and its principal sphere of influence.

CHAPTER IV

IN THE HOUSE OF LORDS. ASCENDANCY OF BUCKINGHAM AND THE 'CABAL'. THE EMBASSY OF 1670

Sir George Savile had thus attained the goal of his immediate ambition, a seat in the House of Lords; but the Parliamentary business of the next two or three years need not long detain us. It is not particularly interesting; and though the new Lord Halifax was regular in his attendance, we can only detect his political bias on three occasions.

1. The Roos Divorce Bill—the first which countenanced remarriage when the validity of the first marriage was not contested—seems to have been regarded as a feeler of Buckingham's—the prelude to the King's divorce and remarriage; and the secondary object thus supposed to underlie its introduction may have affected both debates and votes. Lord Halifax, like his uncles, Henry and William Coventry, opposed the Bill. He was among the eleven Peers—six spiritual and five temporal—who were the most active speakers on their side; and was also one of the few lay Protestants who twice joined the Anglican Bishops, the Duke of York, and the Roman Catholic Peers, in recording his protest.

A valuable synopsis of the final debate on 28 March 1670 has been recently published, founded on the Sandwich papers.[5] From this we gather that during its course a Roman Catholic Peer, in a long and apparently able speech, declared that he knew of but two arguments that could be pleaded in favour of the Bill. (i) It might be regarded as a Christian and conscientious attempt to prevent sinful connections on the part of Lord Roos, should he prove incapable of continence; but on the other hand the same plea might be urged on behalf of all 'brothers in Christ' placed in the same predicament. (ii) It might further be defended as an act of generosity to a noble family, threatened with extinction; but this argument overlooked all the 'many inconveniences' involved in such a precedent. Lord Essex, on the other hand, had cited in support of the Bill such Church Councils as had been held before marriage was forbidden to priests, as favouring the plea of Lord Roos; and had further argued that the Bill might prevent the introduction of foreign practices, such as the murder of faithless wives.

To these arguments Lord Halifax is said to have retorted in a speech which, as the first and one of the most amply reported of this famous orator's efforts, shall be given in full.*

To Lord Essex he replied that: 'Perhaps the Church was a better judge in this matter when the priests were unmarried. For surely the generality of them are not to be supposed unclean. And therefore the argument of preventing sin cannot weigh much, because a great many live holily without marriage; and prayer and fasting and a good climate are good means to keep safe on that point.' He told the story of a traveller who, visiting a monastery and wondering at their strictness and duty, asked them what would become of them if that they laboured after, and obeyed, were not true? To whom they replied: 'What would become of him if it were true?' This Halifax applied as follows: 'What would become of us if we should make a law against the law of God?' To the argument that relief had already once been given by Parliament in a somewhat similar case, he answered: 'that precedents of Parliament were not infallible, for it may be the best thing we have done may have been the repeal of some acts of Parliament'. Again to those who argued that 'Bishops [and] martyrs have been' for such a course, he replied, 'that such was no good argument for they might have done [i.e. judged] ill' in their earlier years; instancing Cranmer concerning whom 'it was notorious that he once recanted, before he was burnt'. He pointed out that 'the general practice had been against [such] second marriage[s] and therefore the proof should lie on the marriage side'. He further complained that: 'this bill hath already done much hurt, it hath put by many private bills [on more important subjects?] wherein men have wanted relief as much as my Lord Roos can want a wife. And it is likely these [divorce?] cases will be more frequent hereafter and take up much of our time.'

He said he feared '[not?] the introduction of the customs of stabbing wives in this climate; but he feared the great encouragement of perjury,...when it shall have this strong motive, viz. of being quit of a wife one is a-weary of and the hopes of obtaining one one loves'.

The inconvenience, on the one hand, is that 'if my lady Roos does

* We accept the authority of the Sandwich MS. But we confess that in tone it is much more suggestive of a Roman Catholic Peer.

not die in convenient time, my Lord Roos cannot marry; but on the other hand, there is a likelihood of inconveniences public and eternal'.

The Bill, however, passed both Houses; Sir William Coventry, and his brother, in the Lower House, voting against it.

2. Next we must mention the action of Lord Halifax concerning the Conventicle Bill which was directed against Protestant Nonconformists; and was distinguished by the severity of its definitions and by the despotic powers it conferred upon Justices of the Peace. Here, again, Lord Halifax voted with the opposition, and was included among the seventeen Lords who entered a special protest.

3. In the third place he appears to have also advocated, again without result, a reform of the Parliamentary privilege system; the abuse of which, in the seventeenth century, was an outstanding disgrace.

Meanwhile, outside Parliament, the Board of Accounts was of course requiring his particular attention. Pepys had appeared before it on 31 January 1667/8; and had found himself received 'with great respect and kindness'; which he reciprocated. 'I do observe', he writes, 'they do go about their business like men resolved to go through with it, and in a very good method, like men of understanding.'

On 3 July he again records a long sitting; and had found the Commissioners were 'hot set on the matter; but I did give them proper and safe answers. Halifax I perceive was industrious on my side on behalf of his uncle Coventry.' The Commission finally reported in October 1669; but the only result was to throw into yet more invidious relief the prevailing mismanagement.

The most arresting feature, however, of the Ministerial situation during these years was the rapid and spectacular, but not surprising, decline of William Coventry's influence. He had immediate reason to regret that he had helped to displace a Minister who, if arrogant and bigoted, was yet a statesman and a patriot, by the meteoric and licentious Buckingham, who was neither. With him, Coventry's relations became quickly and obviously strained. Buckingham had keenly resented Sir William's opposition to a proposed impeachment of the ex-Chancellor; while Sir William's devotion to business soon became a butt for the Duke's unscrupulous ridicule.

Nor was this all. The witty Duke's personal fascination soon gave him direct influence over the King; while Charles, on the other hand, was perfectly aware that to certain still secret but far-reaching projects of his own Sir William would prove an uncompromising obstacle. Thus, doubly out of favour, Coventry, within four months of his apparent admission to power, found himself excluded from the 'Cabinet' Council, and 'without a friend in the whole Court'. The capricious Duke, indeed, still oscillated between insolence and flattery. At one moment we are told he offered to make Coventry Chief Minister of State; but if so, he soon recanted, and the climax was both sudden and characteristic.

In a play which he had written for the King's 'House' (i.e. 'Theatre'), the Duke had inserted an obvious caricature of his colleague. Participation in the general laugh might have turned the edge of the satire; but a sense of humour was not, we gather, Sir William's strong point, and he had suffered much.

Almost immediately (March 1668/9) the Court was startled by a rumour that either Coventry or Halifax had challenged the Duke to a duel. The report had already reached the authorities; and as Coventry when summoned, in consequence, before the Council had refused to incriminate himself, his intended second Harry Savile had been, to the general consternation, relegated to the Gatehouse, and Coventry himself to the Tower. There Lord Halifax had become his first visitor, and there Sir William himself learned that he had been summarily dismissed from the Privy Council. It was not till after a fortnight's incarceration, which Sir William endured with characteristic philosophy, and his second with characteristic hilarity, that both were released—in disgrace.

That the offence was, as we have already hinted, merely a pretext is abundantly clear. 'I am not sorry', wrote Charles to his sister, 'Madame' d'Orléans, 'that Sir William Coventry has given me this good occasion to turn him out of the Council. I do intend to turn him also out of the Treasury. The truth of it is he has been a troublesome man in both places, and I am well rid of him.' What this meant we shall see later.

How indecent was the pretext for his disgrace we can only realize when we note that the proclamation against duelling, upon which it was based, had been elicited by the notorious and fatal duel, fought just over a year before, between Buckingham, the seducer of Lady Shrewsbury, and her injured husband. Lord Halifax, as a kinsman of the family, had been left guardian to its orphaned heir; and relations which, by that event, will have become strained to the uttermost must have become impossible after the disgrace of Coventry, and of Savile's own brother Henry.

Meanwhile, Sir William's place on the Treasury Commission was promptly transferred to Buckingham's new favourite, Sir Thomas Osborne, a former friend of Halifax; and from this time Sir William Coventry, who had barely passed his fortieth year, withdrew as far as possible from public life, satisfied perhaps that the experiment he had once proposed in Pepys's presence 'To see whether [a man could] keep himself up in Court by dealing plainly and walking uprightly' had ended in failure. In the House of Commons, however, from which he could not retire, his high character and statesmanlike moderation retained for him an authority which he rather deprecated. But Parliamentary duties apart, he subsided into the part of a country gentleman, the friend and monitor of innumerable nephews and nieces.

During this period the Parliamentary career of the nephew for whom Coventry showed most concern was being chequered by domestic misfortune. On the night of 16 December 1670 Lady Halifax died—suddenly we must presume, as her husband had attended the House that day. Lord Halifax was left a widower at thirty-seven, with four young children whose ages ranged from three to nine years.

Some four months later (22 April 1671) Parliament was prorogued; and the recess thus begun lasted two years.

So much for Parliamentary affairs during the first three years of Savile's career in the House of Lords; but in fact, during this whole period, the real interest of the country, and, indeed, of all Europe, had been focused on the continental stage.

This, from the date of the Chatham disaster onwards, had become the scene of a startling transformation. For the sudden assault of Louis XIV on the Spanish Netherlands, without even a declaration of war, had betrayed to the world—and especially to his new Dutch allies—both his immediate claim to a hegemony over western Europe, and his ultimate design upon the whole of the Spanish Succession.

Hence of course had followed an immediate rupture between France and the United Provinces, and the emergence of the hardly less momentous problem—what lines would England pursue? Would she take sides with France, or against her?

Actually, Charles had offered his alliance to the highest bidder; and as, at the moment, the States had, in his opinion, returned the most favourable answer, he had closed with their proposals. During January 1667/8, Sir William Temple had been empowered to conclude the celebrated treaty, which, as it also included Sweden, is known to fame as the Triple Alliance.

It says much for the political acumen of Englishmen that the new pact excited a more or less general applause. The warm approval of Halifax followed as a matter of course; and through life he remained faithful to the basic principles of this 'League against Aggression'.

The step, however, had been forced upon Charles II by his necessities, and in direct contradiction to his own political sympathies. Well aware of this, French diplomacy now made the dissolution of the new League its first object. Intrigues to that effect almost immediately began; and had soon become inextricably interwoven with the one great political design which Charles II ever elaborated: the reduction of England, with the assistance of France, to the obedience of the Roman See.[6]

This remarkable project appears to have been but slightly connected with that rather superficial preference for Roman doctrine and practice, so wittily satirized by Halifax in his *Character of Charles*. Natural as this was in one who had lived long under the influence of a Roman Catholic mother and had no reason to love the extreme forms of Protestantism, yet in the intrigues of the years 1670–72, the real motives seem to have been political. What Halifax was dexterously to imply some thirteen or fourteen years later in his *Character of a Trimmer*, is more bluntly expressed by Burnet in the early (contemporary) draft of his posthumously published *History*. 'The King', he says, 'thinks an implicitness in religion is necessary for the safety of government, and he looks upon all inquisitiveness into these things as mischievous to the State.' So convinced, Charles had persuaded himself that the divisions of the sects and the sacerdotalism of the High Church Anglicans, might, if sufficiently stimulated by pressure from abroad, and conciliated by considerable ecclesiastical concessions from Rome, with a toleration to pacify Dissent, render this great reaction a possibility.

The occasion had appeared to him favourable. The Ministerial disappearance of that staunch Protestant, Clarendon, and the then impending disgrace of the equally staunch Coventry, had seemed to clear the ground; and the secret adhesion of the Duke of York to his mother's Church—a fact with which, how we know not,

Halifax became very early acquainted—gave a vigorous impetus to the intrigue.

It was under these circumstances that there had taken place on the Feast of the Conversion of St Paul (25 January) 1668/9, a fortnight before Coventry's dismissal, a mysterious consultation. The protagonists, it is known, were, on the one side, Charles II, the Duke of York, and Lord Arundel, a leading Roman Catholic. On the other, the Ministers Clifford and Arlington. The former, a professed admirer of the 'système Louis Quatorze', declared openly his adhesion to Rome; while the latter, though at this time a professed devotee of the Anglican Church, was to become reconciled to Rome on his death-bed. This conference seems to have brought matters to a head, the Royal brothers avowing, in confidence, their conversion to Roman Catholicism, while remaining openly in Communion with their national Church.

The assistance of Louis XIV had already been claimed; and to facilitate the negotiations, 'Madame' d'Orléans, the devoted sister of Charles II, paid about the middle of 1670 her celebrated visit to Dover; to which Halifax (in *The Character of a Trimmer*)—but in respect of its political aspect only—was to make such pointed references.

Then and there was signed in May–June 1670 the notorious Secret Treaty, to which, alone among the Ministers, both Arlington and Clifford were privy.

In this treaty, Louis XIV, in the first place, required that Charles II should, by the sacrifice of Holland, to whom our faith had been so recently pledged, further the French King's design on the Spanish Succession. In return Louis bound himself, first, to co-operate, with men and money, towards the restoration of the Papal authority in this country. In the second place his most Christian Majesty undertook (*a*) to secure for Great Britain the four islands of the Province of Zealand, and (*b*) to promote the political interests of the very youthful Prince of Orange, nephew of the English King, then still a mere subject of the States. A clause against separate negotiations on the part of the contracting Powers was appended to the treaty.

Here, for the moment, the negotiations paused. But six months later, the avowedly Protestant Ministers—Buckingham, Ashley, and Lauderdale—were entrapped into signing a military convention between the two Powers, expressly directed against the United Provinces. In this convention the ecclesiastical conditions were ignored; but as a first move in that direction His Britannic Majesty issued a totally illegal declaration of Indulgence to all Nonconformists, whether Roman or Protestant.

And then—on 25 February 1672—the war started.

Both steps were extremely unpopular; and the resentment of Halifax knew no bounds. Indignant at the treacherous breach of the newly formed Triple Alliance, his knowledge of the Duke's secret change of religion threw an alarming light on the unconstitutional declaration. The Duke of York had himself openly boasted that the stricter Anglicans must, on their principles of passive obedience, acquiesce in the Royal mandate. But as the Duke of York's biographer himself records, My Lord Halifax replied: 'His Royal Highness would soon see the contrary', for those to whom he referred would, he was sure, 'roar against this declaration with all their might'.

The result justified his warnings. The Lower House, then predominantly and decidedly Anglican, showed such tokens of discontent, that the Government saw the necessity of some conciliatory gesture. As a sop, therefore, to popular resentment, Lord Halifax, and three of his fellow-malcontents in the House of Lords—Lord Essex being the most important—were on 17 April 1672 admitted to the Privy Council. Further, Sir William Coventry's elder brother, Henry, lately Ambassador at Stockholm (and therefore presumably in part responsible for the recent popular Alliance), having already received his letters of recall, was at once appointed to the responsible post of Secretary of State.

On this exchange his nephew congratulated him with a characteristic blend of grace and satire:

Dear Uncle [he wrote on 3 June 1672], Though I sent you no compliments to Sweden, I cannot hold congratulating your return from it. That alone is ground enough for your friends to rejoice with you, and it is not the worse that from the minute you are no more My Lord Ambassador, you will at least be Mr Secretary; upon these terms you may be the better content to part with 'Excellency' and all the worship belonging to your character; since you have something in exchange for it. I expect you will bear it with Christian patience, that you are no more to wait upon the King's person in the Bedchamber, nor represent his person in foreign countries; never more to see Stockholm and for ever to take your leave of Brother Philipson are afflicting things, 'tis confessed, but you must submit to your ill fate and make the best on't. In great earnest there is an universal joy for the King's choice of you; whether that is a compliment to you or no I will not determine; I rather incline to believe it ought to be a matter of humiliation to you, considering how little the world is disposed to approve anything that is good. The truth is, you are popular to a scandal, and I am tempted to love you the less because everyone else is so kind to you. I think I was the first man the King told of his actual choice of you; for upon the first notice of your predecessor's death, I being then in the room he called me to him, and acquainted me with his resolution concerning you. I made the best compliments for you I could at that time; when you come yourself you will make better; and in the meantime pray believe it is none when I assure you of my being, Dear Uncle, Your most affectionate Nephew and humble servant.

It seems even to have been suggested that Halifax himself (had he not been so 'stiff against Popery') might have been appointed Viceroy of Ireland. Probably Halifax would not have coveted an office which had proved so fatal to his uncle Strafford; and in the course of a fairly frequent, but mainly complimentary, correspondence with Lord Essex, who actually obtained the post, we find Lord Halifax congratulating the Earl on being 'the first man that could ever at the same time [so] govern and please such an unruly province, that all sorts of people are satisfied that are fit to be so'.

Meanwhile, however, Halifax himself was being selected for an important but strangely invidious mission.

Already Louis XIV, relying on his half-disclosed compact with England—which had by this time brought him the support of a mobilized English fleet, and the services of an English contingent—had thrown his admirably equipped, and, for those days, enormous army of 100,000 men upon the ill-prepared forces of the Dutch Netherlands. He had, indeed, already occupied, or effectually menaced, five out of the seven United Provinces; and had thus forced the English King's nephew, the very youthful but undaunted Prince of Orange (who, in the vain hope of placating his uncle, had been hurriedly appointed Captain General), to fall back with his meagre army round the Hague and Amsterdam; where he stood prepared to sell as dearly as possible the two remaining provinces.

At this juncture the birth of an illegitimate son to the apparently triumphant Louis seemed to call for the usual complimentary mission on the part of his English ally. This at the same time provided opportunity for new professions of loyalty to an Alliance, which the terrified Dutch politicians, by separate appeals to the English partner, were attempting to undermine. All this was natural; but the choice of a representative proved surprising in the extreme. On 10 June, M. Colbert, the French Ambassador to the Court of St James, informs his Government that a certain Lord

Halifax has been selected for the errand. He has indeed 'de la qualité, de grands biens, et beaucoup d'esprit; il a même témoigné par sa conduite envers moi, le grand respect... qu'il a pour le roi notre maître; *mais il m'a paru jusque's à présent assez contraire à la bonne union qui est entre la France et l'Angleterre*;* though Colbert trusts he, like all others, will succumb to the fascination of his most Christian Majesty's conversation. Two days later M. Colbert adds a pregnant warning: 'Milord Arlington m'a prié de vous avertir, que Milord Halifax qui va trouver le Roi ne sait rien de la grande affaire'—i.e. the Restoration of Popery.

Surprising as the appointment appeared on the surface, it is not so strange if we look into it more closely. It was no doubt part of the general attempt to appease—and possibly to compromise—the opposition. But it is certainly, at first sight, difficult to understand why Lord Halifax should have accepted a mission so little in unison with his known and expressed sentiments. The most likely interpretation is that some one of the Ministers, alarmed by the general dislike of the war, which had become only too obvious, was desirous to hedge; that he wished Halifax to exercise a moderating influence; and that Halifax accepted an uncongenial task with this end in view. Arlington, naturally timid, who, though so deeply involved in the Dover treaty, had Spanish sympathies, and had married a connection of the House of Orange, was in all probability the Minister in question.

The instructions of Lord Halifax, which were signed on 14 June, directed him to make for Bruges; reporting himself meanwhile during the crossing to the Duke of York, then commanding the fleet. From Bruges he was to proceed to the French headquarters, and, with his congratulations on the avowed object of his mission, compliment the King on the happy progress made by his armies against the common foe. He was to report that the Dutch overtures for a separate peace had been repelled; and that the Dutch Ambassador had been dismissed.

He was required, however, in his public discourse to refrain from displaying any aversion to peace proposals, which would be a thing of 'an ill sound both at home and abroad'. While passing through Zealand, however, he was to encourage 'as far as you may without exposing your person to any hazard', any potential proposal for a voluntary surrender, of that, or any other province, to the protection of the English crown.

* Italics our own.

On the other hand, he was to reassure the French King 'in the most convincing terms you can devise, of our entire satisfaction in his friendship, and his whole proceeding ever since the beginning of all our late transactions to this day and of our firm resolution to correspond therewith by all the acts of friendship within our power'.

He was further to remind the King of the conditions in favour of the Prince of Orange and of the timeliness of the existing conjuncture (when a 'dissolution' of the United Provinces seemed at hand) for the fulfilment of the pledges so recently made in his favour. Finally, his most Christian Majesty is to be informed that a British fleet is ready for a descent on the Dutch coast, in collaboration with the French land forces.

Lord Halifax seems to have started on 14/24 or 15/25 June, and after a painfully protracted passage, reached Calais 19/29 June. Thence he reported to Arlington that, to make amends for the delay, 'I intend, though not quite recovered of my sea-sickness, to go this night to Dunkirk, upon the strength of 5 or 6 hours rest I have had in this town'.

The travellers reached Nieuport, accordingly, the following day, and finding the Bruges canal-boat passing through the town went on at once. At Bruges the envoy was detained four days by passport difficulties, and thence wrote twice to Lord Arlington. Of the first letter only the following passage has been recovered: 'It is almost certain that at the rate the King of France now goeth, while I am making a circuit to find him, the country will be gone. The French are within two or three leagues of Amsterdam which, although it hath drowned the country about it, yet the multitude of people, want of fresh water, and above all, fear, will hinder them from doing the utmost for defence.'

The second despatch tells of the popular revolution which was restoring the energetic young Captain-General in the Stateholdership so long held by his ancestors. The passport difficulty once over,

> I am going [writes Halifax] this morning to Sluys and from thence to Middleburgh....I believe it now certain that the Prince of Orange is declared Stadthoulder at Amsterdam, Rotterdam, Dort and Haerlem and the messenger I sent into Zeland saw it done whilst he stayed for my passport. I am told that de Witt who came sick from the Fleet to Dort was forced by the people to sign to the making the Prince Stadthoulder. One of the men that hurt de Witt is beheaded....In Zeland the Burghers of all the Towns, hav[e] sworn to defend themselves to the last and to

part with all money they have to the State if it be necessary. But I suppose if our Fleet cometh out and hath the success we may reasonably hope, it may make them dispense with their rash Oaths. They have taken some men from their Fleet to put into their Garrisons hereabouts which shows they do not intend to engage with us at Sea. I hear now that they are a good deal recovered from their fears at Amsterdam relying upon the water they have let in to secure them. The particulars of Ardenburg and Zutphen I send as I received them in print from Zeland. A Regiment of foot came to-day to this place in very great haste. If their business should be anything more than ordinary it must be known in a few days. If I meet anything in Zeland worth acquainting your Ldpp. with I will send from thence to you. In the meantime I am

My Ld.,

Your Ldpps. most humble and obedient servant

HALIFAX

Bruges, 4 July 1672

We have, however, no means of knowing when, if ever, Lord Arlington perused this letter; for an extraordinary transformation of the Ministerial situation in London was bringing the Foreign Minister hard on the heels of his own Ambassador.

A few days after the departure of Halifax, the French Court, regarding the Dutch defeat as certain, had asked that Charles should send someone to the French camp empowered to treat for peace.

The zeal of the mercurial Duke of Buckingham for the French Alliance had rapidly cooled. He resented the young Duke of Monmouth's appointment, coveted by himself, to the command of our prescribed contingent. He realized, perhaps shared, the very general suspicion—entertained even by our own representatives at Versailles—that Louis, in the flush of success, and in the interest of his own designs on the Spanish Netherlands, intended to bypass our claims to the islands of Zealand. Even Buckingham's temerity had become alarmed by the widespread dislike of the war, and suspicions as to the secret conditions of the Dover treaty; while his vanity had been flattered by private overtures from the Dutch.

Within a week of Lord Halifax's departure Buckingham had become anxious—not, like Halifax, and possibly Arlington, for a speedy cessation of hostilities, but for our own more certain and extensive share in the anticipated booty. This alone, he thought, could reconcile his critics to the continuance of an unpopular war. Negotiations in which England might play the part of a—dishonest—broker, could alone, he fancied, propitiate public opinion.

The overtures which the alarmed States-General had made in severalty to the Allied Powers had now in appearance brought peace within the sphere of practical politics. But though Louis had already requested plenipotentiary powers for Godolphin, our own representative at Versailles, Buckingham, now urged that he himself should be sent thither on a special mission. Charles II yielded; but to bridle Buckingham's unwelcome ardour included Arlington in the Commission; thus leaving the country—Henry Coventry being still at sea—without a Secretary of State.

On 20 July, therefore, Buckingham and Arlington, together with Clifford and Ashley, i.e. the whole available membership of the 'Cabal' or Cabinet, had met the Dutch deputies in a preliminary conference. Therein all recognized their common interest in refuting the extravagant demands of Louis; and there the Dutchmen, unofficially, broached possible terms of peace.

Thereupon the new Ambassadors received their instructions to repair to the French headquarters; and there, in conjunction with the Commissioners of Louis, 'to treat with the...States for satisfaction and accommodating all differences'. Should Lord Halifax have arrived before them, 'You shall', they are told, 'acquaint him with all your instructions, and let him know he is in joint commission with you, and that he act accordingly'.

They were further to insist with His Most Christian Majesty that 'we cannot assent to a peace until we have some effect of the war—namely—the places agreed upon between us for our division', or conditions equivalent. And any Peace Treaty so concluded must include certain conditions in our favour, to which, as Buckingham believed, the Dutch might be prepared to accede.

These were, *in general*, recognition of our right of the flag, and of our Dominion in the British seas; payment for fishing rights therein; an indemnity; the surrender, in permanence, of 'Cautionary Towns' such as Flushing, Sluys, and The Brill, with payment for the English troops to be garrisoned there; concessions in East Indies, etc.

As respects the *interests of the Prince of Orange*, the best terms possible were to be obtained for him. These must include at the very least the offices of Stadtholder, Captain-General, and High Admiral in perpetuity; with descent to his heirs male. But preferably he was also to receive the sovereignty of the Province of Holland, with as much territory in the other Provinces as might consist with the safeguarding of British interests.

Immediately on receiving these instructions, the Ambassadors started.

Leaving them on their way we must now return to the unwitting Lord Halifax, still in ignorance of his own practical supersession. He had left Bruges on the 24th; and travelling by way of Sluys, Cadzant and Flushing to Middleburg in Zealand, he thence addressed to Lord Arlington, whom he supposed still at Whitehall, an important despatch of which we give the salient passages:

...I go away from hence this afternoon and in the meantime what I have observed in this little time, is an extreme aversion in this people of Zealand to the French; your Ldp. will believe they are not very fond of us at this time, yet the Burgers here have amongst other articles resolved, that in case of extremity they will give themselves up to the English; how that extremity will be defined or how far it may be in their power to keep their resolution, if they let the danger come too near them, is a question I cannot determine; that which recommendeth us to them is their greater hatred to the French, and the consideration of preserving their religion, they being here very Zealous Protestants, and universally so, without any mixture of Roman Catholics. I could wish in this and other respects, that if anything should be attempted upon this Island, it might be done by English alone, for in a good conjuncture, half force and half treaty, the K[ing's] business might perhaps be better done by a small number of his own subjects, than by a greater force half made up of French, to whom the aversion is so great, that it would make them desperate and deaf to any treaty; whether this is to be practised or no, your Ldp. best knoweth; I only offer it to your thoughts, which I hope will forgive me. The Prince of Orange's colours flourish everywhere in this place and the people are much pleased with it. He is chosen Stadtholder of Amsterdam and Delft and other places in Holland, in many of them it was done by a kind of violence of the people upon the Magistrates. He is now between Utrecht and Leyden, but I do not hear he hath any considerable force with him. This morning four of the States here gave me a visit; amongst them, Mr Odike, who is just come back from his deputation to the most Christian King. The account he gave me which was before the rest of the States, is, that the King never saw them but referred them to Mr Pompone and Mr de-Louvois, who at first told them nothing could be treated upon till our Master was first consulted, but afterwards proposed the articles I now send to your Ldp. (which are printed here); that upon the deputies asking him what satisfaction the King of England would expect, he told him each party was to keep what they had got, that the English were not in a condition to make such demands as his Master and that they would look only to the business of the Flag, and the fishing; this, I relate as I heard it from the Author, thinking it my duty not to omit to let your Ldp. know it; when I am at my journey's end, I shall presently see whether there is any mistake in this intelligence. The States said much of their ill condition, lamenting the war they have with England and wishing the King would interpose. I kept myself the best I could within the rules prescribed to me, putting them in mind I was a private person here; and in that capacity I told them the King had no fixed resolution to ruin their country, but only to do himself right and that whenever they found themselves in the disposition of proposing anything to his Majesty I did not doubt but they would find him inclined to all reasonable things that might consist with his honour. It would be too long to tell your Ldp. all our discourse, but we parted very kindly. One thing I must not forget they said, which was that if the King of England should now engage with their Fleet, the advantage of his victory would go wholly to the French, since the effect of it would be that all the countries would the sooner yield to him, when they have no hopes* at sea left to support them. I intend to go from hence towards Utrecht this afternoon, being told the King of France is there or near it. They please themselves here with the report of an Army coming out of Germany to their rescue. Their Fleet lieth so near Flushing that I saw it as I came from Sluys. I am my Ld.

Your Ldps. most humble and obedient servant,

HALIFAX

Middleburgh, 5 July 1672 (N.S.)

Meanwhile on this actual date the very Minister to whom, as still awaiting it at Whitehall, this letter was addressed, was forwarding from the Hague to a Ministerial colleague in England a lengthy despatch, accompanied by a letter from Buckingham himself. These gave a vivid picture of the excitement which prevailed throughout Zealand, but more especially at The Hague. There the populace was forcing on the terrified magistrates the elevation of the Prince to the Stadtholdership. Enthusiastic multitudes—much exhilarated by drinking health to the Prince, and confusion to the States, and confident that the English mission was 'partial to the Prince', and 'came to make peace'—had escorted the envoys to their lodging. The Englishmen, regarding the annihilation of the Dutch Republic as a practically accomplished fact, presumed that nothing remained for the young Prince save to ensure that the ruin of his country should involve his own elevation. They expected, therefore, that he would be prepared to extort from his fellow-countrymen the satisfaction of those English demands, which the French, as we believed, were unwilling to implement; and thus, by combined Anglo-Dutch pressure, wrest

* This word may be read either as 'hopes' or 'forces'.

from the victorious French the personal profits proposed by Charles for his nephew. With this end in view, they broke their further progress to the French camp on 25 June/6 July by a visit to the Prince's Leaguer (i.e. camp), 'at a certain place called Newerbrugge...being a pass upon the old Rhine'.

There a momentous collóquy took place which the despatch describes at length. But the very youthful Stadtholder proved intractable. He refused to sacrifice his country's interest to his own; and, as the Prince afterwards told Burnet, dilated so cogently upon the impolicy of the Anglo-French Alliance that the volatile Duke, exclaiming with his accustomed oath that William 'was in the right', offered then and there to sign a treaty between England and the States. Arlington was thunderstruck—night brought counsel—Buckingham recoiled; but the Prince and the Dutch still stood firm. The envoys departed in much mortification; Buckingham to the last urging upon the Prince, that he 'must see' his country 'was lost'; only to evoke from the Prince the historic retort that he would 'never see' that; since he would 'die in the last ditch'.

The embittered Ministers proceeded on their way to Utrecht. Their reception by Louis was gratifying, and they were proportionally impressed.

On that very day Lord Halifax (detained by contrary winds on his passage from Zealand to Rotterdam), followed, in their wake, to the Prince's camp. There, apparently, he first learned the existence of the second Embassy; and thence he despatched his apologies to his new and unexpected colleagues.

So much we learn but no more; though one would give much to know what passed between the young Prince and the budding statesman. They had possibly met a year before, when, as a mere subject of the States, the Prince of Orange had visited his English kindred; but little could either of them have guessed that, sixteen years later, Halifax was to offer the Prince the Royal Crown of England and serve under him as his first Prime Minister. All we hear is that Lord Halifax speedily left the Prince's camp, and reached the French headquarters a day after his predecessors.

There his audience was deferred for two days; that is, *until after the decisive conference between the other Ambassadors and the French Ministers had taken place.* His arrival is cursorily mentioned in their ensuing despatch: 'My Lord Halifax here arrived last night, and will have his audience to-morrow;' at which (after having presented his formal congratulations) 'he will refer himself in the other points of his instructions to what hath been said by us; his Lordship is acquainted with this whole despatch and shall be so with the whole progress of our negociation.'

It is obvious that to acquaint a colleague with the progress of a negotiation, and to concede to him a substantial share in its discussions, are two very different things; and it is certain that while the other envoys (and especially Buckingham) continued intent on reconciling their countrymen to an unpopular policy, by the bait of territorial gains, Lord Halifax continued firm to the principles he had previously avowed. Anxious to withdraw his country, at almost any cost, from a dangerous and impolitic war, and a disastrous alliance, he favoured a conciliatory and purely honorary scale of demands; such as might facilitate an arrangement between the Dutch and English combatants, and lay the foundation of a new Triple Pact.

Four separate strands of evidence prove this to have been, in fact, the policy he advocated.

Firstly, in the following year there appeared in England an anonymous but very able and apparently well-informed attack on the French Alliance.[7] It has been ascribed to Sir William Coventry, but is more probably attributed to Pierre du Moulin, Secretary to the Prince of Orange. The writer challenges the Duke and Arlington, whom he charges with pecuniary corruption, to answer eight queries. Of these, the fourth, inquires 'How far those that were joined in Commission with them, did concur with them in their judgment...?' and whether the dangers of endorsing and accentuating the French demands, together with the importance of the advances made by the Prince and the Dutch, 'were not represented to them; and urged by some who had no other end but to serve their master faithfully'. Finally the fifth article openly suggests this as the reason why 'they opposed so fiercely, my Lord Viscount Halifax (who came a day or two after them) his appearing and acting with them, though commissionated in as...ample a manner as themselves'; while the sixth query roundly demands 'who were those (after my Lord Halifax could be kept out no longer) who went privately to the French Court under several pretences and had still negociations of their own on foot'.

Secondly, Buckingham himself, eighteen months later, in his self-vindication before the House of Commons, fully approves the exaction of severe terms from the States and practically assumes the sole responsibility for this policy.

Thirdly, Lord Arlington is even more explicit. 'I and Halifax', he says, 'were for moderate courses, Buckingham for exorbitances.'

Fourthly, we have a paper of undated, but obviously contemporary notes, in the handwriting of Lord Arlington's Secretary which concludes with these words: 'N.B. Some differences of opinion happened among the Ambassadors as to the framing of conditions on our part, viz. how high or low to go in our demands. *Duke Buckingham* was for all Zealand, Doorne, Cadzant, Sluye and in fine [query: 'a fine'] as high as the highest that had ever been thought of; as being of opinion they must, and would, give it. At least the Nation would expect to have somewhat by the war.' ('He remembered not the Instructions made a lower degree yet, etc.' (? optional).)

'*Earl Halifax* was for a little money and few places, etc.; a peace would be so happy, so grateful, so necessary for the nation. (He) remembered not the instructions were peremptory—in a peace to have this or that, etc.

'*Earl Arlington* was much lower than the Duke of Buckingham, and yet above Lord Halifax, but withal seemed to think there was latitude enough left in the Instructions for their Lordships to vary in some particulars from what seems peremptorily prescribed in it, etc.'

The efforts of the new Privy Councillor were, however, of no effect, when opposed to Buckingham's determination and Arlington's weakness. The terms formulated, apparently within twenty-four hours of his arrival, were couched in Buckingham's sense; with the addition of an item demanding the extradition of political refugees. These terms were transmitted to the Prince with a peremptory credential letter, which was signed by Buckingham, Arlington, and Monmouth only. The Prince responded drily that they were twenty-four hours too late; he had taken the oath to the States the day before and meant to abide by it; the terms offered should be forwarded for the consideration of their High Mightinesses.

Two days later this was done, but the French Ministers exacted from the Englishmen the signature of another engagement, confirming the provisions against a separate peace. This document bears the signature of Halifax, along with those of his fellow-negotiators, but from a letter despatched to the Prince of Orange his signature seems to be absent.[8] The Prince's attempts to obtain better terms appeared at first to offer some prospect of success; but this was illusory; for though Louis consented to some modification of his original demands, the Prince and the States continued to oppose a contemptuous refusal to the proffers of the two Kings.

Whereupon, to the world's astonishment, Louis, on 16/26 July, alarmed by the floods and the threat of German forces on his flank,[9] suddenly returned to Paris. Thus without any formal armistice the United Provinces were respited, and the immediate situation saved.

Brief and abortive as the ambassadorial experience of Halifax had proved to be, it exerted no doubt an influence on his subsequent career, which can hardly be over-estimated. It had enabled him to study the Continental situation at first hand and at the moment of supreme crisis. Into the four weeks it had occupied had been concentrated the decisive moments of half a century. He had seen with his own eyes the initial stages of the great military and political duel between Louis Quatorze and the young Stadtholder, which was only to end thirty years later with the death of the latter; a conflict of which, in the eyes of the protagonists, the English Revolution was a mere episode, and by which the general policy of Lord Halifax himself was to be in so large a measure conditioned.

Meanwhile, shortly after his return from abroad, events of more private interest to Lord Halifax came to the fore. He had been a widower almost two years when, in November 1672, he rather suddenly contracted 'a second matrimonial alliance'—how else can one describe the great marriages of the seventeenth century?—with Gertrude, youngest daughter of a near neighbour, Mr William Pierrepoint of Thoresby, a distinguished Parliamentarian and a fellow-member of the Commission of Accounts.

The second Lady Halifax, two of whose sisters had married his personal friends, had reached the age of 31, and does not appear to have been exceptionally well dowered. But she had the reputation of unusual loveliness; a reputation which, to judge by the exquisite engraving in Dr Maty's *Life* of her grandson, was very well deserved, and which had involved her in some embarrassments. Six years earlier the heir of Lord Bellasis had paid his court to the young beauty. Compelled by his father to marry a rich heiress, he had publicly asserted that Mistress Pierrepoint should never marry any man but him; and though the young lady gave him no encouragement but was 'exactly virtuous', yet on the mere rumour of a treaty of marriage between her and William, afterwards the famous Lord Russell, Sir Henry, on a flimsy pretext had sent him a challenge; and had only withdrawn it on hearing that the treaty had fallen through.

Dr Maty, in his biography of her grandson, the famous Earl of Chesterfield, who was brought up under her care, says her influence was the best to which her grandson's youth was subjected. 'Her mind', he says, 'seems to have been congenial with that of her...lord, and her understanding and wit were still exceeded by the goodness of her heart and by the purity of her taste.'

Mutual esteem and affection are suggested by the rare references to Lady Halifax which occur in her husband's letters, and by the terms of their respective wills.

A daughter, Elizabeth, born in 1675, was the sole surviving issue of this marriage; but the children of her predecessor no doubt found in the second Lady Halifax a kindly stepmother.

CHAPTER V

UNDER DANBY'S ASCENDANCY

THE strange double negotiations we have just described had failed on either count. Both the King of France and the young Stadtholder had proved obdurate. Peace had not been attained; neither the 'peace of territorial aggrandisement', at which Buckingham had aimed, nor the 'negotiated peace' for which Lord Halifax had striven. On the other hand, the real and great 'Popish Plot' concocted between the two Kings—and the heir of one of them—had received a severe check; worse still, the underlying motives of the war and the Indulgence were being gauged, on this side the Channel, with extraordinary accuracy. 'My Lord Arlington', writes the French Ambassador to his Court, 'has shown me [a pamphlet] which gives a perfectly true account of the designs of the King of England.'

M. Barillon, moreover, had foretold, with curious exactness, the consequent action of the two Houses. For when Parliament at length reassembled on 6 February 1672/3, the Administration found itself exposed to a burst of indignation, far stronger, and far more justly directed than the torrent which, five years before, had swept Lord Clarendon away.

The Government at first showed some resolution; and the Chancellor, recently created Lord Shaftesbury, endorsed to the full the overt policy of the two preceding years. But he did so in vain.

The Indulgence was the first target of attack, and the Commons, under the statesmanlike guidance of Sir William Coventry, displayed both firmness and moderation. They freely offered to secure, *by legal means*, that relief to *Protestant* Dissenters which had been the ostensible motive of the Indulgence. In vain did Shaftesbury urge on his Sovereign the rejection of this compromise, and the reassertion of Prerogative. Alarmed for the prospects of supply, Charles, on the advice of the terrified Arlington, referred the legality of his Declaration to the Lords.

In the debate which ensued Lord Halifax took a leading part. Of his oratory on this occasion, however, but one fragment survives; which while showing how little he realized the depth of the King's perfidy, was to embitter up to the last his relations with the heir-presumptive. For, he said, 'if we could make good the Eastern compliment of "O King live for ever" he could trust the King with everything. But since that was so much a compliment that it never could become real, he could not be implicit in his confidence.' From that moment, says Burnet, the Duke conceived a hatred against Halifax, such as Shaftesbury in his most violent moments never subsequently inspired.

The Lords, in effect, supported the Commons; the King (urged thereto by Louis XIV) thereupon prudently cancelled his Declaration; the Chancellor gave free vent to his exasperation. Angry at the weakness of his master, alarmed for his own safety, and, it is believed by some, made aware, by a panic-stricken Arlington, of the real tenor of the Dover treaty, he began advances towards the Opposition; and at the end of the Session was summarily dismissed from office. As leader of that Opposition, his restless and brilliant strategy was soon to make him a power. But it is probable that his kinsmen, Coventry and Halifax, never subsequently regarded him with either complacency or confidence.

The Opposition, meanwhile, was not yet content. The celebrated 'Test Act', whose shibboleth excluded Papists from all offices, civil or military, was specially supported by Halifax and Coventry. It passed both Houses, and received the Royal Assent. But further ominous references to 'Evil Councillors' were by now rife among the bolder spirits in the Lower House. The alarmed Government hurriedly rushed through both Houses an Amnesty Bill, pleadable in bar of an impeachment, and then summarily prorogued.

The more violent threats of the extremists, however, had won no sanction from Sir William, who shrank, with very characteristic sagacity, from precipitating political animosity by the terrible solvent of blood. His moderation, we find, was highly distasteful to his more bitter associates; and his continued intimacy with his brother, the Secretary of State, aroused, we fancy, considerable suspicion among the irreconcilables. He feared, however, to involve his favourite nephew in his own momentary unpopularity. 'I should be glad', he wrote to another nephew, 'to hear from you (for I must not expect it from him) how Lord Halifax hath made up his matters. I hope he is not like myself, out with all sides. Though I do not regret it for myself...yet I do not think it a good posture for a man who desires to be in the world and in business.'

The anxiety of the country now centred upon the immediate question—what effect would the Test Act produce in high government circles? The answer was alarming in the extreme. The Duke of York and his confidant Clifford promptly threw up all their offices, and thus, to the general consternation, declared themselves Papists. Buckingham at once joined the Opposition; Arlington retired into the safe obscurity of the Lord Chamberlainship; and Shaftesbury having already made his peace, the great 'Cabal' was no more.

The remaining Ministers, not unnaturally, saw the advisability of some further conciliatory gestures. Rumour, and his friends at Court, began to suggest as a popular move, the promotion of Lord Halifax to a position of importance. To this, however, the Court remained very averse; and in fine the 'White Staff' of the Treasury was conferred on an old associate of his Yorkshire days. This was Sir Thomas Osborne, better known to history as Lord Danby, Lord Carmarthen, and Duke of Leeds; a man of real, though superficial ability, but, despite a touch of elementary patriotism, both greedy and unscrupulous.

The Session had been a crucial one. Its events had for the first time revealed to Charles with what intensity of dread the nation still regarded Popery; and had also convinced him that the Act debarring him from the employment of Roman Catholic officials must nip in the bud his ecclesiastical projects. From this moment he, unlike his brother, definitely abandoned the 'grande affaire'.

No less clearly did Lord Halifax and his associates visualize the situation. They, too, saw that a plan for the re-establishment, by force and fraud, of an alien ecclesiastical authority had been entirely checkmated by the Test Act. In regarding thenceforth that Act—despite the hardship it inflicted on a deserving minority—as *at that time and under the then existing conditions* an indispensable condition of political and ecclesiastical safety, they argued correctly.

During the following spring Session (1673/4) the Opposition raised another issue, and gained another victory. The determination of the Houses compelled a peace with Holland, on much the terms advocated by Halifax in 1672. His former fellow-plenipotentiaries were (as we have noted before) severely interrogated. An address for the disgrace of Buckingham was duly carried; and the tacit acquittal of Arlington roused much outspoken indignation in the breasts of Halifax, Shaftesbury, and Coventry.

Shaftesbury now showed himself particularly active in the ecclesiastical sphere; and various expedients were suggested, in order to minimize the danger of a Popish reaction. Nor was he alone. Halifax, too, had his expedients; he advocated the disarming of all reputed Papists. The remarriage of the Duke of York with a Princess of the Roman Catholic House of Modena, proposed and arranged by Louis XIV, was very unpopular; and another Peer, Lord Carlisle, on his part, proposed to restrict future Royal marriages to scions of Protestant houses. He and Halifax even suggested that the penalty on any other marriage should be exclusion from the succession. This proposal, being merely *prospective*, of course differed widely from the *retrospective* scheme which was to be so strenuously opposed by Halifax at a later date. The House of Commons, however, while resolving that none of the blood Royal, within certain degrees, should thenceforth marry a Papist, rejected 'with scorn' the proposed penalty.

During the Sessions the Court learned that meetings of Lords Shaftesbury, Halifax and others, with certain members of the House of Commons, had taken place at *The Queen* in King Street. This is said to have eventually developed (or degenerated) into the notorious *Green Ribbon* Club, which was a main source of Shaftesbury's power in the City. They were said at this time to be discussing Popery, Ireland and Scotland, and the possibility of a French invasion.*

A long prorogation—1674–5—for which Louis XIV is believed to have paid the King of England 500,000 crowns—now followed; and this political pause offers us an opportunity of returning to the private affairs of Lord Halifax.

He had already—some time between 1670 and 1672—removed his family from Lincoln's Inn Fields to a more fashionable quarter; having built himself a 'large airy' and stately mansion in the 'New Piazza'. This, the firstfruits of London's West End movement—and known to seventeenth-century slang as 'Little London'—became our 'St James' Square'; in which Nos. 17 and 18 now represent 'Halifax House'. Common fame described the denizens of the Piazza as outvying all the other Squares (nay even 'under the rose' the Court itself) in 'dressing and breeding'. There, within a stone's throw of the Embassies, and in touch with half the political grandees, Lord Halifax was to make his headquarters until the day of his death; spending only brief intervals of retirement and refreshment at Rufford, or later on at Acton.

* Miss Brown's *Shaftesbury*, p. 267, from Carte's *Ormonde*.

It was there, no doubt, that during the winter's recess of 1674–5, we find him engaged with the Moderates of the Established Church (Drs Tillotson and Stillingfleet) on the one side, and the Presbyterians on the other, in abortive negotiations for a proposed Act of ecclesiastical comprehension.

But his interests while in London were not exclusively political or ecclesiastical. He shared to some extent in the new scientific life of the times. On 20 November 1675 he was, on the proposal of Seth Ward, Bishop of Salisbury, elected fellow of the newly formed Royal Society, of which he seems to have remained a member to the close of his life. We hear of his now and then meeting the Secretary, who describes him as 'kind'; and who interested him in hydraulic experiments and the 'equation of days'. Again, in *The Character of a Trimmer* we find Lord Halifax referring to the epoch-making experiments in the transfusion of blood; which had been made with apparent success at one of the new Society's meetings, some twenty years before, but of which only this century—and, indeed, this present war—has reaped the full advantage.

About this time, however, he seems to have been particularly preoccupied by the education of his sons, the eldest of whom was entering his 'teens'.

In conversation, Lord Halifax appears to have been fond of dilating on his own theories of education; and while many of these sound fantastic, others are suggestive of more approved modern methods.

[One] great cause [says 'Saviliana'] of the decay of virtue his Lordship attributed to the wrong education of the youth. His Lordship would have had School Masters to have been old and grave, taken out of all orders of men, Lords for young noblemen, Gentlemen for the young gentry, and so in lower degrees. These men, if unwilling, to be forced by Law into the imployment for a time; the place to be looked upon as one of the most honorable; without any salary at all from schoolboys, only with a stipend from the Government when the men would take it; their chief care being that the youths should be punished for immorality more than for want of proficiency in learning; and that all should be taught to read and to write and to cast accounts, but not any brought up to languages and Sciences, except such as had parts that would answer. And that shoals of such as had not, should be released from study and timely sent home to make Artificers and Soldiers. It being his Lordship's opinion, that nothing distresses the commonwealth so much as half learned men, and that downright quiet ignorance is much to be preferred before restless, conceited knowledge.

We know nothing of the reasons which had prompted him to send his eldest son, when only twelve years of age, to spend a year at Geneva; but though this choice, as the elder Henry once reminded him, had brought Lord Halifax under 'some reproach' at home, for breeding his sons at 'so sanctified a place' it was to be repeated later on in the case of his two younger boys.

The young Henry meanwhile had matriculated at Christ Church, Oxford, 11 April 1674. He did not, however, long remain there, being removed during November 1675, in charge of a French Protestant tutor, to Paris. There he was entered at the 'Academy' of riding and gymnastics which was kept by another Protestant, M. Foubert, and was therefore much frequented by the English in Paris. The lad's training there was supplemented by external teaching in French, Italian, fencing, singing, and military evolutions; while his mornings seem to have been devoted to the study of Latin, and of English law, under the superintendence of his tutor.

We must now, however, return from the domestic affairs of Lord Halifax to the political situation which confronted him, when, on 15 April 1675, the long prorogation came to an end.

The Parliamentary interval had been remarkable for the completed disgrace of Shaftesbury and a rapidly rising predominance of the new Lord Treasurer, Sir Thomas Osborne by this time elevated to the Peerage as Lord Danby.

Between him and Lord Halifax, despite their early familiarity, relations had already become strained; especially perhaps within the precincts of the Privy Council, where Lord Halifax now alone represented the 'Country' party, or Parliamentary Opposition. The breach was no doubt intensified by Danby's obvious anxiety to split up the existing 'Country' party in the Lower House, and thus to create a new 'Court' or 'King's' party. Flattery, propitiation, and bribery, direct or indirect, were the means at his disposal; his success exalted his dexterity; and ere he had been eighteen months in office, the new faction had begun to assume proportions ominous for the Opposition. This change naturally aroused the anxiety of the 'Country' leaders. A new election appeared to offer the only chance of staying reaction, and two months before Parliament met the hopes of the Opposition had begun to centre upon a speedy *Disolution*.

To Danby, on the other hand, the prospect was naturally unwelcome, since such an event threatened to annihilate the tender Parliamentary plant he was so assiduously watering.

He conceived therefore a simple, though ingenious, plan for controlling the formation of parties, actual or to be, in both Houses. He adopted, indeed improved, as against the Opposition, the tactics that Opposition had so successfully employed against the Papists. By means of a Bill introduced in the House of Lords, he proposed to impose on all Justices of the Peace, all officials, and all *Members of either House* a 'Test Oath', hitherto confined to certain other classes of the community. This involved a declaration which denounced the taking up of arms against the King on any pretext whatever; and thus hit such members of the old Presbyterian party as had rallied at the Restoration. It also included a solemn undertaking against all attempts at alteration of the Government whether in Church or State; and might thus be held to bar the most legitimate efforts at reform in either of these directions.

The Session began with an attempt on the part of the Opposition to substitute for the usual Address of Thanks for '*the King's speech*', a Vote of Thanks for '*the Gracious expressions in his Majesty's speech*'; an incident which was to be appreciatively recalled by Halifax, on a similar occasion, some twenty years later.

Long and bitter were the debates which ensued as regards the proposed Test. In these Lord Halifax, under the leadership of his uncle Shaftesbury, took a prominent part. The Lords greatly resented this threat to their own hereditary rights; but in Committee the first point raised was 'whether there should be an Oath at all in the Bill'. This, says a contemporary report (ascribed to Lord Shaftesbury), 'was the only part the Court party defended with reason'; an Oath being the only reason for the Bill's existence. 'Yet', continues the Report, 'the Lord Halifax did, with that quickness, learning and elegance that are inseparable from all his discourses, make appear that as there really was no security to any State by Oaths; so also no private person, much less statesman, would ever order his affairs as relying on it; no man would ever sleep with open doors or unlocked up treasure or plate, should all the town be sworn not to rob; so that the use of multiplying Oaths had only been most commonly to exclude or disturb some honest conscientious men who would never have prejudiced the Government.' This Lord John Russell considered the ablest contribution to the debate.

When the clause denying the lawfulness of resistance came under discussion, it evoked a bold though guarded defence of that ultimate right as the one mark by which a 'limited' can be distinguished from an 'absolute' monarchy. Passionate contests arose also on the question of *ecclesiastical reform.* One Lord demanded whether the Bishops did not claim a power of excommunicating their Prince? They evaded the question, on the plea that they had never done so. Upon which Lord Halifax told them 'That that might well be; for since the Reformation they had hitherto had too great a dependence on the crown to venture on that or any other offence to it.' Finally the Bill, which had been considerably amended, was killed by a suspiciously opportune 'Privilege' quarrel between the Houses, which provoked a fresh prorogation.

During the Session, Lord Halifax had been absent from the Upper House on one occasion only, while Sir William, then at the height of his influence in the Lower House, had been also unusually active. He had supported abortive Bills to exclude, in the first place Papists, in the second place officials, from the House of Commons.

Tired of repeated prorogations, the Opposition now began to agitate yet more vigorously in favour of Dissolution. The 'Long' Parliament of Charles II had already enjoyed a life of unprecedented duration; and there was much complaint of the inconveniences this imposed, and the invidious position of practically perpetual representatives. Lord Halifax, together with Lord Shaftesbury, took a strong line in the matter, and in consequence, six weeks later, Lord Halifax received the final blow of expulsion from the Privy Council. He had been, it would appear, a regular attendant at the meetings, but his presence there had been somewhat anomalous, since he was on the worst possible terms with both the Duke of York and Lord Danby. The former's exasperation cannot have been lessened when on a complaint being made that a Roman priest had attempted a conversion by threats, Lord Halifax sarcastically suggested a hope that similar tactics would be permitted to Protestants *versus* the Papists. But a gibe at Lord Danby seems to have been the final straw among his offences. Danby, it seems, had been the subject of an unsuccessful attempt at bribery. Whereupon Lord Halifax caustically observed that the Treasurer appeared to have rejected the suggestion so mildly as not to have discouraged a second attempt; which was much as if a man should ask for his neighbour's wife, and meet with a civil refusal.

But despite the active collaboration between Shaftesbury and Halifax during this Session, their personal relations were becoming more and more strained. In fact, something like a rift was already observable, within the already thinned ranks of the anti-Court, which was by now also an anti-Danby, Opposition. Shaftesbury was emerging as the head of an extreme section in both Houses, while Halifax in the Lords, and Coventry, then at the height of his reputation in the Commons, guided the more moderate members.

In the next Session the split was still further widened. For Shaftesbury, with characteristic energy, championed in the House of Lords a curious theory, that owing to the length of the recent prorogation, the Parliament no longer possessed a legal existence. Lord Halifax, says Burnet, set himself vehemently though unsuccessfully to oppose the design; 'and did it not without expressing great sharpness against Lord Shaftesbury, who could not be managed in this matter'. Buckingham, however, it was who eventually 'threw [Lord Shaftesbury's] bombshell', being supported only by Shaftesbury himself and two of his friends. Halifax, after marshalling all possible arguments *in favour* of the motion, declared *against* it; and an angry House not only rejected the motion with indignation, but summarily committed to the Tower Buckingham and his three supporters.

Against this last arbitrary proceeding, however, Halifax (who at once visited his uncle) and his followers vigorously protested; and in Burnet's synopsis of their arguments one seems clearly to trace the sardonic wit of the principal speaker himself.

> They said that, if an idle motion was made and checked at first, he that made it might be censured for it, though it was seldom, if ever, to be practised in a free council, *where every man was not bound to be wise nor to make no impertinent* [i.e. *inappropriate*] *motion*; but when the motion was entertained and a debate followed, and a question was put upon it, it was destructive to the freedom of public councils, to call any one to account for it: they might with the same justice call them to an account for their debates and votes; so that no man was safe, unless he could know where the majority would be; here would be a precedent to tip down so many lords at a time; and to garble the House as often as any party should have a great majority.

The justice of his remonstrance was immediately illustrated; since the Country party in the Lords thus lost, during the whole remainder of the Session, the services of three members; and those of Lord Shaftesbury for a whole year.

Only one other event of the Session calls for our attention: Lord Halifax was elected a member of a Committee appointed to inquire into the *licensing of books*. Printing still remained a monopoly of the Stationers' Company, and nothing could be printed without the imprimatur of the official licensers. These were the Lord Chancellor for law books, certain bishops for divinity, physics, and philosophy, and the Secretary of State for history and politics. In practice, however, the pamphleteer L'Estrange, once an agent of the Secretary's Office, decided the issue. The matter is of interest, since it shows that the questions of licensing, of the law of libel, of anonymous publication generally, and perhaps of L'Estrange's invidious position, had been brought before Halifax, at an early date, in a very pointed manner. This may in part account for the anonymous character, guarded language, and often merely manuscript circulation, of his own subsequent pamphlets.

The succeeding Session of 1676–7, on the other hand, was mainly occupied with questions of *foreign* policy. The Five Years' contest between France and the confederacy under William of Orange had reached a climax. The fortunes of war seemed swaying against the Allies; and great anxiety was felt lest Charles II should throw his weight into the French scale. The Commons, led by William Coventry, urged a breach with France, whose forces had been uniformly and menacingly successful in Flanders and Sicily. Charles II demanded £600,000 from the House of Commons, as the preliminary of action on the side of the Allies; the Commons, very prudently, declined to authorize a loan for more than £200,000. Coventry himself stigmatized with great severity the encouragement afforded by the English Government to the levying of English troops for the French Service, a policy for which in fact the French King was surreptitiously paying Charles II; and which was the more dishonest, in that Charles was ostensibly acting as mediator between the French and Dutch.

Lord Halifax, meanwhile, perhaps with the same suspicion in view, had been occupied in an attempt to obtain for the Lords, as well as the Commons, a right to receive the accounts of public money. He probably engineered the eventual compromise; an address to the King saving the rights of the Peers, but conceding the immediate issue to a sense of the exigencies of public businesss.

Much to the general surprise, however, our assiduous politician left London at the Easter recess and remained at Rufford till September. But it is possible that this step, which cost him the brief summer Session, may have been due to reasons of health; he had had a dangerous illness about the time when he was dismissed the Privy Council. These sudden illnesses, after a period of considerable activity were, we shall find, frequent in his career; and lead us to suspect that his constitution was never really robust.

Meanwhile, his brother Harry was, perhaps for the first time in his life, more arduously occupied. The career of that lively personage had been for some years remarkably chequered. Extravagant tastes, a flippant wit, and extremely convivial habits had involved him in perpetual embarrassments, pecuniary and otherwise. He had now begun to think seriously of the future and had become ambitious of a place under Government. But as he was convinced that 'our measures, now at Court, are so taken that it is essential to a man's succeeding there to be of the parliament', the erratic courtier, whose earlier attempts had proved futile, now stood for Newark in the *Treasurer's* interest.

One ludicrous incident had nearly ruined his chances. The House of Commons, anxious to stay the abuse of 'treating'—intensified by the political excitement of the preceding few years and the rapid increase of by-election contests, in a Parliament now sixteen years old—had recently passed a vote by which 'treating' to an extent exceeding the modest sum of ten pounds should have voided any election. The Newark electors, however, saw no reason why legislative virtue should deprive a willing constituency of proffered cakes and ale; they ascribed the obnoxious vote to Harry's interest with his uncle (William?), carried about a grotesque effigy of the 'ten Pound Burgess', and would have burnt it but for the intervention of the authorities. So poor Harry was forced into a wholesale transgression of the salutary restriction; and after an awful week of unlimited 'good ale' and 'ill sack' found himself, to his ingenuous delight—a delight somewhat chequered by the ensuing bill of £100—senior member for the borough. A characteristic letter implores his brother in mock pathetic terms to cultivate the good graces of the worthy electors; and when on 23 May he took his seat, Dorothy, Lady Sunderland, wrote mischievously to Lord Halifax: 'I have heard nothing of your brother; but as soon as he came into the House he placed himself between his two uncles [Secretary Henry Coventry and Sir William] to keep them both from going too much of either side, with his prudence.'

Lord Halifax, on the other hand, as we have already seen, had been absent from this Session, which only lasted five days; but his friends had sent him regular reports of its progress. The recess had been utilized by the representation of both France, and Holland (with her allies), as a breathing space for intrigues, largely, it is said, of a pecuniary nature. Charles in his opening speech had pledged the word of a King that if he were granted a sum of £600,000, it should be spent for the good of the Kingdom. Probably on the motion of Sir William, the Commons had refused the grant, unless and until an alliance with the Confederates should have been actually declared. But, as Thomas Thynne wrote from Longleat to his cousin Halifax:

> I hear our carrying the vote for the naming Holland as an Ally much displeased the Court.... Upon our denying money, the Duke [of York] said he thought the French Ambassador had bribed us to serve his [most Christian] Majesty; and the King would ruin the Royal Family if he made war upon Flanders at this time; the exposition of which you can easily make.... At the Cabinet the Duke moved to have us dissolved, others prorogued, but the more moderate counsels prevail, so that we shall have an answer, but most think a rough one, which in the temper we are will work little, the Country gentlemen being very sour and displeased.... Upon the division of the House several of the Court went with us.

These anticipations were not falsified. On the following day, the King returned a severe answer to the Address, and peremptorily adjourned; so peremptorily indeed that, as Sir William tells Lord Halifax, some cried out 'in a confused manner' that 'the House was not adjourned'.

The Government, however, could not altogether ignore the strength of Parliamentary resentment. Charles, it is true, renewed in the month of August his secret engagements with France; he actually undertook, indeed, in return for a pension of £200,000 to prorogue the obnoxious Parliament for eight months, i.e. till April 1678. But he was already wavering, and signs of the times were soon noted, by the more vigilant observers among the friends of Lord Halifax. They proved good correspondents to that statesman in his forest retreat. Dorothy, Lady Sunderland, for instance, noted that Bentinck, the confidant of the Prince of Orange, had come over on a secret mission. And in September, about the time that Lord Halifax returned to town, a yet more striking portent appeared; the Prince himself followed his confidential emissary.

His allies abroad were greatly alarmed fearing he meant to

desert them; so at any rate the Spanish Ambassador in Rome informed the younger Henry Savile's tutor, then sojourning there with his pupil. In England, of course, speculation was equally rife. 'The Prince of Orange's visit', so wrote Thomas Thynne to Lord Halifax, 'fills us all with discourse; the vulgar proclaim love and marriage, the more discerning Treaties and Peace.' Love may have been absent, and Peace in the balance; but Marriage and Treaties were certainly under discussion.

For the Treasurer, who had always disliked the French intrigues though he had stooped to condone them, was now employing all his influence to effect a marriage between the Prince and his cousin, the Princess. Secret proposals for her hand from the Dauphin are said to have necessitated an immediate decision; and on 24 April 1677, the approaching marriage of the Prince and the Princess was officially announced. Although the young lady was not at the moment next in the succession to her father—a half-brother, who only survived a month, having been born within a few days of her wedding—the Duke was greatly incensed, and only yielded to strong pressure from his brother.

The marriage, in fact, represented at the moment a real political approximation. Charles had actually, though not openly, broken with France. His pension having stopped, the prorogation till April fell through; and when, in January 1677/8, he once more confronted Parliament, the excitement both here and abroad became correspondingly intense.

The Country party, or at least the moderate section represented by Halifax and Coventry, had pinned their hopes on an actual war with France. 'If it shall please God', writes Thomas Thynne to Halifax, 'to incline his Majesty to concur with his people they... seem not to be afraid of war nor what is the necessary concomitant of war, taxes; so universal is their dread of the growth of France;' and it is certain that Charles, for once, had actually resolved on throwing his weight into the popular scale.

His well-known duplicity, however, made it impossible to convince the majority that his conversion was sincere; while Louis XIV, not unnaturally exasperated by the tergiversation of his one-time ally, and alarmed at the prospect of so important an accession to the coalition against him, strained every nerve to prevent this contingency. His Ambassador, M. Barillon, was amply provided with funds to corrupt the unscrupulous. To the presumably incorruptable Members of the extreme 'Country' section, such as Shaftesbury and Russell, to whom foreign policy, compared with domestic exigences always appeared insignificant, he offered appropriate baits. Should war be averted, the French King would exert all his influence at the English Court to secure their immediate aims, namely, a Dissolution of Parliament, the reduction of the forces raised for the war, and the disgrace of Danby, on whom France burned to avenge the marriage of Princess Mary.

In this unstatesmanlike intrigue, neither Coventry nor Halifax were in any way involved. Coventry who, says Temple, 'had the most credit of any man in the House of Commons, and I think the most deservedly, not only for his great abilities but for having been turned out of the Council and Treasury to make way for the ...designs of the Cabal...had been ever since opposite to the French Alliance and bent upon engaging England in a war with that crown'. While Harry Savile, writing to his brother, refers to 'yourself and all such anti-courtiers...*who grounded their policies upon the continuance of the war*'.

But their policy was thwarted by the suspicions and deliberate tactics of their more extreme associates, and by the vacillating shifts to which Charles once more resorted. Between March and July it is possible to detect five separate fluctuations in his policy, or at least in his professions.

Louis XIV, however, at length realized that peace, for the moment, was the only possible solution; and on 31 July 1679, the six years' war, and three years of protracted negotiation, ended with the peace of Nimeguen.

By this pacification the Prince of Orange did not indeed secure the status of absolute security which he had demanded for his country; but he had attained such a measure of success as could not have been anticipated, even by Lord Halifax, in 1670.

Bitter, on the other hand, was the disappointment of William Coventry, who, dejected by an at least partial failure in the policy he had pursued, no less than by advancing years and increasing ill-health, began once more to talk of retirement from political life.

With the peace of Nimeguen begins a new period. For it concluded one episode in the great European struggle; and a fresh chapter opens with the depositions on 28 September of the notorious Titus Oates.

CHAPTER VI

THE 'POPISH PLOT'. FALL OF DANBY. THE OPPOSITION IN OFFICE

WHILE reprobating the foul calumnies of Oates, and the undiscriminating fury they excited, we must not blind ourselves to the fact that the Protestantism of the later seventeenth century had just and ample cause for fear and for suspicion. During the preceding century that faith had been practically wiped out of existence in Bohemia, in Italy, and in Spain. During the reign of our Mary I a double attempt had been initiated, both at home and from abroad, to extirpate it here. During the ten years which had elapsed between 1669 and 1679 a practically continuous series of attempts had been made to reduce this country to the obedience of the Roman See; for to the secret Treaty of Dover (the real 'Popish Plot'), of which the existence was strongly suspected, there had succeeded those intrigues between Coleman and the extreme Jesuit party, which were revealed by his correspondence. The whole reign of James II was to be devoted to further efforts in that direction; rendered the more ominous because they ran parallel to the more terrible and effective measures of his cousin and ally, 'le grand monarque', on the other side of the Channel.

The first depositions of Oates, however (September 1678), attracted little attention. Accident, none the less, revealed their purport to Gilbert Burnet, a young Scottish Episcopalian, who, after a breach with Lauderdale, had moved south; and already ranked as one of the most admired among London preachers. He had been from the first in touch with the Opposition leaders, to whom he now communicated the rumours. The majority derided them; but, observes Burnet, 'Lord Halifax...said [that] considering the suspicion all people had of the Duke's religion, he believed every discovery of that sort would raise a flame which the Court would not be able to manage'. His prophecy was only too abundantly justified; for these reports, reinforced by the mysterious death of the magistrate Godfrey, and the discovery of alarming documents among the papers of a former secretary to the Duchess of York, soon aroused a frenzy of suspicion.

The inquiry into this affair occupied the House of Lords during the major part of the following Session. Halifax was at least as actively engaged as Shaftesbury, Buckingham, or Essex. 'None', writes James II's biographer indeed, 'so violent a driver of it as he.' Here, however, that writer goes too far. Halifax, it is true (misled perhaps by strange rumours as to Somerset House), did support the scandalous attack upon the Queen; but (so Burnet tells us) he deprecated the institution of criminal proceedings on the sole authority of such witnesses. For when Burnet had himself remonstrated on that aspect of the matter with several of the Opposition leaders, Shaftesbury said that 'we must support the evidence, and all those who undermined the credit of the witnesses were to be looked on as public enemies'. Holles, on the other hand, showed more moderation 'than could have been expected'; and, adds Burnet, 'Lord Halifax was of the same mind'.

On another count Halifax pursued the so-called 'Trimming' policy for which he was soon to become proverbial. For on the one hand he opposed the Act, from which the Duke of York with difficulty obtained exemption; and which was for the ensuing 150 years to exclude Papists from the House of Lords. He thus incurred some unpopularity among the more extreme party, which was voiced in the Lower House by a creature of Shaftesbury's. But, on the other hand, he *concurred* in an address for the removal of the Duke 'from the King's presence and counsel'. This address emanated from both Houses, and evoked from the King the reply: That while he was ready to sanction provisions for the security of the Protestant religion under a Popish Successor, he should veto any attempt to tamper with the Succession. This incident foreshadows the future division of parties on the 'Exclusion' issue.

Such was the state of affairs, so far as the 'Plot' was concerned, at the end of November 1678. Concurrently with these events, however, the attacks on Lord Danby had assumed a new and sinister form. Montague, our representative at Versailles, had been recently recalled; and attributing this rebuff to the Treasurer's influence, had planned revenge. He determined on betraying to the Opposition the part—a minor one—which Danby had played in the pecuniary dealings between the French and English Courts.

The French Government readily collaborated in this intrigue against the Minister who had eventually given 'check' to its King; and Versailles undertook to recompense Montague by a secret pension. The latter therefore acted throughout in collusion with Barillon, French Ambassador at the Court of St James.

The historian Dalrymple, on the faith of Barillon's despatches, has described Halifax as also engaged in conscious co-operation with Barillon over this affair. But Barillon's own language does not bear this out; the Frenchman merely plumes himself on exerting an (indirect) influence over Halifax through the medium—strange to relate—of Algernon Sidney.

That stern Republican (an uncle of the first Lady Halifax) had lived abroad after the Restoration, mainly in France. While visiting Paris, he had met the younger Henry Savile, then, as we have seen, there domiciled with his tutor; and had courted, with pathetic urgency, the society of his sister's grandson. 'We waited', writes the tutor, 'on Colonel Sidney...who was extraordinary kind to Mr Savile...and...said, once he got Mr Savile at Nerac in Guienne where he lives...he would keep him as long as he could before he would let him go....' This intercourse also involved an introduction to the elder Harry Savile, then passing through Paris; who, by his influence with Secretary Coventry, succeeded in securing for Sidney that permission to revisit England, which Sidney—as he informed his benefactor with passionate gratitude—valued, as he would have valued the saving of his life.

Sidney had thus returned to England in 1677, of course, under an implied pledge of political neutrality; but the outburst of the Popish Plot agitation in the following year seems to have recalled him to political life.

He had naturally made the acquaintance of Savile's brother, Lord Halifax, his own nephew by marriage, had conceived for him a strong admiration, and had courted his society. They had, indeed, something in common. Both were able men, regarding politics from a philosophic as well as an empirical point of view, and Halifax, as we know, toyed, at least in conversation, and even in print, with Republican ideals. But the differences between them were far greater than the resemblance.

The position of Sidney at this moment seems curiously anomalous. A rigid Republican in theory, his Republicanism entailed a hatred for the House of Orange, and thus deflected his sympathies towards the Prince's main enemy, France. Gratitude to the land which had sheltered him in his exile increased these sympathies, and issued in a strange infatuation for Louis XIV. Thus, Sidney was certainly, at this very time, acting with Barillon in his intrigue against Danby. It seems, however, very absurd to suppose that in this affair he can have exercised any influence over Halifax, who needed no spur to exasperate him against Danby, and was from first to last diametrically opposed to all collaboration with France.

The coalition against Danby, meanwhile, had just received an important acquisition. The Duke of Monmouth, Commander-in-Chief of the Army, was then at the very zenith of his meteoric career. His wealth—he had been married to a Scottish heiress, the 'Duchess' of Scott's *Lay*—his charm of person and manner, the influence he possessed over his infatuated father, the military reputation he had gained abroad, and the appearance of his name on the Black List of the Popish Plot imposture, had rendered him a power to be reckoned with. He was at this time at odds, on various accounts, with several powerful personages; with Lord Danby who had married his daughter to a rival half-brother—with Lord Lauderdale, respecting Scottish affairs—and with the Duke of York regarding military appointments. He therefore threw in his lot with the Opposition.

It must be remembered that the rumours of his legitimacy, which had been current from his childhood, and which may have possibly originated in some indecent parody of a marriage ceremony, had never, so far, been seriously taken; and he joined the Opposition simply as a great Noble, who was also a favourite at Court. But designing men, Shaftesbury and Montague included, and even the young Duke himself, were beginning to be the objects of whispered suspicion on this count.

Charles II, however, who never in any way countenanced the report, may have looked with leniency on the young Duke's new intimacies, which promised him at least one friend in the Opposition camp.

Under such increasingly favourable circumstances, Montague shot his bolt. Papers which he produced before the House of Commons convicted Danby—and his Master—of an offer to betray the interests of Holland; in collusion with the French King, and in return for a secret payment of £900,000 to the Privy Purse. The fury of the House may be imagined; and on 23 December, Sir Henry Capel (the brother of Lord Essex) impeached at the bar of the House of Lords, and in the name of the Commons of England, the compromised Lord Treasurer. Lord Halifax took an active part in the subsequent proceedings, which culminated, during the next Session, in Danby's committal to the Tower; where he was to languish, untried, for a period of some five years.

In the meantime, Charles, alarmed for the safety of his Minister, hastened to prorogue Parliament. It was, moreover, on the advice of Danby, who thus hoped to conciliate the Opposition, almost immediately dissolved; and writs were at once issued for the election of a new Parliament. No General Election, as we are already aware, had taken place for eighteen years; so it is easy to imagine the intensity of the excitement which ensued.

At this juncture an event occurred of some moment as respects our more intimate knowledge of Lord Halifax. His brother-in-law, Lord Sunderland, the son of 'Saccharissa' and a diplomatist of some standing, had been created Secretary of State; and to his influence we may doubtless ascribe the appointment of Harry Savile the elder as his successor at Versailles. To this circumstance we owe a delightful and characteristic correspondence between the brothers, while the country gained a capable and conscientious representative. For patriotism, as Harry himself ingenuously observed, is apt to steal upon your diplomatist, however 'foppish' —'in despite of his teeth'.

The result of the polls, however, soon monopolized attention, and it was not favourable to the men in power. Of late, the Court, at a pinch, thanks to Danby's manœuvres, had been able to control 150 votes. Thirty was the utmost on which it could now rely; and Halifax naturally ranked among the most influential leaders of the new Opposition majority.

Danby, then still at large, redoubled the attempts at conciliation; disbanding continued; the Duke of York, having skilfully extracted from his brother a public declaration of his nephew's illegitimacy, was himself ostentatiously despatched to Brussels; while, on the very eve of the Session, it became known that Danby himself would retire from the Treasury, *with the title of Marquis.*

This unlucky rider nullified the propitiatory effect of all the preceding concessions. A storm of protest arose, and Lord Shaftesbury, in the Upper House, was the first to attack the obnoxious patent.

Charles had just left the throne and stood, after his fashion, technically unrecognized, by the fire, when Lord Halifax rose in support. Fixing his eyes on the august spectator, he ironically refuted the motion. Lord Shaftesbury must be the victim of a 'flamm' report. It was impossible that the King could have been prevailed on to do an act so ungrateful to his people; but should it indeed prove true—were such advancement to be the recompense of treason—the thing was 'not to be borne'. 'My God!' cried Charles bitterly, 'and I must bear it and say nothing.'

His Lordship's own view of the matter is contained in his first letter to our new Envoy in Paris:

VISCOUNT HALIFAX *to* HENRY SAVILE

20/30 *March* 1678/9

I make use of this minute to write by this gentleman who is just now going towards you. It will be no news to you by that time this reaches you that my Ld. Treasurer hath resolved to lay down his staff; and it will be as little to tell you that the world is still jealous he may take it up again in convenient time, or else keep such a station near the King as may make him the same omnipotent figure as before under the disguise of some other name. This, you may imagine, the hard-hearted Commons of England will be very willing to prevent, and therefore in all probability they will go on with their impeachment....I am call'd upon in haste, and therefore can add no more. Adieu. Yours.

My old Lady Sunderland hath been very ill, and is not yet out of danger.

With these proceedings against Danby there were closely interwoven further investigations into 'The Plot'. Halifax, together with Shaftesbury, showed himself 'eminent in pleading for indulgence to tender-conscienced Protestants, and severity against Papists'; sitting, for instance, on a Committee for clearing London altogether of Papists.

The political revolution consequent on the fall of Danby, meanwhile, was only just beginning. For the Opposition had become practically master of the situation, and the Court was proportionately alarmed. Only three important personages appeared to possess both influence over the King and credit with the nation. These were first the Duke of Monmouth; secondly, the newly appointed Secretary of State, the smooth and subtle Sunderland; and thirdly, Sir William Temple, the sponsor of the Triple Alliance, who had just returned from a diplomatic mission. Conscious of the extent to which Temple, by his responsibility for the popular pact, had recommended himself to the nation, Charles now pressed him to accept office. The wary diplomatist, however, constitutionally averse from risks, contrived to evade compliance.

He was, none the less, fully conscious of the acute crisis through which the nation was passing. Danby, he saw, had ruined himself by two errors. He had attempted to monopolize authority; and had, however unwillingly, become involved in the meshes of Anglo-French intrigue. Thence had arisen envy and mistrust. Both, he thought, might be obviated, were the existing Privy Council to be replaced by a new one, larger, more respected, and more representative of all shades of opinion. From this he would only except Shaftesbury, whom he regarded with inveterate suspicion. A Council so constituted might also, he hoped, tend to restrict the growing influence of Monmouth, which he regarded with considerable misgiving.

Such, we imagine, is the simple explanation of a scheme to which both Macaulay and Von Ranke have ascribed subtle constitutional intentions.

Temple, however, was anticipated by Sunderland and Monmouth, who had formed a similar scheme, and were the first to act. They began by placing Lord Essex—a *persona grata* with the Opposition, and a capable financier—at the head of a new Treasury board. The step was popular; the Commons, at the instance of William Coventry, passed a vote of thanks for it; and further acceptable changes were anticipated. The friends of Halifax, of course, expected his further elevation, but these hopes were premature. Temple, indeed, had proposed Halifax for one of the new appointments, but had at first found that the King 'kicked at him more than [at] any of the rest'. Of this fact Halifax was perfectly well aware, as a letter to his brother sufficiently shows. It is dated 10/20 April 1679:

I had yours last night, and deliver'd both the enclosed to my Ld. of Essex....I find you suppose me amongst others by this time restored to grace at Court, but I am so ill at making steps as they call it, and the good impressions that have been made of me do so remain that you may reckon me amongst the incurable, except there be a miracle made on purpose for me, and that you will say is not very likely. Your late friend [Lord Danby] taketh up all our time and is almost as great a grievance to us now he is falling as he was whilst he remain'd in power. Our house is gentle, but the House of Commons, being a true representative of England, are stiff and surly in the point, not to be softened by conferences, nor persuaded by expedients; though we are to make one trial more to see whether they will relent. I hope you have made a good change, as well as the nation, by having the treasurer turned into a commission where you have friends that at least will be just to you; but if they go no further I doubt that will hardly serve your turn, especially if you go [on a Court progress] with an equipage suitable to your excellency's character....

Temple, however, persisted. 'Upon several representations', he writes, 'of his family, his abilities, his estate and credit* as well as [his] talent to ridicule and unravel whatever he was spited at, I thought his Majesty had been contented with it.' Soon, however, 'he raised new difficulties upon it; and appeared a great while invincible in it, though we all joined in the defence of it; and at last I told the King we would fall upon our knees to gain a point that we all thought necessary for his service'. Monmouth, in private, seconded these appeals; but even he said, he found as great a difficulty in overcoming the King's prejudice 'as ever in anything he studied to bring the King to'. Charles, indeed, eventually yielded; but—presumably at the solicitation of Monmouth, Sunderland and Essex, and to the infinite mortification of Temple—he not only restored to the list the name of Lord Shaftesbury, but also revived in his favour the office of Lord President.

Algernon Sidney's gratitude to Henry Savile had taken the acceptable form of regular news-letters, which were particularly welcome, as official communications proved deplorably scanty. He had hailed the new era with no little satisfaction; and immediately prophesied that Halifax, Sunderland and Essex would, if united, control the policy of the administration. Reresby, too, a north country Member of Parliament, who was more and more attaching himself to the person of Halifax, tells us that in the Upper House the influence of Halifax was hardly, if at all, inferior to that of Lord Shaftesbury; while no man had a better interest in the House of Commons, or a better character for consistency. Essex and Halifax (adds Henry Sidney) 'are of that reputation that nobody can blame them for any one action in their whole lives'. Once more the report that Halifax was in the running for the Vice-royalty of Ireland became current; although (according to Carte's *Ormonde*) Halifax 'took occasion to declare to Sir W. Coventry, that he never thought of it, nor would he take it, if it were offered him'; since under the Duke of Ormonde it 'was in very good hands (he thought) for the King's service, and wished it might so continue'. His brother saw grimmer objections. 'I wish you', hints Henry Savile from Paris, 'better fortune than our great-uncle found there; though I think you go in a time when you will run as great hazards as any of your predecessors, and for that reason the glaring outside of that preferment does not please me so much as

* Henry Sidney once computed that Essex, Sunderland and Halifax, put together, had more land than the King.

if...you had a less honourable, provided a less hazardous station.' Hazards apart, in fact, the Viceroyalty of Ireland (then worth £30,000 a year) held at that date much the same place in public estimation as does the Viceroyalty of India to-day. It was the greatest place in the gift of Government; but involved temporary exile, and absence from the political arena at home.

Meanwhile, the new Council of State, wherein the Country party had a numerical superiority, was taking shape, and Halifax, of course, became one of the 'Committee for Foreign Affairs'; the formation of which, despite the promise of the King to avoid 'Cabals', became, for administrative reasons, immediately inevitable.

As this embryo 'Cabinet' included—together with Halifax and Temple, Sunderland and Essex—the then apparently inseparable combination of Monmouth, Shaftesbury, and the latter's then intimate, Lord Russell, its explosive probabilities were obvious; and in fact, within a few days, it had split into two parties. Temple himself assumed responsibility for negotiations, which consolidated, against the phalanx headed by Lord Shaftesbury, a 'Triumvirate' composed of Halifax, Essex and Sunderland. He represents Sunderland as his first recruit, Essex as brought in by Sunderland.

'My Lord Halifax', he continues, 'appearing unsatisfied by observing where the King's confidence was, I proposed...to receive him into all our consultations which I thought would both enter him into credit with the King and give us more ease in the course of his affairs....Lord Essex received this overture with his usual dryness; Lord Sunderland opposed it a good deal. He said "I should not find Lord Halifax the person I took him for, but one that would draw with nobody, and still climbing to the top himself".' Notwithstanding this underhand insinuation—for Sunderland was ostensibly on the best terms with his brother-in-law—Halifax was admitted; and the Triumvirate (with Temple in the background) continued, he says, to act for some weeks in complete harmony.

We seem, however, to observe in the excellent Temple a certain tendency to exaggerate his own importance. The division he describes seems to have developed on perfectly natural lines.

The split apparently dates from 28 April, only five days after the institution of the Council; when Lord Russell brought up to the House of Lords a vote of the House of Commons explicitly defining the prospect of a *Popish Succession* as the main peril of the political situation; and from the King's reaction, which was immediate.

For his Majesty, only two days after this 'Exclusion' vote, forestalled the Exclusionists. He offered, in a speech to the two Houses, the following 'Limitations' on the power of a Popish Successor: That on a demise of the Crown all preferment, ecclesiastical or secular, should, during the life of such a successor, become vested in the control of Parliament; provision being made for its automatic meeting.

On this question the Conservative instincts appropriate to a successful diplomatic career seem to have reinforced the hereditary loyalty of the Temple family. Essex, on his part, was influenced by constitutional scruples, which the Exclusionists eventually overcame. Lord Sunderland, as usual, adhered to the party which seemed to him the strongest; and Halifax from the first showed a determined antagonism to the policy of Exclusion which seems to have excited not a little surprise. He was known to be on bad terms with the Duke of York; and he had never attempted to conceal his contempt for the school of political thought which invested the institution of hereditary monarchy with supernatural sanctions. At this very moment he was cautioning Temple against Filmer's theory of 'paternal dominion', lest he should, by supporting it, threaten 'the rights of the people'; and he had long lain under the imputation of a (theoretical) Republicanism. 'He had often', writes Burnet, enquired 'who takes a coachman to drive because his father was a good coachman?... Yet he was now', adds Burnet, 'jealous of a small slip in the Succession.' So uncompromising indeed was his language that several among his friends 'took great pains on him, to divert him from opposing it so furiously as he did'. What then were his motives?

The reports of the subsequent Exclusion Debates which have come down to us are of so scanty a nature that his motives must remain in good measure conjectural. But we observe at once, first, that the 'Limitation' policy was the more practicable; for it had already secured the adhesion of the King.

In the second place this policy opposed a complete bar to the pretensions of the Duke of Monmouth, at the moment espoused almost ostentatiously by Lord Shaftesbury. If it is possible that aristocratic pride, which resented the pretensions of a bastard, had some share in the decision of Halifax, this was reinforced by the most solid political motives. Deeply concerned with the serious issues which the European crisis involved, he looked forward with very real expectation to the day when William of Orange, in right of his marriage with the heiress presumptive, should succeed to a paramount influence over the counsels of England. Thirdly, it is certain that Halifax feared the possibility of Civil War, that too frequent result of a disputed succession, and a culmination of which he, his family, and his country had already had so painful an experience. In this he was presumably justified; since the actual dispossession of James II, after a far more menacing crisis, did entail on us, though at long intervals, two civil wars, fortunately of brief extent and duration.

And lastly we seem to trace in the career of Lord Halifax a strong disinclination to *ex post parte* interference with individual rights. He had already, as we have seen, vindicated the *hereditary* legislative privileges of the Popish Peers; while, on the other hand, by supporting the Test Act, which denied to Papists the opportunity of an *official* career, he had practically asserted for the nation a right to restrict the *exercise of executive functions.* He could therefore argue without inconsistency for the retention by James of the *title* of King, and *the possession of the hereditary revenues*, while advocating a limitation of *political* powers in the case of so dangerous a successor.

Matters had reached this stage when Halifax wrote to acknowledge the congratulations of his brother on the political transformation scene. 'I confess', so the envoy writes, 'I think you have reason enough to be satisfied with the fall of the late great man from his high station; but I think I understand both your nature and your style better than to believe the silly stories that are spread here of the jests you made and the triumph you showed at his first being brought to the bar of your house, and therefore I take pains to vindicate you'; a task in which he had the help of Lady Scroope, a Roman Catholic lady then in Paris, who had the reputation of being both a courtier and a wit. Moreover, the warm-hearted uncle expresses his regret that his eldest nephew is to make so short a stay with him in Paris; though (so he concludes his playful reproaches) 'His Majesty having trusted his business with a man, has not this long time been an argument for you to trust anything else with him, especially your son and heir'.

Lord Halifax answers as follows:

VISCOUNT HALIFAX *to* HENRY SAVILE

May Day 1/10

It seemeth you had the knowledge of my preferment before I could tell it you, so little did I apprehend myself to be likely to be readmitted into the state of grace, as you might perceive by the stile of my last, in which I assure you I did not dissemble with you. To undertake the being useful to my friends in the station I am in, would be a piece of arrogance very unfit for a councellour of a new edition; but if ever such a miracle should come to pass, as that from such a degree of disfavour as I have lain under I should come to have any credit, no doubt but our envoyé in France might rely upon a friend at court. I am already brib'd to it, by your zeal to justify me against such scandalous accusations as that you mention in your letter, yet I am not so much offended at the lie as I am pleased that my Lady Scroope defendeth me. Pray improve my thanks to her in the best manner, and tell her the right she doth me in her opinion doth more than make amends for all the injustice I can receive from her whole party. The peace of the North being so far advanced maketh our jealousy of France so much the greater; his army being now at liberty and we having yet provided nothing to secure us but the abilities of our envoyé. I suppose Harry may now be with you if no accident has made his journey slower. I have confined him to ten days or a fortnight's stay in Paris; in which time you will be able to search him, so as to send me his perfect character along with him. And pray take some pains in it, it being of some moment to me that I should not mistake his humour, which is less discoverable by a father than by any other man less concerned. I cannot blame you for fearing a journey with a court; I know few things would give me more terror, but it must be done, and I dare rely upon you for making it as easy to you as the matter will bear. We are here every day upon high points: God send us once at an end of them! Impeachments of ministers, trials of peers for their life, discourses and votes too concerning the heir presumptive, are the only things our thoughts are employed about. And I that have dream't this half year of the silence and retirement of old Rufford, find myself engaged in an active and an angry world, and must rather take my part in it with grief than avoid it with scandal. Whatever passes is sent to you of course; so that I shall never write any news to you except you bid me. My Lord Sunderland is very kind, and I value his being so to the degree I ought. I need not tell you how much you owe him, but remember it is no small things for men at court to speak kindly of their friends when they are at a distance. I leave you to your triumphs for your great wedding; and that I may close with a pleasing line to you, I was told by a Frenchman that *Monsieur Savile fait les affaires de son maître le plus habilement du monde.* Adieu.

The next letter refers to a small diplomatic success which Henry Savile regarded with the most ingenuous delight. He had complained in dignified fashion of the stiffness with which he was treated, and had recommended a retaliation on M. Barillon:

VISCOUNT HALIFAX *to* HENRY SAVILE

12/22 *May* 1679

I find by your letter to my Lord Sunderland that your nephew is come to Paris, and am not sorry to see you do not altogether dislike him. Your opinion of him more at large I expect when he cometh over; in the mean time, though you will hear it from better hands, I will not omit to tell you that your letter to Mr Secretary Coventry was read at Council, where it received so much applause that I hope it will encourage you to deserve more upon all occasions you shall have to send any account of your transactions; and as the best evidence that your dispatch is approved, it hath produced an order which will not only be for your credit and vindication, but will give universal satisfaction to every body here, there being few things that gave more offence than the too familiar admittance of embassadours, especially of those from France, to speak of business to the King. Now, though it happeneth well for your credit here that you are the occasion of having this regulated, yet I hope you will not impute more to yourself in it than is necessary in the place you are in, that you may not draw a disadvantage upon yourself by seeming to resent too much what hath been done to you in relation to your own particular. You see a new councellor will be advising, though whilst I am writing I conclude you will think fit to do this without my putting you in mind of it. We begin to hope the French will not discompose us this year, since it is so far advanced, and that such a diligent watchman as we will suppose you to be doth not give us any alarum of it. There is no need of anything from abroad to give us exercise, being sufficiently employed at home in parlt., where things are started every day that will make the world conclude we are in a more quarrelsome humour than I hope will be found when men have had a little time to grow cool. The particulars of everything will be sent to you by my Lord Sunderland, who telleth me he taketh care you may know all we do. I write this whilst we are at Councill, which you therefore ought to take kindly, and think I have acquitted myself pretty well to you, though I add no more than I am, etc.

HALIFAX

Meanwhile, if the Triumvirate possessed the Ascendancy in Council, Lord Shaftesbury had secured, through his supporters, a preponderating influence in the Lower House. There the 'Limitations' favoured by the Triumvirate were accordingly rejected; and after a critical debate during which Sir William Coventry, in a remarkable and statesmanlike speech, had supported the policy of his nephew, a *Bill of Exclusion* had passed on 22 May its second reading.

Nor was this the only rock ahead. A dispute had arisen between the two Houses regarding the preliminaries to the trial of Danby, and the Peers charged with participation in the 'Popish Plot'. Here the whole Country party in the House of Lords, Halifax and Shaftesbury included, voted against Lord Danby. Both Houses remaining obstinate, business had come to a standstill; and the Triumvirate—with Temple—resolved on a prorogation.

This course seems to have been advisable, the violence of the contest considered; but the *method* taken proved unfortunate in the extreme. A majority in Council for the step was quite anticipated, once its members had been duly warned; but when, in Temple's absence, and in consequence of some disturbing rumours, the King, by advice of the Triumvirate, peremptorily, and without forewarning, cut short the Session, the reverse was the case.

Before doing so, however, Charles II gave the Royal Assent to the famous 'Habeas Corpus Act', which had hitherto invariably succumbed to one of the innumerable preceding prorogations. Fame has generally attributed this Act to the influence of Lord Shaftesbury, to whom, probably enough, its *inception* may be ascribed; but it was definitely stated during the subsequent 'Exclusion Debates', and with even greater probability, that the Royal Assent on this occasion was procured by Lord Halifax.

In its result, however, the failure to warn the Council, and thus prepare its members for the step which the leaders saw to be essential, if unpopular, proved fatal. The rage of Shaftesbury knew no bounds; and he swore aloud in the House of Lords 'that he would have the heads' of his Majesty's advisers—including of course his nephew Halifax. 'Spiteful repartees' between the two diversified proceedings in Council; and Monmouth having 'broken all measures' with Lord Essex 'with whom he had been long in the last confidence', the Council Chamber became the scene of unbridled recrimination.

The Triumvirate, however, for the time, continued to carry all before it; and could, at the moment, rely on the Royal support. Temple the King saw himself forced to respect. Sunderland, a clever administrator, proved the most adroit of courtiers; and Halifax, to the general surprise, rose rapidly in the Royal favour. He 'studied' according to Burnet 'to manage the King's spirit and gain an ascendant there; which he did' (adds Burnet) 'by his lively and libertine [i.e. free-thinking] conversation'.

What then was the policy of this 'Triumvirate'? Let us turn

in the first place to its domestic policy. 'We thought', says Temple, 'of such Acts of Council as might express his Majesty's care for suppressing of Popery even in the intervals of Parliament.' On one point alone, says Temple, they disagreed. This was whether several Roman Catholic priests, convicted—under certain obsolete penal laws, long since suspended *in terrorem*—merely for executing their priestly functions, should be respited, or 'left to the law' as demanded by the House of Commons.

Their execution, says Temple, 'I thought wholly unjust, without giving them warning by proclamation. . . since the connivance had lasted now through three Kings' reigns; upon this point Lord Halifax and I had so sharp a debate at Lord Sunderland's lodgings that he told me, if I would not concur in points which were so necessary for the people's satisfaction, he would tell everybody I was a papist; and upon his affirming that the Plot must be handled as if it were true, whether it were so or not, in those points which were so generally believed by city or country, as well as both Houses, I replied with some heat, that the plot was a matter long on foot before I came over into England; that to understand it, one must have been here to observe all the motions of it, which not having done I would have nothing to do with it; in other things I was content to join with them, where they thought I could be of use to the King's service; and when they thought there was none I was. . . very glad to leave his Majesty's affairs in so good hands as theirs'.

We have thought it right to give this incident as related in Temple's own words. It leaves on the mind a most painful impression; but the reputation of Halifax for justice and humanity stands in other respects upon so high a plane, the cynical indifference as to the truth or falsehood of the plot is so unlike his avowed views—and we may add, so much more akin to those ascribed to Shaftesbury—that we should perhaps refrain from laying undue stress upon the details of this conversation. For it was avowedly conducted in circumstances of mutual irritation. It was eventually reported years later by one of the disputants, writing, moreover, under the influence of an intervening alienation. 'We may doubt', with Hallam, 'whether Temple has represented this quite exactly.'

The incident, whatever its nature, occasioned no breach between the parties. Lord Halifax and his brother-in-law Sunderland, in fact, by Temple's own showing, urged Temple 'to come into the Secretary's place.' This Halifax himself had refused; professing himself 'weary of the business, since he could find no temper like to grow in the next Session. . . between the King' and the Houses.

He had even offered to bring the matter of the Secretaryship 'to a point' with his uncle Coventry, as concerned the money payment then usual on such occasions.

Meanwhile the expressed opinions of Lord Halifax may be found in the following letter to his brother; who, at a previous stage in the correspondence, had described his nephew as handsome and gentlemanlike, with a complexion like his father's, though tanned by a Spanish journey; and only feared lest the youth might, in later years, emulate his own rotundity. Now, however, Savile had dispatched a further communication to the father by the hands of the young gentleman himself thus acknowledged.

VISCOUNT HALIFAX *to* HENRY SAVILE

2/12 *June* 1679

I had yours yesterday by the young gentleman, who telleth me he will write this post to you. I find him full of his acknowledgements for your kindness to him, by which you have gain'd a friend, if that were worth any thing. I suspend my judgement till I see more of him; in the mean time I will only tell you I am not discouraged by what I have seen already, and finding him so much leaner than I expected was a welcome disappointment to me. His Madrid complexion I hope will not last always, but that our climate will unbake him, and then his person will be tolerable. But to go on to answer your letter in the several parts of it: You may be assured that whatever I observe in your letters that may be liable to exception you shall know of it, it being an unkind piece of tenderness to conceal anything of that nature.... I agree much with you in what you say concerning the Duke,* and if the parlt. had continued I should have had the opportunity of shewing moderation, which was never more advisable, for many reasons, than upon this occasion. It becomes the zeal of the French clergy to press their King to a persecution by way of revenge upon us here; but I will hope wiser things of the governmt. there than that so unreasonable a thing should prevail. However, if the fear of it putteth thoughts into the Protestants of removing hither, I am sure we must renounce all good sense if we do not encourage them by all possible invitations. It hath ever been so much my principle that I have wonder'd at our neglecting a thing we ought to seek; and those that have not zeal enough to endeavour it for the preserving our religion might have wit enough to do it for the increasing our trade. But to think of any greater designs† is not fit for our age: we may please ourselves with dreaming of such things, but we must never hope to get further. For that which concerneth an amnesty to the King's subjects that did not obey the King's

* Savile had feared too much severity to him might throw him into the arms of the French.

† Such as the King declaring himself Protector of the Protestants of Europe, as Savile had suggested.

proclamation the last year, if they are Protestants, I think it a very fitt thing, and shall move to have it consider'd. As for the printing Coleman's trial, I doubt your zeal may go a little too fast in it. You are to consider there are several expressions against popery that his Christian Majty. will never allow to be publish'd by his authority, and to make a request which would be deny'd might be of much worse consequence than the letting it alone; so that you are not to wonder if Mr Secretary doth not encourage you in a thing he himself doth not approve. I hope the notoriety of the fact, as our lawyers call it, is evidence enough of the plott; and yet it is in vain to hope it will ever be confess'd by those that say still there never was any such thing as the Massacre at Paris, or the Gunpowder Treason in England. The story of your Irish priest* is a very odd one, and I shall not conceal it, though we do not need here any further proofs of the good intentions of our popish countrymen abroad. I hope you will use ordinary cautions for your safety in all events; as for extraordinary ones, and such as bring great trouble with them, a man must count ill that thinketh life worth them. You need not much fear the having a chaplain imposed upon you; besides the charge, it would be an incumbrance, for which I should pity you; but I do not at all apprehend you will be put to such a trial of your patience. I approve your going to [the Protestant temple at] Charenton, and your countenancing the Protestants, which I think the principall work of an English minister in France; but I am apt to believe it may make the court there very weary of you, it being a method that they have of late been so little used to that they take it for an injury. This is enough for once, and, being at the bottom of my paper, I will leave you to your better entertainments. Adieu.

Meanwhile, besides its domestic anxieties the Council was harassed by foreign complications; and in this department alone both parties in the Ministry found themselves at one. An alliance with the States became the immediate object of all; and a very appropriate agent appeared in the person of Algernon Sidney's younger brother, 'le beau Sidney' of Grammont's *Memoirs*. Between him and the Duke of York a personal feud existed, Sidney having professed a too obvious admiration for the first Duchess of York. In him dissipated habits and considerable social gifts veiled the tact of a go-between and some diplomatic ability. As Colonel of an English regiment in the Dutch service, he had gained the favour of the Prince of Orange, which he repaid by a lasting attachment. He was now openly entrusted with the proposal of a common guarantee for the integrity of the Spanish Netherlands; and, in private, with a suggestion of the 'Triumvirate' that, as a counterpoise to the presence and popularity of the

* Who had advised revenge upon the English Protestants in France, should the Popish Peers be convicted.

Duke of Monmouth, the Prince of Orange should prepare for a visit to England. In anticipation of this he was to be created Duke of Gloucester, with a seat in the Privy Council. Halifax was particularly interested in this suggestion, and Sidney tells us that Essex and Halifax 'spoke much to the advantage' of the Prince. Halifax, in especial, insisted that each Minister in turn must have some private conversation with Sidney concerning the Stadtholder; and had added 'that every honest man would be for him, unless he were a mad man meaning the setting up of popery and arbitrary government'.

Sidney's departure was precipitated by a very characteristic incident. The Ministry saw reason to suppose that the Sovereign, in direct defiance of his avowed policy, was engaging, in collusion with the Duke of York, then at Brussels, in a secret negotiation with the French Ambassador. This time it was on the basis of a three years' pension, a three years' alliance and a three years' intermission of Parliament; and we find that before this intrigue collapsed, a few months later, the unscrupulous Sunderland, who professed a peculiar solicitude for the Dutch Alliance, had become deeply implicated.

In the third place the new Council found itself no less seriously involved in Scottish complications. That Kingdom was known to be seething with political discontent. The tyranny and misgovernment of Secretary Lauderdale were matters of notoriety, and had disgusted English opinion of almost every shade. Temple had urged, though in vain, the omission of Lauderdale from the reorganized Privy Council; the Commons had petitioned, also in vain, for his removal. A deputation of Scottish noblemen had now obtained the promise of a hearing in the presence of the King, of Halifax and of Essex. But while the matter impended, startling intelligence arrived. A chance encounter between soldiers and the armed members of a field conventicle had 'set the heather on fire'.

The news reached London during a sitting of the Privy Council. Russell started to his feet, and, amid general approval, denounced Lord Lauderdale as the true cause of the revolt. 'Sit down, my Lord,' cried Charles with a sneer, 'this is no place for addresses.' But at a second Council held the same day, remonstrances no less forcible became general; Halifax and Temple, indignant at the King's unblushing patronage of Lauderdale, even threatened to resign. Nor was the exasperation removed when the King announced his intention of sending north the *Duke of Monmouth*, with the additional title of Commander-in-Chief for Scotland, and with orders to repress the rebellion. To the Triumvirate, this concentration of power in the hands of a possible pretender seemed perilous in the extreme; while Lord Shaftesbury, on his part, realized to the full that the task thus imposed on his proposed instrument was, at the least, highly invidious. But Charles had determined; and, on 15 June, the young general started north.

Four days later, Lord Halifax wrote to Henry Savile:

19/29 *June* 1679

. . . Our fears in relation to Scotland lessen every day, for, though the rebels are together in a body to a considerable number, yet they are so ill-arm'd and disciplin'd, it is to be presumed that the King's forces, which now are 10,000 men, will not find much difficulty in suppressing them. The D. of Monmouth is by this time at Edinburgh, and it is hoped that we may have such an account from thence by the next express as may make our preparations here unnecessary. When this storm is allay'd, the King intendeth to go to Windsor, and I have it in my thoughts, though it is not without some doubt, to make a short visit to poor old Rufford; for which my passion increaseth proportionably to the difficulties that arise in getting to it. The peace concluded with the Elector of Brandenburgh maketh France the more terrible, now it is absolutely at leisure to do whatever their own strength or their neighbours' weakness may tempt them to do. I am interrupted whilst I am writing this to you, so that I make an end something sooner than I intended, though I have nothing at present to say that you should lament my omitting it. Yours.

Six days later news reached London of the victory at Bothwell Bridge, by which the Duke of Monmouth had put an end to the revolt.

Meanwhile, a startling decision had been taken at Court; it was resolved to dissolve the five months' Parliament, and call a new one. The origin of these tactics has been ascribed by Burnet to the King; and by Temple (who acquiesced in them) to the King indeed, but at the instance of Halifax and Essex; who feared the Duke's success in Scotland might give additional energy to the Monmouth-Shaftesbury alliance. It was settled between the consultants that at the next Council the King should propose a question: 'Whether Parliament be further prorogued or dissolved.' It was considered that if the King's own party (i.e. the officials) and the friends of the Triumvirate should be duly primed, Shaftesbury and the Duke would secure no more than four votes for a mere prorogation ; and Temple declares that Halifax, Essex, and the King undertook the task. But, once more, when the critical day arrived, Temple realized that, either through negligence or forgetfulness on their part, the subject had not been broached to a single member of the Board. Unprepared for the intentions of the King and the moderate leaders, not a voice, save those of Temple, and the Triumvirate itself, supported the policy of dissolution. Charles, however, promptly declared for that step; whereupon the Council broke up 'with the greatest rage in the world' on the part of the Exclusionist members, and to 'the general dissatisfaction of the whole board'. Thus, by this second piece of carelessness or indifference, whatever unpopularity might attach to the decision was concentrated on Temple and the Triumvirate.

Four days later Lord Halifax wrote as follows to his brother:

VISCOUNT HALIFAX *to* HENRY SAVILE

London, 7/17 *July* 1679

My being at Windsor since I had your last hath made my answer so slow to you; and to do it now in method, I must tell you as to your first point concerning my journey to Rufford, that I doubt you may spare your envy to me for it, since I am likely to make none, or so very short a one as will only serve to grieve me for not being able to make it longer. Your nephew seeméth to be in great impatience till he seeth it, and I think there is no better receipt to make him love it than the taking care he may not be cloy'd with it. I hope we shall both join in justifying our usurpation against the Benedictines, and, how little zealous soever we may be in other respects, we may be relyed upon, from our tenure, to be most unmoveable Protestants. I cannot blame you for being a little stirr'd to see men's unbelief so ill placed as to think there is no plot here. There are late evidences very material to justify Mr Ireland's being in town at the time Mr Oates said he was; and yet that was the principal thing insisted upon by the papists to blemish his testimony. How you and my Lady Scroope can agree upon this matter I am not able to imagine, and especially to live in the same house, which maketh the wonder great. Here is lately come out in print, amongst other libels, an 'Advice to a Painter',[10] which was written some years since and went about, but now by the liberty of the press is made publick, which for many reasons I am sorry for. The Scotch lords are to be heard to-morrow morning, and the King hath appointed me amongst others to be present at it. The D. of Monmouth hath leave to come back, all being now very quiet in Scotland.... I hear you have been in some fears you might be supplanted by an embassadour, but my ld. telleth me he sent you the King's answer to put your thoughts at quiet in that particular. Here is Monsieur Flamarin from Monsieur, to give notice of Mademoiselle's marriage, but I do not find he saw you before he came from Paris, which I thought was to be of course upon such occasions. Next Thursday at Hampton Court, the resolution will be taken about the time of meeting of the parlt.; in the mean time I leave you to the enjoyment of your beloved town of Paris, and so kiss your hands.

The hearing of the Scottish lords inimical to Lauderdale took place, as arranged, in the presence of Halifax and Essex. It lasted eight hours; both the Lords spoke warmly for the complainants, Halifax in especial animadverting upon acts of flagrant illegality, which their abettors could only defend by pleading prerogative. 'He told the King', says Algernon Sidney, 'he saw the Scottish nation was more free than the English'; a startling assertion, though it is true that Scottish writers were apt to make very extensive claims as regards the *theoretical* powers of Parliament. The petitioners, as the two Lords told Burnet, proved their case to demonstration, and gained, it would seem, very general sympathy; but Charles with cool effrontery maintained that while 'many damned things' had been objected against Lauderdale, nothing had been advanced that was detrimental to his own service.

Rumours of the intention to dissolve Parliament were already rife; and Halifax suspected the garrulity of the Chancellor as their source. But the decision as to the date of the actual publication had been deferred to a subsequent meeting, which took place three days later at Hampton Court. Lord Halifax went down with Sunderland and Henry Sidney; and during the sitting the Duke of Monmouth arrived from Scotland, having played his cards extremely well. He had at once enhanced his military reputation, and obtained, by his humane and sympathetic treatment of the vanquished, an enthusiastic popularity.

At the Council Charles asserted his authority; the dissolution became a certainty; a public announcement was made; but though the issue of writs for the purpose of an Autumn Session of a new Parliament followed immediately, Sir William Coventry was greatly perturbed. He only trusted that Halifax, 'for whom I have so much concern', was not responsible. 'Beware', he wrote to him, 'of the reputation of a [sole?] Minister; it is the worst place for a man in your circumstances, between Berwick and the Mount in Cornwall.'

Thomas Thynne wrote in even greater anxiety; and Algernon Sidney, in a letter to Henry Savile, declared the Triumvirate was universally credited with the new policy. They begin 'to be spoken of all over England in the same manner as Danby, and, I fear, may be impeached the next Parliament upon this point, and the war in Scotland'.

The general odium was increased, in the case of Halifax, by a singularly inopportune honour: on 17 July Charles declared in Council the elevation of Halifax to the rank of Earl.

The views which the recipient of this extremely ill-timed promotion held, or affected to hold, are contained in the following letter to his brother:

THE EARL OF HALIFAX *to* HENRY SAVILE

17/27 *July* 1679

I had sent you the first news of the dissolution of the parliament, but that H. Thynne promised to do it, so that I relied upon him, and I suppose he did not fail you. It is to be presumed you make comments upon it at Paris, as we do at London, though not just the same; and you may be sure that those who are near the King have their share of the censure that ever attendeth things of this nature. You would think it a strange thing to have it from other hands, and not from mine, that the King, resolving to add my Ld. Roberts and my Ld. Gerrard* to the Earls' bench, hath though fit to let me keep them company. I keep the same name still, and intend your nephew shall take that of the barony, which is Eland: if any young woman that is a good match may be found that can be fool enough to like him the better for it, this piece of preferment hath something in it; else it is to me of very little moment more than as it is a mark of the King's favour, which maketh everything valuable. I am often at Windsor, where much of the time is taken up about your friend† Ld. Lauderdale, who is defending himself against the Scotch Lords, who have brought up their lawyers to report their complaints; and, though perhaps, after the hearing they have had, all things will not proceed so as they might expect in relation to their own particulars, yet it is believed they will have the satisfaction of seeing their great adversary removed, but when and in what manner is a thing of more uncertainty. Our cousin Coventry is marry'd to Ld. Wiltshire, and the wedding kept with great solemnity according to the fashion of old England. I do not find your nephew hath any great stomach to matrimony, and I am inclined to let him follow his own genius, having so many years before him, that he may throw away a little time with the less disadvantage. There is nothing to tell you from hence worth the making this longer, and so I take my leave. Yours.

Ten days later he wrote again on the financial affairs of his brother, and added:

The parliament here is put off for ten days longer, for which other reasons are given out, but the true one is Newmarket. My Ld. Sunderland is gone for a week to Althorpe, and I stay here till he returneth. My

* A follower of Shaftesbury.

† This is satirical.

small tenement is so remote that I cannot so easily divert myself with such small journeys, and I now begin to doubt the summer will pass without my seeing poor old Rufford, now that I have made it deserve a visit better than ever it did before. If I had my choice free, I should prefer being there before this place with all its glory. There is a certain charm in that we call our own that maketh us value it above its true price; but I must lie under the mortification of an absent lover, and am not like to give any other expression at present of my kindness...; I leave you to the triumphs and diversions of your great wedding, and to your particular enjoyments of Father Patrick, and so kiss your hands.

As regards his brother's reference to the charm of Rufford, Henry Savile, in his answer, makes a rather palpable hit: 'Your philosophic contemplation of not seeing Rufford makes my worship smile; when a lover is absent by his own choice it is a sign of very moderate passion, and such has yours always been for Nottinghamshire.'

By this time the new elections constituted the main and absorbing topic; and it was on this occasion that Sir John Reresby frankly transferred his allegiance from Lord Danby to Halifax. 'And now', as Burnet says, 'the hatred between the Earl of Shaftesbury [and Lord Halifax] broke out into many violent and indecent instances.' On Lord Shaftesbury's side more anger appeared, and more contempt on Lord Halifax's; while either strove to form an interest in the forthcoming Parliament. Halifax, in reply to a letter from his cousin Thynne, pleading the writer's desire to retire from politics, wrote urging upon him, not without success, the rescinding of that resolution; and thereupon expressed his satisfaction.

VISCOUNT HALIFAX *to* MR THOMAS THYNNE

(This

for THOMAS THINNE Esq. at Drayton to bee left at Colshill, Warwickshire.)

31 *July* 1679

Dear Cosen—Besides your kindnesse to mee in prevailing against your own inclinations at my request...you are doing the most publique service that can bee to the Nation, by making use of your interest to get reasonable men chosen for the Plt. and if the rest of England had as good a prospect of elections as you have for 2 counties, I durst almost undertake, that not-withstanding all the discouraging circumstances wee live under, things might bee brought to such a settlement, as that wee might at least sleep secure from any sudden destruction. The world is at present a good deal heated, and I have just interest enough at Court, to entitle mee to a part of the fury of the Coffee houses; I need not tell you that they are incouraged by some of my small friends,* which I need not describe to you; my method shall bee to let the storme have its course, and when wee grow calme againe, I do not doubt but I shall bee able to wipe of the dirt that hath been throwne upon mee; Sr. W. Coventry will not bee perswaded to stand which I am sorry for, but you know hee is not easily to bee mooved.... The King is gone to the Downs and said hee would go no further, but how farre his kindnesse to the sea may tempt him to stay out longer than hee intended, I cannot determine.

I am, my dearest cosen
most faithfull and humble servant
HALIFAX

Henry Savile meanwhile was congratulating his brother on his new title; providing always, as he shrewdly observes, the time do not prove 'a little improper' for his Majesty's favour to 'appear to his Privy Councillors'. He regrets, however, the second title of Eland. 'I cannot conceive how either the sound or antiquity of the name can please you better than your own'; and the original line having come to an 'unfortunate (not to be so "foppish" as to say a "sinful") end', Halifax may be thankful that he escapes the dread liabilities of the 'third and fourth' generations. In the absence of data he declines to discuss the dissolution; and makes a cryptic reference to a 'fair lady', for whom a year before Halifax had been in danger of a duel, and who was possessed of such a 'hound' of a husband that she could not possibly be in the wrong.

Lord Halifax replied as follows:

Windsor, 11/21 *August* 1679

I find by yours that the late dissolution hath given some of us fame abroad as well as at home. It is some kind of preferment to be rail'd at, and I do not know whether I shall ever get any further; in the mean time I have argued myself into so much philosophy upon this occasion, that I am neither disquieted nor alarum'd by it. [He excuses the choice of Eland as a title, by the plea that a 'Lady Savile' might possibly be mistaken for a knight's wife], an objection I have often heard amongst the women, and so I let it prevail with me. I approve the continuance of your zeal to vindicate our proceedings in the plot against the scandals that are thrown upon them; and if you will needs publish some counterpoison to the infamous reports that are made of us, I cannot think of a shorter way than the translating into French a very good pamphlet lately come out as an answer to those very speeches you mention, which were made by the Jesuits at their execution. I will talk with somebody about it; but I, being

* I.e. Lord Shaftesbury, who was diminutive in person.

your younger brother in zeal, may perhaps not be so quick in it as to satisfy your impatience and therefore I would not discourage you from what other ways you think fit to take to keep up the credit of our religion.... I am pleased to see your earnestness for a fair lady, though it is not necessary to me, who do already think it would be a sin not to be partial to her in the dispute with her husband; and yet I have not that reason for which you and my Ld. Newport are to be suspected and envied. Sir W. Coventry will not be perswaded to stand for this parlt., making use of his ill health for an excuse. Your friend my Ld. Daincourt will try at Newark, but sayeth he will not be at any charge, which maketh me doubt his success; for I doubt your noble friends there will not much approve a dry election, as a thing of ill example, and tending to introduce presbytery, by the way of small beer, besides the detriment it may bring to his Matys. revenue of excise.... Algernon Sydney is chosen at Amersham; but I hear there is a double return, which will create more dispute. This is a very different scene from your preparations at Paris for the great wedding, which maketh you all there play the fool in another kind, I must not say a worse, because of my known quarrel to fine clothes, which maketh me a party, and then I must not be a judge. The Duke hath desired my Lady Anne may go over to him for a month or two, and I hear the King complieth with it. I have nothing more to tell you, so that the kindest thing is to make an end. Yours.

We must now inquire as to the progress of the negotiations with the States, whence Henry Sidney wrote hopefully; but his suggestions did not meet with complete approval here, as they involved direct relations with Spain, whose procrastination and incompetence had become proverbial.

THE EARL OF HALIFAX *to* MR [HENRY] SIDNEY

London, 18 *August* 1679

I am to thank you for two of yours, the last of which was delivered first to me. I will say little to the kind part of either of them, my good opinion of you having been so long fixed,... and I could wish no more for the good of the world than that the public friendships were as well established where we would place them. You will have it from better hands that the project you mention is not approved of here; and, presuming you will be told the reasons at the same time, I do believe you will acquiesce in them. Other men may propose to themselves other hopes, but mine are all restrained to the person and character of the Prince, whose interest with the States and influence upon the country is that which must keep things firm and steady; and, without that, I look upon every thing there as floating and changeable, and their government would be as unsafe to build an alliance, as most of their ground is to build a house upon. But from the good sense and vigour of the Prince I hope every thing; and pray, as the best and kindest office you can do me, endeavour to represent me as

I am towards him, and you shall not run any hazard of forfeiting your credit with him by engaging for me. You will remember to say something for me to Monsieur Van Beuninghen: thus you see how little scruple I make to trouble you with my small commissions.

I go to Windsor to-morrow for some days, being forced to live between both, neither here nor there, which is not so pleasant a method as that I should make it my choice; but it must be submitted to. When the elections are all made, we shall be able to give some judgment of the complexion of the Parliament, and so give a near guess what we are to hope and fear from their meeting.

We dined the other day at Sheen, where you were remembered, as you shall ever be, with particular kindness, by

Your most faithful, humble servant,

HALIFAX

The meetings of the Council had been adjourned till after Michaelmas. Sir William Temple and Lord Shaftesbury (who felt himself practically superseded) both left town. 'I recommended', says Temple, 'the common cares to the [Triumvirate] whose attendance, I knew, would not fail at Court; two from their offices and the third [Halifax] from his humour, which he owned always must have business to employ it, or would else be uneasy.'

All three lords were accordingly at Windsor when on 22 August Charles, who had caught a chill out hawking, fell suddenly and seriously ill.

During two or three days the general consternation defies description; wild rumours of poison prevailed in the city, and panic terror reigned supreme. People, says Temple, 'looked upon anything, that should [at the time] happen ill to the King, as an end of the world'. The legal successor was abroad; the prospect of his succession aroused, on every hand, grave misgivings; and among the 'Exclusionists' a fanatical repugnance, which seemed to threaten civil war.

Meanwhile the Duke of Monmouth might almost have seemed to have the ball at his feet. His military reputation was at its height; he commanded the entire standing force of the two Kingdoms; he was also Lord Lieutenant of both Staffordshire and the East Riding, and governor of Hull. In Scotland he inspired a grateful devotion, even among the Covenanters he had subdued; while the populace of England, won by his personal charm and the romantic legend of this 'claimant's' birth and wrongs, traced, in his wild youth and martial prowess, a half-superstitious resemblance to the then first of our national heroes; to 'Harry—

of Monmouth'. Politically, the support of Shaftesbury, the most daring of contemporary statesmen, was assured him; with it, perhaps, at such a moment, the support of many less extreme.

The adroit Sunderland had retained personal relations with Shaftesbury; but Lords Essex and Halifax felt that the triumph of Shaftesbury and his candidate must involve not only national disaster, but irrevocable ruin for themselves. They learned that the young Duke was urging his father to forbid, in express terms, the Duke of York's return. And therefore they promptly obtained from the King, not without the cognizance of two of the Duke of York's supporters, an order commanding James to repair at once—in all secrecy, and as of his own initiative—to Windsor. Even Temple was not in the secret. Charles by this time was recovering; and the two conspirators, somewhat ashamed perhaps of their precipitance, were not a little alarmed at the possibilities it let loose.

Their position, indeed, was one of extreme embarrassment. The gulf which yawned between them and the Duke—apart from the one point of the succession—was far wider than the breach which by now separated them from Shaftesbury and his supporters. For both Moderates and Exclusionists shared the traditions of the Country party; while, to the Duke, that party, with all its work, was anathema. He regarded the Moderates as men who sought the same ends as the Exclusionists, though by another way. The policy they had pursued during the last few months—repressive measures against Popery, negotiations with Holland, the attack on Lauderdale—disgusted him. His personal hostility to Halifax had not declined. He had long regarded that Lord and Essex as 'men that did not love a monarchy as it was in England'. He congratulated one of his followers on an attempt to prejudice the King against the Triumvirate in general; had with difficulty forced himself to send Halifax a civil message; and admits he had once told him: 'I looked on him as one of the dangerousest men I knew.'

At this critical moment Halifax wrote again to his brother:

THE EARL OF HALIFAX *to* HENRY SAVILE

Windsor, 28 *August* (7 *September*) 1679

I had yours yesterday, and before I answer any part of it I must for my own vindication tell you I had sent you an early notice of the King's being ill, if some of your kind friends had not assured me they would do it, by which I was secure that you would not be left in ignorance by my omitting it. The first beginning of his sickness gave us some fears, his continued health making it appear a very new thing to us as well as to him; and then the consequence at such a criticall time did so strike men that they were not left at liberty to judge of it with indifference; but now that he is better, and men's thoughts are a little more quieted, we are in better humour, and if we may believe either the doctors or all other appearances and symptoms there is no cause left to apprehend any danger. The doctors have yesterday given him a remedy which they say will prevent any more fits coming upon him.* [As regards Savile's own expenses at the coming festivities in honour of the Spanish marriage Lord Halifax has secured for him a grant of £500 for wedding clothes.] I can easily acquitt you from the guilt of loving fine cloaths for their own sake; it is a crime our family hath very little to answer for; but you must be fine in your publick capacity; and for our credit you must give an advantageous pattern of our wealth by the richness of your embroidery; and of our wit by the choice of your ribbons. Heaven direct you and your tailor so that your poor country may not suffer by you! Adieu, yours.

Meanwhile the Duke of York had started at once from Brussels; and arrived, incognito, early in the morning, at the earliest possible date. He was thus the first to inform his brother of his own arrival. Charles affected surprise; James, in an audible voice, assumed the entire responsibility for the step. As for the younger Duke, who returned later from hunting, his surprise and annoyance could not be disguised. While as regards Lord Halifax, who was responding to a business letter from Henry Thynne, we find him at once informing his correspondent that 'two hours since, whilst we were at the King's rising, the Duke came in, very much to his surprise as well as ours....Pray write this piece of news to Sir William.'

This decidedly disingenuous attitude was preserved, even as against Temple, who, when he subsequently learned the truth, bitterly resented it. On first hearing the news, he had sympathized with the probable dismay of the Triumvirate. 'Next day', he writes, 'I went to Windsor, and the first person I met was Lord Halifax coming down from Court on foot, and with a face full of trouble; and as soon as he saw me, with hands lift up two or three times; upon which I stopped, and alighting asked what was the matter; he told me, I knew all as well as he; that the Duke was come; that everybody was amazed; but where we were or what would be next, nobody knew; he bade me go on to Court before the King went out; said he was going to his lodging to sit and think over this new world; but desired we might meet [with] my Lord Sunderland, after dinner.'

* The Jesuits' powder, i.e. quinine.

Temple had every right to resent the dissimulation with which he had been treated; but the vexation and bewilderment, which Temple dismisses as assumed, were no doubt real enough. The Triumvirate stood exactly in the position of a conjuror who has raised a spirit he knows not how to lay; but they did their best.

Within thirty-six hours of his return, the three Ministers (accompanied by the two friends of the Duke who had been advised of the summons from the first) waited upon James. By the mouth of Sunderland (probably as the least obnoxious) he was informed that the recovery of the King rendered the Duke's immediate departure both possible and eminently advisable; and the deputation offered to obtain from the King, as a counterpoise, the expatriation of the Duke of Monmouth. This last ingenious expedient settled the matter; the King's assent was obtained, and a few days later the Duke of Monmouth, much to his astonishment and disgust, found himself required to resign his commission as Captain-General and to leave the country for an indefinite period.

The Triumvirate had thus trumped the cards of both their contingent political adversaries; but brief indeed was their triumph. Scarce had they breathed again before the Duke of York began to intrigue for a softening of the terms in his own case. The substitution of Scotland for Brussels had the ready acquiescence of Essex, the reluctant consent of Halifax, and the underhand encouragement of Sunderland; who further engaged in a treacherous understanding with James, by which his journey was soon to be ostensibly *broken*, but in reality *terminated*, in *London*.

Of this Halifax had no knowledge; but his anxieties remained poignant, both from a personal and political point of view. The Duke had evidently re-established his influence over the King, and this boded ill for the Moderates and their policy. On the other hand, they were completely at odds with the Exclusionist wing of their own party. The prorogation and dissolution, with the current suspicion of their complicity in the Duke's return, had still further impaired their popularity. 'I know not', writes Algernon Sidney to Henry Savile, 'how much your friends and mine do grow at Court, nor whether the gains they may expect to make there, will countervail what they lose in the nation; but I do think myself assured that two of them, who were generally as well esteemed as any men I know, are now as ill spoken of as any; and the asperity one of these showed against the Papists is most bitterly retorted upon him.'

Harassed as he was by disappointment and apprehension, Halifax was now further afflicted by a serious and apparently dangerous illness. It was said that he excused himself for not waiting on Shaftesbury when returning to town, on the plea that he had a violent fit of the strangury; to which Shaftesbury sarcastically retorted: it was no doubt Ormonde (i.e. a supposed desire of Halifax for the Viceroyalty) which lay heavy on his stomach. Certainly after the return of the Court to town about the middle of September his condition became such as caused grave anxiety to his friends. Temple, who visited him during the earlier days of his complaint, writes rather sarcastically: 'I saw plainly', he says, 'his distempter was not what he called it: his head looked very full, but very unquiet; and when we were left alone, all our talk was by snatches; sickness, ill humour, hate of town and business, ridiculousness of human life; and whenever I turned anything to the present affairs after our usual manner, nothing but action of hands or eyes, wonder and signs of trouble, and then silence.' Burnet, who apparently visited him in his ecclesiastical capacity, is more sympathetic. 'Lord Halifax', he writes in his contemporary record, 'fell ill, much from vexation of mind; his spirits were oppressed, a deep melancholy seizing him; for a fortnight together I was once a day with him, and found then he had deeper impressions of religion on him [than those who knew the rest of his life would have thought him capable of]. Some foolish people gave it out that he was mad; but I never knew him so near a state of true wisdom as he was at that time....He was', he adds, 'offered to be Secretary of State but he refused it'. Some (including Shaftesbury and Sheffield, Lord Mulgrave, the satirist) 'gave out that he pretended' (i.e. desired) 'to be Lord Lieutenant of Ireland, and was uneasy when that was denied him; but he said to me that it was offered him and he had refused it. He did not love, he said, a new scene, nor to dine with sound of trumpet and thirty-six dishes of meat on his table. He likewise saw that Lord Essex had a mind to be again there; and he was confident he was better fitted for it than he himself was.' Burnet's assiduity occasioned some comment. 'It was said I had heightened his disaffection to the Court....I was with him only as a divine.'

All this time the Dutch treaty had remained in suspense. 'Nobody', wrote Henry Sidney to the Earl, 'will do any business, little or great, with an Englishman till they know certainly the condition of the King's health and what reception the Duke hath had....I showed [the Prince] part of your letter, and upon it had a good deal of discourse with him of you, which you may easily imagine was not to your disadvantage; he hath desired me to say a great deal for him to you, which I will be sure to do one of these days.'

The answer of Halifax was somewhat oracular:

London, 19 *September* 1679

I have been indisposed and am so still, which, though it be some excuse for me that I have been so slow in answering your last, yet it must not keep me any longer from doing that which I have always so much mind to do. I do not wonder that what hath happened here lately set everybody's thoughts at work where you are; and no doubt till these riddles are cleared, we must expect nobody will be in temper to take any measures with us. But my Lord of Sunderland hath from time to time acquainted you with the state of our world, and by that enabled you to lessen if not destroy the fears that have been raised in Holland upon the late occasions, and when the things are executed, which are intended, I hope the conclusion of these matters will give as much satisfaction as the beginning of them afforded occasion for jealousy and dispute. You cannot give me a greater mark of your kindness than your continuing to do me good offices where I am so ambitious to be well, and I do not doubt you will get so good an interest there yourself, as that, besides your own satisfaction, it will be an advantage and a furtherance to those things that are designed.

It is no small mark of the Prince's credit that he hath been able to draw Monsieur Van Beuninghen from his opinion, to which he is naturally partial enough, if I do not mistake him; therefore, if our disagreements here, when the Parliament meeteth, do not prove to be such as will discourage all our friends abroad from dealing with us, I am in hopes we may join in the means for our preservation, notwithstanding the arts as well [as] the power of France, which are both great arguments to discompose any model that can be made against them. We say here that the Duke of Monmouth will go next week, and the Duke a day after him. The King seemeth inclined to go to Newmarket; his inclination is so strong for it, that it is an ill way of making one's court to dissuade him from it, though most wish he would stay in town for more reasons besides his health.

I am ever your most faithful Servant,

HALIFAX

In the event the Duke of Monmouth left England for Holland on 24 September, while his uncle insisted on remaining here till the following day. Further instances of his recovering influence followed in quick succession.

Parliament was once more prorogued for a fortnight. Scotland had been substituted for Brussels as the Duke's temporary place of residence; and on 13 October, to the utter consternation of Halifax and Essex, but in accordance with the secret connivance of Sunderland already mentioned, the yacht bringing back the Duke and his family landed them at Whitehall. Two days later Lord Shaftesbury was dismissed the Council.

This blow, no doubt, the Moderates could bear with equanimity; but it was otherwise when Charles, in Council, announced his intention of postponing the so often prorogued Session, by further short prorogations, *for a year*. 'All at Council', says Temple, 'were stunned at this surprising resolution.' Temple himself was exasperated into a public and spirited remonstrance; Halifax (still apparently confined to his house) 'expostulated severely upon it with some that were sent to him from the King'.

The mortification of Halifax and Essex may be imagined and was only mitigated by their success in getting the Duke of York, after a brief respite, dispatched to Scotland; though not till his patronage of a forged 'Protestant' plot, in which Halifax, Essex and Shaftesbury were all said to be implicated, had still further embittered relations between the whole Country party and the Duke.

Meanwhile, Henry Savile was complaining bitterly, though in his usual witty vein, of the 'stupid ignorance' in which he had been left. From Sunderland he had received *but two letters since the beginning of his mission*; he had heard of his brother's illness merely by chance; as regards political affairs he lived in absolute darkness. 'I am fain', he says, 'to nibble in my discourses of England like the ass munching thistles.' Though 'tied to those interests that inclination as well as nature direct me to follow', he was unable to refute the most obvious calumnies; and knew not 'from those I intend to shout with whether I was to cry a Y[ork] or a M[onmouth]'. Nor did his expostulation evoke an entirely luminous reply from his brother.

THE EARL OF HALIFAX *to* HENRY SAVILE

London, 30 *October*/9 *November* 1679

I was not till now well enough to write to you; but those that had informed you of my being recover'd were a little too hasty, for I am but now creeping out of a distemper that hath afflicted me cruelly; and I have the same contemplation upon it as you have, that things of this kind are apt to grow upon us with our age, which maketh me desirous to take the more time for my cure, in hope to alter the habit of my blood, and take away that sharpness which it hath ever been subject to. It is not strange to me that censures are thrown at random upon men who are thought to be in business, and they must be content to receive the shot, and yet are bound up by their circumstances from making their defence. You may answer to yr. self and every body else that I will always mean well, and though I may committ errours they will be such as have no guilt in them, if a man can be justifyed by good intentions. It is not easy to acquaint you with the details of some things at this distance, though my Lord Sunderland hath always told me he took care you should know everything that was done, as far as it was communicable; and, though I find by yours his correspondence with you is not very quick, yet I desire you will not complain of it, not so much as within yourself, both in respect of my Lds. nature, that is apt to neglect forms; and, which is a better reason, because he is so essentially kind to you, that you must not allow yr. self to see those omissions, which perhaps would stare in your face if they came from one to whom you were not so much obliged. I must now tell you that I am very sorry to hear that some liberties you have taken of speech not agreeing with the clymate where you are, are so ill taken, that it is observed the King of France plainly resenteth it by the manner of his behaviour to you; that alone is enough to render your life there less pleasant to you; but that is not the worst, for you like all other men must presume you have enemies, who, if they can blaze and aggravate the indiscretion of your bringing this upon you, it may perhaps have an effect here to your prejudice, and, by lessening the opinion of your conduct, may help to exclude you from any pretentions you may have at your return.

The gravity of advising is as little pleasant to me as it is to any man in the world, but my kindness to you would not hold, and so it hath broken out upon you.

H. Sidney is just now come from Holland; and the Duke gone three days since for Scotland. Adieu.

On 29 October/8 November our diplomatist writes again under a renewed sense of injury. He hears that M. Barillon has been intriguing for his recall, and, moreover, that Halifax himself (though his brother will not believe the story) has 'spoke with trouble' concerning Henry's 'manner of living' at Paris 'in point of debauchery. Sure I am', exclaims the aggrieved Minister, 'that no part of my life has been so sober.' The answer to this appeal runs as follows:

THE EARL OF HALIFAX *to* HENRY SAVILE

London, 13/23 *October* (*November*) 1679

I am willing to take this opportunity of Mr Temple's going over to send you an answer to the letter received last from you. I find you had written upon the same occasion to several other of your friends, and we all concur in the opinion that you take the alarum too hot, and that you suspect some for your competitors who are very far from having any ambition to succeed you. H. Sidney assureth us it never came into his thoughts, and I hope Mr Churchill, whatever inclination he may have to be a minister, will never give such a price for it as the supplanting a friend. What your reasons are of being so fond of it are unknown to me, and I remember there is no disputing about tastes, so I do not enter into the enquiry; it shall suffice me that you like your post, and it must make me contribute all I can to keep you there. As for what you hear of my censures upon you for your debauchery, I hope you do not believe a word of it. I hope I am not so negligent as quite to forget in what style it is fitt for men to speak of their friends; and I cannot imagine upon what such a lye could be grafted, except it be from my lamenting to some friends upon the occasion of what I writ in my last, that you should be so open in any French company as to expose yourself to any prejudice by the discourse you might have with them, it being so sure they would tell the least thing they would hope to make their court by. I am told too that Mr Barillon denyeth he ever said anything concerning you, so that your friends agree it would not at all be proper to speak to him concerning it, since it would have no other effect than the making a great matter of that which will not prove so if it be left alone. My condition of health mendeth, but, like most other good things, very slowly, the weather being so sharp that it helpeth to keep me back. All here send you their complements, and I am ever yours.

Meanwhile, the Anglo-Dutch negotiations had completely failed; and Henry Sidney, at home on leave, noted that the postponement of Parliament was generally held as an abandonment of anything resembling a popular policy. The Moderates were all horribly dissatisfied; the Duke's party governed; Temple had retired to the country; Halifax he found still 'sick and out of humour'—'strongly discontented'—'melancholy and uncertain what to do'. The Treasury had been offered him, but in vain. Sunderland was intriguing with Lord Shaftesbury; Essex had resigned from the Treasury; 'Lord Halifax', says Temple, '...commended him for it; and told me his resolution to go down into the country; and though he could not plant melons as I did, being in the North, yet he would plant carrots and cucumbers rather than trouble himself any more about public affairs.' He had, however, resumed his attendance at Council; but the whole Triumvirate complained that they had now no share in the King's counsels.

Matters in effect went from bad to worse. The Duke of Monmouth suddenly complicated the political tangle by an unauthorized return from the Continent, and lost all his offices; whereon he openly joined Shaftesbury and assumed the full status of an 'Exclusion' leader.

Henry Savile meanwhile was excusing himself to his brother for a supposedly exaggerated solicitude concerning his own reputation, by saying that the position he occupied was positively his last chance of 'making a figure in the world'.

His brother responded as follows:

13/23 *December* 1679

I had yours yesterday, and shall say nothing to the business that hath given you so much disquiet, since your thoughts seem to be calm'd as to that particular; and as for your friends' jealousies that something of the report concerning you might be true, you ought to forgive them, as flowing from their kindness to you, and being acquainted with your natural liberty of speech. Some little breakings out over a bottle of wine might not be thought impossible; but now that is past, and such a report being made will make you the more cautious, and it proving false will make your friends less credulous in anything of this kind for the future that concerneth you.

He adds that he is trying to find a purchaser for Savile's place in the Bedchamber, but there were difficulties in the way.

In December another attempt to engage Halifax in the active business of Government had failed and the Earl wrote again to his brother:

8/18 *January* 1679–80

I do not know what you have done to your nephew, but he is full of kindness for you, and presumeth much upon yours; which maketh him not only willing to go from hence, but impatient till he is with you; and I do with less difficulty comply with him, since the parlt. is put off, which would have been an entertainment of some use as well as pleasure to him. I hope that when he is left to himself without the encumbrance of a governour, he will make a good use of that liberty, and think himself so much the more obliged to improve, to avoid miscarrying under his own conduct; though I presume he will not think fit to insist so much upon his right to dispose of himself as not to give it up to you whenever you will be so kind as to advise him. Our world here is so over-run with the politicks, the fools' heads so heated, and the knaves so busy, that a wasp's nest is a quieter place to sleep in than this town is to live in; which maketh me so weary of it that you must not wonder if you hear that, notwithstanding my passion for London, that hath been little inferior to yours for Paris, I go very early this Spring into the country; where, besides other invitations, I shall have that of seeing my small works at Rufford, having yet only had the pleasure of disbursing for them. I confess I dream of the country, as men do of small beer when they are in a fever; and at this time poor old Rufford with all its wrinkles hath more charms for me than any thing London can shew me. How long Paris will keep you in love with it I do not know; but I am mistaken if at last Barroughby* doth not get the better of it. My uncle Packington is lately dead, but whether you or your nephew will think fit at this distance to mourn for him is left to your better judgements. I am for ever yours.

Almost immediately after writing this letter Lord Halifax seems to have left town, and it would appear abruptly, for Sir William Coventry's country house; his wife and family remaining in London. By 30 January he had 'stolen down from Sir William Coventry's to Rufford and none of his friends pretend to know whether he will come up any more'. So wrote Temple to Henry Sidney.

His motives may be inferred from events which quickly followed on his departure. The King resolved to recall his brother from Scotland; whereupon by Shaftesbury's advice four of his principal followers retired from the Privy Council.

By leaving town, Halifax had avoided the inconvenience of fraternizing with any party.

* A small estate belonging to Mr Savile.

CHAPTER VII

IN RETREAT: FEBRUARY TO SEPTEMBER 1680

THE experiment patronized by Temple had thus completely failed. The new Privy Council had been rent from top to bottom on the 'Exclusion' question; and no one of first-rate importance remained in office. Lord Sunderland, who alone among the Triumvirate still remained at his post, had held the Seals but little over a year. In practice, he depended on the intermittent attendance of Lord Essex, and the unimpressive support of two young and recent accessions to the Treasury Board. These were Sidney Gudolphin and 'Lory' Hyde; Mr Hyde's importance at the moment consisting in the fact that he was brother-in-law to the Duke of York.

These three, sometimes described as the 'Second Triumvirate', and more frequently and satirically as 'The Chits', were thus confronted by two recalcitrant factions: firstly, the extreme 'Exclusionists' who had been driven, or had seceded, from the Council on that issue; and secondly, the Moderates who, while opposed to the policy of Exclusion, had broken with the Government upon the second visit of the Duke of York, and the indefinite postponement of a Parliamentary Session.

Lord Halifax, as we have seen, had succeeded in retiring to the country, without committing himself to any of the dissentient parties; and it was consequently the aim of all three to contest his valuable adhesion. Throughout the seven months, therefore, during which he remained in the north, each did its utmost to propitiate the recluse of Rufford.

His Lordship no doubt responded in due form to these various attentions; but unfortunately few of his letters during this period seem to have been preserved.

Lord Sunderland, for his part, astutely employed the very acceptable intermediacy of his delightful mother, Dorothy, Lady Sunderland, the friend and, by his first marriage, the mother-in-law, of Halifax. Her object was to secure his return to town, and collaboration with the new Triumvirate; and at the first she attempted to persuade herself and others that such was his intention. Her letters, which Lord Halifax has carefully preserved and numbered, have been more than once published, They contain, besides the political gossip of the day, expressions of a 'passionate' affection for her son-in-law; and her belief that the King 'will disappoint those that are enemies to the King and peace by...acts of justice, moderation, and observing the laws and using no tricks, but dealing sincerely, openly, without any secrets, especially such as passed between my Lord Danby and Mr Montague....They say there shall be no more underhand dealings to gain Parliament men.' The 'Chits', in their anxiety to propitiate the moderate Opposition, were now become much concerned as to a new alliance with Holland; 'I am never better pleased', adds Lady Sunderland, 'than when I am told things will be done that my Lord Halifax will approve; for then I am sure they are good.'

In the meantime the right wing of the Opposition seceders, represented by Coventry, Thynne, and at this time Burnet, were equally assiduous in their approaches. The last-named, however, in the absence of his former mentor, Halifax, kept veering more and more towards the 'Exclusion' section. All, however, deprecated, with equal urgency, any approximation between Halifax and the 'Chits'. They recognized, with increasing anxiety, the unpopularity which Halifax had incurred during the course of the preceding summer; they trusted that his opposition to the long prorogation and his breach with the Duke might serve to modify the unfavourable impression thus created; and they believed that by remaining in the country until the meeting of Parliament he should most clearly express the reality of his discontent.

Meanwhile we ask ourselves in what manner Lord Halifax himself was employing this unexpected vacation. It is clear in the first place that, after a season of serious ill-health, he felt himself much in need of a period of relaxation and recuperation. We have already suggested the possibility that his constitution may never have been very robust. This might account for his apparent indifference to field sports, his steady rejection of all posts entailing heavy routine responsibilities, and perhaps for an almost austere abstemiousness which seems to have been marked. No one could have less resembled the average country gentleman of his day, and his only interest in provincial life seems to have been in the improvements he had contrived about this period to his own domain. He is credited with having repaired one front of the old mansion, and with having diverted the course of a stream running through the grounds.

For intellectual intercourse or correspondence he can have had little opportunity. Dr Burnet, indeed, during this interval, corresponded with him weekly. Burnet's share of the correspondence (that of Halifax has not been recovered), which has been edited by the present writer,[11] amounts in fact to a series of political news-letters, interspersed with expressions of admiration for his correspondent, and continued concern as regards his supposed religious heterodoxy.

In his *History* Burnet alludes to the subject in the following terms:

> He passed for a bold and determined atheist; though he often protested to me that he was not one; and said 'he believed there was not one in the world'. He confessed he could not swallow down everything that divines imposed on the world; he was a Christian in submission; he believed as much as he could, and he hoped God would not lay it to his charge if he could not digest iron as an ostrich did, nor take unto his belief things that would burst him. If he had any scruples they were not sought for nor cherished by him; for he never read an atheistic book.

Moreover, Burnet may not have been the only divine who, during this period, engaged him in theological discussion. This, the last long interval Lord Halifax was destined to spend at Rufford, will also have offered the last long opportunity for intimate conversation between Halifax and Mompesson, his parson and chaplain while there. The summary of his beliefs as Mompesson understood them is embodied for us in his 'Saviliana' and may be appropriately inserted here. He begins as follows:

> It is the misfortune of great men that they are thought to entertain low-ebbing thoughts of Religion, when they do lay open the wrong methods by which it is managed. His Lordship suspected broad symptoms of allay in the Church, to the present decay and the possible future ruin of Christianity; but to my certain knowledge, of Religion itself he had a noble and a lively sense. I will instance only in things which I had from his Lordship's own mouth. Of all the books in the world, even historical, morals, and of the Laws, My Lord clearly gave the preference to the Bible, whether considered in the matter or stile, in the more than natural eloquence or the extreme good principles of it. His Lordship designed to have writ Notes upon it, and had one intersheeted for that purpose, but was from time to time prevented by business. In the historical books of the old testament, he admired the prodigious variety of events; In the prophets, the noble descriptions and figures; In the whole book the extreme mild Character which God Almighty gives of himself, by his most tender addresses to mankind, in these and the like expressions, *Why will you die, O house of Israel, O that my people had hearkened unto me*....
>
> His Lordship had also a very great veneration for our blessed Saviour.

He observed in him the same high Character of Divinity as in his Father, by the same infinite kindness towards mankind. At this answer of his amongst others, *you know not what manner of Spirit you are of*, I saw him once transported with admiration. He wondered that no Divine had writ his life, when so many men infinitely below him, even considered barely as a man, made so good a figure in Plutarch. His Lordship thought, the Commentaries or Memoirs of his words and actions in the Gospels would afford most excellent materials to the undertaker. And as for the Christian Religion, it was his Lordship's opinion, that all the wise-men, Lawgivers and Philosophers in the world could never contrive such another; It being absolutely the best method and surest way to Happines; The best procurer of health and long life to the body by sobriety, of tranquillity to the mind by contentedness and patience, of love and esteem from men by good nature and serviceableness; the only thing in the world that could keep a man modest in prosperity and undejected in adversity; Besides the hopes of a better life which his Lordship did firmly entertain; not only from Revelation, but also from natural arguments, particularly from the short life of the greatest and best men, the seeming unjust distribution of Providence, and the equality of the wise and the fool in death; which to his Lordship appeared great incongruity in Nature, were it not for another State. In which manner of arguing his Lordship seems to have followed the steps of the wise observer of the Vanity of the World.

But this real respect for Religion did not hinder his Lordship being* faulty in some of the methods, by which it is recommended to the World. He loved the Clergy, but he would sometimes give broad hints of dislike, of the lives and carriage of some of them. He was a great admirer of eloquent discourses, some preachers I have heard him commend and recommend to his familiars; yet he did, upon occasions complain of the too great number of undigested declamations in the pulpit, and that *velvet cushions* too often served for *woollen sermons*, as his Lordship was pleased merrily to express himself.... He was of opinion that making the revenue of the Church [a] property to private Clergymen, had made them men of this world, and by consequence brought disrespect upon their office; whereas in ancient times their profession was more awfull by reason that inclination and a kind of vow, not hope of preferment, made Divines. And as wise men have complained that, giving orders to Monks in the Roman Church has made them degenerate from their first institution, his Lordship thought that giving temporals in property to men in orders, had enervated the primitive vertue, for which the Apostles and their immediate successors were so venerable. And as for learned books and sermons, printed and preacht by Clergymen either vicious or dabbling too much in secular affairs, his Lordship used to compare them to the dry maxims of old Philosophers, which tho' excellent in themselves, yet lay unregarded and even despised; for coming from men who lived contrary to them, and whilst they taught one thing acted quite another.

* We should probably read 'seeing it to be'.

As regards more mundane subjects meanwhile, our only certain lights as to the doings of Lord Halifax during this interval are to be derived from his regular correspondence with his brother Harry.

His first letter to Savile from Rufford is dated 2/12 February 1680:

I am once more got to my old tenement; which I had not seen since I had given order to renew and repair it. It looketh now somewhat better than when you was last here; and, besides the charms of your native soil, it hath something more to recommend itself to your kindness than when it was so mixt with the old ruins of the abbey that it look'd like a medley of superstition and sacriledge, and, though I have still left some decay'd part of old building, yet there are none of the rags of Rome remaining. It is now all heresy, which in my mind looketh pretty well, and I have at least as much reverence for it now as I had when it was encumbered with those sanctified ruins. In short, with all the faults that belong to such a mishapen building patch'd up at so many several times, and notwithstanding the forest hath not its best cloaths at this time of the year, I find something here which pleaseth me. Whether it be the general disease of loving home, or whether for the sake of variety, since I have been so long absent as to make my own house a new thing to me, or by comparing it to other places where one is less at ease, I will not determine; the best reason I can give is, that I grow every day fitter for a coal fire and a country parlour, being come now to the worst part of my elder brothership in having so much a greater share of years than you that it may make amends for the inequality of the division in other respects. The greatest pleasure I have now to hope for dependeth much upon the good advice you will give your nephew, who never shall have any injunctions from me but such as he ought for his own sake to impose upon himself. I think him so capable of succeeding well in the world that it is pity he should miscarry by a wrong setting out at first; therefore pray let us have a care of his launching, for there is the greatest danger for young men in this age. I bid Gosling acquaint you with the particulars, by which I suppose you will not be dissatisfy'd with my part. It may be a real kindness to inform him sometimes of such things as pass through your hands as are not great secrets, and yet may give him a taste and quicken his appetite to know what passeth in the world. He promised me to read books of treaties and negotiations, in which you may not only encourage but direct him very much to his advantage. It is a great matter for a growing man to apply himself to read what may be of some use, which may be done with as much pleasure at least as in loosing time upon *nouvelles* and *entretiens*, things only fit for young fellows and their wenches to read till the hour of assignation cometh for a more substantial entertainment....Your company would not have been unwelcome at Sr. Wm. Coventryes, where we could have entertain'd you a little of things that have pass'd in our world, to make you a return to the account you would have given us of France,...

THE EARL OF HALIFAX *to* HENRY SAVILE

Rufford, 20 *February*/2 *March* 1679–80

I am glad to find that your nephew groweth in your opinion. He is now at the true age of forming himself, and with your assistance and encouragement, I think in the best place for doing it; therefore I hope he will intend it, and think it worth his pains to go about it, I am sure he hath a great belief of yr. kindness, and that will give you the power of persuading when there is occasion for it; so that I rely very much upon you in all that concerneth him. This is somewhat a greater trust than that of leaving it to you to make my complements wherever you think it necessary, as indeed it was to Mr Colbert upon such an occasion. I have proposed your demoiselle to my wife, and I find her not averse to taking her, only she, having no exceptions to the servants she hath, cannot put any away without a fault, only to make room, a method, though often used in courts, not so allowable in private families. Upon the first change I will put my wife in mind again, and if your woman is not otherwise disposed she may come; if she is, there is no hurt done. In the meantime my credit with the French Protestants I owe wholly to you; your zeal being so notorious that it throweth a lustre upon all your poor relations. It is enough to be akin to a man that goeth twice a day to Charenton. Heaven reward you for giving such countenance to the Gospel! Sure when you come home and find my Lady Scroope return'd from hearing 4 masses in a morning at Nostre Dame you are both very merry; for I take it to be an equal laughing match between you about your respective devotions. Pray make her my complements, and let this be one of them. We watch here to know how poysoning goeth on at Paris, thinking it may concern us in time, since we are likely to receive hereafter that with other fashions. Methinks you should not lose this opportunity of retrenching your table, you being a man of too much importance to be out of the danger of ratsbane. These things maketh our forest brains turn round; we are apt to think some new evil spirits are broke loose into the world to confound it. Our hope is that Mr Savile, being a Nottinghamshire man, and once burgess of Newark, will by his influence secure us from the calamities that threaten the rest of mankind; if you do we shall be bound to pray for your worship, and so I leave you.

Private and family affairs occupy a good deal of the envoy's attention at this period. His own title to the small estate of Barrowby was being at the moment contested; and he was sincerely concerned in the matrimonial future of his nephew, Lord Eland. Proposals had been made on behalf of the Marquis de Gouvernet, a wealthy and long-descended Protestant gentleman of Dauphigny, who, sharing the fears which, four years before the Revocation of 'The Edict', agitated his co-religionists, was anxious to marry her in England. The young lady, whom Savile describes as fourteen years of age, 'very pretty' and 'as modestly bred as ever I saw', would carry with her 'a portion of 25,000 pounds'.

To these topics Lord Halifax refers in his replies:

THE EARL OF HALIFAX *to* HENRY SAVILE

Rufford, 1/11 *March* 1679–80

To receive two letters in so short a time from a publick minister, ought to be very kindly taken by a country gentleman, and in gratitude I must in the first place answer that which concerneth you, which is about the suit commenced, or rather renewed, against you. From what pass'd formerly in it, I hope you are not in any danger, but you may be sure that no care shall be wanting to do all that is possible to make a defence, if it should be necessary, which I can hardly think it will be,...Yr. aversion to the remaining in debt must needs produce good effects, for in these cases resolving strongly goeth a great way. Men will find out some way or other of doing whatever they have a very great Mind to, and I think the parting with your place is none of the worst expedients, but you cannot reasonably expect at this time Mr Neale's rate for it. I see your kindness to your nephew maketh you think his being in the house with you no incumbrance, so that you are to be left to do what you will in it. I come now to your second letter, which is upon a very kind subject, there being nothing I have in my prospect to please me so much as the settling your nephew to his own satisfaction and the advantage of our family. The proposal you make is in this respect tempting, that by furnishing me with a considerable sum in present I may be enabled to give a large and liberal allowance, without which a young man married in this age liveth with such straitness that it begetteth uneasiness and dissatisfaction, and from thence flow a thousand inconveniences, of which we have almost as many examples as there are marriages, whilst the father is living; but on the other side, there are many objections to be made; as first, the alliance, though very honourable, is of no manner of use or support to an English family. Then their way of treating about portions is very different from ours; the husband generally hath only the use, and the principal is to go to the children. But more than all this, in the age we live in, and considering our sky looketh very changeable, and that we do not know what kind of weather we may have, the argument of alliance may grow much stronger, and it may so happen that in a shuffling and distracted time, your nephew may by a wise and reasonable choice, by a thing well timed, do a great deal towards the preservation of his family, if the times be such as to require it. I confess this amongst other arguments hath ever made me the less pressing upon him to marry....

Indeed, if Harry himself had such a liking to the person as might make him wish for my approbation, it would have great weight with me; but you saying he knoweth nothing what you write, I take him to be wholly unconcerned. In the mean time the thing is so fair, as it is represented to you, that before one would take an absolute resolution it deserveth [further] enquiry.

I must now give you a friendly advertisement, and, though you may think it a little thing, you must not laugh at me. I hear by accident that you write into England with some freedom of a lady you converse with, and you are so happy in your writing talent that things are repeated and whisper'd for secrets to so many that they will cease to be so at last; but you will remember that the more we deserve jests, the less we bear them, and the more they are commended, so much more they are resented.

My wife and daughter are very much your servants.

THE SAME *to* THE SAME

Rufford, 29 *March*/8 *April* 1680

Your last was more than ordinarily welcome to me, by holding out some possibility of seeing you if you come into England. I will not let myself hope it too much, for fear of being disappointed, knowing how many excuses a man in your circumstances may have for not taking such a journey. If the charms of your native soil can overcome those difficulties I shall be very glad of it, and old Rufford will put on her very best looks to receive you; but if it should so happen that you cannot, without great inconvenience, spare time for so long a visit, I will meet you halfway, that after so long an absence I may at least have some few hours' talk with you. We shall then have opportunity to discourse fully about the matter you proposed.... I see you are a very constant man to your nephew.... I believe he is more apt to be faulty in little circumstances than in great ones, and therefore he must be put in mind that there is a necessary subjection to forms which young men are to submitt to; and at the same time [that] it may be very reasonable to laugh at them, it is yet more so to practice them. Little words and motions of respect and civility do often recommend a man more to the company than the knowledge of all the liberall sciences; but the truth is, all good sense hath something of the clown in it, and therefore though it is not to be suppressed it must be soften'd so as to comply with that great beast the world, which is too strong for any man, though never so much in the right, to go to cuffs with. You guess right both of the lady and the friend you correspond with. I conclude what you write is shew'd by way of applause, and not out of ill meaning, therefore you are to use reasonable caution, but not to take any other notice of it. Wife and daughter kiss your hands and I am, *vous pouvez croire*.

THE SAME *to* THE SAME

Rufford, 24 *April*/4 *May* 1680

Yours by this post was very welcome to me in curing the fears I had for Harry, which were raised from the knowledge I have of his constitution being, like mine, hot, and apt to take more fire than ordinary upon any distemper. I think it will be adviseable for him to rest a little after it in some place out of Paris, at his own choice, before he taketh any long journey. Besides, by the complexion of things, one can hardly be secure that Flanders will be a quiet place this summer; and then it would be an unpleasant progress. I am sorry you have put back my hopes of seeing you;...

The talk goeth here that Flanders is to be sold, but I hardly believe it, not that the Spaniards would not part with it, but that France will not give money for what they may have without it. If it should be either given or sold, I think it a wise piece of revenge of Spain upon those who would not preserve it, though more nearly concerned. I forget I am at Rufford, as ill a climate for politicks as for melons. Upon recollection I leave you to your state contemplations, and am ever yours.

Meanwhile the adhesion of Lord Halifax was more and more urgently courted by the Ministers. Lord Sunderland was specially insistent; and since Lord Halifax declined to go south, his brother-in-law suggested a conference at Althorpe. The mere rumour of this created a great commotion in political circles; but when Halifax was at length induced to consent, business detained Lord Sunderland in London.

THE EARL OF HALIFAX *to* HENRY SAVILE

Rufford, 31 *May*/10 *June* 1680

Your last filled me with the expectation of seeing you ere long, but by the letters from London my hopes are blasted. It being determined it seemeth, for reasons of state, that you are for the present to remain where you are. In the mean time you are a man of that importance, that the news both at home and from abroad speaketh of your being recall'd, and a successor named, with as much formality as if there were something in it. One piece of intelligence I confess I am not a little pleased with, which is, that upon a contest you had with His Christian Majesty (we will suppose it was for the honour of England or the advancement of the Protestant religion) he thought fit to give you a cuff on the ear. This was discoursed amongst the most sober newsmongers of St James's Park, as a real truth, and you cannot imagine how such a thing as this advanceth your reputation amongst all true lovers of the gospel. The King of France hath great pleasure to see how all the world trembleth under him, for I suppose it a satisfaction suitable to his heroic mind; but for my own particular, was I in his place, I could find out a hundred things that would please me more than to keep Flanders and Germany from sleeping for fear of him. These great preparations must have some matter to work upon, and by what I see, wherever he falleth, all the revenge they have upon him is by an immediate yielding to take away the relish of his victory.

The delay of the Althorpe meeting meanwhile was allowing free course to the gossip of the coffee houses; and Halifax seems to have employed his cousin Sir Thomas Thynne to collect the suffrages of his friends on the subject. Sir Thomas found opinions divided, but himself urgently advised that Lord Halifax should not leave Rufford till Parliament met.

Despite these remonstrances the visit so long discussed took place, however, eventually. The Ministers went down to Althorpe in a body, accompanied by Henry Sidney, who had just returned from Holland, and who remained at Althorpe a week. 'We gave', he writes in his *Diary*, Lord Halifax 'so great satisfaction that he will again come amongst us. He enquired much after the Prince of Orange....They think his being here will put an awe upon people, and hinder them from being stark staring mad....The King will desire no money, unless his alliances will require it; he will have all acts for securing them against popery, but will not meddle with the Succession. He will have the Parliament meet sooner than was intended.' The gist of this of course is that Halifax was ready to collaborate with the second Triumvirate, but only if run on the same lines as had been professed by the first.

Lord Halifax returned from Althorpe after a visit of about a week; and the excitement created by it was such as had been anticipated. Sir William Coventry, who was then staying at Rufford, had only delayed his departure in order to hear the result; Sir Thomas Thynne and Dr Burnet wrote guardedly, but with noticeable stiffness. Lord Halifax found it necessary to reassure his friends, by a kind of circular letter, which intimated that he had no immediate intention of returning to town or resuming an active part in affairs; and this transaction was represented to Lord Sunderland in a very unfavourable light. He wrote:

> I received your letter with greate Satisfaction and will take care that the next time you come to altrope your ague shall have (?) no kinde of encouragement. I have been told by severall People that you have writ to some heere that you had met dangerous Company but you would take care not to be caught, and much more to that Purpose. I made no answer to it but that I did [not?] thinke that was your Stile; it being ill suited to Men who did not care to catch any body. I write no newes because I knowe you will heare from otheres all, and fifty times more than I can thinke of or have heard. I am intirely yours.

His mother, Dorothy, Lady Sunderland, was peculiarly incensed by the tenor of this report—so much so as to draw, apparently, a remonstrance from Lord Halifax. But she was easily placated, and soon her letters to Halifax did not lack more agreeable topics. She retails the encomiums of Lord Eland which the ever active Lady

Scroope reports from Paris; he had won golden opinions, and had shown himself greatly attracted by the fair Protestant heiress. The elder Henry pays a brief visit to England; and the unwonted slenderness of his person, together with the foresight which had induced him to bring over a handsome present for the Royal Mistress, appear to have afforded Lady Sunderland equal satisfaction.

Much to the disappointment of Lord Halifax, however, a meeting between the brothers had to be postponed.

THE EARL OF HALIFAX *to* HENRY SAVILE

Rufford, 3/13 *July* 1680

It is a cruel thing your stay in England should be so limited that it is impossible for me to hope to see you, a thing I wish for many reasons, there being a great many things of several kinds both private and publick that it might be of some use as well as satisfaction to us to talk of. But you are a man of that importance to the world that all your minutes are precious, and so your poor country friends must be content. In the mean time we rely upon you that you will stop the K. of France from doing any hurt in Flanders, supposing you have power with him, notwithstanding your late disputes. Your countermand about the couple of pads was unnecessary; for the truth is, it is almost as possible to get a horse that flyeth as a horse that paceth, I mean one that doth it well, so rare that kind of creature is grown amongst us; and for my own stock, you know how I used to be provided, though I intend for Harry's sake to have my stable better furnished. If I had ever a one fit for you he should be at your service without the help of a third person to intercede for it. If you have a mind to tell me anything you do not think fit to trust the post with, my servant in town will be able to convey it safely to me; you will let me know whether you can get your tether lengthened, and the time you are certainly to return again. Adieu.

A few weeks later the Earl was actually in London. 'Lord Halifax came to town on Thursday', writes Rachel Lady Russell to her husband, Sept. 17. 'The town says he is to hear all sides and then choose wisely....My sister', she adds (in playful reference to Lord Russell's early courtship of Mistress Pierrepoint), 'says Lady Halifax has lost no beauty in the country and takes care you may know it.'

CHAPTER VIII

THE EXCLUSION CONTEST OF 1680/1

'To hear all sides and then choose wisely!' Lady Russell's conclusion reveals to us how successfully Lord Halifax had maintained his attitude of reserve. 'I had', writes Sir William Coventry, 'a letter this day from L.H. wherein...he saith...that the Country Party are *far from being displeased either with his coming up or going to Council.**...I...do heartily wish he may not take the civility of men's expressions, with whom he speaks...for the sense of the party....I have since thought of Lord H. and doe conclude one so discerning as he cannot (after warning) mistake so far his measures ...and...sees some point on which to redintegrate himself.'

On the other side Sunderland and Sidney, calling together at Halifax House, thought Lord Halifax 'in good humour and willing to comply'. But in what did Sidney expect his compliance?

At the Althorpe meeting, as we know, Lord Halifax had promised to support the Ministers upon certain definite issues, which were but the development of the Earl's own original policy. These included, first, the substitution of 'Limitations' for the Exclusion; and secondly, a firm alliance with the United Provinces. Meanwhile he had continued to maintain close relations with the Moderates of the old Country party, and had not lost touch even with some who ranked with the extreme section. We may infer that he hoped to rally the more reasonable members of all the political groups round an Administration pledged to a moderate and patriotic policy.

But while the outlook of Halifax had not changed, that of Sunderland and Sidney had undergone a complete transformation.

Some days after the Althorpe interview, an attempt on the part of Lord Shaftesbury to indict the Duke of York as a Papist, and the Duchess of Portsmouth as a National Nuisance, had revealed to the timorous mind of Sunderland the increased strength and daring of the Exclusion party; which had, indeed, gained enormously through the events of the preceding year. The general uneasiness had at length culminated in a fever of enthusiasm for a measure, the sweeping and definite character of which appealed

* The passage printed in italics is underlined in the original.

with peculiar force to the ignorant and zealous; while motives of prudence or conviction were drawing into the vortex many of those who had previously stood aloof. Lord Essex, for instance, had finally drifted with the tide. Sir William Temple, while maintaining in public his attitude of complete neutrality, regarded the passage of the measure as certain. He saw in an entire surrender to the Exclusionists the only hope for a reconciliation between Court and People; the indispensable preliminary of the strong foreign policy which was still his main interest. Henry Sidney had reached the same conclusion; while many others, who in principle remained anti-Exclusionist, shrank from incurring a futile odium for a cause they regarded as lost.

Nor was this all. Within the strictest circle of the Court the defections had become alarming. Even the Duchess of Portsmouth—with whom the Duke of York had inopportunely quarrelled—had been terrified by the attack of July. She had hastened to propitiate 'the Faction' and espoused its cause with fervour. Moreover, the King (it was whispered) had begun to waver. Relations between himself and his brother had not been invariably cordial; the influence of the Duchess was notorious; while the secret offers of the Exclusionist party, made through her intermediacy, were munificent in the extreme. Six hundred thousand pounds and the right of naming a successor is a regal bribe indeed.

Under these circumstances Lord Sunderland, who, as virtual Prime Minister, expected to become the main target of obloquy, had resolved to quit a ship which he believed to be sinking. Having opened secret negotiations, he had effected a definite, though private, understanding with the Exclusionists. The truth cannot have long escaped Lord Halifax's penetration, and he was thus compelled to reconsider his own political policy.

It is curious to note how nearly his dilemma coincided in form with the problem which, in 1886, was to confront the right wing of the English Liberal Party, headed, one notes, by a descendant of Lord Halifax himself. Was he to abandon the standpoint which he had hitherto maintained, and adopt a policy which might necessitate a civil war, and eventually undermine the reversionary interest of the Prince of Orange?

As regards the first point, there can be little difference of opinion. Had the Exclusion Bill passed into law, it is practically certain that the Duke of York, supported by a vigorous minority of Old Cavaliers, of Roman Catholics, and of Jure Divino Anglicans, would have raised the standard of revolt; and could have relied not only on the gold of France but on the political sanction of Parliaments both in Scotland and Ireland. Eight or nine years later, when the criminal folly of James had alienated the most loyal, his deposition was to occasion civil distractions in both those kingdoms; while his adherents and those of his family were to constitute for over fifty years a standing menace to peace. In 1680 the struggle would have been more equal; since the issues to be faced were then problematic rather than actual.

Meanwhile the 'Limitation' policy offered, at this stage in the controversy, a fair prospect of success. James was probably the only man in England, his own co-religionists not excepted, who would not have admitted the desirability of some restriction of the Royal prerogative, while in Papist hands; were it only to propitiate the Protestant majority. The Royal assent, and with it that of the whole Court, and of the Jure Divino Anglicans, were secured beforehand. 'Lord Halifax', says Burnet, 'assured me that any Limitations... that should leave the title of King to the Duke, though it should be little more than a mere title, might be obtained of the King; but that he was positive and fixed against the Exclusion.' The enemies of Halifax, of course, 'imputed' this unwonted firmness 'to his management'; but however this may be, it is clear that Charles, though credited with at least a momentary hesitation, displayed, in public, throughout the crisis, a very unexpected decision. Thus it is at least probable that, had the Exclusionists accepted the proposed compromise, James II would have eventually succeeded to a purely titular sovereignty. Hence his mortal hatred for the Limitation project, as contrasted with the Bill of Exclusion. The one scheme would have *formally* deprived him of a crown; the other, while *in practice* effecting the same object, would have deprived him of power wherewith to regain his authority.

The second issue, which relates to the interest of the House of Orange, appears more complicated. According to the Bill as eventually drafted, the Prince's position would have been improved rather than threatened, his wife's reversion being no longer postponed to that of her father. On this the more recent Ministerial seceders laid stress. They insisted that the pretensions of Monmouth were purely chimerical, and, indeed, his avowed adherents in the House of Commons did not certainly exceed a dozen.

But so superficial a view excluded certain considerations, very vividly present to both Halifax and Shaftesbury. Fear of York had become among the more ardent Exclusionists the predominant motive, and the question of his substitute a matter of very secondary importance. Charles, if driven to bay, might well have preferred his son to his nephew. If so, the young man's pretensions, emphasized this very summer by the 'Black Box' rumours, might have prevailed; more especially, since Monmouth had attracted the enthusiasm of the populace, to whom the Prince of Orange, and even the Princess Mary, were but names.

His enemies, of course, adduced more intimate reasons for the obstinacy of Lord Halifax. Jealousy of Lord Sunderland (a suggestion which probably emanated from Sunderland himself)—vanity and ambition—hatred of the Earl of Shaftesbury—were all alleged as motives; and perhaps the latter may have 'sharpened', though it did not originate, his opposition.

On the other hand, it is clear that the argument of personal safety, which had so strongly appealed to Lord Sunderland, was as cogent, indeed more so, in the case of Lord Halifax. 'He's a stout man', writes a contemporary, 'that dares offer a negative first.' He knew, none better—for it was the constant theme of his friends—how sullen and bitter a resentment had been elicited throughout the Exclusionist wing of the old Country party by his share in the acts of the Triumvirate. The defection of Sunderland and Essex had left him as the sole magnet of political vengeance; and an impeachment for high treason might involve, at the very least, a preliminary imprisonment of years. His own long and intimate connection with the Country party only aggravated the perils of the prospect. For the fate of his uncle Strafford had been ominously recalled during this very year; when Rushworth had published his own stenographic report of that statesman's trial, accompanied by a laudatory dedication to his nephew Lord Halifax.[12] So sinister a correlation can hardly have failed to remind the latter that no hatred is so intense as that evoked by a reputed renegade.

Meanwhile, the way of escape lay invitingly open. His protracted absence from the political scene would easily cast over a change of front the halo of calm reconsideration. These reflections, of course, were very obvious to lookers on; the Exclusionists, we imagine, entertained little doubt of his ultimate recantation. One is forced to believe that Sunderland felt secure on the point; and in fact even the Duke of York seems to have despaired of the statesman's support. Even after the opening of Parliament he preserved a somewhat delusive reticence, continuing to co-operate on minor issues with all sections of the Country party. To one man, however, he had already declared himself. The following letter to his cousin Thomas Thynne is dated a fortnight before the meeting of Parliament:

THE EARL OF HALIFAX *to* SIR THOMAS THYNNE

5 *October* 1680

...I beleeve that though I found at my arrivall a new Scene in State matters, yet it is the same as when you left the town, so that I shall not be able to give any information that is new to you. But I confesse I was a little surprised to see such a change in some of the Court in relation to the Duke; I am told there is now as much anger against him at Whitehall as there can be at the other end of the town, so industrious his Highness hath been to spoyle his own business; the waves beat so high against him, that great part of the world will not hear of any thing lesse than exclusion. For my own part I neither am nor will be under any obligations that might restraine the freedom of my opinion concerning him; but yet if there is any possibility of making ourselves safe by lower expedients, I had rather use them, than venture upon so strong a remedy, as the disinheriting the next heir of the Crown. Upon this occasion I have been thinking what is proper for a friend to advise you as to your own particular. If you do not come at the very first sitting [of Parliament], the country party will bee angry and perhaps treat you as roughly as they have done some of your friends; If you do come, in all probability the first business will bee to proceed against the Duke, and if you have the same tendernesse you used to have in point of decency towards him, you will bee in great difficulties to know how to behave your selfe: for my own sake I wish you here for a thousand reasons, but as things are, I do not know, whether it may not bee adviseable for you, to hearken a little for a week or 10 dayes, whilst the Plt. sitteth, after their method of proceeding, and upon that forme your resolutions of coming up. And though others may do it better, I shall not omitt to give you the best lights I can; presuming upon the safety of this conveyance by the Carryer of Colshill. In the meantime I can tell you, the Town sayeth as confidently the K. will quit his brother, as those of his party say the contrary: a fine world, and a happy prospect of things, when our remedies are little lesse to be feared, than our disease; I am, Dear Sr. for ever Yours.

Meanwhile, on coming to town, Lord Halifax himself had resumed his attendance at Council; where his first action was calculated to increase the animosity of the very Prince whose interests he was intending to support. He proposed that before the Session should begin, the Duke of York should withdraw from the political scene. The Duke was naturally furious. Halifax he stigmatized as 'an Atheist' who 'had no bowels' and had hitherto been no good friend to the Monarchy. His remonstrances, however, were futile, and the Duke left for Scotland the day before the opening of Parliament.

The King, in a brief speech, dilated on the alliance with Spain, urged the further investigation of 'the Plot', and dwelt on his financial necessities. He promised such securities for the Protestant religion as might consist with preserving the succession in its due and legal course of descent; and pleaded with some pathos for political concord, in the interests of all Europe, no less than in those of England.

The Plot was the first topic to be taken into consideration by the Upper House. Lord Halifax—still ranking as one of the Country party—seems to have once more championed the intemperate Bill, framed to drive the Papists from London. This passed the Lords, but dropped very fortunately with the next prorogation.

Meanwhile a Bill of Exclusion was already passing through its stages in an impatient House of Commons. By 8 November it was in Committee, and rumour began to insist that the King would eventually yield.

That evening Charles held a meeting of the Council. Time, it was felt, now pressed; and it seems to have been on this occasion that both Halifax and Sunderland unmasked. The King displayed (as is said, at the instance of Halifax) unusual vigour; and repeated, before the House of Commons, his unalterable determination to stand by his brother. It was in vain; for three days later, by an overwhelming majority, the Bill of Exclusion passed the House of Commons.

A mysterious lull in the proceedings now took place, which was either occasioned by, or utilized for, an attempt to coerce Lord Halifax; the news of whose intended opposition had spread like wildfire.

'I got', says Burnet, 'many meetings [to be] appointed between Lord Halifax and some leading men; in which, as he tried to divert them from the Exclusion, so they studied to persuade him to it.' The arguments of the Exclusionists were, it seems, of a forcible character. 'I am full of my Lord Halifax,' writes Dorothy Lady Sunderland, 'and will tell what perhaps nobody else will, that, a day or two before the Duke's bill was carried to the Lords, one of the great actors came to him (as a friend, I suppose) to tell him if he did speak against it he would be impeached by the House of

Commons, or an address made to the King to remove him from his great place of Privy Counselor; he answered, neither threatenings nor promises should hinder him from speaking his mind.... In a point, he says, he has studied more than ever he did, and would have been glad if he could have gone the popular and safe way.'

The futility of these negotiations, therefore, soon became evident; and on the morning of 18 November, the zeal of Lord Russell, to whom the Bill had been entrusted, precipitated the final issue. Snatching the parchment from the table of the House of Commons, he hastened towards the House of Lords, a confused body of supporters streaming after him. And as (his somewhat heavy features aglow, no doubt, with the almost fanatical enthusiasm of the moment) he read aloud to their lordships the ominous title of the Bill, a shout of applause arose from the throng behind. An attempt to adjourn the House, which was initiated by the Exclusionist Peers, met with defeat at the hands of the Courtiers; and the House went at once into Committee for the purposes of freer discussion.

Then ensued a scene, the most striking, perhaps, of a by no means inanimate period. The debate gradually evolved itself into an oratorical duel between the two finest speakers of their own generation. Bound by the ties of affinity and of long political association—alienated by recent animosities and jealousies which had long reached their height—the two champions, for the greater part of seven hours, in presence of the King and of the representatives of the people, surging behind the bar, debated the succession to the imperial crown of England. Lord Shaftesbury displayed to the full his extraordinary oratorical powers; but, by the consent of friends and foes alike, Lord Halifax surpassed him. 'Shaftesbury', writes a contemporary, 'was never so outdone before.' 'Lord Halifax', says Barillon, 'stood up to Lord Shaftesbury, and answered him every time he spoke.' 'He gained', records Burnet, 'great honour in the debate; and had a visible superiority to Lord Shaftesbury in the opinion of the whole house: and that was to him triumph enough.' 'Halifax', observes James II's biographer, no doubt upon the authority of men who had been actually present, 'spoke incomparably, and bore the burden of the day in the committee. He answered Shaftesbury and Essex, as oft as they spoke. He spoke, at least, sixteen times, letting slip no good occasion. His reasons were so strong, that they convinced every body that was not resolved not to hear.' 'His Lordship', says Peterborough, 'that day...did outdo himself.' 'He made', says Reresby, 'so fine and so powerful a defence that he only (for so all confessed) persuaded the whole House.' 'Old men', says Macaulay, 'who lived to admire the eloquence of Pulteney in its meridian, and that of Pitt in its splendid dawn, still murmured that they had heard nothing like the great speeches of Lord Halifax on the Exclusion Bill.'

Of this magnificent effort, how little remains to us. Miss Brown has indeed recently unearthed in the Bodleian Library some most interesting notes of the debate, attributed conjecturally to Lord Huntingdon.[13] These are elliptical, fragmentary, and sometimes undecipherable; the MS. terminates abruptly; and while it throws much light on the views of a number of those who contributed to the debate, the report cannot be regarded as giving any adequate picture of the debate as a whole. For the speakers against the Bill are much more liberally reported than those in favour; while as regards the protagonists Shaftesbury and Halifax—of whom the latter is elsewhere credited with nearly a score of speeches—the report makes them responsible for only two or three apiece.

These, however—together with two or three intervening speeches of Lord Essex who, though reputed an Exclusionist, seems to have been prepared to compromise—form a more or less connected whole, and may best serve our purpose.

The suggestions of Lord Essex appear to have implied that the Bill should not be thrown out but amended. He admitted, indeed, that the Duke of York had still a following in Ireland 'and the Plantations' (Colonies). But if so, was *Exclusion* (he asked) the only expedient available? What about a fresh indictment, such as had been recently quashed? It would, in any case, be unwise to throw out the Bill, without debating and voting on possible alterations.

Lord Shaftesbury is represented as putting two queries to the House:

(1) Is an 'Exclusion' vote within the competence of the House?
(2) Is it expedient?

Lord Halifax apparently replied to him in a speech more fully reported here than any other, though the opening sentence is cryptic. 'Lord Shaftesbury' (he said) 'has been in so many changes that it is charity to fear; for he fears not. I believe the Parliament has a power [to Exclude?] rather than not; it is a right however that will be taken up' (i.e. contested).

For what follows immediately, we may preferably accept a longer version, given in the Biography of James II. It seems to be derived from contemporary letters. There it is said that Halifax urged—'How imprudent it would be to declare the Duke an enemy to the State, who was actually at the head of a powerful Nation [Scotland]; where there was an army too; that in Ireland his power was no less considerable, where there was 10 or 15 Papists for one Protestant; that he had great interest in the Fleet; and credit with the English troops.'

Resuming the Huntingdon version, we find Halifax reported as suggesting that, should the Bill entail a (civil?) war, the Duke might 'fall on us' with the assistance of the Irish, and the English Papists. Ireland, he said, was 'in a dangerous condition; not a gun mounted'. Yet he feared the Bill would provoke the Duke to throw in his lot with the Irish; this might cause a breach between England and Scotland (which had made a figure in the world, even when separated from England). That the Duke was a Papist, Halifax of course recognized; and the Duke must suffer the consequences. Not a penny of public money must be granted to the Duke, or to any Papist successor; and thus he could not do much harm. 'If this Bill doth pass', moreover, it will be only a beginning; another Bill may be brought in which would go much further (i.e. to the elevation of Monmouth?). Then follows another cryptic passage: 'Was there never an argument against the Prince of Orange's aims at the Sovereignty of Guelderland? Fleets and armies [have ere now?] corrupted men.... Will you be satisfied if confiding men* be not placed in† offices of trust? If the Duke should make any endeavour to return, to whom could he address himself, except those in power, who must all be against him?'

Lord Essex seems to have replied that since, under existing circumstances, a Protestant King, supported by Protestant laws, could hardly hold his own against Popery, and the people submit meekly; what would happen under a Papist?

Lord Shaftesbury appears to have retorted to Lord Halifax that Scotland would soon co-operate with England, if the 'load that lies upon them' (i.e. Lauderdale?) were taken away. What then? Are we to live in fear of the French and the Irish, and act 'craftily'

* Does he mean confidential followers of the Duke, or co-religionists?

† Query 'are excluded by the Bill from'.

so as not to exasperate them? When once we know that the King is ready to declare war, all Protestant States will be ready to join in. Are Popery or rebellion necessary alternatives?

Lord Essex argued again for the *amendment* of the Bill. All the House was agreed that something must be done for religion, 'and that the Crown must not be left with that plenitude of power, as the laws of the land now stand'. If so, let the Lords now consider what limitations they would offer, before the Bill is thrown out; because, if the Bill is thrown out, and the expedients found insufficient, what confusion shall we be in? It would be to tempt God if we do not something to secure religion.

From this suggestion Lord Halifax dissented. 'This notion is unparliamentary and impractical.' He 'is against Exclusion as so bad that it is impossible to mend the Bill and therefore it signifies nothing to retain the Bill. It is not agreeable to the debates among mankind [query *to the universal rules of debate*] that before a Bill is offered [query *put to the vote*] one should have to find expedients.'

So ends our only version of the Halifax speeches.

As the day wore on, however, it became abundantly evident that the eloquence of Halifax was gaining an ascendancy over the mind of the House. The debate became more and more violent, and in his excitement Lord Peterborough, so some declare, laid his hand, by an illustrative gesture, on the hilt of his sword. An instant of wild confusion followed, and it seemed, for a few seconds, as if a debate at the sword's point actually impended. In the midst of the turmoil, so some say, several of the more violent Exclusionists closed upon Lord Halifax, 'being resolved to make sure of him in case any violence had been offered'. Lord Dartmouth, who heard the story long after from Lord Winchester, understood that Winchester himself was one of them; but in this at any rate, as Mr de Beer points out, he must have been mistaken, as Lord Winchester appears to have been absent from all these debates.

The danger of an absolute collision was, however, fortunately averted and the sitting reached a less bloody conclusion; for when, at a very late hour the same evening, the House divided, the Bill was rejected, on the first reading, by a majority of thirty-three.

Seldom, perhaps, is the ultimate fate of a Bill decided by even the most splendid displays of Parliamentary eloquence. But the number of waverers was on this occasion unusually large; and though Mr de Beer[14] after close investigation, maintains that the forces of the Court must in the long run have triumphed, he agrees that the summary defeat of the Bill, after one day's debate, was due to Lord Halifax.

To him alone contemporary opinion, almost universally, ascribed the result. 'At present', writes the wife of that late recruit to the Exclusion policy, Lord Sunderland, '*Lord Halifax is the King's favourite*, and *hated* more than ever the *Lord Treasurer* was, and has really deserved it, for *he* has *undone* all.' The fury of the Exclusionists is, indeed, the best evidence of their opinion; it was the fury of men foiled in the moment of expected victory. That Lord Halifax appreciated fully the peril of his political situation appears from a passage in a letter of introduction addressed to his brother in Paris which bears the date of this momentous day. 'Our world here is so heated that you must not be surprised though you should hear I am in the disfavour of those from whom I never yet deserved ill; if innocence can be a protection, you need never be in pain for me and so I kiss your hands.'

On the following day the House of Lords went again into Committee to consider 'heads for the effectual securing of the Protestant religion', i.e. substitutes for the Exclusion Bill. Lord Shaftesbury proposed the King's divorce and remarriage. As the French Ambassador wrote:

Lord Halifax, wishing to undo the effect of what had been proposed by Lord Shaftesbury about the exclusion of the Duke of York and the divorce, said that all these proposals were based only on private interests, and had no object but to bring about the success of unjust and chimerical pretensions. He said much else which could only apply to the Duke of Monmouth, and he added that there were more secret and dangerous designs, and insinuated, without naming the Duchess of Portsmouth, that she had views for her son, and that she had hopes also for herself, and that it was these designs which made her shake the whole machine.

Lord Shaftesbury, impatient at such a speech, told Lord Halifax that he of course did not believe that the Duke of York was a Catholic, since he combated with such warmth the reasonable precaution, which the nation desired to take against him.

To this Lord Halifax replied: 'I know that the Duke of York is a Roman Catholic; and I am one of the first who knew it, and I feared the consequences of it at the time when that Lord, who has interrupted me, affixed the seal to a declaration for establishing liberty of conscience in favour of Papists, and at the time also when that Lord was working with zeal and with success for the rupture of the Triple Alliance.'

This answer much disconcerted Lord Shaftesbury, who however did not give up pressing his point...as vehemently as before.

On his part Lord Halifax proposed the banishment of the Duke to a distance of 500 miles from England, either during the King's life, or for an express period of five years. This only excited the ridicule of the Exclusionists and was of course very coldly received by the Duke's partisans. The biographer of James II thinks this suggestion was not quite seriously intended; but on the Duke himself it made an extremely disagreeable impression, though he prevailed upon himself to write Lord Halifax a civil letter.

Lord Essex's suggestion that an *Association* should be formed (as under Edward III and Queen Elizabeth) for the maintenance of such precautions as should be adopted, and should be fortified by the grant of 'cautionary towns', was accepted by the Committee, but regarded by the King as a 'deposing of himself...and...worse than the Exclusion'. Indeed, Halifax himself frequently observed to Dr Burnet that 'this whole management looked like a design to unite the King more entirely to the Duke, instead of separating him from him; the King came to think that he himself was levelled at chiefly, though for decency's sake his brother was only named'.

Meanwhile, in the Lower House ominous murmurs were foretelling another storm; and on the first possible opportunity Montague moved, first for a vote declaring Halifax an enemy to the King and Kingdom; and secondly for an Address to the King praying that he would be pleased to remove 'George Earl of Halifax from his Councils'.

After an acrimonious debate—during which one speaker declared 'I would rather have his head than any Popish Lord's in the Tower', while Temple played a timorous part, and Russell sat silent—the result seemed a foregone conclusion. Proceedings had been unusually protracted, and the House of Lords adjourned while the sitting was still in progress. As Lord Halifax passed through Westminster Hall he learned the nature of the business which still detained the Commons. With ostentatious indifference he proceeded, as he said, 'to his dinner', declining all converse in the precincts 'lest men should say he was making friends'.

A motion for adjournment was negatived by 219 to 95, 80 members walking out of the House; a remarkable fact, as the third reading of the Exclusion Bill had been passed *without a division.* The resolution in favour of the Address was then carried to a Committee appointed to draft it. This brought the sitting to a close; but in the afternoon, as Dorothy Lady Sunderland tells us, Halifax House 'was full of House of Commons men....He says he will speak his mind and not be hanged so long as there is law in

England....I am not well' (she concludes); 'pardon this narrative. I were a beast if I were not concerned for so perfect and constant a good friend' as her son-in-law had always proved to herself.

Sir William Coventry displayed similar anxiety, and an almost pusillanimous desire that his nephew should bend to the storm and retire from the Council.

> I...you know have long wished him out. The times are so uncertain, and humours are in so high a fermentation that I cannot see how a man of moderation can take joy in acting. I have written to my Lord to beg him to have a watch upon himself that the opposition of his enemies may not thrust him into another party, but that he keep upon a national bottom, which at last will prevail...contenting himself to keep up his own spirit and value by acting with freedom in the House of Lords, according to the national interest. Whilst we are jangling, I foresee the Sovereign Princes will despair of us and run into France, from whence will come an irreparable ruin.

On 22 November the Address was reported. It ascribed the dissolution of the last Parliament, and 'the frequent prorogations' of the existing one, to 'the evil and pernicious Counsels of George Earl of Halifax', and desired that his Majesty 'would be graciously pleased to remove' the said George Earl of Halifax 'from his Presence and Councils for ever'.

The friends of Halifax now endeavoured to recommit, and thus shelve, the Address. During the last Parliament, urged Sir Thomas Clarges, 'we had quartering soldiers taken away by a clause in the Tax-Bill; and we had the *Habeas Corpus* Bill passed, and both by this Lord's mediation, which was worth forty Prorogations. They were exposed to the Council and had all the forms observed, and it was happy they passed, and I know that this Lord had a great hand in it.'

The Address was duly presented to the King and laid before the Council. Lord Halifax offered to retire, but Charles refused to accept his resignation. Lord Essex supported the Address; Lord Sunderland ostensibly opposed it. But after Council (so Temple reports, on Sunderland's own showing)

> Lord Halifax went to Lord Sunderland's lodgings, where they fell into discourse of what had passed; and Lord Sunderland told him that though he had given his opinion at Council as he thought became him, yet if such an address should ever be made against himself, he should certainly desire leave of the King to retire, as a thing that would be for his service. Upon this Lord Halifax fell into such a passion that he went out of the room. And from that time they hardly lived in any common civility when they met.

The King, in his formal answer, found the Address liable to several exceptions, as to which 'having a great desire to preserve all possible good understanding with this House' he forbore to enter into particulars. He added that he did not find in the Address sufficient grounds for removing Lord Halifax; but would leave to his own legal defence either that Lord, or any other Lord, against whom the Commons should 'in a due and regular course prove any crime'.

Dorothy Lady Sunderland believed that the major part of the House were ashamed and sorry for the line they had taken. She declared that both Shaftesbury and Russell disowned any share in it, and that even Montague dared not make a second speech in the debate. 'A great many who differ from my Lord Halifax as to the Bill, say few besides him that come within Whitehall could decide [query *divide*] the House at this time.'

Upon Lord Halifax, meanwhile, these events had made, it is clear, a profound and painful impression. Prepared as he had been to face some temporary odium, it was not without a shock that he realized in how great a degree the virulence of the extreme factions had invaded the ranks of the old Country party. The following letter, despite its apparent philosophy, clearly reveals this:

The Earl of Halifax *to* Henry Savile

13/23 *December* 1680

You will before this have one of mine which giveth you some account of my late preferment in the House of Commons, who were pleased to make me a man of more importance than I am, the better to entitle me to the honour of being addressed against. I am not worth the notice they have been pleased to take of me, and I do not doubt of outliving the disadvantage this may seem to throw upon me, being resolved to give such evidence of myself, if I should continue to have any part in the publick business, as shall cure the suspicions men may have taken of me in a heat, for differing with them in some of their darling points, to which they are at present so wedded that no reason can be admitted in contradiction to them. Your kindness maketh this appear a heavier thing than either it is in itself, or than I apprehend it; the circumstances that attended it are more than the thing itself and yet I have borne it without much disquiet. I must only cast about for a new set of friends, for my old ones have been so very zealous for the publick that some of them thought it as meritorious to persecute me as others believed it excusable to desert me; the history of it I reserve till I see you, and in the meantime whatever may be said from any other hand to lay any blame upon me, let it not find any great credit with you; for I dare undertake when you hear all you shall not need to make use of any partiality to incline you to judge of my side. I had a letter this day from your nephew dated at Turin, in his way to Venice. My Ld. Dorchester and Ld. Coventry are dead, which may give you the opportunity of mourning if you care for it. Yours.

The significant hint concerning 'new friends' demands our special attention. It is evident that the ungovernable fury of the Exclusionists was now (as Sir William Coventry had feared) driving Halifax, almost and perforce, into the arms of the Hydes, the Reresbys and the Musgraves—men with whom at heart he had very little in common, but who had rallied courageously to his defence. He was, in fact—though by no means so wholeheartedly—placed in the position which had confronted his own father at the moment of Strafford's impeachment; and he evidently feared that events were tending towards the same dire solution, i.e. towards a second Civil War.

Sir John Reresby throws considerable light upon this aspect of the question. On 24 November he records:

My Lord Halifax told me that he had no ways deserved this heat of the Commons against him. I said he ought not to be concerned, for he had got more friends by it than he had lost.... He said he would venture his life with those friends. [On 28 November he wrote] I went to wait on my Lord Halifax, who, after the great service he had lately done the Crown...was looked upon as the rising man and first favorite. He carried me with him in his coach to Whitehall: the next day he invited me to dinner with him in private. He told me it was to be feared some unhappy differences might arise in the nation from these disputes about the succession; and in case it should come to a war, it might be convenient to form something of a party in one's thoughts. He told me that he knew very well there was but one other and myself that had any considerable interest in my neighbourhood; asked me my opinion how their inclinations stood. [Reresby promised to bring the Earl a formal statement.] I did so [adds Reresby] and he did agree with me that the loyal interest was not only much more numerous, but consisted of more wealthy and active men; and that those who were so busy in Parliament against the Court, were men of little power or esteem in their country.

Meanwhile a Bill of 'Expedients', which was to replace the defunct Exclusion Bill and for which Lord Halifax was believed to be mainly responsible, was passing through the House of Lords; and the severity of its provisions called forth some sarcasm on the part of the Exclusionists. Parliament was to meet automatically within six months of a Papist Succession; and the Bill further entailed, during the anticipated reign of a Papist, the entire suspension of the Royal right of veto, the temporary surrender of all ecclesiastical patronage, and the appointment of all officials by Parliament or its nominees. The Duke of York was at once to vacate his seat in the House of Lords, and all offices which he had still retained. To him these expedients were, not unnaturally, even more distasteful than the Exclusion; and the Prince of Orange, then in close touch with the Exclusion party through Henry Sidney and the Sunderlands, was being tutored by them into the belief that prerogatives reft from a Popish Monarch would hardly be regained by a Protestant.

The Dutch Ambassador accordingly received instructions to remonstrate with Lord Halifax on this head; and a despatch records his interview. Lord Halifax, he says, replied that he was the very attached servant of the Prince who, he trusted, was convinced of this, and whom he had always considered as the only Prince on whom the Protestant party could rely. That from this point of view he had always entertained a very personal veneration for his Highness; and that he was ready to express himself so openly that the Ambassador must see that his protestations were genuine. That he for his part knew well that the Duke could never bear rule over England—that he never would [so] bear rule,* that he himself would be the first to oppose it; but that the Prince would do well on his part to be on his guard against persons who would deceive him—who had private aims—and who only desired to obtain the passage of the Exclusion Act against the Duke of York, in order to prove beyond doubt that Parliament had the power to make such an Exclusion. That the measure once passed, this cabal, deriving its precedent therefrom, would consequently in the course of two or three years, and in another Parliament, endeavour to effect further Exclusions; and to place the Duke of Monmouth on the throne, in whose interest all this was being done. That he said this as the humble servant of his Highness; and that these precautions could do no injury to his Royal Highness, being solely designed against James Duke of York. The Dutchman had continued to argue in favour of an Exclusion, and to invoke precedents in its favour; but Lord Halifax answered that it was all one, that the Parliament would by that show that it could alter the Succession; and that if the Dutchman was the friend and partisan of His Highness he ought above all to prevent this; lest, under some pretext in that His Highness was a foreigner, etc. he should be injured in his

* I.e. have more than nominal authority.

rights. The Ambassador, though by no means convinced by these arguments, could not move Lord Halifax; who would only say that he felt certain an accommodation would take place and that suitable expedients would be found.

Meanwhile, public attention was being diverted to the trial of the first of the accused Popish Lords. Lord Stafford was cousin to Lord Halifax. He was also the first to be tried in Westminster Hall, under an impeachment for high treason, since the trial of Lord Strafford forty years before; and many feared it portended the same terrible issue—civil war. The 'Plot' witnesses repeated anew the perjuries which had already brought so many victims to the gallows; and though the discrepancies were glaring, their assurance staggered some who were not altogether disposed to credulity. The unfortunate prisoner—old, infirm, unaided—made but a feeble defence, and was convicted by a majority of twenty-four. To the credit of Lord Halifax be it said that he was one of the thirty-one Peers who, rising each in his place, with his hand upon his breast, pronounced his 'Not guilty upon my honour'.

That some of his friends did not share his conviction, or inclined to censure him for braving a second time the anger of the Commons, we shall learn later. On such a subject, however, one friend at least could be trusted to support him. 'If a man do according to his conscience,' wrote Sir William Coventry, 'the quiet of that is above any other to be acquired in this world. God preserve him... and us all.'

On 29 December Lord Stafford, with courage and dignity, suffered upon Tower Hill. That same day Reresby dined with Lord Halifax. 'He said to me,' records Reresby, '"Well, if it come to a war, you and I must go together."' Reresby urged his own claims to a foreign appointment. Halifax replied, 'We must have you [here?] in business; we have need of such men nearer home.'

The Commons now offered, in return for the Bill of Exclusion, and a subsidiary Bill of Association, a handsome pecuniary supply. Some supposed that Charles would have yielded; but Lord Halifax told Reresby 'that it was like offering a man money to cut off his nose'; which a man would not suffer for a greater sum.

In the House of Lords, however, the Earl enlarged upon the excellent effect which would accrue from a spontaneous liberality; a position which Lord Shaftesbury vehemently opposed.

On 4 January the King returned a definite refusal. The debate upon this answer was deferred for three days; and Lord Halifax in the interval received intelligible hints of the upshot.

THE EARL OF HALIFAX *to* HENRY SAVILE

6/16 *January* 1680–1

Your answer to mine by Mr Nelson is in a style that of all others ought to be the most welcome to me. I like kindness best when it is in so plain a dress, and to be told by a brother, and, which is more, by a friend, what the world sayeth or thinketh of me; though their censures of me may be mistaken, yet I cannot be so in judging yr. part to proceed only from true and perfect kindness, which I assure you is not thrown away upon me. Your opinion that I am in the right may be too partial, but that I think myself so, you may undertake for me, and I shall not deceive you; and if the points lately in question are errours on my side, I have this to say in my excuse, that I have hardly one friend that was not till very lately of that very opinion which is now accounted a mortal heresy; so that if by a greater measure of grace than I pretend to they have outran me by their sudden conversion, they ought to have been gentler to a weak brother than I have found them. If I could tell you the several steps of their behaviour to me you would wonder they do not turn papists; since there is no other church in the world charitable enough to give them absolution for it. I would not much doubt of satisfying you in the great objections made against me, if I had time to discourse with you; but a letter cannot be made long enough to give you a clear light into things of this kind. You will I am sure give me some kind of credit when I tell you I am not such a volunteer in philosophy as to provoke such a storm as hath fallen upon me, from a mistaken principle of bravery [i.e. bravado]—to do a thing only because it is dangerous; but when upon enquiry I think myself in the right, I confess I have an obstinate kind of morality, which I hope may make amends for my want of devotion. It seems the foreign ministers have had my picture drawn by their correspondents not very much to my advantage. I guess who were the painters, and think I am not mistaken in it. Where all this will end, either in relation to myself or to the publick, God in Heaven only knoweth. I am at this hour threatned with more thunder from the House of Commons to-morrow; whether it will be so or in what manner I do not yet know, but where there is infinite anger there is reason to expect the worst;* for which I have recourse still to my small philosophy, and have not only the comfort of innocence to support me, but the impossibility of avoiding any strokes of this kind without such indecencies (to give no worse term) as I can never digest: and, though I agree with you this is not an age for a man to follow the strict morality of better times, yet sure mankind is not yet so debased but that there will ever be found some few men who will scorn to join in concert with the publick voice, when it is not well grounded; and even that popular fury which may now blow in my face will perhaps with a little patience

* He probably means impeachment.

not only abate, but turn against these very men that now appear against me. I am interrupted, and so can only tell you I am for ever yours.

The debate of 7 January answered the forebodings of Lord Halifax. From the first it took the form of a renewed assault upon himself; and the tone of the discussion was menacing in the extreme. Sir Henry Capel, brother to Lord Essex, spoke with remarkable violence; to which Lord Russell demurred. Some called Halifax a renegade to his political principles, some a Papist, some (apparently) an Atheist. His late accession in dignity was thrown in his face; he was charged with aiming to be 'a Premier Minister of State' which 'our Government will not admit of'. Burnet tells us how his step-father, Chicheley, moved that Burnet himself might be sent for, to satisfy the House as to the truth of his religion. 'I wish', adds the Doctor, 'I could have said as much to have persuaded them that he was a good Christian, as that he was no Papist.'

The House eventually resolved to insist on the Exclusion, and to refuse Supply in the meantime. It followed this up by a Resolution that the advisers of the last Royal Message had given 'pernicious counsel'; that George Earl of Halifax, was one of them, 'and is a Promoter of Popery and an enemy to the King and Kingdom'. It further resolved that an Address should be presented for the removal of five of the Duke's supporters by name.

The King's retort was a ten days' prorogation. Reresby says:

> The same day waiting on the Lord Halifax, he complained of the unjust severity of the Commons against him in their vote, which was that he was a promoter of popery and betrayer of the liberties of the people. He said that were a man never so innocent, it coming from the representatives of the people, it was too heavy for any single person to bear; therefore, he had thoughts to retire from Court, but that he would go his own pace, and not just be kicked out when they pleased. And in case the King should at any time have occasion to use him in what was just, he should be ready to serve him.... At the same time he complained of the unsteadiness of the King's temper, that whilst he seemed to approve the counsel you gave him, he hearkened to other counsels at a back door; which made him wavering and slow to resolve (and people afraid to serve him).

The question now arose in Council whether the prorogation should be the prelude to a dissolution. Against this Lord Halifax argued strongly, and for several reasons. The step was certain to be laid at his own door. It must cut short the proceedings on the House of Lords 'Expedients', which had by now been strengthened by two additions: the first that the Duke should be banished during the King's life; the second, that Foreign and Irish affairs, under a Popish Government, should be controlled by Parliament. Lastly a rumour prevailed that a dissolution would be the prelude to the release of Danby, and Lord Halifax, says Reresby, 'was jealous ...that my Lord Danby would come out of the Tower and be received again into counsels. If that happened, he resolved to retire, and advised me not to press to be in employment till things were upon another foot.'

The arguments of Halifax were, however, overruled in Council; but, on the other hand, and perhaps on his initiative, the proclamation which dissolved Parliament summoned a new Parliament to Oxford, for the 21st of the ensuing March.

THE EARL OF HALIFAX *to* HENRY SAVILE

20/30 *January* 1680–1

You have given full evidence of your kindness by your fears for me, which I suppose may increase when you hear of the dissolution of a Parliament. You may believe me when I tell you, this is not to be imputed to me, though I am far from arraigning the better judgments of those with whom I may differ in this particular. If it should happen, which is not unlikely, that I should go down to Rufford, you will be further convinced in this matter; and if I could talk with you, I should as little doubt of doing it in that of my Ld. Stafford, in which you are possessed I see by the powerfull majority, which is not at all times found to be in the right. A man must never hope a pardon for small sins if he will digest great ones, and where blood is in the case there is not, or at least ought not to be, any room for prudence. That an honest man is a very scurvy calling I agree with you; but having used it so long I do not know how to change, but must be content to keep to it with all its hazards and inconveniences. By what you say concerning my late friends, I find a statesman hath as much charity out of interest as a Christian hath from his religion, and is as easily reconciled to his enemies whenever the scene changeth, and that it suiteth well with his affairs. I confess I, who am slow to anger, when I am once thoroughly injured, am apt enough to retain it, not so far as to revenge myself, but only to remember, and not easily to trust again. Your bill of naturalization* did not want my help while the Parlt. sat, but, greater matters depending, it could not be dispatch'd; when the next meeteth I do not doubt but it will pass, if the session continueth any time.

Next day, Reresby dined with Lord Halifax and thought the Earl 'seemed to hold his resolution to retire', but meanwhile he had recommended Reresby to 'his particular friend' Mr Hyde. His Lordship added that 'he was not at all dissatisfied with the King',

* I.e. for Huguenot refugees.

but feared the Duke's 'prevalency' with him would 'carry things too far'.

In point of fact, the Duke and his ostensible champion now stood on by no means friendly terms. At the very moment when the Commons were accusing Lord Halifax of Popery the Duke believed that he was designing a general banishment of Roman Catholics. James also, and very properly, resented the urgency with which Lord Halifax had adjured him to renounce Popery; and feared he was against the Duke's own return to England. He further believed that the advice of Halifax had secured a fresh meeting of Parliament to which James himself was opposed. 'He might', he wrote, 'have relied on me, I having given him all the assurances of being his friend I could do.'

Meanwhile, on 24 January, the Exclusionist members of the Privy Council were dismissed; Sunderland being warned that his own resignation of the Seals was imperative. It was perhaps for this that Lord Halifax had waited on in London; for on the following day, just before starting for Rufford, he wrote as follows to his brother:

THE EARL OF HALIFAX *to* HENRY SAVILE

London, 25 *January*/4 *February* 1680–1

Your kind repeated earnestness to rescue me from the dangers you apprehend I am in from the general anger that hath of late been raised against me, coming from the warmth of your heart, as I am sure it doth, is a welcome though an unnecessary evidence of your mind towards me. . . . I have had the good luck to have every unpopular thing imputed to me in the first place, and by going a straight way without any byas, or engaging in any faction, one part of the world hath been much more violent against me than the other hath been in my defence. All these disadvantages did not move me so as to quit my ground whilst the Parlt. sat. I thought myself restrain'd by a necessary point of honour not to do that by compulsion which perhaps in itself was the thing in the world I most desired; but now that the Parlt. is dissolved, I am going down to Rufford to breathe a little, and enjoy some quiet, which will be a very welcome thing to me; and when we meet again at Oxford I must venture to go into the storm, and receive the shot once more of an angry House of Commons, except they should by a miracle grow into a better temper than is naturally expected from them. I shall at least have some respite, though I assure you it was not my choice. I am for ever yours.

The disgrace of the other Councillors was of course imputed to him. 'Lord Halifax', wrote Sunderland's wife vindictively to Henry Sidney, her reputed lover, 'said he would stay in town till my Lord were ousted, and then he would be gone, which he accordingly is to-day, but with two faces; for he tells the King he will certainly be at Oxford, and to the town he professes he will be torn to pieces before he will have anything to do with it.' Finally, she insinuates with shrewd dexterity that the real aim is the ruin of the friends *of the Prince of Orange*.

The King, at any rate, expressed no doubts as to the intentions of Halifax. 'His Majesty', wrote Lord Peterborough, 'did lately speak of your Lordship with great expression of esteem and kindness; and said, that notwithstanding the reports of the town, he did not doubt but you would be the same in the Parliament at Oxford that you had been in that of Westminster.' In reply Lord Halifax professed that his 'thoughts in relation to the public' would require 'some very powerfull argument' to effect their alteration; 'but I who have had the ill fortune to turn papist and yet know nothing of it myself, can answer for nothing, but that, which is impossible for me to fail in, I mean by being ever', etc. etc.

During the recess Reresby saw a good deal of Lord Halifax and had two long and very confidential talks with the Earl. In the first 'His Lordship told me', says Reresby, 'the King would not call a Parliament so speedily as was believed'; and that

the King was slow to resolve where any difficulty arose. That he intended to go to Parliament whenever it assembled, but that afterwards he would leave the Court and business, except his Majesty would be advised to do such things as were for the public good, change some officers about him and take such in their room as would act according to the present counsels. For it would ruin all if his Majesty continued to advise with those of one interest this day and hearken to those of another to-morrow; nor could his ministers be safe under such uncertainties. And if he would be advised, it was in the King's power to make all his opponents tremble.

On the second occasion 'My Lord told me some began to question whether or no the King would remain constant to his brother, or take part with the Duke of Monmouth, who was now treating to make his peace.'

Meanwhile, Henry Savile was urging his brother (in a letter not now extant) to put forth some sort of vindication of his own policy.

Lord Halifax replies as follows:

THE EARL OF HALIFAX *to* HENRY SAVILE

Rufford, 5/15 *February* 1680–1

I had yours the last post, and am glad to find by it that Sr. Thomas Thynne hath stated my case, so as to set me right in your opinion. You know that, besides the perpetual imployment I had whilst I was in town, I am naturally not very good at dilating—half laziness and half honesty. I do not take so much pains to vindicate myself as perhaps a wiser man would do, and, being secure of your justice to me, I know you would take my word for my being an honest man.... I do not agree to the expedient you recommend to me for my fuller vindication. The precedent you mention doth not come home to me. That lord, as he could pen an apology better, so he wanted it more than I do, for I assure you if I am a criminal I am an impudent one, and if you had been upon the place, you would have seen me much less out of countenance than those that pursued me. I think that I am not mistaken when I tell you the greatest part of them are far from being proud of what they have done as to my particular; for where a thing wanteth a true foundation in justice it cannot be long lived, let the authority be never so great that would give it countenance, and make it pass in the world.... As for any that have dealt ill with me from whom I had no reason to expect it, I leave them to the vengeance of their repenting thoughts, which must at one time or other represent their ungenerous proceeding in a worse and an uglier shape than either a vote or an address ever appear'd to me. I am now at old Rufford, where the quiet I enjoy is so pleasant, after the late hurricane I have escaped from in town, that I think myself in a new world, and if wishes were not vain things, and resolutions little better in so uncertain an age as this, I would neither intend nor desire any thing but what I have here—silence and retreat; but if the Parlt. sitteth at Oxford, by vertue of my peership, I am under the obligation of venturing once more to run the gantlet, and I am so ill at any undecent evasion of that which I think my duty, that if I should go about it I should do it very scurvily, which maketh me run hazards in these cases that more dexterous men would perhaps find means to escape.

I came through your corporation of Newark, where I find you might be chosen preferably to any other pretender; but, having so good an excuse as a foreign imployment, I suppose you will not lose it at this time. The quiet station you are in is not to be quitted to come into a storm, and thrust yourself into the difficulties that must always attend a courtier who will be of the House of Commons. I speak against myself in this, since if you were there I should not only have a kind advocate, but a good one too to help me, if there should be occasion. Will you not let a man that is grown famous for giving ill counsel send you this short piece of advice, which in this changeable time is not to declare yourself too positively of any party? I do not mean to unfix your Protestantship; in that be as firm as you please, but in problems of state, where men may or may not be in the right, do not deserve the good opinion of one side so entirely as to forfeit your credit with the other. When you and I meet I can confirm this doctrine by an instance that you will not disallow. Adieu, yours.

THE SAME *to* THE SAME

Rufford, 16/26 *February* 1680–1

I am a debtor for two of yours. . . . I find my 'Not guilty' is a fault that groweth less with you, and that I am already half absolved in your opinion for my part in that business; if I know you aright, I think a little more time will undeceive you as much in the other parts of my charge. . . . The changes made lately at court have removed some of your friends, but those who are now thought to have the greatest credit are, I believe, well enough inclined to continue all kinds of good offices to you; yet if at any time you can think, that at this distance, and in my present circumstances, it may be of use to you that I should say any thing concerning you, upon the least notice I am ready to obey. . . . In the mean time if your approbation of a calm and an easy life is not the effect of some sudden rapture, but a contemplation raised from a steady and deliberate thought, I could say more to encourage you to continue it than perhaps is fit to preach to a man in your circumstances, that is in the way of succeeding in a busy world. You are to take heed of Horace, who, though he supp'd with Augustus at W. Chiffinch's,[15] could not keep in a thousand sentences, of which every one well thought upon is enough to destroy not only the preferment, but the very calling, of a statesman or a courtier. You are not to hearken in this case to the voice of the charmer, charm he never so wisely; and yet I lament with you from the bottom of my heart that there must be no mean between such brothers as use one another scurvily at home, and such who, though united by their kindness, are divided by different circumstances and imployments, and instead of the pleasure of living under the same roof must be content with a kind absence, which is well, but it is absence still. . . .

THE SAME *to* THE SAME

Rufford, 9/19 *March* 1680

I have yours of the 8th, your style. . . . How far your Charenton prayers will prevail for a man that is voted a promoter of Popery I do not know, but I would not discourage your devotion let it be never so much misapplied. . . . If your circumstances will permit it, I would offer it to you to ask leave to come over for ten days, and it must be done immediately, because of the uncertainty of the continuance of the Parliament. The end [i.e. object] of this is that you may see and consider the scene now that it is changed, examine how many of your old friends deserve to be kept, and what new ones are necessary to be made, settle yourself in your master's mind, and offer some antidotes against the poison some may endeavour to infuse into it. You must not be so humble as not to think yourself big enough to be talked of. . . . This meeting at Oxford is very critical; there may be short turns and sudden changes. . . .

We have seen that among the friends of Halifax great differences of opinion had existed as to the wisdom of his decision to retire temporarily from the political scene. This at any rate is certain, that whatever changes he might anticipate in the future, his absence from London was facilitating certain immediate intrigues, very much opposed to all his hopes and aspirations.

In effect, unknown to Halifax, then and thereafter, secret negotiations were being once more initiated with the Court of Versailles. They were warmly advocated by the Duke of York, who, from his seat of dignified exile, was energetically urging, through his confidant Mr Churchill, not only the Duke's own recall, but a monetary treaty with France which would render Parliamentary meetings unnecessary; together with a further strengthening of the prerogative, and 'resolute counsels' in general. These instructions, we are not surprised to learn, were accompanied by a warning to Churchill to take care 'how he communicate these matters to Lord Halifax as not likely to enter into such measures'.

These 'measures', in fact, culminated in the secret compact, *verbally* concluded a few days before the actual meeting of Parliament. By this the King of England was accorded a payment, in three annual instalments, of 3,000,000 French crowns—about £150,000. In return he conceded the sacrifice of the Spanish Alliance and 'the prevention of Parliament from counteracting his engagements'—a very transparent euphemism. Thus the policy of the Exclusionists and their ally, the Prince of Orange, had only succeeded in diverting Charles II once again from the anti-Gallican policy (which since the marriage of Princess Mary he had more or less consistently pursued) into the arms of the French King.

Meanwhile the unwitting Lord Halifax himself was fostering, if he did not originate, a fresh alternative to the Exclusion. This was that on the death of Charles II the Duke should indeed succeed to the title of King, but that the powers of Government should be transferred to the Princess of Orange with the title of Regent.

This ingenious plan seemed to solve many difficulties. The King approved; it conciliated the rather fine-spun scruples of the *Jure Divino* men. It assured the interests of the Prince of Orange and was free from the Republican tendency charged upon the earlier 'Limitation' schemes.

The recess was now drawing to a close; and when towards the end of March Lord Halifax left Rufford for Oxford, he passed along highways thronged by excited travellers. Many of the leading Members of Parliament were followed by bevies of retainers, and themselves rode armed to the teeth, as if repairing, so Hume puts it, to a Polish diet. A regiment of horse, meanwhile, had been posted along the Windsor road to secure, if necessary, the King's retreat.

In Oxford itself, the undergraduates had been despatched to their respective homes. The schools had been turned into temporary Houses of Parliament; the Colleges provided lodgings for Members and their servants.

On 21 March the King opened the proceedings in a remarkable and statesmanlike speech; which produces on the present writer a strong impression that it had been revised, if not composed, by Lord Halifax.

> The unwarrantable proceedings [it began] of the last House of Commons, were the occasion of my parting with my last Parliament; *for I, who will never use arbitrary government myself, am resolved never to suffer it in others*.... It is as much My Interest, and shall be as much My Care, as yours, to preserve the Liberty of the Subject; because the Crown can never be safe when that is in Danger.... I let you see, by My calling this Parliament so soon, that no Irregularities in Parliament shall make me out of Love with them; and by this Means offer you another Opportunity of providing for our Security here, by giving that Countenance and Protection to our Neighbours and Allies, which you cannot but know they expect from us, and extremely stand in Need of at this Instant.

The King's former warnings with regard to the Exclusion were next repeated, but were accompanied by a significant reference to 'Expedients' by which the 'Administration of the Government may remain in Protestant Hands'. Finally, the speech concludes: 'I may the more reasonably require that you make the Laws of the Land your Rule, because I am resolved they shall be Mine.'

Whatever his own part in it, how little can Lord Halifax have realized, as he listened to this princely adjuration, that the lying lips which pronounced it had just sold to a foreign Prince the Assembly which they addressed, and the Allies for whom they pleaded.

In the House of Lords there next occurred the strange episode of the lost Bill for the ease of Protestant dissenters; during the debate on which Lord Halifax rebuked the Bishops for their opposition to the measure. Then we find Lord Halifax opposing an attempt to procure the release of Lord Danby—on the plea of ill-health—as inopportune and irregular, since previous consent of the House of Commons had not been obtained.

In that House, meanwhile, a debate on the introduction of a fresh Exclusion Bill had been deferred, until the 'Expedients' should have been brought forward in the Upper House. During this pause, Shaftesbury obtained an interview with the King in the precincts of the House of Lords; and, it is believed, offered to accept the Regency proposition; on condition that Monmouth, not the Princess of Orange, should be the Regent named. The King at once refused, and the crucial debate in the Lower House therefore took place immediately. The Regency scheme was put forward, and very badly received; and the House at once resolved to pursue the policy of Exclusion.

Lord Halifax seems to have desired that the House of Lords should await the advent of the Exclusion Bill, while initiating fresh efforts for a compromise. But Charles forestalled him. During an intervening Sunday he made no sign; on the Monday he suddenly dissolved; and, ere the members had recovered from a stupor of astonishment, had reached Windsor.

Previous to his departure, however, Lord Halifax had obtained an audience; wherein he may have suggested the issue of an explanatory Declaration, and may even have presented some suggestions as to its form. All that we *know*, however, is that he then and there recommended Reresby to his Majesty's favour; wrote at once to his brother as follows; and left the same evening for Bibury, Sir William Coventry's seat:

THE EARL OF HALIFAX *to* HENRY SAVILE

Oxford, 29 *March*/8 *April* 1681

I have just now received yours, and would not have thought it necessary to return so quick an answer to it, but that I conceive it proper to acquaint you that this morning the Parlt. was dissolved after having sat only a week; but there were such foundations lay'd for heat and dispute, that the King thought it advisable to part with them. Things of this kind are sure to have comments made upon them, and it is not proper at this distance to enlarge upon this subject, so that you must be content to reserve the satisfying your curiosity, till you come over...though I shall not perhaps be in town when you come, intending to return to Rufford. ...Yet I hope you will have time enough allowed you to contrive how we may meet.

CHAPTER IX

IN THE GOVERNMENT 1681–1685

PART I. PRELIMINARY; RUFFORD, MARCH TO MAY 1681

AT BIBURY, where he met some political friends, Lord Halifax will have received the full sympathy of his host. For the Knight, though so strongly attached to the Country party, had deeply regretted the recent violence of the Parliamentary Opposition; and was now decidedly in favour of a reconciliation between the Moderates and the Court. His nephew left Bibury for Rufford on 4/14 April, and next day wrote as follows to his brother at Paris: 'I am come home again sooner than I expected...had not writ now, but that just now Mr Hyde sendeth me word, leave is given you to come over...so that I am only to wish you a good journey, and to put you in mind that, besides the necessity there is for many reasons that I should see you before you return, old Rufford...expecteth a visit from you.' The envoy, however, could only propose to meet him at some intermediate trysting place; but Lord Halifax urged that since 'your kindness will bring you half-way', the Earl's coach should also meet him half-way. 'I do in the name of Rufford desire you will make the whole journey, let your stay here be never so short.' 'I do not', he adds, 'stand upon any forms with you but it would just at this time be more inconvenient to me than ordinary to stir from hence.'

Were his preoccupations of a literary nature? Recent discoveries made it more than possible that he was just then engaged in preparing his first published (though anonymous) pamphlet for the press.

We have already suggested that Halifax, before leaving Oxford, may have proposed to the King the preparation of some form of proclamation, explanatory of the recent and unexpected Dissolution; and may even have sketched the outlines of such a pronouncement. But though the Declaration actually signed by the King in Council on 8/18 April, with orders for its publication in all Churches and Chapels, is on the whole a moderate and statesmanlike presentation of the Royal case, as it may have appeared to a man like Halifax, we have no warrant for claiming the whole as his work. Presumably various Members of the Council will have pressed their own views as to the nature, order and treatment of the topics employed. Moreover, a commentator, who appears to have had some inside knowledge, maintains that a draft of the Declaration had been shown to Barillon two days before the order for publication; and professes to detect French idioms in the style.

But this commentator (as pointedly) refers to its rather unusual, though not unique, use of the word 'Right'—as synonymous with 'Justice'—which is certainly very characteristic of *Halifax*. 'One of the penmen of the Declaration', he says, 'has done himself and the Nation Right...by using his ordinary phrase upon this occasion. The person is well known without naming him, who always tells men they have done themselves no Right when he is resolved to do them none.'

This Declaration called forth several retorts. In all probability the first of these was the anonymous *Letter from a Person of Quality*, which seems to have appeared about the end of April. This in its turn evoked *Some Observations on a late Libel, called a Letter from a Person of Quality*, etc., which is also anonymous; but which Mr Hugh Macdonald now ascribes to Lord Halifax.

In his excellent reprint of this pamphlet (Cambridge University Press, 1941) Mr Macdonald, as the present writer believes, has fully proved his case. He has found two copies of the little work, bearing this ascription in an obviously contemporary hand; and though this could not be considered in any way conclusive, the internal evidence is also strong. Mr Macdonald lays special stress on its almost invariable use of the termination 'eth' rather than 's' in the third person singular of the present tense, which, as the reader will have already observed, is remarkably characteristic of Lord Halifax. Yet it was so rapidly becoming quite archaic that in the first (and unauthorized) printed edition of the *Character of the Trimmer, the printers modernized the unfashionable termination throughout*; while Addison some thirty years later was feelingly to deplore its almost complete disuse. In the second place, Mr Macdonald lays most emphasis on that rare use of the word 'Right' as a synonym for 'Justice', by which, as we have seen, one writer had already attempted to identify the author of the Declaration with Lord Halifax.

And what, we may ask, were the motives of Lord Halifax in undertaking this task? His brother, we know, had a short time before advised him to draw up an apology *for his own policy*; which advice Lord Halifax had deprecated, on more than one account.

But whether or no he had had a hand in the Declaration himself, he may have welcomed the opportunity for indirect self-defence in this vindication of a Royal policy, of which he himself had been to a great extent the author.

The *Observations* themselves, evidently written in haste and under the influence of personal embitterment, are not of any great interest, political or literary. Here and there we find, indeed, flashes of the scathing Savilian wit; but in general the pamphlet is so markedly inferior to his other works, that some have been tempted to query Mr Macdonald's verdict. But in a Life of Halifax it claims its own place; since it expresses his immediate point of view at an important crisis of his career, and may include reminiscences of his great Exclusion speeches. It reads, in fact, rather like a speech or series of speeches than a political tract. The note of passion, so completely absent from his acknowledged writings, is unmistakable here. Personal allusions by name, never met with in his other pamphlets, but which were apparently characteristic of his speeches, are a remarkable feature; and those speakers who had been foremost in denouncing Lord Halifax on the Exclusion issue receive marked and direct castigation. We are specially struck by a passage on Lord Shaftesbury's handling of the Papist Plot; and by reflections on the vote which had declared Lord Halifax 'an enemy to the King and Kingdom'.

If we accept, literally, the pamphleteer's own description of the work as written 'in the country', we must presume that it was completed before the middle of May. For on 17 May Lord Halifax received an urgent appeal from Lord Hyde: 'For God's sake, my Lord, come up, *or you will not find me here*'; which adjuration was reinforced two days later by a peremptory summons from the King.* Why was this?

The Continental situation—owing to a renewed act of aggression on the part of Louis XIV—had suddenly become acute.

PART II. 'FIRST MINISTER', MAY 1681 TO MARCH 1681/2

THE Continental situation, however, though the ultimate, was not the prime cause of the Royal summons. The point immediately at issue was the question of the Duke of York's projected return from a dignified exile in Scotland; a point on which Charles had definitely deferred his decision, with the expressed intention of consulting

* See *Cal. St Pap. Dom.* 1681, p. 287 (Mr Macdonald's reference).

Lord Halifax. This delay, and its cause, were equally offensive to the impatient Duke; who resented the 'excessive credit' which the Earl enjoyed; and who fulminated against the 'timorous' nature of his counsels, and the unsatisfactoriness of 'men of expedients' as a class.

Lord Halifax meanwhile was acquainting his brother (who had been hurriedly recalled to his post in Paris) with his change of plans:

THE EARL OF HALIFAX *to* HENRY SAVILE

Windsor, 26 *June*/6 *July* 1681

I am in debt to you for yours since your arrival at Paris, and deferred my answer in hopes I might have given you some account of my Ld. Windsor's* treaty with his friend for your place.... Your letters were read to the King and approved.... My Lord Hyde's letter... telleth you... how much a moral reflection of yours was applauded, first by our master, and then by all the company; you may see by this, we have a conceit left still, notwithstanding the condition of Christendom, and the late elections of the Sheriffs.†... But that which will be the greatest news to you, my family is coming up this week, and I must lose the joy of being in the country now that the rain hath made it so delicious. Adieu.

Curious to relate, this sudden departure was to be the prelude of a protracted sojourn in London. Five years were to elapse, and Charles II had passed away ere Lord Halifax saw Rufford again. Circumstances, in fact, forced on him a ministerial responsibility which, we imagine, he was not very loth to assume; so that from the moment of his arrival in town until the advent of the Duke of York, ten months later, Lord Halifax, though in official rank a mere Privy Councillor, was regarded as 'the entire Favourite'—'the Chief Favourite and Minister'. His predominance, however, was rather apparent than effective; for, as we have seen, there were underground influences at work by which his sagacious counsels were perpetually neutralized.

The dissolution of the Oxford Parliament had indeed marked the beginning of a new era. The ascendancy of the Exclusionists—or 'Whigs' as they began to be contemptuously called, after the conventiclers of the west of Scotland—had passed its zenith, and the reaction had set in. Men saw how narrowly a civil conflict had been averted; they remembered the Long Parliament of Charles I, with its consequences; and they reflected, in the words of a re-

* Brother-in-law of the Saviles.

† Which had been favourable to the Opposition.

markable pamphlet often, though erroneously, attributed to Halifax himself, that the tyranny of many is even more insupportable than the tyranny of one. An unreasonable fanaticism was now succeeded by a loyalty as extreme. The new 'Tories' (whose nickname, derived from the wild outlaws of Ireland, appears this summer, for the first time, in the correspondence of Lord Halifax) had as little in common with Lord Halifax as the 'Whigs' they supplanted; and his contempt for the servility of some congratulatory addresses was expressed in a ribald sarcasm which became very current; he said that the petitioners for a Parliament 'spat in the King's face' and their adversaries 'spat in his mouth'.

The comparatively brief period of the Minister's somewhat precarious ascendancy involved therefore three preoccupations. For while he was concerned (1) to hold in check the spirit of reaction and (2) to keep, therefore, at a convenient distance its avowed champion, the Duke; it was at least equally important, from a national point of view, to frustrate the aims of the King of France, in his renewed attempts to obtain the hegemony of Europe.

The immediate, though not the most important, task was of course to deflect the importunities of the Duke of York. For some weeks, however, Lord Halifax was more successful than usual in placating this opponent. For if Halifax obstructed, and with success, the Duke's immediate recall, he declared with equal decision against the readmission of the Duke of Monmouth to Court; which had been proposed as a counterpoise; and he advised the postponement of Parliament until even beyond the ensuing winter. The Duke's confidence in him improved; but he still conceived Lord Halifax as less favourable to his return than any other of the 'Cabinet Council'. And when, in August, the Duke once more requested leave for a visit, if only of some days' duration, the negotiation was deliberately concealed from Lord Halifax. A letter inadvertently shown by Lord Conway betrayed the intrigue, and Lord Halifax did not affect to disguise his annoyance. He wrote immediately to the Duke himself, 'assureing him that nothing could be more unwelcome to him in the world than to have the honour of his commands, and at the same time the misfortune of thinking it not for his Highness's seruice that they should be complyd with'. The influence of Lord Halifax still decided the King; permission was again refused; and, moreover, Lord Hyde was despatched to the north on a special mission peculiarly distasteful to His Highness. For Lord Hyde's instructions directed him to inform the Duke that his return to Court must be contingent on his conforming to the Protestant faith. Hyde was empowered to hint that, in case of obstinacy, it might become impossible to support the Duke further; and to promise that, if His Highness would but yield so far as to attend the services of the Church of England, he should be at once recalled. Hyde, who, despite the favours he enjoyed at the hands of the Duke, remained a staunch Anglican, pressed this expedient from his heart; and Lord Halifax, at whose instance the attempt had probably been made, wrote with the utmost uncompromising plainness. He said,

> That all the good part of England, seconded My Lord Hide's errand with their wishes, and tho it was a tender point which no one durst venture to press home, yet he could not hold (out of the abundance of his zeal for his prosperity) from assureing him, he should think it a greater miracle than had happen(ed) since the Apostles' time, to weather the storme which his enemies had rais'd against him, without taking away the arms he had put into their hands; that the hopes of this, had been hithertoo the support of his friends, and preserved them in his interest, but that if once they dispair'd of it, he must expect all men would desert his cause, as they would a town that could no longer be defended, and that his enemies would triumph for a victory not of their gaining, but his giving.

Such expostulations, to the credit of James be it said, were, of course, absolutely futile.

Meanwhile the attention of Halifax was claimed as urgently by a far more alarming issue. The three years which had elapsed since the Nimeguen pacification had been years of precarious and troubled peace. The vast aims of Louis XIV had been scotched, not killed. And the verbal compact which he had made with Charles II on the eve of the Oxford Parliament—a compact of which no Englishman but Hyde was aware—had been in fact a preparatory move towards new designs. Hardly had it been completed ere he put forward a claim to the Duchy of Luxembourg, with its great çitadel, 'the fortress of the Spanish Netherlands'; and about the time that Halifax returned to London, his fresh pretensions upon Chimay were ostentatiously flaunted.

This was the situation which now confronted Charles II on the one hand, and his Ministers on the other.

These flagrant acts of 'aggression' in times of peace had of course excited the most violent agitations on the part of the threatened powers, and more especially of Spain and the United Provinces; who naturally demanded that their nominal ally—the

King of England—should endorse and support their vigorous expostulations.

All through the complicated and prolonged diplomatic wrangles which followed, and which lasted nearly a year, Charles II stood confronted by the discrepancies of his incompatible double engagements; and wound his way through these by a skilful use of his usual defensive weapons, duplicity, prevarication, and procrastination.

The position of the Prince of Orange, though almost equally embarrassing, was faced with his usual unbroken courage. He was still under the influence of the Exclusion policy, which had been urged upon him by the Sunderlands and the younger Sidney; yet he could not but be aware how much this impaired his position at the English Court, which it was so much his interest and that of the United Provinces to conciliate. Henry Sidney, as usual, acted as his go-between, and his reports were not altogether favourable to Halifax. 'Nobody', he wrote, 'hath any credit but the Duke's creatures....My Lord Halifax is greatly incensed against the House of Commons, and must stick to the Court (for he hath not a friend anywhere else) and is therefore obliged sometimes to comply against his inclination.' Both Halifax and Hyde, however, agreed that only a villain or a fool would desire to see a quarrel between the King and the Prince; which would destroy not only the nation and all the Royal family, but all Europe as well. Halifax for his part (added Sidney) 'made great professions of being entirely in your interest, and said you were the only interest one could build upon. That what he had done last winter', i.e. his share in the Exclusion debates, 'was to carry on your interest and for his part he would never think of any other'. Halifax was also of opinion that a visit of the Prince of Orange might do good. The Prince duly received and availed himself of the invitation, but he complicated matters by injudicious approaches to the men of the Exclusion party; for his advances, though intended to facilitate their reconciliation with the Court, were greatly distrusted in that quarter; and, moreover, proved quite unsuccessful, owing in great part to the inexorability of Lord Russell.

The visit, however, seemed to have had certain good results. The Prince's urgency finally compelled Charles to pledge himself in the first place that he would join the States in a vigorous remonstrance addressed to Louis XIV; secondly, that he would, if necessary, assist in regarrisoning the denuded fortresses of the

Netherlands; and thirdly that in case of an actual invasion of the Flemish frontier he would forthwith summon his Parliament and openly break with France.

Moreover, the intercourse which necessarily took place between the Prince and Halifax improved their mutual relations, and resulted in a correspondence to which we shall refer later on; while even before the Prince left England, the Privy Councillor could write as follows to his own brother in Paris:

THE EARL OF HALIFAX *to* HENRY SAVILE

London, 28 *July*/7 *August* 1681

I have yours by Sr. R. Mason, and have seen that which you wrote to Secretary Jenkins, and they both afford considerable matter of reflexion; and for what you direct more particularly to myself I need not tell you how kindly I take it; and, though perhaps my suspicions may not be altogether so strong as yours, yet sure there is ground enough for me to have my cautions, being under such circumstances as I am, and having enemies of so many several colours. I know no better expedient to secure myself against all events than to build upon the same foundation, and live by the same maxims I have ever done since my being in business; and to take care that in all my actions there may be so much of the Protestant and the Englishman as may silence the objections of my being a papist or a pensioner. In particular I shall endeavour to justify my Protestantship by doing all that is in my power towards the encouragement of those that shall take sanctuary here out of France; though even in that, our present condition consider'd, there is great tenderness to be used in the manner of it; that we may give no occasion for a higher persecution against them there; or by disputing a prince's power over his own subjects draw a question upon us which would hardly be decided in our favour; and we are not strong enough to support our having the wrong end of an argument. Upon this occasion I must give you a hint to be wary in your expressions, without abating any thing of your due zeal for religion; for instance, in one of yours to the Secretary you took occasion, from the translation of Plunket's speech into French, to say somewhat, which, if your memory can recollect, your judgment will scarce allow....The Prince of Orange is here, and speaketh of you very kindly. His stay will be very short, but long enough to inform himself better of our affairs than he could have done by receiving his lights from the best of his correspondents....

Soon Lord Halifax was writing again to the following effect:

THE SAME *to* THE SAME

London, 11/21 *August* 1681

I wrote by way of advance, being to go to-morrow early to Hampton Court, without being sure of returning hither time enough to write to you.

...To your next paragraph, I will say no more than that I am never likely to be a French pensioner further than another kind vote may make me, so that I must sit down with the honour of such a noble character without the aim of ever being the richer for it; in the meantime your part to me is so kind, that I must encourage you to continue it as often as you have the occasion; and I assure you, the hints you give me shall stay in my thoughts, so that I do not doubt but they may be very usefull to me. ...Upon your last proposal, in which you seem so earnest, where you desire an addition of character, and for very good reasons relating to the publick, and the dignity of the crown, besides the arguments that may concern yourself in it, I moved the King, my Ld. Hyde being present; and without disallowing your reasons, it is not thought fit to be done, from the argument of expence; which perhaps might have been over ruled in this single case, if it had not been urged that this would be a precedent to send embassadours to other places, which would lay a burthen upon the treasury it is not at present in condition to bear. This being so, I thought fit to represent to the King that I was sure he was too gracious to you, and too well satisfied with your service, to let you lie under such a mortification as this might perhaps be to you; and that if the uneasiness it might bring upon you should make you desire to return home, yr. coming would look like a disgrace; except you had the countenance of some other imployment to secure you from any such misconstruction. Then putting him in mind of the Admiralty, he presently fell into it; and said he would make a new commission where you and Sr. John Chicheley should be taken in; he spoke it in a manner that I think you may rely upon it. It is yet a secret, and so you are to treat it; my opinion is, you should immediately take notice of this to the King, and desire to be recall'd that you may give him thanks, and serve him here; for I conclude you will judge this a more desirable thing than the tinsel of an embassy; besides it will ease you of a thousand difficulties and vexations the present posture of things abroad must necessarily throw upon those that are imploy'd in them. Adieu.

The Same *to* The Same

London, 25 *August*/4 *September* 1681

I have been slower in answering your last from Paris from the hopes I had to have got before this a letter from the King himself to you, which he hath promised; but you know it is not very easy to prevail with him to keep his time upon such occasions. Your continuing to be so earnest for an addition of character, though against my own opinion, made me move again in it; but you over-value my power if you think I have enough to carry this point, for though there's all the disposition you could wish to gratify you as to your own particular, the objections against what you desire are so rooted in the King that they are not to be removed.... I am far from sorry for it, for your sake and in your consideration wholly, having no interest of my own to bias me; though your offer is very kind to dispose yourself to wave all other arguments, if I apprehend you might be useful to me here. There is nothing of that in the case, but upon viewing your present circumstances, and forseeing what may probably happen to you in the station where you are, I should not think it an unreasonable advice to you to leave it, even without the prospect of any thing here....

In the next letter we are introduced to more weighty business. Henry Savile for his part has had to report a serious affray between his servants and those of a great French noble; while the projected remonstrance of the Allies to the Crown of France looms in the offing. It had been drafted mainly by Halifax; and substituted for an earlier version, on account of certain assurances received from M. Barillon; and it had been described in the Dutch despatches as in full accordance with the wishes of the States, being couched 'in terms the most civil and acceptable, yet forcible and significant withal'. Lord Halifax comments as follows, Sept. 1/11, 1681:

...I hear of the adventure which hath lately happened to you, though I wonder there are no letters from you concerning it; by the account that is given by the French Embassadour, your servants are absolutely justified, and the fault lay'd where it ought to be; besides that the King of France resolveth to pursue the offenders with all severity, and to do every thing else that may give you entire reparation in all kinds. I come now from the Spanish Embassadour's, where we have had a conference with him and the Dutch Embassadour concerning a joint memorial to be presented by you and the Dutch Minister at Paris, and in a little time it will be drawn up and sent to you.

THE SAME *to* THE SAME

London, 8/18 *September* 1681

You will receive by this post from Mr. Secretary Jenkins a memorial agreed upon here by the Spanish and Dutch Embassadours, and to be delivered jointly by you and the Dutch Minister to the King of France. I believe you will judge that in the condition we are in it is fit to use a gentler style than might be proper if we were stronger; and therefore, our circumstances considered, it cannot be expected we should have said more, and perhaps the prince you have to deal with may think we have said too much. It seemeth there is a precedent for this method of a joint memorial, the same having been done by Monsieur Van Beuninghen and Sr. John Trevor. I have seen the account you give of your own adventure, and as your proceeding is approved here, so I do not doubt but the King of France will do you exact justice, according to the strictness of his own nature as well as his method of governing; so that probably some of the offenders may be prefer'd to the gallows. In that case I thought it no disservice to you to move the King you might have full power to intercede for them, or let them alone, as you should judge most reasonable, or as you find yourself disposed to return the civilities of the house of Lorraine to you upon this occasion. Whilst I am writing, yours of the 9th cometh to me, by which I find you are not inclined to interrupt the course of justice. However it can do no harm to have it in your power. The King went this morning to Newmarket.

In the next he betrays his unconquerable distaste for these periodic removals to Newmarket. For racing he cared nothing, and the accommodation was very indifferent.

THE SAME *to* THE SAME

London, 26 *September*/6 *October* 1681

I have not yet been at Newmarket, though I think I could not have escaped it any longer, if I had not a very scurvy reason to excuse me, a small indisposition that maketh me unfit for a journey, especially when I have so little mind to it. Last night I saw your letter to Secretary Jenkins, which mentioneth the delivery of your memorial. In your last you seemed to be of opinion that it was not seasonable at this time; but if you had seen the importunity of the Spanish Embassadour here, and which is more of the Prince of Orange, who writ quarrelling letters because it was not despatched, I am persuaded you would as we do, conclude it was unavoidable; and by what I can see, it is still more justify'd by the late proceedings of the French at Courtray, besides Casal and Strasbourg, that must help to rouze the world out of their sleep. Though in the distracted condition the confederates are in it may be doubted whether it is not now too late for them to do anything towards their security.

His next letter is to Lord Hyde:

London, 27 *September* 1681

I had so great a mind to follow you, that, as it usually happeneth, I am disappointed in it; my distemper, though somewhat abated, yet still continuing so much that I do not know how to venture upon a journey; but to supply my place you will have the Spanish ambassador, who goeth full of complaints, for which you are to prepare yourself. He is resolved to try again about Portugal, a business so rooted in his head, that neither Strasbourgh, Casal, nor Luxembourgh, can put it out of his head. I think, if you could persuade the King to speak plainly to the French ambassador concerning what is passed at Courtray, it might perhaps have more effect than any other means that could be used; besides that his doing it in a right manner, would be of good relish both here and abroad. I have not seen either of our East India men since you went, but I am told by one who had it from them, that they intend, upon Wednesday next, to have it moved that the Company shall give a yearly present to the King of 10000£.... It will be well you should know the King's mind fully in it before you return, and to take care beforehand to engage him that whatever is given may be fixed to a public use, without being diverted....

His correspondence with the Prince of Orange now begins:

...I need say nothing of the memoriall lately delivered in France, the States Embassadour being now with you, from whom you will receave a full account of it; [in] the mean time the besieging Strasbourgh and the purchase of Cazal at the same time giveth such an alarum as must awaken those that are the most asleep; and foe what concerneth us neerer, as a more immediate danger to this part of the world, the Spanish embassadour informeth us that the proceedings of the French commissaries at Courtray are of such a nature that there must be something done very suddenly, or else the conferences will have no kind of effect for the preservation of what remaines to the King of Spayne in the Low-Countries. Your Highnesse knoweth my thoughts perfectly upon this matter, and I have had them so long that I shall not easily bee brought to vary from them, no more than from my resolutions of being ever

Your Highnesses most obedient servant,

London, 27 *September* 1681 HALIFAX

Three days after the date of this letter the apprehensions of Lord Halifax were abundantly justified, by the news that Strasbourgh, the key of Germany, had surrendered in time of peace to French troops. The Prince of Orange at once addressed Lord Halifax in terms of extreme urgency, and Lord Halifax answered as follows:

Your Highnesses first letter found mee here and, upon the receipt of it, I made hast to Newmarket, to shew it to the King, who, upon consideration of what your Highnesse had written, gave me order to send this answer from him, that hee continueth in the same dispositions hee was in, when your Highnesse was here, in relation to the affairs abroad; that, in the condition he is in, he hath no reason to bee forward to provoke or draw upon himself the necessity of a war; quite contrary, it is his interest to avoid it, as far as it may bee done by fayre and honourable means; yet, in case of any such further progresse of the King of France as shall appear to bee a plaine violation of the peace in relation to the Spanish Netherlands, for the preservation of which His Majesty and the States are most immediately concerned, he will bee ready to joyne with the States in taking such measures as shall bee judged most proper upon such an occasion; and will call a Parliament, and do all other things that may inable him the more effectually to help his Allyes....Mr Van Beuningen ...hath represented the condition of Christendome to us to bee, as it is too apparent, melancholy enough; and yet your Highnesse seemeth to bee yet more despairing, which I am very sorry for; yet cannot but hope that God Almighty intendeth better things for you than are in your present prospect. Your Highnesse knoweth my thoughts upon this whole matter, and therefore cannot doubt of my endeavouring, as farre as lyeth in mee, to promote anything that may tend to our common security; and, wherever I shall bee so happy as to agree in opinion with your Highnesse concern-

ing it, no man shall outdo me in my ze[a]l nor in any thing else that may shew how ambitious I am to serve you.
London, 11 *October* 1681

The efforts of the Prince of Orange were well seconded by the Dutch representatives, who five days later handed into the Court of St James a formal memorial, requesting the King of England to join in a long-projected 'League of Guarantee' to the terms of the Nimeguen Treaty; and 'so to arrange his internal affairs'—a polite euphemism for assembling his Parliament—'as that the vast resources of his flourishing realm might be at his disposal'.

This memorial was referred to a Commission comprising the inner Committee of the Privy Council (Lord Halifax, Lord Hyde, the Secretaries, etc.), and while it was under their very prolonged consideration, Lord Halifax on 4 November 1681 wrote thus to the Prince:

> ...I am sorry to find you are under great[er] discouragements, in relation to what is expected from England, than I hope there is ground for. Your Highnesse hath so much experience in things of this kind, and are so well acquainted with the necessary delayes that belong to them, that I am sure you will not make any hasty inferences, because a proposition is not immediately accepted....If in every circumstance the King doth not come up to that which is required of him, I hope the best interpretation will be put upon it; and if there shall bee such foundation laid as here after more may bee built upon it, his Ma. will bee the best incouraged to it, by seeing that the steps hee is now willing to make are well receaved. Your Highnesse is so discerning as to know all my meaning by this little hint and it is unnecessary for mee to tell you that nothing would contribute more to the losse of every thing abroad, than the seeming to despayre of England, which in that respect can never bee justifyed, whilst there remaineth any reasonable ground of hoping better things of us.

But Lord Halifax had not, of course, been admitted into the real explanation of the 'delays' to which he referred. They had been caused by the necessity under which Charles lay of submitting his answer to the criticism of M. Barillon. The reply, eventually 'passed' by this censor, again suggested that the Treaty of Guarantee should rather emanate from the German Princes whom it more immediately concerned. But it offered to follow their example, should the principal authorities of the Empire show the way; and promised, with specific formality, that any claim pressed 'par voye de fait' upon the Spanish Netherlands, or any part of it, should be countered by a summons to Parliament, with a view to effecting 'whatever may be held necessary for the succour of his confederates'. Barillon had been somewhat alarmed by the apparent scope of this answer, but Charles himself and Hyde had reassured him, by disavowing in express terms any intention of fulfilling the promises thus made; reminding him, appropriately enough, that a declaration, if intended to deceive, must, while offering every loophole for evasion, appear ostensibly cordial.

The reply, thus concocted, was delivered on 8 November, and the same day, Lord Halifax wrote to the Prince of Orange:

It will not, I presume, bee unwelcome to your Highnesse, who hath seemed of late to have so little hopes of us, to know that the Memoriall given this day to the Embassadours hath given them so much satisfaction that they have thought fit to give his Ma. thanks for it, and therefore it cannot be doubted but your Highnesse will give it your approbation; and, if so, I hope the melancholy thoughts you have of late been possessed with, will bee dispelled and give way to a cheerefuller and more incouraging prospect of the condition of the world. I was willing to prepare your Highnesse for the worst, in what I have said to you, since monsieur van Beuninghen's coming over; that you might raither bee disappointed on the better side than raise your expectations, whilst there was a possibility they might not be answered. I would beg of your Highnesse that you would immediately write to the King to approove what is done, as being one of the best means to incourage him to continue in the good dispositions hee hath at present....

London, 8 *November* 1681

It is almost pathetic to see an honest and able statesman so completely duped; but Halifax was only one of many. The Prince of Orange and the Dutch ambassador were at the moment equally deceived.

It is clear, indeed, that Lord Halifax at this juncture seriously contemplated the probability of a European conflict. French troops still threatened Luxembourg; at any moment this country might find itself called upon to fulfil the Royal pledge. In view of this contingency Lord Halifax was prepared with a scheme of internal reconciliation, at once broad and sagacious.

The tide of popularity had by this time decidedly turned against the Exclusionists. In the eyes of Lord Halifax, this in itself gave the opportunity for conciliation; which would be rendered more essential by the advent of a state of national emergency. He had already, during the summer, declared against the arrest of Lord Shaftesbury (2 July), and his committal to the Tower, though both events had been generally laid on his shoulders. 'I must' (so he had written to his brother in the middle of August) 'first tell you the world abroad maketh both my Ld. Shaftesbury and myself much greater men than we are, and draw inferences from the success of things one way or other that are not bound to follow. The matter is not so criticall as they apprehend it, and I will only tell you that I am far from thinking either the King or those near him to depend so much upon the event of this matter as it is represented to you at this distance; so that I have none of those inward disquiets you might reasonably suppose, if I took myself to be so nearly concerned.'

But now, despite his representations, at the moment when the reply to the Dutch remonstrance had just been given in, the actual trial of Lord Shaftesbury, on an indictment for High Treason, impended in the near future; and there was strong reason to suppose that a Grand Jury, packed by 'Whig' Sheriffs, would ignore the Bill against him. Shaftesbury, on the other hand, knew that a 'true bill', should it be found, must place him at the mercy of the Crown; which appointed the Lord Steward's Court, the tribunal reserved, in the intervals of Parliament, for Peers; and he offered, if released without trial, to retire to his own estates, or to go abroad, or to settle on his property in Carolina, in which he was greatly interested.

Lord Halifax strongly advised that these advances should be reciprocated. 'People', so he told Reresby, who had repeated some rumours on the subject, 'were too ready to pass their judgement; but if it were so, what could the King do better? He had as good be set at liberty upon terms as by a jury, which would be sure to acquit him should he be brought to trial, though never so guilty. Nor could he do the King that harm if he were out, as such an act of mercy and legality would do him good.'

This important concession, however, formed but a subordinate part of the schemes conceived by Lord Halifax. He foreshadowed more comprehensive overtures, and seems to have hinted at an amnesty for political prisoners of every shade from Danby, and the imprisoned Roman Catholic Lords, to Shaftesbury himself. 'I have been informed', wrote Barillon, '[that] Lord Halifax has this project in his head, and that he talks on every occasion like a man who has no other design than to reconcile the King of England with his people'; a project, of course, equally abhorrent to Barillon and to his Master.

Even the concurrence of the Duke of York in an immediate summons of Parliament might—so Lord Halifax imagined—have been purchased by permission to attend its deliberations. 'Hitherto', so he wrote to the Duke, 'it had been an unspeakable trouble to him, that he could not get the better of his own thoughts when they stood in opposition to his Highness' commands, but that now he was so happy as to think nothing more reasonable, than what he so much desired, and that he should be present when the Parliament met, to answer for himself in case they had the confidence to lay any thing to his charge.'

Meanwhile Lord Halifax was himself practising the leniency he preached to others. Reresby, who had obtained private intimation that several of the Earl's associates in the Ministry had, underhand, encouraged the attacks on him in the Westminster Parliament, now conveyed that intimation to the Minister. 'This my Lord took as a service done him, since at the least he knew thereby how to avoid and beware of them in future.' At the same time, adds Reresby, 'I brought a gentleman to my Lord to ask pardon for some things that he had been reported to have said of his lordship ...and I remember his expression to him was, "Sir, if you have not said the words, I am very glad of it; if you have, I am so too, that you find cause to be of another mind."...And [comments Reresby] the truth is, not only from policy (which teaches us that we ought to let no man be our enemy when we can help it), but from his disposition, I never saw any man more ready to forgive than himself.'

As regards the humane course of action which he was now urging upon the Government, it would be absurd to attempt evaluation of a policy which never was tried. Yet it is permissible to surmise that, at the period in question, suggestions of this nature afforded some reasonable prospect of success. Leniency would almost certainly have secured for the Government the neutrality, at least, of Shaftesbury. The 'swing of the pendulum' promised a favourable result, in case of a general election; and the desire for a strong and a patriotic foreign policy had become very general. Several of the Exclusion leaders were prepared to make terms, and even to give large sums in return for readmission to Court; and others would have ensured liberal Supplies in return for a summons of Parliament and an act of general indemnity. Russell, it is probable, would still have led an uncompromising minority; but it does really appear probable, both that a satisfactory *via media* might have been discovered in the matter of the Succession, and that Supplies would have been voted, which would have enabled Charles to take a dignified and independent part in the Continental controversy. On

13 October, Lord Halifax in fact told Reresby that 'if it were not for the King of France's interest here he did not question but to put England into a very happy state and condition in a short time'.

But even if he sometimes glanced along the way to conciliation, Charles, as we know, still in private ranked as Chief of the 'King of France's interest'; and Louis XIV now intimated to him and his confidant, Hyde, with uncompromising plainness, his intention of securing Luxembourg at all hazards. He reinforced his pressure by the seductive argument of the purse. On 1 November, in return for a subsidy of a million livres, Charles and his confidant secretly undertook that the pretensions of Louis upon Luxembourg should meet with no hindrance on the part of England.

It was not without reluctance that the nefarious step was taken. The two conspirators were perfectly aware of the dangers it entailed. They thus risked the confidence of the country and the Allies, and the support of Halifax, whose assistance they dared not forego. For it was about this time that Halifax, in pursuit of his conciliatory projects, had introduced Dr Burnet to the King; who had mendaciously assured the divine that he desired his services no longer than he himself should be true to the Church and the law. 'Lord Halifax', says Burnet, 'upon that added, that the King knew he served him on the same terms; *and was to make his stops.*'

But, in the end, all such considerations notwithstanding, the counsels of this sagacious adviser were to be set at nought in domestic, no less than in foreign, affairs. Dryden, whose famous and inflammatory satire of *Absalom and Achitophel* had been deliberately published a few days before the actual prosecution of Lord Shaftesbury, might well eulogize Halifax as

> *Jotham* of piercing wit and pregnant thought,
> Endued by nature and by learning taught
> To move assemblies, who but only tried
> The worse awhile, then chose the better side,
> Nor chose alone, but turned the balance too
> So much the weight of one brave man can do.

But it was in defiance of 'Jotham's' expostulation that Lord Shaftesbury was put to the bar a few days later; only to be acquitted by a Westminster Grand Jury, and, in consequence, unconditionally released. The opposition of Lord Halifax to the prosecution seems to have become known; and his adversaries began to remember that they were kinsmen, and to suspect collusion between them. But as Reresby says, 'My Lord Halifax denied [it] to me very seriously, and said he would speedily convince the world of the contrary by his demeanour in that particular.' He may have alluded to the impending dismissal of the Duke of Monmouth from the Mastership of the Horse which took place a week later.

The bargain between the Courts of France and England continued of course to be the secret of the high contracting parties, and the delusive Continental consultations continued as before.

Luxembourg, meanwhile, remained invested and threatened with a regular siege; French and Spanish forces had been actually in contact near Bruges. The Spaniards and the Dutch not unnaturally regarded this as an actual breach of the peace. Lord Halifax, say the Dutch reports, spoke in exactly the same sense as regards the necessity for an exact observance of the treaties, and of the pledges given; but he seems to have expressed uncertainty as to whether the facts were correctly reported, and to have advised a delay till the actual meeting of Parliament. Charles concurred; and a compromise was effected on the basis of a fresh remonstrance to Versailles to be supported if unsuccessful by an appeal to Parliament.

Lord Halifax wrote at once to his brother:

London, 1/11 *December* 1681

In answer to your last, I think you have reason to turn your thoughts towards home, it being time to be weary of the station you are in; especially when there is such a prospect of things abroad as may reasonably discourage you from staying much longer in your present employment.* And therefore I continue my endeavours to get you another here, and hope in a little time it may be brought about: but till it is, I desire you will not move for lodgings or anything else. For though I am come late to the trade of a courtier, yet I know so much of it, that it is not skillfull to press for too many things at once; and at a time when an extraordinary thing is to be done for you, and a rule broken that you may be admitted, to mention a thing that hath so unwelcome a sound at court as every thing must have where money is expected. I assure you there is no friendship in the Treasury in these cases; and your late noble friend of blessed memory hath taken sufficient care there should be no room left for doing good turns, even to the smallest proportions. I have been so sensible of the necessity I should have lodgings in Whitehall, that I have the King's promise to have the first that are to be had; but in the meantime I content myself with a little garret, where I may write a letter and retire sometimes for half an hour, which I find to be very convenient whilst I am under the necessity of spending a good many hours of the day at Court.

* He means of course a declaration of war.

I think we shall shortly send you another memorial upon the business at Luxembourg, which is so extraordinary that it groweth to be above our digestion, though we have of late been pretty well used to swallow. Yours etc.

This letter was followed by another to the Prince of Orange, dated 2 December 1681:

I should have hoped that his Ma. answer to the States Embassadours would have given your Highnesse satisfaction in all the parts of it, since it hath in a good measure silenced the objections of those here who seldome fayle to strike at the weak part of any thing that is done by the Government. ...I cannot pretend that my opinion should have much weight, but I do truly believe that, if upon the representation intended to bee made to the King of France, there shall not bee some reasonable satisfaction given in the matter of Luxembourgh, his Ma. will call a Parliament, without which hee is in no condition of making good the least of his ingagements to his Allys. Your Highnesse shall never bee disappointed in the beleefe you have that I will contribute my endeavours, in my small capacity, to all the publique ends that may put us in such a condition at home as may inable us to help our friends abroad....

The memorial presented by the representatives of England and Holland is believed to have been the work of Halifax; but as it is couched in the usual polite formulas of diplomacy it does not seem necessary to quote it, even as a proof of his Lordship's command of the French language.

To his brother he wrote as follows:

London, 5/15 *December* 1681

Mr Secretary Jenkins telleth me he writeth to you by this post and sendeth you the memorial which is intended to be deliver'd by the Dutch Embassadour and yourself in conjunction; I do not know what success it will have, but I am sure a great deal dependeth upon it, for it is certain if the K. of France will not be perswaded to leave the town of Luxembourgh at liberty, we are engaged here to call a Parliament, and in case that by a miracle we should grow wise and agree, the French might perhaps repent the having forced us into our right senses. I believe you are not sorry that in such a case as this a memorial is sent ready drawn to you, since it secureth you from any blame that might else be thrown upon you by saying too much or too little; besides that you would bear the greatest part of the weight, by any thing that I hear of Embassadour Starembergh. I hear the gentleman that was thought of to purchase your place in the Bedchamber hath changed his mind, so that your friends must endeavour to find out another chapman. I hope you will furnish yourself with a good stock of papers concerning the finances and the marine against you come over, they being things I shall be very glad to have copies of, because they may be usefull to me upon many occasions. Adieu.

The situation was now regarded with very general alarm; Charles himself was obliged to remonstrate with M. Barillon in tones of significant urgency; M. Barillon on his part was compelled to suggest that the *razing* of the great fortress might effect a compromise.

Halifax wrote at once to his brother:

London, 15/25 *December* 1681

I had yours yesterday, in which you mention the receipt of the memorial sent from hence, that will I suppose be delivered immediately upon the arrivall of the Dutch Embassadour. It will be well if it should move your great monarch to act a little less like a conqueror than he doth now in time of peace, and to offer some expedient which may be better approv'd by the Spaniards than the razing Luxembourg. I cannot think it will depend upon any thing that is done concerning that particular place so much as about the King of France his present inclinations in generall, whether the world is to have war or peace. We are not in a posture to wish the first; but if a Parliament is call'd in such an exigency, I do not know but men might grow wiser, and agree to act more vigourously than would otherwise be expected from them. I will do my best to enquire out a chapman for your place, though the Court at present lyeth under such a scandal of non-payment that men's dealing with it is much discouraged. You may be sure my own interest shall no more be an argument to me in this than in any thing else where you are concerned....

Lord Halifax, as we have seen, had long been warning his brother, not only that he had no chance of the Ambassadorship, but that his post as Envoy was not a very secure one; and very real expectations of a possible, and, indeed, early breach of the peace, may by this time have rendered him less averse from informing Harry of his recall—of course as a person not sufficiently complacent to French interests.

London, 2/12 *January* 1681

I have not been unmindfull of you, though it is some time since you heard from me. This day order is given for a new commission of the Admiralty, in which you and Sr. John Chicheley are to be added; and I am enquiring what can be alledged for your precedence in your capacity of Vice-Chamberlain, that you may suffer no diminution, if anything of that kind belongeth to you of right;...I was not sorry to receive the King's commands this day to tell you he would have you return home within a month or six weeks to give place to your successour, my Ld. Preston; who goeth under the same character you have, and is not likely to obtain a greater whilst he stayeth abroad; so that you will not have the mortification of seeing that allow'd to another which you could not obtain. I don't know how far your passion for a fair lady may make your return at this time uneasy to you; but I am such a clown as to think there are two reasons to make a man at least content to leave a mistress; for anger if she is not kind, and to cure a surfeit if she is; but this is such unmanly doctrine that I will not provoke you with any more of it.... We expected to have heard before this the memorial had been deliver'd, but I suppose the Dutch Embassadour may have stay'd longer upon the way than he intended. In case such an answer shall be given to it (which is most probable) as will immediately produce the calling a parliament, you are to consider whether you will send to your corporation of Newark; not that I would perswade you to it, if you ask my opinion; only the advertisement may be seasonable, and you may do as you see cause.

Louis peremptorily and insolently refused to accept a *joint* memorial, so Lord Halifax despatched fresh instructions to Henry Savile.

8/18 *January* 1681

This cometh to you by the express you sent to us, and, though the objection made to a joint memorial is a little extraordinary, considering they have received one of the same kind lately without taking any exceptions; yet, since his Christian Majesty will not allow that method, he must be comply'd with in his own; and there is no more to be done but to follow the directions you will receive from Mr. Secretary, to put the plural number into the singular wch. was intended to have been presented jointly: this manner of proceeding doth not afford any great hopes of a good answer, but, let it be what it will, it will be good to have it as soon as may be, that we may be able to take our resolutions here accordingly....

The depression of Halifax was natural, for the indictment of Shaftesbury had greatly compromised his hopes for an accommodation at home, and the support of the confederated powers abroad. He did not, however, relax in his efforts. The Duke of York had become extremely anxious, as he had written his confidant Legge. 'So long', he declared, 'as Lord Halifax continues in such credit, I can expect no good....I hope the two foreign ministers you named, with the help of Lord Halifax will not wheedle us into a war; if they do I know the monarchy will be in great danger, and they not the better for it.'

At length, indeed, Charles had found himself obliged to contemplate, at least in appearance, the possibility of a breach with France. Secretary Jenkins and Lord Hyde opposed this policy in the Commission for Foreign Affairs; on the plea that money was wanting to defray the charges of war. But Lord Halifax defended the policy with extreme urgency according to a contemporary report; saying

His Majesty may be sure to have money, when once bravely engaged against one whom the country so much abhorreth; and if he be not engaged therein before the Parliament sit, they will advance no money for any design whatsoever. Therefore, if his Royal Highness have a public command in his design, he will then have it in his own breast to unite the people again; and if this be long deferred, I assure you it may prove dangerous both to the government and trade. The French King will in a little time, if he be let alone, grow so potent as not to need our help or value our hatred; and when once it is done, and the Ministers despatched, as well to Holland as France, to acquaint them early with it, lest they pretend jealousy—I say when that is done, we may safely have a Parliament, and just before that must secure Shaftesbury. As for the Duke of Monmouth, he cannot hurt the progress of this affair, and I wish his Royal Highness prove but compliable in this, then we trample all those little pretenders in pieces.

But his Majesty's resolution, whether actual or delusive, was but a flash in the pan; and despite pressure on the part of the Dutch, which overpassed the usual limits of diplomatic decorum, the policy of procrastination, for a period of nearly two months, resumed its sway.

Throughout England meanwhile the extreme urgency of the crisis was fully appreciated, and it was no secret that grave divergence of opinion existed in Ministerial circles. Sir John Reresby says:

Now was the great expectation whether a Parliament would be called or not, the Ministers of State not agreeing in the thing. My Lord Halifax argued for it for these reasons—that all Christendom desired it, France only excepted, and nothing ought to discourage it at home, but the fear that they might fly upon high points; which, if they did, the King might dismiss or dissolve them when he pleased, and show the world that it was their fault, not his [; and] that he endeavoured to give satisfaction to his people by frequent Parliaments. But if the King and they agreed, his Majesty would then gain the great point to be united at home, and formidable abroad. Seymour and Hyde [adds Sir John] that were more in the Duke's interest, were against it, fearing that not only the succession, but themselves, might be attacked in the next Parliament.

Suddenly, however, about 17/27 March an unexpected solution occurred. Louis XIV solemnly announced through M. Barillon, that in view of the alarming progress made in Hungary by the Turkish infidels, he was prepared not only to raise the siege of Luxembourg, but also to submit the questions at issue between himself and Spain *to the arbitrage of the English King*.

All the circumstances of the case considered, the pretext of magnanimity could only be described as transparent. 'His Christian generosity', wrote Halifax himself some years later, 'made the world smile', and the real motives of this theatrical abnegation were eagerly canvassed. The States plumed themselves on their own (rather tardy) pressure; but Lord Halifax—both at the time and later—specifically ascribes the step to the action—the no doubt reluctant action—of Charles. 'The true ground of [this] retiring', says *The Character of a Trimmer*, 'is worth our observation; for at the instance of the Confederates, offices were done, and Memorials given, but all ineffectual till the word *Parliament* was put into them. That powerful word had such an effect that even at that distance it raised the siege: which may convince us of what efficacy the King of England's words are, when he will give them their full weight, and threaten with his Parliament.' This very explicit assertion admits of but one interpretation. King Charles, we must suppose, while ostensibly repudiating his obligations, did actually, though privately (and, we may presume, under pressure from Lord Halifax), convey to the French Court an intimation that, unless the siege should be raised, he could no longer resist the force of public opinion.

The passage, quoted above and written in 1684, is substantiated by admissions of Charles, of the Duke, and of Lords Hyde and Conway; and also of Lord Halifax himself, as described in contemporary Dutch reports. But the Dutchmen were no more aware than Halifax himself that the action, though actually taken, was what moderns describe as 'eyewash'; that Louis had but drawn back to leap the better; and that *Charles himself had originally suggested the arbitration as a means of awarding Luxembourg to France.* Halifax himself was again so far deceived as to write to the Prince himself, complaining that the King was maligned:

THE EARL OF HALIFAX *to* THE PRINCE OF ORANGE

4 *April* 1682

I had not given your Highnesse so much respite, but that the things which have happened, since I writ last, might appear so ill and give you such an impression of us here that I did not know but, whilst that dissatisfaction remained in your mind, I might be involved in it; and therefore nothing could be more welcome than the assurance your Highnesse is pleased to give mee that I am still in possession of the same place in your favorable thoughts you have ever afforded mee. I am the same man in relation to the publique, and am yet lesse to be altered in my respects to your Highnesse in particular; and, one of the greatest obligations I could possibly receave, was the opennesse and freedome you were pleased to use towards mee at Windsor.... In the mean time it is unnecessary for mee to lay before you that the posture of things is extreamly changed, since what hath passed at Luxembourgh; which, as it is a great step towards the establishment of the publique peace, so I hope it will bee improved, as much as may be, in order to that end; and since the King hath had such a part in bringing this about, hee deserveth all imaginable incouragements from his Allyes, who are the more obliged to do him right in this, by their having been so hard upon him in their censures, before hee gave this evidence of his zele for the preservation of Flanders. Your Highnesse will, I am sure, not bee wanting in this, because it is not onely a justice and a respect, in neither of which you can ever fayle, but that it is really of a publique consequence that his Ma. and your Highnesse should in all circumstances bee intirely satisfyed with one another....

THE EARL OF HALIFAX *to* THE PRINCE OF ORANGE

Your Highnesse will have had an account from Mr van Beuninghen how the King receaved your letter, which I was very glad to see; though perhaps hee did not consent to every particular expression in it, upon the whole it must have a good effect, by shewing his Majesty that you take paines to satisfy him.... In order to this, I do, out of the fulnesse of my heart, beg leave to offer this caution to you that you must take away the possibility of the Kings being persuaded that any who are known to bee contrary to his interests here, can have any credit or influence with your Highnesse; for such an apprehension, once admitted into his mind so as to take root in it, would destroy the inclinations hee otherwise must have to meet and cherish your friendship. You must forgive mee, if I own my fears that your Highnesses generosity in being slow and unwilling to beleeve ill of men, may have rendered you more lyable to bee misled and misinformed in our affayres here, by some that are too much swayed by their particular interests to represent things truly to you; and this appeareth so much cleerer to the world every day that I am persuaded, if your Highnesse saw it as wee do, you would bee convinced that even the best things they pretend are promoted and pressed by them for ill ends, and from reasons that are not justifyable. I do not say this out of any particular sharpnesse of my own towards men that may have used mee unkindly, but as it is a great truth, which I affirme with the same indifferency as if I never had any occasion to complayne of them. Mens expectations are for the present suspended, till the answer cometh from Spayne concerning the arbitration, which being accepted by the King for good ends, will I hope bee so interpreted by his Allyes. The King's recovery from a small distemper putteth every body here in good humour, and will, I am sure, bee welcome newes to your Highnesse, to whose favorable thoughts I most humbly recommend myselfe.

Windsor, 2 *June* 1682

The relief of Luxembourg however, temporary and delusive as it was, constitutes the sole real triumph of the Minister's predominance, which was now drawing to a close. For the Duke of York was becoming increasingly clamorous for his own recall. He resented with almost equal asperity the Minister's opposition to his own return, his anxiety for a meeting of Parliament, his advocacy of a breach with France, and his conciliatory policy towards Protestant dissenters and 'Whigs'. He wrote angrily to his confidant Legge:

> I never could understand his politics, and am sure they were never calculated for the meridian of a monarchy; and though he be such a hero in a House of Lords and has a tongue which makes him considered there, he is less than other men out of his sphere, and will I doubt run the King into such inconveniences that I fear will be fatal to the Crown, and even to his Lordship too though he doth not think it....

Halifax retorted with severe, if sarcastic, deference; and told Reresby

> that it was well if the Duke's being too hasty in that matter did not turn to his injury; that he had a sort of hungry servants about him that were still pressing his return, and would never let him alone till, out of interest to themselves, they put him upon that which would turn to the prejudice of their master by the ill-timing of it...there was great partiality in the judgment of men as to his particular, for in justice they should as well take notice of things done to the advantage of the Duke as what appeared to be otherwise; but nobody commended the Ministers [for the dismissal of Monmouth from his last remaining office] which would prove a great bar to his return near the King, and the greatest service one could do to his highness was to prevent the Duke of Monmouth's coming to Court.

During the course of the winter, moreover, affairs in Scotland were to engineer a fresh breach between Lord Halifax and the Duke. Urged by the greedy and unscrupulous enemies of the Earl of Argyll, and apparently also by motives of personal resentment, James had, early in December 1681, countenanced the iniquitous condemnation of the Earl for evading a 'Test'. Lord Halifax had indeed already warned one Scottish Lord, who was 'looked on as a man that was setting himself at the head of the party in opposition to the Government', against attempting to take that line, since 'he might easily foresee what the consequences of that would be'; but at the instance of Burnet he had expostulated with the King on Argyll's behalf. It was currently reported in Scotland how he had told the King to his face that 'he knew not the Scotch law but by the English law' the 'Explanation' (or proviso) to the 'Test', for which Argyll had been condemned to death, 'could not hang his dog'; and he had even consented to co-operate in the matter with his dying enemy Lauderdale. He had soon, indeed, assured himself, on the best authority, that the Duke did not really design the crowning wickedness of a judicial murder; but when, apprehending the immediate execution of his sentence, the Earl broke prison, Lord Halifax renewed his solicitations on behalf of his son, Lord Lorne. They had little effect, save as exasperating the Duke of York; who highly resented this 'meddling', and was anxious to conduct his correspondence with the English Court through his brother-in-law, Hyde, alone. But Lord Halifax, 'looking upon himself as the Privy Minister', composedly returned that it was not 'possible to govern one ship if he knew not what course the other steered'; and James, though bitterly mortified, dared not break with him.

As the spring advanced, however, the Duke found it desirable to employ another and more potent influence. Lord Halifax, who had hitherto refused to visit the Duchess of Portsmouth or attend the King to her lodgings, had been recently compelled by the Royal command to do both. But the reconciliation was purely formal; and James, by playing on her cupidity, had obtained leave to pay his respects at Court. It was then at Newmarket, whither Halifax a few days later repaired, having offered Sir John Reresby a seat in his coach. The Earl spoke much and freely on the way. He had recently told Sir John that 'those that belonged to the Duke of York made him mad, for that there were few among them that had common sense', and had further animadverted upon the 'hardships he lay under in the administration of public concerns from the great indiscretions of some near the King, whom, notwithstanding the King very well knew and laughed at in private', yet he intrusted them with great affairs. And now he informed Reresby of the former correspondence between himself and the Duke on the subject of his religion; notwithstanding which 'he doubted not but his highness would receive him with kindness'. In all he said, exclaims his admiring companion, the statesman expressed 'the wonted goodness, honour and discretion with which he always both spoke and acted; for certainly', adds Reresby, 'there never lived a man in the world of more wit and judgment'.

At Newmarket the two spent about a week, sharing the same lodgings, and also the crowding and discomfort of which Reresby gives an amusing picture; and which must have intensified the distaste which Halifax had always expressed for the great racing centre.

His reception, as he had expected, was favourable. The Duke of York, after 'great expressions of respect and kindness', granted Halifax a long private audience. The Minister frankly asked whether he was to appear before the Duke as a criminal or no? But James 'received him so graciously and seemed by his great attention to his good offices not to remember the ill ones, that my Lord was reassured' and appeared to be 'entirely satisfied with his reception'. At bottom, however, he was 'neither changed in his opinion nor his conduct'; a fact which he betrayed by at once urging—quite ineffectually—that the Duke should receive immediate orders to resume his post in Scotland.

For though on 3 May the Duke indeed went north again, it was merely to fetch his wife; and in the meantime, trouble threatened Halifax from exactly the opposite quarter. The Duke of Monmouth, whose recent dismissal from his last Court appointment had been favoured by Lord Halifax, had seized the occasion of his uncle's impending absence to make certain overtures towards his father; who, incensed at some expressions in his application, forbade his servants to consort with the Duke any longer. On the following Sunday, 21 May, as the worshippers left St Martin's, the young Duke, while still within the sacred precincts, accosted the Minister; and, requesting him to step aside, inquired in a heated manner why his Lordship had moved in Council for the offensive proclamation? 'Pray', retorted Halifax, 'who told your Grace I had done so?' The Duke refusing this information, Lord Halifax rejoined, 'Then since your Grace is upon those terms, I do not think fit to tell your Grace whether I made such a motion or no.' The Duke hereupon lost his self-command; proceeded with much asperity to intimate that his lordship's society at least could be well dispensed with; and added with a threatening accent that elsewhere he could have expressed himself more plainly. His lordship retorted that he should be happy to resume the subject when, where, and in what manner his Grace should please.

So public an altercation between such protagonists naturally attracted considerable attention. A duel appeared to impend; and Sir John Reresby, a noted fire-eater, at once placed his services at the disposal of the Earl. Lord Halifax made answer, 'that if that were [necessary] he would make use of somebody he esteemed less'—the seconds in the seventeenth century, as is well known, often fighting as desperately as their principals. But, continued Lord Halifax, he 'did not conceive himself obliged to fight [i.e. challenge] upon that account, though he should be ready to defend himself [i.e. accept a challenge] for he carried a sword by his side'. The affair, however, went no further. The King, highly incensed, compelled Lord Halifax to retail the occurrence in Council; and exonerated the Earl from all responsibility for the prohibition, which he again endorsed. The young Duke, on calmer reflection, became convinced that his suspicions had been erroneous. The storm in the teacup thus quietly subsided, and the relations of the young Duke with the Opposition became if possible more intimate than ever.

Another incident of this spring, though doubtless political, has its amusing side. Some time in February, funeral tickets had been dispersed to many of the principal nobility, requesting them to send their coaches and six to 'accompany the body of George, Earl of Halifax, out of town'. History does not relate how far the witty victim appreciated this practical insinuation of an impending political extinction.

Part III. Ascendancy of the Duke of York, March 1682 to August 1684

Lord Halifax, about a week after the Duke's departure for Scotland, had told Reresby, not only that he was himself 'very steady for a Parliament', but also that he thought the Duke had got no advantage in the King's good graces by his journey into England. His expectations were, however, frustrated by the event. On 27 May 1682, after an extremely hazardous voyage, during which the question of the succession had been very nearly settled, in a tragic enough fashion, by the disastrous shipwreck of the *Gloucester* frigate in Yarmouth Road, the Duke and his family completed their return journey. From this moment onward, Lord Halifax ceased to be, either in appearance or in reality, the principal Minister. By 5 August our Ambassador in Paris was describing Lord Hyde as 'first Minister of State to the King of England', while in reality it was Hyde's brother-in-law, the Duke of York (who at first, however, effected to decline public business) that became the managing spirit. His imperious temper and decided views exercised a certain coercion upon the mind of his Royal brother, whose disposition, naturally easy, had become more indolent with advancing years. 'Your advice and your resolution', wrote Louis XIV to the Duke, 'will henceforth be very necessary to confirm the King of Great Britain, in his resolve to make use of the means which I offer him to establish peace, and to render unshakable the ties of friendship towards which you have so largely contributed. M. Barillon will inform you more fully of our intentions.'

Yet, despite the Duke's ascendancy, Lord Halifax remained a member of the interior or 'Cabinet' Council; and Charles himself, it is evident, continued to treat the Minister with an outward consideration, which was generally held to betoken a personal, and even an affectionate, partiality.

Your Lordship [says Dryden] held a principal place in his esteem, and perhaps the first in his affection, during his latter troubles...an exact knower of mankind and a perfect distinguisher of their talents...whatever his favourites of state might be, yet those of his affection were men of wit....But in the latter part of his life...his secret thoughts were communicated but to few...who were *amici omnium horarum*, able to advise him in a serious consult...and afterwards capable of entertaining him with pleasant discourse....He confined himself to a small number of bosom friends, amongst whom the world is much mistaken if your lordship was not first.

That Charles appreciated the agreeable qualities of his Minister, and the personal deference which, transferred by others to his more energetic brother, Halifax, almost alone among the courtiers, still rendered to his Sovereign, is very probable. Lord Halifax himself, however, as is clear from the fourth section of his *Character of Charles II*, regarded the King's apparent kindness as a pure matter of policy; and knew that his own services were in general retained merely as a slight counterpoise to more aggressive factions, whose violence inspired the shrewd though by now inert monarch with occasional alarm. The counsels of the Minister, indeed, now and then prevailed when some outstanding instance of the Duke's domineering temper had roused the tardy resentment of his brother; and we shall presently give reason for our belief that at the death of Charles II a very remarkable revolution in his favour was progressing.

Yet, in spite of his reduced influence, the apparent favour of the Sovereign, however limited its scope, evoked against Halifax a crop of anonymous lampoons of remarkable virulence. One, *The Impartial Trimmer* exclaimed, with peculiar irrelevancy, that

> Degenerate Rome and Spain deserve to outbrave us
> If Hyde or Halifax can e'er enslave us.

A second threatens him with the fate of Danby, and a third stigmatizes him as one 'whose crimes now furnish fame' and who

> That he all villains might exceed
> His honour sold for what he did not need.
> An Atheist once, now popery has professed
> Finding that suit with his good morals best.
> He's sold his country, and his King abused,
> Joined with scorned Chits he's innocence accused
> And is at last even by those Chits refused.

Meanwhile, his power was being further reduced by the intrigues of one among those very 'Chits'. His brother-in-law, Sunderland, who had so pusillanimously 'ratted' to the Exclusion interest, had thenceforth unscrupulously reviled the comrade who had 'stood to his guns'; so that Halifax, though so habitually placable, now 'hated him beyond expression'. But Sunderland, on his part, had long and bitterly rued his ill-times apostasy, and was now intriguing for pardon and restoration. The Duke of York had repelled his advances with the coldness they deserved; but the Duchess of Portsmouth proved more compliant. Charmed by the prospect of a Minister at her devotion, she had prevailed upon the King's good nature. Sunderland 'kissed hands' on 26 July, and Halifax was compelled, in the apartment of the Duchess, to endure his fulsome embraces and professions of lasting friendship.

But worse seemed likely to follow. On 9 August a vacancy occurred in the office of Lord Privy Seal. Lord Halifax had never held office as the term is usually understood, but his claims were of course transcendent, and he had an actual promise of the first vacancy. Astonishing to relate, however, the urgency of the Duchess and his own undeniable departmental abilities brought Sunderland's pretensions to the fore. Other claims came also into competition; and it is probable that the Marquisate conferred upon Halifax on 17 August represents an attempt to 'buy him off' by a merely titular promotion. Halifax, however, declined to accept a dignity which he had not sought, as a substitute for political claims; and therefore, after a delay of two months, he was gazetted Lord Privy Seal with a salary of £3000 a year.

The post was one which suited him to perfection. The precedence it conferred was calculated to gratify a man who looked for place, not emolument; though the salary was in fact relatively large. As regards comparative importance, it ranked far higher than at present in the scale of Ministerial ambition, without exacting the severe application to the details of official routine, for which Halifax, we suspect, despite his business capacity, had little taste. But Lord Halifax had no intention of confining himself to the sphere of his official duties; and the foreign situation, as usual, absorbed the larger share of his attention.

He had lost, as we know, a faithful ally at the centre of affairs. The actual departure of Henry Savile from Paris had taken place about the end of February, Lord Halifax having written as follows to hasten his return:

THE EARL OF HALIFAX *to* HENRY SAVILE

London, 20 *February*/2 *March* 1681–2

I saw the King sign your letters of revocation this night; and Mr Secretary promiseth to send them away by this post, so that I hope you will come over as soon as ever you receive them, all other impediments being so fully removed. My Lady Portsmouth intendeth to begin her journey, as I hear, the 2*d*. week in March, by which time you may be here if you have a mind to make haste home....

Lord Preston, Savile's successor, had been originally in the service of the Duke of York, to whom no doubt he owed his appointment. But the post, as in the case of Henry Savile, served to stimulate a possibly hitherto dormant patriotism; and his want of pliability soon rendered Lord Preston as obnoxious as his predecessor to the authorities at Versailles. From the home Government he received little support; and he soon discovered that Lord Halifax, alone among the Ministers, endorsed his international anxieties. Letters, however, if transmitted by the ordinary post, or *en clair*, were not safe from official inspection on either side of the water; Lord Preston was soon driven to suggest to his noble correspondent the employment of a cypher; and even so, the two could only communicate, with any approach to freedom, through occasional channels.

The first evidence of this intercourse occurs in June of this year. The Spanish Government was still evincing a stubborn and well-justified reluctance to accept the arbitrage of the English King. 'It appeared', wrote Halifax himself some two years later, 'that notwithstanding [the King's] merits . . . in saving Luxembourg, the remembrance of what had passed before, had left such an ill taste in their mouths that they could not relish our being put into a condition to dispose of their interests.' It was now therefore the turn of Spain to postpone the final answer by studied delays, while the King of France responded to these procrastinating tactics by ostentatious military preparations. 'This Court', wrote Preston to Halifax 3/13 June, 'expresseth great inclination to peace, but is preparing with great diligence for war.' In answer Lord Halifax observes:

London, 15 *June* 1682

. . . The Court of France doeth wisely to wish peace, and at the same time to prepare for warre; this method hath of late given them conquests without fighting, and except the rest of the world will resolve to take the example, they must knock under, and never pretend to contest. . . .

Lord Preston's next extant contribution related to a supposed French plot for seizing Ireland, and to the French King's insolent interference with the Stadtholders prerogative as Prince of Orange. To this Lord Halifax replied thus:

My Lord . . . the last information you sent over is considerable and your care in it is approved. Means will bee used to pursue the enquiry according to the hints that are given, and after all, if it should at last proove to be lesse materiall than it seemeth to be at the first appearance, your Ldps part in it is such as must recommend you to his Matyes. good opinion. . . . What is lately done at Orange either showeth great anger to the prince or a mind to mortify him into more complyance. Our home affayres alwayes seem calme in a long Vacation, but by Michaelmas terme, I suppose the noise and clamour against the Govt. will bee revived . . . .

To the Prince himself he wrote:

THE MARQUIS OF HALIFAX *to* THE PRINCE OF ORANGE

I do not know a stronger motive to make mee wish I had credit at Court than that I might serve your Highnesse with it; not that I think upon the present occasion there is any need of it, the King being of himselfe so well disposed to do you all the good offices in his power, though I dare not answer for the successe of them, . . . I shall say nothing of our affayres at home; onely that, if your Highnesse could bee here to see the advances made by our publique spirited men to get into the Court, you would bee convinced of the truth of what I have told you concerning their sincerity and good meaning, as fully as I hope you are of my zele to your service.

The last paragraph, we presume, refers to the stages by which Sunderland was worming himself still further into business.

For months these diplomatic altercations continued, since the King of France, like more recent 'dictators', was willing to postpone war, so long as the possibility remained of obtaining his objects by open menace and unscrupulous diplomacy. The Dutch representatives sided strongly with Spain; but the English Ministers continued to argue that under existing circumstances—the weakness of Spain, the divisions of Germany, the fears of Holland, the dubious position of affairs in England—Spain must submit to the French terms.

In this attitude Lord Halifax found himself compelled to acquiesce. With the French interest in the ascendant at the English Court, to expect strong action for the Allies would have been madness; and its open advocacy could have only entailed a cruel disappointment to Spain. In a long conversation with the Dutch representative which took place on 27 October/6 November, Lord Halifax, for instance, regretted that the State should continue their importunities to the King of England, though they knew that despite his good inclination, the state of his affairs, and the determination of the King of France, rendered further remonstrances useless; and that therefore the King of Spain, considering the perplexed condition of his affairs, and the Turkish menace to Germany, ought to accept the arbitration demanded. This aspect of affairs should, he added, be presented to the Allies, without touching on the impotence to which he was condemned by the state of his internal affairs; or on the painful necessity of a peaceful settlement, if he were to succeed in attaining a position in which he will be able to dispose of the resources of his kingdom (the accepted periphrasis for 'call a Parliament'). Lord Halifax also deprecated as unprecedented and indecent the demand of assurances as to future action, which could only do harm both as regards the French, 'and his Majesty's own discontented subjects'; and he urged the Ambassador 'with much kindness and confidence'—on the ground of his (the speaker's) sincere zeal for the interests of the States ('of which', adds the Dutchman, 'I am entirely convinced')—to refrain from further representations, which must compel the King to a formal resolution and a written response—in the negative.

In his official correspondence he preserved the same tone; and on the French King's deferring (as Louis professed, at the instance of the English King) the date of his ultimatum, Lord Halifax wrote as follows to Lord Preston, who had just sent congratulations on his correspondent's new post.

London, 4 *December* 1682

My Ld.,—I am to acknowledge your favour to mee, and to assure you, that I should take the more pleasure in the station I am in, if it might give mee better opportunities of serving your Ldp.; and therefore when ever you can think mee of use to you, your directions shall find mee very well prepared to observe them. The prolongation of the term lately obtained from France by our Master, is the likeliest means to keep the world in peace; but it is not yet known how it will work in Spain and Holland, where there is at the same time a fear of a war, and yet a great Slowness to use the most probable methods to prevent it. A little more time must needs open the scene; and the world will at least bee put out of the suspence it is now in for the event of things, the Spring being so criticall a time, that wee shall be able then to guesse, what the weather will bee for the rest of the year. Your Ldp. hath a difficult province enough, which I am not sorry for, because you will have so much the more credit, by acquitting your selfe so well, as I am sure you will do; and as often as there shall be occasion of doing you right here, you may depend upon it, from,

My Ld,

Your most faithfull humble servant,

HALIFAX

The Spaniards, however, remained obdurate; and with their usual want of tact, seized this moment for picking a quarrel on a point of privilege with our Ambassador at Madrid. To this Lord Halifax referred in his succeeding letter to Lord Preston:

London, 26 *December*, 1682

My Ld.,—It seemeth the Ministers of Spaine now in Paris were rightly informed of the intentions of their own Court, when they expressed such an aversion to the Arbitrage; for by what wee hear from Madrid, as well as by their extraordinary proceeding towards Sr. Harry Goodrick, it appeareth they are resolved not to agree to it, and yet at the same time are sufficiently apprehensive of the ill consequences a war may bring upon them. And now they would fayne put it upon the King my master (to whom it least belongeth) to find out some other expedient after they have reiected that which hee offered them. I read your letter to his Maty. who very well approoveth your Ldp's answer to the proposall made to you of calling a Parliament. Hee resolveth to keep that intirely in his own power, and to choose his own time, without consulting either any foreigne princes or their Ministers in a thing of which hee conceaveth him self to be much a more proper judge than they can pretend to be. And as for the Kings asking a farther delay from the K. of France, hee is not satisfied it would bee of much use; and therefore I believe will be very slow in doing any thing of that kind, except he should have more reason to hope than he hath had yet, that in case it was granted, it might produce a good effect. I am to congratulate the satisfaction your Ldp. will have, when all your family is together, after your having been so long divided from it and wish you happinesse in all other kinds, being,

My Ld, Your most faithfull humble servant,
HALIFAX

But while in his formal official correspondence the sentiments of Halifax were thus shrouded by the decent mantle of Ministerial reserve, they found vent in the secret correspondence with Preston which the latter had initiated. By 24 March 1682/3, the (as he believed) deliberate refusal of a leave of absence, on which Preston had counted for an opportunity of consulting Lord Halifax, drove the Envoy to the hazardous expedient of sending the Marquis through the post, *though under cover*, a confidential letter *en clair*. In this he warned the Lord Privy Seal that a French emissary was starting for England with, as he believed, private instructions, and proceeded to suggest:

> I have some reason to believe that they are not designed either in favour of your lordship or of Mr Secretary Jenkins; you have both the misfortune not to be too much in the good graces of this Court...it can do your lordship no harm to be upon your guard, and to keep your eyes open for a while, and I hope your lordship will endeavour to keep your ground for the good of England, tho' it be to your own loss. I am a stranger to many things which pass in England at present, but I am very well satisfied of your lordship's care of us all, and I wish your designs success. If this reacheth you I hope your lordship will let it pass no farther.

Eight months later (5 October 1683) (this time by means of a private hand) Lord Preston transmitted to Lord Halifax another confidential despatch, which was of extraordinary length. He observes

> I should oftener impart things which are observable and of consequence to be remarked here if I had not found out that advices of this kind are not agreeable at home, and that I have suffered by sometimes giving of them; so that I may freely say to your lordship, I am often more sollicitous what to suppress than what to write. Therefore nothing but your lordship's commands (to whom I have so many obligations) could have drawn from me at this time some things which will make the subject of this letter.

Upon this exordium there follows an elaborate indictment of the policy of France, as shown in her relations with foreign States. The Envoy dwells upon the continued encroachments in Flanders, which, he adds, were long since foretold by Halifax himself; and upon the just determination of Spain to avoid an arbitrage which, by involving the loss of Luxembourg, might enable Louis to terrorize the German Electorate, and become, in course of time, Emperor of the West. Lord Preston further insists upon the unscrupulous fashion in which France intrigued for the dissolution of whatever Government or coalition dared withstand her, and upon her determination to obtain by threats or stratagem what her exhausted finances rendered her averse from attempting by force of arms. He points out that while France obviously maintained relations with Whig or Exclusionist circles in England (relations upon which Preston, by the way, lays absurdly exaggerated stress), the Envoy is yet tormented by reports of an understanding, and even of a league offensive and defensive, between Charles and Louis, of which M. Barillon was the supposed channel—a suspicion of which we have long since gauged the absolute accuracy.

To this outspoken dispatch no answer from Lord Halifax is known to exist. But his real views on the situation are given with sufficient vigour in *The Character of a Trimmer*, which was written fifteen months later. In the section which deals with foreign affairs, the insolent superiority of France is stigmatized with an almost tragic force; while the feeble dependent attitude of the English Court becomes an occasion for the bitterest and most contemptuous satire, not unmingled with a characteristic infusion of sardonic innuendo:

> Our great earnestness also to persuade the Confederates to consent to [the arbitration] was so unusual and so suspicious a method, that it might naturally make them believe, that France spake to them by our mouth... and so little care hath been taken to cure this, or other jealousies the Confederates may have entertained, that quite contrary, their Ministers here every day take fresh alarms from what they observe in small, as well as in greater circumstances....Thus we now stand, far from being innocent spectators of our neighbour's ruin; and by a fatal mistake, forgetting what a certain fore-runner it is to our own....It is not partiality (the Minister assures us) which moveth him; but the just fear, which all reasonable men must [have] of an overgrown power....He hath no such peevish obstinacy as to reject all correspondence with France, because we ought to be apprehensive of the too great power of it. He would not have the King's friendship to the Confederates extended to the involving him in any unreasonable or dangerous engagements; neither would he have him lay aside the consideration of his better establishment at home, out of his excessive zeal to serve his allies abroad; but sure there might be a mean between these two opposite extremes; and it may be wished

that our friendship with France should at least be so bounded, that it may consist with the honour as well as the interest of England.... When England might ride Admiral at the head of the Confederates, to look like the 'Kitchen Yacht' to the 'Grand Louis' is but a scurvy figure for us to make in the map of Christendom.

And the Marquis proceeds to lament with pathetic energy 'that the life and vigour which should move us against our enemies, is miserably applied to tear our own bowels'; that 'by a fatality which seemeth peculiar to us' we 'misplace our active rage one against the other whilst we are turned into statues on that side where lieth our greatest danger', etc.

Having thus carried on our account of foreign affairs to October 1683, we must proceed to trace the conduct of Lord Halifax in relation to domestic matters during the same period.

In England the return of the Duke of York had exaggerated the rebound from 'Whig' or 'Exclusionist' principles, and had intensified the 'High Prerogative' or 'Tory' reaction, of which the Duke of York was the most thorough-paced exponent. It had thus exasperated the bitterness of party hate, and cut short the conciliatory trend which Halifax had initiated.

But despite this, Lord Halifax had not relaxed in his efforts to 'bring over' rather than 'stamp out' the extreme or Exclusionist party; and his conciliatory zeal found one very curious vent. On 10 August 1682, he had given in marriage 'Nan', his only daughter by his first marriage (and the darling of her grandmother Sunderland), to Lord Vaughan, heir to the Earldom of Carbery. The bridegroom, in this case, seems to have had no other attraction save that of being a recent and valuable convert from Exclusionism. Nor was this his Lordship's only attempt in this direction.. Later in the year we find him laying siege to his old friend Dr Burnet; who, though a tardy convert to Exclusionist views, refused to abandon his new principles, or the society of those who held them, even when tempted by an offer of the Mastership of the Temple. The Lord Privy Seal actually 'carried' Burnet to the King, with what Burnet justly describes as 'a very extraordinary' (though possibly sarcastic) compliment, namely, 'that he did not bring me to the King to put me in his good opinion so much as to put the King in my good opinion'. It was during this conversation that Halifax described the King as 'head of his Church'; to which the King answered that he did not desire to be head of Nothing. 'For indeed', adds Burnet, 'he (? Halifax) was of no Church.'

To this negotiation the following letter belongs:

THE MARQUIS OF HALIFAX *to* DR BURNET

16 *October* 1682

Sir,—Though I was tender in advising you to wave anything you might think advantageous for you, yet since you have thought fit to do it, I am at liberty to approve it: And I only desire you will not make too hasty resolutions concerning yourself, and not be carried so far by the sudden motions of a self-denying generosity, as to shut the door against those advantages, which you may expect with justice, and may receive without indecency. Only a little patience is requisite, and in the mean time no greater restraint upon your behaviour and conversation, than every prudent man, under your character and circumstances would chuse voluntarily to impose on himself. For what concerns me, or any part I might have, in endeavouring to serve you, I had rather you should hear it from any body, than from myself; and though you should never hear it from any body, I expect from your justice you should suppose it. Your withdrawing yourself from your old Friends, on this corrupted side of the Town, is that which I can neither approve for my own sake, nor for yours: For besides many other objections, such a total separation will make you by degrees think less equally, both of men and things, than you have hitherto professed to do, in what relates to the Publick. I have no jealousies of this kind for myself in particular, being resolved, at what distance soever, to deserve your believing me unalterably

Your faithful humble servant

HALIFAX

'Thus', says Burnet, 'I was in favour again, but I could not hold it....I would [not] give over conversing with my friends.'

But Halifax was almost alone in his efforts. Coercion, rather than conciliation, was the motto of the Government to which he now belonged. The year 1682 was marked by a determined and successful attempt, on the part of the Government, to break the power of the Whigs in their principal stronghold—the municipalities. Tory Sheriffs were foisted upon the City; and this step, by giving the Court entire subsequent control over the selection of juries in the metropolis, excited to madness the terrors of the defeated Whigs; and gave the first impetus to that network of secret intrigue comprehensively known to history as the 'Rye House Plot'.

In these manipulations Lord Halifax does not seem to have taken a conspicuous part—though of course the contemporary lampooners credited him with a share in this, as in all other, unpopular courses. One pamphleteer even ascribes to this occasion his epigram: 'That he foresaw there would be hanging, and was resolved to hang last.'

But the Government had other shafts in the same quiver. It was resolved so to remodel the municipal corporations of the Kingdom as to exclude Whigs, both from influence in boroughs and from the exercise of the Parliamentary franchise therein. Upon pretences of the most transparent triviality the validity of the City Charter—that is, of the entire franchises possessed by the Corporation of London—was called into question; and, thanks to the subserviency of a Judicial Bench holding office 'during pleasure', these proceedings, about the close of the year 1683, culminated in a forfeiture of the privileges in question. Similar actions, or the fear of them, soon brought a large proportion of the provincial municipalities into a dependence upon the Crown.

Here again, responsibility for this campaign was foisted upon Lord Halifax by his political opponents. But when, after the Revolution, the question was specifically raised in the so-called 'Murder Committee' (of which the object was to clear the way for an impeachment of Lord Halifax, or at least for his forced retirement from Office) only one piece of evidence was produced, though strong pressure seems to have been employed to procure such. A well-known medical man, of pronounced Whig proclivities, deposed to having met Lord Halifax in the gallery at Whitehall and asked him 'whether he thought the Aldermen were to blame, who defended the City Charter?'

To this very leading question, Halifax, so the witness believed, had answered in the negative; but had added 'that the King must, or will'—the doctor thought it was 'will'—'have the Charter'.

To this evidence Lord Halifax seems to have retorted: 'The first part of it is well enough; the Aldermen are not to be blamed. But it doth not hang together; for note, they deserved to be blamed, if the last words have any sense in them. If the King *must* have it, then it implies the Law will give it him; if the King *will* have it, how could I or anybody help it?' Neither the evidence nor the comment appear impressive. But it is remarkable that in *The Character of a Trimmer*, written perhaps two years later, which castigates with as much freedom as skill the errors of the Administration at this time, the question of the Charters is not raised. Yet a majority—sixty-six—of the new Charters passed his office; the surrender of the Nottingham Charter was made into the hands of the King, Secretary Jenkins and Lord Halifax, the two latter having been charged with the redrafting of a new one. Again, when the Whig magnates of York, anxious to conciliate the Court without surrendering their charter, offered through Reresby (1) to elect a Tory Lord Mayor out of course, (2) the return of Tory members at the next election, (3) the replacement of an obnoxious High Steward by the Duke of York or Lord Halifax, the latter approved the appointment of a Tory Lord Mayor. He thought it, however, not safe to 'venture the King's letter upon it to the Corporation unless the success was absolutely certain', and this because *affairs went so well above (especially that of the Quo Warranto against the City Charter) that all other Corporations would truckle'.* As regards the Stewardship, Halifax deprecated the choice of the Duke of York; but professed his own willingness to accept the office, provided 'he did not himself appear in the matter, and should, in case the thing miscarried, be able to show a considerable minority in his favour'.

On the whole it would seem as if, though Lord Halifax in all probability did not *originate* the policy, may have disapproved it *internally*, and may even have remonstrated *in private*, he did not openly oppose it. The charge is a very serious one, as the attack on the independence of the municipalities constituted, as Lord Halifax was to realize under James II, a most serious shock to the principle of self-government. He *may* have believed that these 'regulations' would render the King less averse to a speedy session of Parliament; and would, moreover, by excluding the more violent Exclusionists, conduce to a national reunion. The opinion was not perhaps altogether unfounded; but in any case the price to be paid for these advantages appears extravagant in the extreme.[16]

Meanwhile his own influence was being still further undermined by a severe administrative set-back. About the end of January 1684, 'the Seals' (i.e. a Secretaryship of State) became vacant. They were bestowed on Lord Sunderland, who some three months earlier had succeeded in obtaining readmission into the Privy Council. The King, indeed, still extended his apparent favour to Lord Halifax; he was still the only man who shared with the Duke of York and the old Duke of Ormonde the right of entry, without leave previously asked, into the Royal Bedchamber. But it was quite otherwise with the Duke of York; who (as Halifax bitterly remarked to Reresby) now extended to Lord Sunderland, who had done all he could against the Duke in the last two Parliaments, more favour than he showed to Halifax, who had done all he could to serve him.

Nor was this the last mortification which awaited him; since a few weeks later the Duke of York was formally readmitted to the Privy Council, an event which of course increased his already overweening preponderance in the counsels of the nation.

It would appear that Lord Halifax ascribed the York-Sunderland reconciliation to the intervention of the Duke's brother-in-law, 'Lory' Hyde, newly created Earl of Rochester. This must have exasperated a feud which arose from acute political differences and was now developing itself in the financial arena. We gather that some year or two earlier the Treasury, in a moment of pressure, had borrowed from the farmers of the Chimney Tax; who, in repayment of the loan, were allowed to farm a certain portion of that tax upon special terms. These advantages, in consequence of fraudulent representations on the part of these farmers (or, as they are usually termed, Commissioners) of the Hearth-money, were grossly disproportionate; and early in 1682/3 a man named Shales, one of the Commission, pointed out that the arrangement involved immense loss to the revenue. He first applied to Rochester, and offered to undertake the farm at an advance which is variously estimated at £20,000, £30,000 and £50,000. Rochester dismissed the suggestion and Shales then carried his complaints and suggestions to the Lord Privy Seal. Halifax, under the impression —which seems to have been correct—that Rochester was the victim rather than the accomplice of the farmers, urged that Lord to investigate the matter. Rochester, however, who was notorious for a passionate temper, resented this interference, and this with a violence which begot the most sinister interpretations in the minds of all concerned, the Marquis included. The latter opened the matter in Council, and declared 'that the farmers ought to be exchequered; and their farm, as a deceit of the King, laid aside; and they, as managers, to become accountants and, having allowance for their pains and charges, the surplus to be answered to the King'. The Treasury, on its side, defended the farmers, and the question seemed decided in their favour. The fury of Rochester, however, was not appeased by success; he roughly asserted that Halifax accused him of corruption, and 'would neither see, hear, nor endure any thing or person that was not clear on his side'.

Lord Halifax, in conversation with Sir John Reresby, retorted that 'he would keep in his corner and hear what was offered for the King's service and not be afraid to declare what he heard to his Majesty's disadvantage, whoever was concerned in it; and whenever he had power, he would distinguish between his friends and those who were not so'. He persisted in his endeavours, and the question was soon reopened.

On 19 February 'the fraud...came to be argued by counsel on both sides before the King'. It is difficult to understand the exact nature and the precise result of the inquiry. Reresby contends that the charge was proved; others maintain that Shales (the informant) had failed to establish his contention, and that the Treasury had scored a great triumph. On the whole, we are inclined to conclude (*a*) that Shales, in the opinion of such persons as were not biased in favour of the incriminated officials, had proved his assertion by the testimony of independent evidence; (*b*) that his statements did not tally with the books of the Commissioners; (*c*) that Lord Rochester refused to admit the possibility of falsifications and the consequent necessity for a further investigation; (*d*) that his interest, as head of the Treasury Commission, prevailed; (*e*) that under these circumstances the legal authorities pronounced the former contract valid, and decided that it could not be annulled in favour of the new tender; and that (*f*) Lord Halifax in consequence pressed the matter no farther.

The triumph of the Rochester faction was not, however, complete; 'whereas some of that lord's friends did reflect upon my Lord Halifax, as too busy in making that discovery, the King justified him so far as to say of him openly that day in Court, upon the trial, that his lordship had done nothing in that affair but by his order and approbation'.

The affair created a considerable stir, and his confidant Reresby considered that Halifax had a very general applause for his conduct, especially in '*the City*'; though opinion in '*Court and Town*' was 'infinitely divided. Those that had any dependence upon payments out of the exchequer durst not but seem to side with Lord Rochester; those that were thinking, serious men, who were independent and wished well to the Government, commended the zeal and courage of my Lord Privy Seal, who would not see £40,000 of the King's money misemployed, and who durst complain of it, where so great a man with his dependents were made enemies by it.'

We find Sir Thomas Thynne (by this time Lord Weymouth) informing his cousin Halifax that the 'common newsletters' had been much occupied with the matter. He hoped, so he added, that his Lordship 'though no great admirer of the sport' will be sometimes at Newmarket. 'You know', he adds, 'that has always been a place where changes have been prest; and having little other support than what your innocence and merit give you, you may find benefit in being present yourself.'

Meanwhile Lord Halifax himself was informing Sir John Reresby

that the Duke had assured him that he was not concerned in the least in the difference between him and Lord Rochester. My lord replied he was sure his highness would never do an ill thing towards him; and if he did, that his lordship would never do anything to oppose him,* but he could not serve him with the same zeal, and he might at some time repent he had lost his service to the degree he desired to use it for him; that he had done in all this no more than he was commanded to do by the King, and who was there so great in the kingdom to be displeased with a man's acting according to the King's command? that he found they had a mind, meaning Rochester, to be rid of him, and would possibly endeavour to make his station uneasy, but they should not remove him; first, because he would stay to serve the King, and secondly, to disappoint those that endeavoured to contrive his absence; that all his lordship had attempted to do in this matter was to save the King's money, and could there be a greater service to his Highness in future than that? that the King had made him a bigger man than he deserved to be, but he was a gentleman, and that his highness ought to consider those that had escutcheons as well as those that had none (three of the Duke's chief favourites, viz. Legge, Churchill, and Hyde, being scarce gentlemen). For his part, that he would never say any thing but truth to his highness; but though it might look a little plain, yet nothing could carry more respect in the bottom, than truth, with much to the same effect. To which the Duke replied that whatever he said did seem very reasonable; that he was sensible of great obligations he had to his lordship, and would never forget them, but would serve him in what lay in his power, and his lordship should find it.

The same day his lordship said he had spoken to my lady Duchess of Portsmouth, and told her, upon some discourse, that he found, in case of need of his Majesty's favour, he was not to expect many friends from that side of Whitehall; that she replied, that some that had been much his friends came thither sometimes (meaning Rochester), and she hoped they would be so again. His lordship replied that he doubted much, however, of her intercession in such a strait, and hoped he should avoid coming into the danger of making use of it; at which she blushed, and seemed to be in some confusion. He said further that were he as young as he had been, he could be as well with her as others.

* I.e. in the matter of the Succession.

About May, Halifax seems to have interfered in the settlement of the Irish revenue. The farm having expired, Ormonde, who considered the farmers oppressive and unpunctual, urged that it should not be renewed. Rochester sided with him; but the farmers offered large advances, and were, so Carte asserts, 'secretly encouraged by the Marquis of Halifax...who set up for a general reformer of all abuses put upon the King, not only in the management, but in the disposal of his revenue; and who was in hopes that he should have an advantage to accuse the lords of the treasury for rejecting the proposals, if the King should not make so much of his revenue by management as the farmers had offered...it was at last resolved to put it into management'.

Finance, indeed, seems to have been at this time a principal political interest to Lord Halifax. For it also appears that he was regarded as the instigator of a new financial scheme which promised to increase the revenue by nearly one-fourth; and that, according to Reresby, 'my Lord Rochester as much underhand discouraged this, in as much as he sent to some of the richest citizens desiring them not to concern their estates'.

This scheme apparently included an offer on the part of Halifax and others to farm the entire revenue at an increase of £200,000 per annum, and to advance the Exchequer immediately £600,000 at 6 per cent. whereby the King was to be enabled to pay off an equivalent debt (for which he was now paying 10, 12 or 14 per cent.); the sum being gradually deducted from the annual payments of the farmers. A large surplus would thus remain for the discharge of the King's debts, especially arrears in wages and salaries. In consequence Halifax was 'much considered', especially no doubt by the unfortunate officials, whose salaries were thus in balance. The King, however (why does not appear), opposed the scheme; and Halifax, early in the day, withdrew his support from it, 'because it would entrench too much on my Lord Rochester'. The consideration would seem to have occurred to Lord Halifax rather late in the day; and we confess that the Lord Privy Seal, for all his virtues and merits, may have been distinctly exasperating as a colleague.

On the other hand, the relations between Reresby and his patron seem to have been at this time unusually intimate.

On 20 March 1682/3 he records:

My Lord Privy Seal and I went to Hyde Park. He told me he hoped I did not repent of my coming up at his request, since I could not have been so well satisfied how affairs went, both public and private, without being there; that he knew not how long he should keep his station (being driven at so fiercely by some); but he did think he had the King his friend, and could not believe that he would part with him for having committed no fault, except it were one to obey his commands; assuring me that he would ever use his interest, so long as it continued, to serve me.... But, said he, times may come, if the Court should fall into French councils,... and if that come to pass, I must quit [my station], for I have greater endeavours against me from the other side of the water than from home. ... When I came into the country he bade me turn the report of his disgrace into raillery, till he gave me notice of his retreat, which he would do early if he found it was not to be avoided.

A few days later Reresby reported that Lord Danby, who had already remained three years in the Tower, spoke 'obligingly' of the Lord Privy Seal, especially of his attempts to procure a Parliament; on which the hopes of the prisoner were now fixed, as the means upon which was based his only hope of release. Nor had the Earl refrained from reflections upon Rochester and his party, with the untrustworthy 'interest' on which they relied. Lord Halifax took the information, we do not doubt, with a grain of salt, but met the overture in a friendly spirit, for his enmity to Danby was by now 'much abated'.

He told me [says Sir John] he had enemies enough besides, and that his displeasure against him was now ceased; but he would not make more enemies by being his friend, as he had formerly done by being his enemy. So that I found [proceeds Reresby] my lord Privy Seal making up his interest on one side, as my Lord Rochester was endeavouring on the other; for he had also sent for Mr Seymour to return to Court, and had promised to be his friend. My Lord Privy Seal told me that Seymour had made some proposals to close with him, and that a reconciliation was endeavoured by Rochester's friends between the two lords. I told his lordship that, in my poor opinion, he had better stand upon his own interest than join with either; for he had now gotten a national interest by what he had done, in opposition to Rochester. In case he closed there again, he might lose that; and if he could support himself separate, he might keep both; or in case he fell, the King would find the want of him so much, he could not be long spared from Court. He said it would be hard for him to continue there with these men, for it was their interest to remove him. They would be apt to play tricks for their own advantage; and knew so long as he was in a station to be informed of such carriages, he should ever reveal them to his Majesty. He said further, that if they should get the King to themselves, they could not long keep him, for he had one quality that would preserve him from being very long in ill hands; which was he would hear all persons, and admit of informations by the back door, when those that seemed favourites little dreamed of it. He lamented the interest that the Duchess of Portsmouth had with the King, she betraying him to France, not only as to his councils, but in his affections. He said the King was too passive in these things; and that it was his greatest fault that he would not be persuaded to resent some things which he clearly saw, as he ought, and keep up that height which belonged to his dignity.

In fine, the Minister warned Sir John to make as many friends as possible.

Upon the whole matter [concludes Reresby] I perceived my Lord Privy Seal had the better and most approved cause, and my Lord Rochester the better interest. The first weighed more in parts, in his family, estate, and his reputation in the nation; the other weighed more, though undeservedly, with the Duke of York, the Duchess of Portsmouth, my Lord of Ormond, and most of those at Court, who depended upon the King's purse, of which his lordship was the chief dispenser. And the fear was that the diligence of these so near the King might work upon him, so as to relinquish my Lord Privy Seal; who depended upon no other person nor interest but his own, and those services that he not only had performed, but was best able to render the Crown.

And what, may we ask, was the effect of these events upon the estimate of Halifax entertained by the *opponents* of the Court? The extremists seem to have blamed him for attempting the improvement of the revenue, because it might render the King less dependent on Parliament. Among the more judicious and moderate, however, these endeavours certainly enhanced his reputation. Indeed, to use his own words, these courted the Marquis at such a rate that he feared 'it might occasion a jealousy elsewhere'. At an interview between Lord Halifax and Burnet, which took place, probably at the Statesman's instance—for Burnet, to use his own words, 'went no more near any that belonged to the Court'—Lord Halifax told the story of the Hearth-money inquiry. The Doctor asked the Lord Privy Seal how he stood with the King. 'He answered', says Burnet, 'that neither he nor I had the making of the King; God had made him of a particular composition. He said, he knew, what the King said to himself: I', says Burnet, 'asked him if he knew likewise what he said to others.'

Matters seem to have remained much in this state till, in the following June 1683, the so-called 'Rye House' revelations burst upon the country.

Lord Shaftesbury, after his release, had more than shared those fears of his party, which had been excited by the election of Tory

Sheriffs and the attack on the Charters. He had thrown himself with half-crazy vehemence into schemes of insurrection current among the extreme sections of 'the Whigs', more especially in the City of London. But his efforts had met with the strongest opposition from the more moderate of his former associates, in especial from Lord Russell and the Duke of Monmouth. His plans collapsing, he had fled to Holland, where he had died a few weeks later; and contemporaries had commented on the fact that Lord Halifax, with his other relations, had assumed mourning for his death. But the agitation he had set on foot remained seething in City circles; and came to include an actual plot to murder the King and Duke while passing the 'Rye House', which had been concocted by the desperadoes of the party.

Meanwhile, in the highest ranks of the Opposition, certain meetings had been originated by Lord Howard of Escrick, a prominent member of Shaftesbury's immediate following. An unscrupulous political adventurer, though of attractive manners, he had obtained some ascendancy over the minds of Essex, Monmouth, and Algernon Sidney; in the latter case, by the profession of Republican principles; and all three are known to have attended his meetings. Lord Russell had been present at some of them under protest; moved, it is probable, by a kindly solicitude for the Duke of Monmouth, whose susceptibility to external pressure he had been forced to realize. The proceedings of this debating club, for it was little more, assuredly never constituted any real peril to the Government; and a few weeks before the final crash it appears to have died a natural death. There is, however, scarcely a doubt that at these meetings a good deal of treasonable talk had taken place; or that Howard, Sidney, and Hampden the Younger, had decidedly favoured an appeal to arms.

It was early in June 1683 that an informer revealed to the authorities the existence of the assassination conspiracy, with the intrigues among Shaftesbury's former following in the City of London. Some of the latter, warned in time, implored Russell to give the signal for revolt; he responded 'that it was better some private men should suffer than the public should be precipitated'. Further evidence, in fact, soon compromised the members of Lord Howard's circle. Lord Essex, Hampden, and Algernon Sidney were apprehended and committed to the Tower. The Duke of Monmouth absconded; Lord Russell refused to do so; and Lord Howard, who was found in hiding, soon turned King's evidence.

The 'assassination' plotters were promptly tried and convicted. Proceedings were then instituted against the Howard group. Of these, Lord Essex committed suicide in the Tower; and on evidence singularly meagre, technically invalid, and mainly contributed by Howard, Lord Russell received on 14 July sentence of death.

Of Lord Russell it may be said, to transfer an epigram of Miss Edgeworth, that if his abilities were nothing extraordinary, his character was first rate. A casual acquaintance once described him as 'a man for whom, of all the men I have known, one would have been most willing to have died'; and the event confirmed this judgment. For while Russell showed himself almost nervously apprehensive lest he should compromise his friends, the latter outdid themselves in efforts to save him. Remorse, it was known, had intensified the despair of Essex, who had forced upon Russell the fatal introduction to Howard. Meanwhile, Lord Cavendish exhausted a fertile imagination in quixotic schemes of evasion and rescue, and the Duke of Monmouth offered to 'come in and run fortunes' with the doomed man; who tranquilly responded that it would do him no good that his friends should die with him.

The character of the prisoner, indeed, commanded almost universal respect. Even the personal adherents of the Duke of York saw in Lady Russell the daughter of the eminent Cavalier, Lord Southampton; for both Rochester and Dartmouth, it is known, made application in the highest quarters.

Lord Halifax, on his part, showed particular concern. His motives, both from a personal and a political point of view, were indeed cogent. Lady Russell was cousin to his first wife, and sister-in-law (by a former marriage) to his married daughter. That he believed in both the legal and moral innocence of the condemned man is practically certain; whose execution, as he could not but foresee, must arouse a passion of resentment, and raise the sufferer to a very alarming height in the roll of political martyrdom.

These considerations no doubt reinforced that 'Tenderness' in matters of blood for which Halifax was renowned; and the Lord Privy Seal 'showed a very compassionate concern' for his former colleague and 'all the readiness to serve him that could be wished'. The Duchess of Portsmouth (as Halifax has himself reported) 'said to Lord Montague, that if others had been as earnest as Lord Halifax with the King, Lord Russell might have been saved'. It was to Halifax that Tillotson and Burnet ('confident his lordship would do the Lord Russell all the good he could') at once directed their application, when circumstances suggested, erroneously, that Russell was prepared to recant his former opinions concerning the limits of political obedience. And, finally, Russell himself, from the condemned cell, 'did send thanks to the Lord Halifax for his humanity and kindness to him'.

The concern of Halifax did not cease with the execution of his old comrade; for his good offices were actively employed on behalf of the dead man's family. So urgent and successful were his representations that almost the first letter which Lady Russell compelled herself to write, after the fatal day of her widowhood, was a letter of thanks to the Lord Privy Seal; since, as she so touchingly writes, nothing but gratitude, and the fear of seeming ungrateful for all his kindness, could have forced her, at such a moment, to make the effort. Her postscript asks his advice as to the pitiful formalities which her tragic situation demanded.

Lord Halifax answered as follows on 16 October:

Madam,—It is enough that my zeal to serve you is favourably received; but it doth not deserve so much notice as your Ladyship is pleased to take of it. I am ready to give myself a better title than yet I have to such obliging acknowledgements, whenever you will give me the opportunity, by laying your commands on me. In the mean time, I will not offer anything to your Ladyship's thoughts, to soften or allay the violence of your affliction; since your own excellent temper, and the great measure of reason you are blessed with, will best furnish you with the means of doing it. I have not seen Colonel Russell, to speak with him, concerning the letter your Ladyship mentioned; but, according to my present thoughts, if he delivereth a compliment from you to his Majesty, by your order, it may be less liable to inconvenience, or exception, from any thing that is put on paper. I must tell your Ladyship, there has been such a stir kept about setting up the scutcheon,* and so much weight laid upon it by some, who might have been more sparing for your sake, though they would not be it for mine, that I am clearly of opinion, it is adviseable to stay yet, for a considerable time, before any thing is moved in the other business. There are some other particulars which confirm me in this opinion, that I shall give you an account of when I have the honour to wait on you: for I would by no means have your Ladyship exposed to the danger of a refusal; which is best prevented by taking a seasonable time, and letting the wrong impressions wear out that may have been given for the present.

In pursuance of the liberty I had from your Ladyship, I left it to my Lord Keeper to set down what was to be given to the Sergeant, and he

* The so-called 'hatchment' over a dead man's door.

hath ordered £20 which I have desired your servant to pay, that you may receive no further trouble in it.

I am, Madam,

Your Ladyship's most humble and obedient Servant,

HALIFAX

He was equally assiduous in his efforts on behalf of Algernon Sidney, to whom he stood of course in an even nearer relationship. 'I did', he says himself, 'upon all occasions give him the best advice I could, for the applying himself before his trial'; and he appeals to the evidence of Henry Sidney, who could bear witness that Algernon considered Halifax as good a friend as any he had in the world. Similar testimony was forthcoming from Sidney's confidential servant; who could depose (and eventually did depose) that though his master for some weeks after his arrest wanted even a change of linen, yet the valet himself, knowing that the Marquis of Halifax was his kinsman, 'applied myself to him; and by his means obtained relief from some of those grievances, and by his Lordship's means I had the liberty to visit Col. Sidney during his imprisonment'.

Nor were the efforts of Lord Halifax confined to the amelioration of individual misery. His sagacity perceived from the first the seriousness of the political conjuncture. From a 'Moderate' point of view the results of the 'Rye House' revelations had been disastrous in the extreme; and the impetus thereby given to the spirit of reaction—to the rampant and rabid 'Toryism' of the *Observator* and its compeers—gave ground for most anxious misgiving. With the ineffectual importunity of a political Cassandra, Lord Halifax insisted that a policy of frank and cordial conciliation could alone extract from the circumstances of the moment a permanent advantage. Renewed urgency for the meeting of Parliament was apparent in all his demeanour; and he never tired of representing that, as the Royalist enthusiasm of the instant gave every prospect of a satisfactory Session, so the issue of writs would be regarded as the omen and pledge of a popular and constitutional policy. Nor did he fail to insinuate that since, under the provisions of the Triennial Act, the session could not be deferred beyond March, a previous summons would be at once graceful and politic.

The suggestions of the Marquis, which derived no doubt additional energy from the very critical posture of Continental affairs, were promptly reported at the Court of Versailles, and excited the usual comments.

'I was told upon Sunday last', writes Lord Preston on 6/16 October, 'by a Minister, that they have accounts from England that upon a consultation whether the King should at this time call a Parliament or not, your lordship and Secretary Jenkins were for it, and that my Lords of Sunderland and Rochester opposed it; which method I can assure your lordship is making of Court here.' That Halifax, at one moment, did not despair of success is shown by the following letter; which also bears witness to the profound anxiety with which he beheld the advance of the Turkish arms, favoured by the unscrupulous diplomacy of France:

FROM THE MARQUESS OF HALIFAX, LORD PRIVY SEAL
(*to* THE EARL OF CHESTERFIELD)

23 *August* 1683

...I may go so far as to wish your Lordship may find no such charms in the country as to make you renounce the town; which with all its faults, (of which it never had more than now) hath still something to recommend it especially in winter....Then it is we will hope your Lordship may come up, even without summons to a Parliament. In the meantime, we begin to be afraid to hear from Vienna. The appearances are a little melancholy, tho' we are comforted with a great army gathering together for its relief; but, if it should move so slowly, as to let the place bee lost, it would be a scurvy after-game for that part of Christendome. Whatever becometh of the world, I must ever bee

My Lord, etc.

Impressed by the urgency of the crisis and by a sense of his own comparative impotence, Lord Halifax was ready to grasp at any available means of transforming the situation; as, by the introduction of some personal element which might neutralize the pernicious influence of the Duke of York. The Duke of Monmouth, as we knew, had absconded; and his generous offer to 'come in and run fortunes' with Lord Russell had been as generously declined.

He had lurked in England all the summer with the secret connivance of his father; and Lord Bruce, a personal friend of the Duke's, describes vividly and pathetically how, when the Duke's name had appeared in a proclamation for the arrest of the plotters, the King had sent for Bruce, told him that 'James' was concealed at Teddington (the abode of his mistress, Lady Wentworth) and ordered Bruce to effect the arrest. Lord Bruce, grasping the situation, gravely responded that the character of the house and its surroundings rendered this impracticable. The King, with transparent delight, had acquiesced in the simple artifice; nor did he ever cease to show his sense of the young man's kindly subterfuge.

Whether or no such, or even more obvious, hints were received by Lord Halifax, it is clear that from the first he was ready to entertain the hope of establishing a hold upon the sluggish energies of the King, by means of the only real affection of his later years; an affection which Halifax has himself described as 'extravagant'. By this means no doubt he hoped a road might be opened to a policy of general conciliation. But this strategy was open to two objections. Though Monmouth had at this time certainly abandoned the ambitious dreams which only outside pressure induced him ultimately to resume, the Duke of York could not be supposed to regard his restoration to favour as other than a menace to himself. The second, and still more sinister light in which others might regard his patronage, we shall realize later on.

The stages of the affair as recorded in Monmouth's own diary were as follows. About three months after his evasion, the Duke of Monmouth, it is clear, came secretly up to London. Lord Halifax paid him a surreptitious visit an hour before midnight; bringing him a message from the King to this effect; that he was unable to believe the Duke had been privy to the murder plot, but that he must, with a view to the Duke's own advantage, affect to do so. Lord Halifax, with some difficulty, induced the young Duke to write a letter to the King, which letter Lord Halifax took away unread, though Monmouth had purposely left it unsealed. In this the Duke passionately repudiates complicity in the murder scheme; and professes that he had, on the contrary, once risked his life for the King and Duke of York. The King's answer 'was very kind', and a few days later he granted his son an interview and received him 'pretty well'. At a second interview, whereat Halifax was present, the King was again 'very kind'. It was probably after this interview, as Monmouth ('wrapped in a cloak') left the presence, he was recognized by an over-zealous officer; whose breathless report to the King, brought him a 'disdainful' snub from Charles II, who never forgave this officiousness.

A little later Halifax told Monmouth that his business should be 'done to his mind' in a week; that the Queen was his friend, and had spoken favourably of him before the Duke and Duchess of York; 'which', he said, 'the King took very kindly and had expressed it so to her'.

The next task of the conspirators—for so we must call them—

was to break the affair to the Duke of York; and Halifax brought Monmouth the draft of a letter to the King which the young man was to sign, and which was to be shown to the Duke of York. Monmouth—prudently—begged it should never leave the King's hands. Halifax agreed, but said that if the Duke demanded a copy it could not well be refused, and Monmouth yielded perforce.

This letter was certainly composed by Lord Halifax, and we notice first the elegant and stilted periods assigned to a by no means cultured client; secondly, that the professions of penitence, though full, are vague; and thirdly, that the negotiation is represented as originating in the Duke of Monmouth's voluntary submission without any kind of extraneous intervention. We give the salient passages, as follows:

You must allow me, Sir, still to importune you, not without hopes of prevailing at last upon your generosity, so as it may get the better of your anger to me. I am half destracted, sir, with the thought of having offended you.... The character I lie under is too heavy for me to bear,—even death itself would be a relief to me could I have it without the aggravation of leaving the world under your displeasure. I must therefore throw myself upon your compassion, which being a virtue so agreeable to your nature, I hope your child, sir, will not be an unfortunate instance of your denying it when 'tis implored. I confess, sir, *I have been in fault, misled,* and insensibly engaged in things of which the consequence was not enough understood by me; yet I can say I never had a *criminal thought* against your Majesty.... Your Majesty will consider, that whilst I was under the *apprehension of great anger and violence against me,* it might easily betray me into very fatal mistakes; but now...everything *like a fault* towards your Majesty appeareth to me in...a reproaching and terrifying shape... I humbly beg, sir, to be admitted to your feet, and to be disposed of as you direct, not only now, but for the remainder of my life. But...your Majesty will permit me to offer to you. Whether you will let pass anything as a penalty upon me which may lay a stain upon my innocent children? Whether you will make me undergo the ignominy of a trial?... and...give me the cruel punishment of hearing myself arraigned for treason against such a King and such a father? and whether my being carried to the Tower...can have any effect but an unnecessary mortification...and some kind of blemish, too, to my family?...

Neither do I imagine to receive your pardon any otherwise than by the intercession of the Duke, *whom I acknowledge to have offended,* and am prepared to submit myself in the humblest manner; and therefore beg your Majesty would direct how I am to apply myself to him, and I shall do it, not as an outward form, but with all the sincerity of the world.... Dear Sir, be pleased to revive, by a kind answer, the most miserable, disconsolate creature now living. MONMOUTH.

Meanwhile, and parallel, as it were, to this curious underhand treaty, a drama of more tragic intensity was proceeding in the light of day. The trial of Algernon Sidney had been hitherto deferred because the evidence against him was legally insufficient, and in hopes that further testimony would become available. When this expectation proved futile, the Government, relying on some totally irrelevant papers, and the unscrupulous partiality of the new Chief Justice (Jeffreys), determined to prosecute. It thus afforded to a man of dauntless courage and intellectual vigour the very theatre which displayed those qualities to the highest advantage; and conferred political immortality upon a theorist of genius, who had never in life possessed any serious political influence.

That Halifax was opposed to this course we may be assured. 'I did upon all occasions give him the best advice I could...after his condemnation for the petitioning for his pardon.' Of Sidney's petitions, one at least seems to have reached the King through the hand of the Lord Privy Seal himself—after, it would appear, Sunderland had characteristically declined to present it;—and Burnet identifies it with the manly outspoken appeal, in which Sidney had applied to the King for the justice refused him in Court. And when a year later, in *The Character of a Trimmer*, Halifax speaks of 'laws, mangled, disguised, made speak quite another language than their own;...thrown from the dignity of protecting mankind to the disgraceful office of destroying them', it is impossible to avoid the conviction that his thoughts had reverted to the trial of Algernon Sidney.

Three days after Sidney's conviction, Charles, with the reluctant assent of his brother, declared in Council his intention of pardoning the Duke of Monmouth, on his submission. Lord Halifax brought Monmouth the order to surrender, and 'cautioned me to play my part, to avoid questions as much as possible, and to seem absolutely converted' (no doubt in the matter of the Succession) 'to [the Duke of York's] interest'. He bade him also 'bear with some words that might seem harsh'. The Duke duly surrendered himself in person at the Secretary's office, where the Council was sitting; and there, in presence of his father and uncle, made a full submission, with a confession, of which the actual value is doubtful; since it would appear that he had understood this confession was not to be published, and had been specially warned against contravening any (statements and questions?) his uncle might propound. He was then dismissed to his lodgings in custody of a Sergeant-at-Arms.

The news spread rapidly and created intense excitement, all the more so since details were unknown except to the principals, and contradictory rumours abounded. Reresby questioned the Lord Privy Seal; Lord Halifax sedately responded that he had no doubt there would be 'various interpretations and guesses, by whose intercession chiefly it came to pass'. Reresby answered that it was ascribed to the influence of the Duchess of Portsmouth and Lord Sunderland, and to the intercession of the Duke of York. 'My Lord', proceeds Reresby, 'said that was a mistake, for the Duke of York and his interest had opposed it to the last; and did own that he himself had chiefly laboured in it and brought it to pass. He gave me several reasons as well public as private for so doing, not so fit to be here mentioned. By this,' adds Sir John, 'it appeared that, notwithstanding the great interest against this Lord, he reserved a great power with the King. I found by his lordship that the Duke of Monmouth had confessed the truth of the Plot to the King and Duke, but would not give any public evidence against the conspirators.' Reresby, however, laid shrewd enough stress on the part played by the King's own affection, which revealed itself in lavish caresses. The young Duke's return had thus, in effect, all the appearance of a triumph, and inflicted a serious mortification upon the Duke of York and the party of reaction.

The Duke of York acted with promptitude and vigour; severe pressure was applied to the King, and two days after his submission, the Duke of Monmouth was placarded in the *Gazette* in terms which certainly suggested that he had practically turned King's evidence.

This strategy, as Ralph points out, demands our highest admiration. James was no genius, but he had effectually checkmated the ablest man of his day; since to Halifax the move was as embarrassing as to the young Duke himself. It had been tacitly understood between the Duke of Monmouth and the Minister that any admissions which the younger man might make should remain sacred; and on the first suspicion of the publication, though his pardon had not yet passed the Seals, the Duke of Monmouth turned restive. Lord Halifax, whose design appeared threatened with immediate shipwreck, remonstrated earnestly with his client. He assured him that the publication had been wrung from the King by the importunity of his Grace's enemies; and pointed out that the bailing of the prisoners in custody, which necessarily impended (according to the provisions of the Habeas Corpus Act) within forty-eight hours of the existing date, would exonerate the Duke from the infamous charge of treachery. Burnet, who always insists upon the supreme importance of this matter, is strongly of opinion that had Monmouth followed the advice of his new mentor, 'it would have given a great turn to affairs'.

The expostulations of Lord Halifax were impotent to curb the Duke's impetuosity; and scarcely had his pardon passed the Seal ere the young man was ridiculing, with the utmost imprudence, the statements of the *Gazette*. His reckless denials, which, moreover, certainly overstepped the bounds of truth, compelled his father to assume the show at least of resentment; and the Duke received summary directions to deliver a written acknowledgment of his confession.

Lord Halifax (says Burnet) pressed him to write a letter to the King. '...*Plot* was a general word that might signify as much or little as a man pleased: they had certainly dangerous consultations among them, which might be well called plots. He said, the service he might do his friends by such a general letter, and by his gaining the King's heart upon it, would quickly balance the seeming prejudice that such a general acknowledgement would bring them under, which could do them no hurt.'

The Duke eventually presented to the Committee of Council a paper, which does not seem to be extant, but which the Cabinet found to be 'finely worded'; and which Ralph not improbably ascribes to Halifax himself. It was pronounced, however, by no means sufficiently explicit; and a draft was eventually produced which the King required his son to sign, on penalty of instant disgrace. The Marquis again exerted his influence; he came to the Duke of Monmouth's lodgings, and was closeted with the young Duke and his wife in her apartments. Friends were waiting in the ante-room; the Duke came out to them once or twice; and eventually admitted that Halifax had persuaded him to endorse the document in question, engaging that his Majesty should never let it be seen, and assuring the young man that now was the time to gain his father's favour. The Duke of Monmouth accordingly resigned to his father a holograph copy of the statement prepared by the Council. But he was haunted by painful qualms lest his action should incriminate his fellows, and immediately submitted the original draft to Mr John Hampden, who, having been just released upon bail, was still awaiting his trial. As evidence the paper was absolutely worthless; but the unwarrantable use which, during the recent trial of Sidney, had been made of irrelevant documents had created a general terror. Mr Hampden sent word to the Duke that he looked on the sheet as his death-warrant. Overwhelmed with horror, the Duke immediately recanted, imploring Lord Halifax to recover the dangerous document. The King remonstrated, but on his son's reiterated importunity he at length, with great irritation, ordered Halifax to restore the paper and send the applicant to Hell. A few hours later the Vice-Chamberlain was sent to forbid him the Court; and the same day, with stoic indifference, Algernon Sidney suffered on Tower Hill.

As regards the incriminating paper, Reresby records:

> My Lord Privy Seal said to me that the manner of doing it was something hard (as it was required) but he ought to have submitted entirely to the King in it. I found his lordship was concerned (as he had reason to be, being looked upon as his friend in the matter of his admittance) that he was so obstinate....I found the Duke of York was much displeased with my Lord Privy Seal, though he showed it not openly, that he was not consulted on the affair of bringing in the Duke of Monmouth; and it was my Lord Privy Seal's expression that the Duke would never forgive him....
>
> [December 11] It was much reported in town that my Lord Privy Seal was not well with the King upon the late affair with the Duke of Monmouth, and that he met with discouragements at Court to so great a degree as to make him leave business. My lord told me, upon my acquainting him with this, that he had met with discouragements from some, but not from the King, for he was as well there as ever; and that there would be a further production of affairs, in a little time, than was expected, and so pointed at the thing that I guessed what he meant. [Reresby subsequently heard, from a third hand, how the Duke of York had complained] that if my Lord Privy Seal had no friendship for him, yet, as being the King's brother, he might have told him of the design, and not have brought in Monmouth without acquainting him with it in the least; that he could never forget the former services done by my Lord Privy Seal; but he took a method to bring it to pass were it possible, for to his knowledge he was yet labouring to reunite the King and the Duke of Monmouth. [The Marquis hereupon told Reresby] that this complaint from the Duke looked as if he had a mind to be upon better measures with him; but that he had not seen the Duke of Monmouth since he last went from Court, and that, he only acting in that affair by the King's commands, could not acquaint the Duke with it when his Majesty would not allow him to do it.

Meanwhile the motives of the Marquis were assailed from the

opposite quarter. Among the extreme 'Whigs'—and we may instance, more especially, the case of John Hampden himself—the whole incident created the most sinister impression; and excited a frenzy of hatred which exploded, some five years later, to considerable effect. In such circles it was positively believed that the Marquis had intervened with the sole object of procuring evidence against the remaining culprits. Absurd as was the legend, it derived superficial corroboration from the course of subsequent events. Upon his breach with the Duke of Monmouth, the King—or, more properly, the Duke of York—chose to contend that the understanding by which the young Duke had been exempted from appearing against his associates was *ipso facto* rescinded; and in the exercise of somewhat sharp practice he was subpoenaed towards the end of January to give evidence against John Hampden. Upon this, and probably with his father's connivance, the Duke, a second time absconding, eventually fled the country; and when, on 6 February, Mr Hampden was brought to the bar, the Duke of Monmouth, the first witness for the Crown, was summoned in vain. The two witnesses requisite by statute in trials for high treason were not, therefore, forthcoming. Mr Hampden, on the evidence of Lord Howard, was consequently tried for misdemeanour only; and condemned to a fine of £40,000, which for him spelt perpetual imprisonment—at least, till the death of his father.

Meanwhile, Lord Halifax had found himself as much perturbed by the Continental as by the domestic situation, each, of course, reacting on the other. At the moment when the siege of Vienna by the Turks engrossed all the energies of the Empire, France had endeavoured to coerce the Escurial by occupying, in time of ostensible peace, the richest provinces of the Spanish Netherlands. These she had refused to release unless indemnified by the cession of Luxembourg or even more valuable 'equivalents'.

Yet, even at this so threatening (and as it must have appeared almost desperate) crisis the French faction which now predominated at the English Court looked on supinely; and in the United Provinces a pusillanimous policy thwarted, with similar indifference, the energies of the Prince of Orange.

The feelings of Lord Halifax on this head had been expressed to Lord Preston on 28 November as in a confidential answer to a confidential despatch, both being conveyed by the safe hand of Lord Preston's Private Secretary.

My Ld.—If Mr Tempest had given mee longer warning I should have inlarged my selfe more, and made the full use of so good an opportunity. I agree with your Ldp. by my observation, that France hath really no mind to the Warre, and will never forgive the Prince of Orange for doing that which they call forcing them into it; And perhaps were their more secret thoughts known, as things have fallen out, they wish they had never insisted upon their pretentions in Flanders...and the thing I would be informed by your Ldp. in this case is, whether by your observations of the temper of that Court, they might not be prevayled with to restore what they have taken, and to quit their groundlesse claymes in Flanders, provided it bee done at our King's importunity for the better grace, and to save the appearances. This would go very much against the stomach of such a mighty Conqueror; and yet if the effect of doing it, might be the making Spayne and Holland less warm in pursuing the interests of Germany, when their own were provided for, and by that means let France bee at more liberty to make their party good in that part of the world, it would perhaps bee no ill bargaine to them. Pray let me know your private opinion whether such a thing is possible in the case above mentioned. Your Ldp. hath I suppose had an account of the late disorders in the lower end of the Gallery,* from those who have more skill than I have in things of that kind; I lament that so much noise was made in the manner of it,... and the undecent discourses, the world is full of upon this subject; which would have lasted much longer, if a new thing had not happened, that draweth everybodyes thoughts towards it; it is the D. of Monmouth's being receaved again and pardoned. You may imagine what oppositions must bee made to it before it was done, and what inferences drawn from it afterwards; things of this kind are ever thought Mysteries, and deep reasons must bee assigned for that which was so little expected, but I beleeve there is no more than this, that Nature hath prevayled, and the Father forgot what hee had committed against the King, by a distinction between his naturall and his politique capacity. He hath made an intire submission, and to the Duke, too, and it is to bee presumed, that after having recovered such a fall, hee will no more put himselfe in the danger of a relapse, for which no cure can reasonably bee expected. As this is sufficiently talked of here, I do not doubt but reflections are made upon it at Paris; I desire therefore your nicest observation of all the discourses relating to this businesse, since they may bee of great use to your selfe, as well as a satisfaction to mee; these collateral things may give great lights to the main businesse, and the disturbance they may receave by any considerable alteration in our Court, may perhaps, in spite of their secrecy, give you a window into their scheme, so that you may gather by rationall inferences, more than they would ever think fit to impart to you. This may bee an occasion for your Ldp. to talk with all your French acquaintance round, as soon as you can, that you may have their first reflections,

* The Duchess of Portsmouth's apartments. The Grand Prior of France was suspected of an intrigue with her.

and not give them time to consider what they should tell, and what they should conceal from you. My curiosity to bee informed in this or any thing else is not so great, as to desire an account, except it bee conveyed by a safe hand; in the mean time and ever, I am

My dear LdS

Most faithfull humble servant,

HALIFAX

The time was now drawing near when at the latest, under the terms of the Triennial Act, a Parliament was required to assemble. On 10 January Lord Halifax told Sir John Reresby:

> ...he had been very earnest with the King for a Parliament, but to no purpose; that he had used for arguments that, though the King had slipped his opportunity of calling one soon after the last plot, when he could not have missed of one according to his own desire; if he feared, not to have a good one now, the longer it was deferred the worse it would be; till at the last it might be used as an argument never to call one at all. That nothing ought to be so dear to him as to keep his word with the people; that the law required a Parliament to be called every three years; that his Majesty had promised upon the last dissolution to observe the laws, by a proclamation setting forth the reasons, at the same time, why he had dissolved that Parliament; that the general use of such proclamation was that he intended to call another within the three years, and that he feared an ill construction might be made of his not doing accordingly; that though the anti-monarchical party was very low and discouraged, yet this might raise discontent in another party, those which were for the service of the Crown, but for his Majesty observing the laws at the same time, especially where they had his royal word for it. However, if his Majesty thought fit to do it, he would not relinquish his service, but if he could find out any reasons as an excuse for his not doing so, would study to do it.

The last sentence Lingard stigmatizes—and not, we think, without justice—as 'very courtly'. It is, indeed, a question whether on such a point Lord Halifax would not have enhanced his reputation by a formal retirement. The principle of Ministerial solidarity was not, of course (as Macaulay so convincingly urges), at that period accepted; and the Marquis, moreover, knew—none better—that his resignation would have constituted in effect a long-desired triumph for the Court of France and the reactionary party. But perhaps the most salient argument in favour of official tenacity is supplied by the sudden changes to which the Court atmosphere was liable, and of which the advent was often as rapid as it was unforeseen.

The Marquis, at any rate, undeterred by repeated failures, pursued his attempts at reinforcing the moderate party. With this view he exerted himself for the release of the imprisoned Lord Danby, his animosity against whom had lessened in the course of recent developments. As in this he was supported, though from utterly different motives, by the Duke of York himself, the opposition of Lords Rochester and Sunderland, together with that of France, proved futile.

Chief Justice Jeffreys therefore took upon himself, rightly according to Hallam, to reverse a former decision of the Courts; and, after a preliminary imprisonment of five years, Lord Danby found himself released on bail. The same day he kissed hands at Court, and Reresby relates that Halifax coming in soon after 'the two lords saluted one another but slightly. The next day,' he adds, 'going from the Privy Seal to wait on the Earl, my Lord bid me give him his service and tell him he should have taken a more particular notice of him, but that he thought it might not prove so well for his service.' The Earl, who for the present had resolved to decline business, fully endorsed this view.

The arrival of Lord Dartmouth from Tangier offered about this time a fresh opportunity for intrigue on the part of the rival factions; but his lordship considered himself strong enough to stand on his own legs. On this Lord Halifax told Reresby that

> everybody had not wit and strength to stand alone, that it was true he had done so, which he attributed to the King's kindness to him, and his good fortune, and to some measures (especially that of not seeking his own gain or profit) which his lordship in his [pecuniary?] circumstances was not so well qualified to follow; and that he [Halifax] had at the last this advantage by it, that he hoped ere long to find his greatest opponents court him for their friend (meaning Lords Rochester and Sunderland) for at this time it was given out that they began to disagree.

But despite all his efforts during the early part of 1684 the star of Halifax steadily and sensibly declined, and it was visible, says Reresby, that he was 'less in business than before'. The appointment of Godolphin as Secretary of State was regarded as a triumph for the Rochester faction. And though Halifax the same day told Reresby that while all these interests continued adverse to him 'the King was as kind to him as ever', yet a few weeks later he received, through his brother, a fresh 'slap in the face'. For on 7 May 1684 his Majesty superseded the Admiralty Commission, on which Harry Savile still retained the seat so long an object of his ambition; and declared his Royal intention of managing naval affairs in future by the advice and assistance of the Duke of York. This arrangement was welcomed in the Service, where the Duke's application and knowledge of detail were regretfully remembered; but its political implications were emphasized when, a fortnight later, the Duke, without taking the oath, formally resumed his seat on the Privy Council.

And while, in England, the influence of the Papist heir-presumptive appeared predominant, on the Continent, France stood supreme. Her rivals, England included, were paralysed by internal dissensions, all fomented by the intrigues of France. And though Spain at length declared war against the insolent and unscrupulous aggressor, its decrepitude prevented any effective operation.

It was at this juncture that (once more through private channels) Lords Halifax and Preston resumed their confidential correspondence.

The personal affairs of Preston were the immediate topic; but Preston had proposed to Halifax that if the Ambassador himself should be compelled to resign, it might be of importance to his correspondent to have a successor in whom he might confide; and for this he suggested Lord Eland, of whose abilities and industry he expressed a very favourable opinion.

In his answer Lord Halifax concerns himself mainly with the future of Lord Preston, but his references to his own son are remarkably dry. He says

> My son is obliged to your Lordship for the favourable opinion you have of him, and it would be well for him if he could deserve it; he hath not yet given evidence enough of his application to anything to engage him where so much is necessary; but your Lordship's kindness both to him and to me is the greater by so much as he is less fit for anything of that kind.

He goes on:

> As to the public affairs, this is the most critical conjuncture that hath happened a great while; France believing the disorders in Holland will reduce the Prince of Orange to give in to their proposals; whilst the other side yet flatter themselves, the resolutions will continue of rejecting a peace upon such disadvantageous terms as it is offered to them. We go on as you left us, there appearing no change in our inclinations, which must be so clear to your Lordship by what you observe, where you are, as well as by that which you hear from hence, that it needeth not be any further explained to you. I will add no more at present than that—I am, etc. HALIFAX.

The forebodings of Halifax were only too abundantly justified. At the end of May 1684, Luxembourg, the object of so many solicitudes, succumbed at last to the French arms; while Spain and the Emperor, abandoned and defeated, had to accept the humiliation of a twenty-years truce, with an endorsement of all the previous encroachments of France.

The sentiments of Lord Halifax, as respects this ignominious catastrophe, were indignantly though anonymously expressed, some six months later, in the famous *Character of a Trimmer*. But they were never in doubt; and the hatred he inspired at the French Court showed itself at this moment in a singular though trivial interference with his family affairs.

The views of Lord Halifax upon marriage were very much those prevalent among men of his rank in the seventeenth century, when the interests of the family were almost always regarded as paramount over those of the individuals concerned. Two years before he had, as we have seen, married his daughter 'Nan'; described by him as 'a gentlewoman not immodestly bred, with £10,000 and no debts upon her'; who, if she approved a suitor enough to be his, would, he hoped, 'perfectly conform' to a husband's 'inclinations and circumstances'. The husband of his choice had been Lord Vaughan, a widower, only six months younger than her father; a man of some ability, but of whom current reports had little to say that was favourable. The marriage had excited considerable comment; the only motives which are apparent on the surface being political conciliation on the one hand, and a mortgaged estate on the other.

At the time of which we speak, another contract was in question. His eldest son, a man of some ability as a wit and poetaster, had for some years, as we have gathered from a letter previously quoted, completely emancipated himself from the control of a father, whose letters had shown so much solicitude on his behalf; and had been spending his time, at least mainly, abroad, in a course of unbridled dissipation. In March 1683/4, however, through the good offices of Lady Vaughan and Henry Savile, a reconciliation had taken place. Lord Eland, hitherto averse from marriage, had now fallen desperately in love with the beautiful Huguenot heiress, to whom he had been at an earlier date so indifferent, and had obtained his father's approval. 'Her portion', he had written to his father, 'is what your Lordship desires, and her wit and person are such, that I am confident...you will not regret having given your consent.' The marriage treaty, in which the elder Henry, who went to Paris for the purpose, took an active part, seems to have been very protracted. The lady's mother considered the settlement insufficient, her portion being £20,000 and the corresponding allowance but £2000 a year. She was also apprehensive as to the relations between father and son, as Halifax had declared that, since no one could foresee how a husband would turn out, he desired to retain the power of increasing (if necessary) his daughter-in-law's income, in his own hands. At length, however, the marriage took place, and Henry Savile went over once more with a yacht to meet the young couple and the lady's family; all of whom (with the 'Revocation of the Edict' impending) desired to settle in England.

The travellers brought three coaches, seventeen horses, and an amount of personal baggage—mainly, of course, clothes—which inspired the unfortunate uncle with positive terror. He wrote to his brother,

> I send you these two enclosed lists of their goods. The first, enumerating their clothes, seemed to me so extravagant (though it be matter of fact that all have been worn) that I thought it best to enumerate their ballots (packages), and leave it to your credit at the Custom House that their yacht may be met in the river with an order to have their goods searched at their own house; a very usual practice to others, and would be hard to refuse to these strangers.

At the last moment, however, the whole 'caravan' (as Harry calls it), with the exception of Lord and Lady Eland, her mother and Henry Savile himself, were detained in France 'by his most Christian Majesty for reasons best known to himself'. Lord Weymouth, in a letter to Lord Halifax, remarks that his Lordship is accustomed to such 'traverses' from 'that quarter' and that he believes 'your Philosophy digests them very easily'. But if the circumstance had nothing strange for contemporaries, modern readers must be somewhat surprised to find the 'Grand Monarque', in the plenitude of his power, suspected of stooping to evince, by petty personal slights, resentment against an incorruptible opponent.

His arrogance, however, shown as it was in all possible directions, naturally excited a corresponding alarm and resentment.

PART IV. THE REVULSION OF JULY 1684 TO FEBRUARY 1684/5

OUR last episode left the King of France and his ally, the Duke of York, at the pinnacle of power; but the very fullness of their triumph was to beget a revulsion by which their policy was to be seriously menaced. We cannot doubt that the victorious Triumvirate—the King of France, the Duke of York and his brother-in-law, Lord Rochester—had at length presumed too far on the easy temper of King Charles. For as Louis XIV, confident in the European predominance he had at last obtained, now deliberately discontinued the pension with which he had purchased the adhesion of the English King; so the overbearing temper of the heir-presumptive, and the peremptory manners of the Minister, had reached a height at which, in the opinion of his Britannic Majesty, they required a decisive check. He was thus impelled, and by a double motive, to patronize Lord Halifax, the consistent opponent of the French and the High 'Tory' interests.

The first symptoms of a change are discernible in July 1684, when, a vacancy having occurred in the Treasury Commission, Lord Rochester hoped, by obtaining the coveted post of Lord Treasurer, to supersede the Commission entirely. Much to his disgust, however, the existing arrangement continued; while the Marquis of Halifax and Lord Keeper North, without Lord Rochester's privity, procured the appointment of their respective relatives, Dudley North and H. F. Thynne, to seats on the Board. The incident created extraordinary excitement, not confined to this country. Across the Channel it elicited considerable alarm; since the triumph of Lord Halifax, which it was supposed to portend, appeared the omen of a Parliamentary Session, and possibly of a rupture between the Crowns.

Nor did the first blow remain long unseconded. About the end of August the Presidency of the Council, the dignified sinecure of the Ministry, fell vacant. Public opinion, anticipating the occasion, had presumed that Lord Halifax would be ceremoniously sacrificed to the ambition of Seymour, who desired the Privy Seal. Far other, however, was the actual disposition. To the general astonishment, no less than to his own, Lord Rochester found himself removed from his lucrative and influential position as First Lord of the Treasury to the comparatively impotent dignity of Lord President. His friends stood aghast at this renewed testimony to the increasing influence of his rival; who expressed the situation in a sarcastic epigram which has become proverbial: 'He said, he had heard of many kicked downstairs', but never before 'of any that was kicked upstairs.' Upon this engrossing topic the Marquis wrote to Sir John Reresby as follows: 'You may believe I am not displeased to see such an adversary removed from the only place that could give him power and advantage; and he beareth it with so little philosophy, that, if I had ill nature enough for it, there is occasion given me to triumph. You see I cannot hinder myself from imparting my satisfaction to so good a friend.'

'The wonder', as Reresby says, 'was how the finger of my Lord Privy Seal was able to effect this against the shoulder of the Duke of York, who continued Rochester's constant friend'; and so mortified, indeed, was Lord Rochester at this unexpected reverse that he seized an opportunity, which soon offered, of effecting a dignified retreat.

In consequence of manœuvres with which Lord Halifax had no concern, it had been arranged that a vacancy should be created within the course of a few months in the government of Ireland; and during October or November 1684, Lord Rochester accepted the reversion of an appointment, which he regarded as honourable exile.

This virtual disgrace, as we have already hinted, must be regarded as the prelude of a proposed Ministerial revolution which was never actually effected. It is certain that during the final months of 1684 secret negotiations were in progress which involved the renewed relegation of the Duke of York, under all the forms of respect, to provincial banishment at Holyrood; and we surmise, with little fear of error, that Lord Halifax was to replace his Royal Highness as 'chief favourite and Minister', with the promise, express or implied, of a free hand in affairs both foreign and domestic.

The *dramatis personae* of this intrigue seems to have been: in the first place, Lord Halifax, whose interest in the scheme is apparent; secondly, the Duke of Monmouth, whose interest is equally obvious; thirdly, the Prince of Orange, whose interest lay entirely in the foreign situation, which the revulsion might improve; fourthly, the King, whose somewhat sluggish interest in freeing himself from political fetters was to be stimulated by the hope of recovering the society of his beloved son. And in the last place, we recognize the part played by the Queen, whose value as an unassuming and unsuspected intermediary had been proved during the preceding year. Then she had merely intervened on the side of her husband's son, for whom she entertained a rather pathetic kindness, but now other motives may have supervened. Their previous collaboration in the Monmouth negotiation of the preceding year had, perhaps for the first time, involved her and her husband in a common concern; and it had certainly brought her into more close association with Lord Halifax. His personal assiduity and fascination, and his determined enmity for the Duchess of Portsmouth, had clearly, long ere this, obliterated from the Queen's mind his conduct towards herself during the 'Popish Plot' frenzy.[17] In the April preceding (1684) he had been appointed her Chancellor, and their relations from this time forth appear to have been most cordial. Moreover, rumour attributed to Queen Catherine some measure of anti-Gallican sympathies; and also some resentment at the state of pupilage to his brother, into which her husband seemed to have fallen.

The earlier stages of the combination are hidden from us, but this much is clear:

I. About the end of November 1684, the Duke of York received his brother's instructions to proceed north during the ensuing February; ostensibly that he might preside over a session of the Scottish Parliament.

II. Further, on 10 November 1684, the Duke of Monmouth had left Diren, the seat of the Prince of Orange. There, ever since his retreat to the Continent, he had been received with a distinction which had, without doubt, the at least tacit sanction of King Charles. It is also certain that he had then travelled secretly (though not without arousing suspicion) to England, where (so rumour averred) he had seen his father; and that he had returned to Holland on 10 December. His diary bears witness to the fact of a private correspondence with Halifax, and Halifax himself testifies that they were 'on very good terms'.

III. We find also that the existence of such an intrigue was strongly suspected, both (*a*) at The Hague and (*b*) at Versailles. For (*a*) d'Avaux, French Ambassador at The Hague, had become convinced that a desire existed on the part of his Britannic Majesty for more intimate relations with the Prince of Orange than had existed since the Exclusion era. He further maintained that this desire was actively fostered by Lord Halifax, who wished to restore both the Prince and the Duke of Monmouth to the good graces of the King; and d'Avaux believed that it was Lord Halifax who had primed them both as to the course they should pursue. He further insisted 'That the aim of my Lord Halifax was to remove the Duke of York from the management of affairs, to procure the dismissal of my Lord Rochester; to introduce the Prince of Orange into the management of affairs and acting in concert with him to become First Minister.' M. d'Avaux maintained that the Duke of Monmouth's part in the intrigue was to recommend the Prince to King Charles, and that his friends expected success. D'Avaux, moreover, understood that a visit from the Prince was actually expected, so soon as the Duke of York should set out for Scotland. All these facts and surmises M. d'Avaux had transmitted by indirect means to the Duke of York himself.

Meanwhile (*b*) at Versailles (where these reports excited great alarm) the Duke of York was from his side insinuating that differences between the Kings were being 'improved' by Halifax and the enemies of France. Thereupon Louis at once took measures, political as well as financial, to revive his former influence over the Court of St James.

Such is the evidence at our disposal. But how far Charles II sincerely contemplated such an extreme reversal of policy as seems to have been anticipated by Lord Halifax, his well-known duplicity forbids us to decide; he may but have sought new hush-money from France.

A special reason for distrust might seem to emanate from a passage which occurs in Burnet's original *Memoirs*, which passage, however, we believe to be erroneous. He there tells us that *at this time* Halifax 'discovered the King's inclinations to Popery so plainly, that he was in great apprehension'. But there seems to be in the passage some confusion of circumstances and dates. Burnet himself had just returned from a brief visit to Paris, and had retailed to Halifax rumours, there current, as to the English King's anticipated secession to the Roman Church. This will, of course, have occasioned discussion; in the course of which Burnet may have realized, for the first time, those suspicions which Halifax (as his subsequent *Character* of the Monarch shows) had long entertained. The curious story of the Roman Missionary, his attempt to convert Halifax, and the latter's sarcastic reference to a supposed Roman Miracle, must have occurred, as Airey points out, nearly twenty years earlier, and can only have been *related* by Halifax at this time.

Other anecdotes referring to the year 1684 do indeed introduce us to schemes in favour of the Roman Communion, which extracted important protests from the Minister, but these certainly did not *originate* from the King, though they secured his sanction.

These designs included: (1) Suggestions as to a Repeal of the Recusancy Laws which emanated from Chief Justice Jeffreys, then a favourite of the Duke of York. To these Lord Halifax, while acquiescing in the proposed release of such 'Popish Plot' prisoners as were obviously innocent, demurred entirely, unless Parliamentary sanction should have been previously obtained. (2) The appointment of Roman Catholic officers to commands in the Irish Army; which had been originally advocated (for differing reasons) by Lord Sunderland, and the Papist Richard Talbot, afterwards well known as Lord Tyrconnel; but they certainly obtained the Royal sanction.

On this last point Halifax was absolutely firm, although the first beneficiary proposed, who was a connection of Lord Sunderland, was also one of his own. The King, having dilated on his merits, Halifax suggested they might be recompensed by a pension; and asked whether the King considered the proposed appointment to be in accordance with the law? The King responded that the laws of Ireland had less obligatory force than those of England. Lord Halifax offered to dispute that question with any opponent; reminded the King that the army had been raised by a Protestant Parliament to support a Protestant interest; and asked whether his Majesty wished to create an impression that, where his hands were not tied, he would show all possible favour to Papists? The King retorted that he cared little what people said or would say; the Marquis returned, that, while it was a just piece of greatness in the King not to mind what his *enemies* said, he trusted the King would never despise what his *friends* said, especially when they seemed to have reason on their side. The King repeated the Minister's remark to the officer concerned, who was naturally irate; and Halifax thus obtained fresh proof of his Sovereign's want of discretion.

But a much more outstanding issue was raised about the same time on a different topic, and as to this the Minister showed the same courage. The Charters of the New England colonies had been recently revoked, and about the end of November 1684 the question of a fresh Constitution for the provinces concerned came under discussion at the Cabinet Council. It was debated whether provincial assemblies should be established, or whether arbitrary powers should be vested in a Governor and Council, subject to orders from the home Government.

'The Marquis of Halifax', writes M. Barillon (who had just received, by despatch dated 1 December, fresh instructions to press for the disgrace of the Minister), 'took upon him to contend with great warmth, that there should be no doubt whatever but that the same laws, which are in force in England, should also be established in a country inhabited by Englishmen. On this he enlarged very much and omitted no argument by which it could be proved, that an absolute government is neither so happy nor so safe, as that which is tempered by laws, and which sets bounds to the authority of the prince. He exaggerated the inconveniences of a sovereign power and plainly declared that he could not make up his mind to live under a King, who should have it in his power to take, when ever he thought proper, the money he has in his pocket. The speech was strongly opposed by all the other Ministers', and especially so by Judge Jeffreys, who maintained with characteristic effrontery that 'whoso capitulateth, rebelleth'; meaning that the attempt to define, after any fashion, the function of the Sovereign is equivalent to revolt. In the event, as Barillon tells us, 'it was determined not to subject the Governor and Council to convoke general assemblies of the people, for the purpose of laying on taxes, and regulating other matters of importance'. The Ambassador adds that his Royal Highness made use of the episode (which Barillon himself dismissed as relatively unimportant) in order to convince his brother of the 'inconsistency and danger' involved in employing one so much opposed to the interest of monarchy as Lord Halifax. The French Court rose to the occasion. 'Les raisonnemens du Sr. Halifax', replied Louis, 'sur la manière de gouverner la Nouvelle Angleterre ne meritent guères la confiance que le Roy d'Angleterre a en luy, et je ne suis pas surpris d'apprendre que le Duc d'York en ait bien fait remarquer les conséquences au Roy son frère.'

Perhaps, however, the most significant feature of the situation is this; we cannot fail to trace a connection between the supposedly impending political revolution and the appearance *in MS. form* of the second, and most celebrated, among the works which we owe to Lord Halifax.

The authorship of *The Character of a Trimmer* was for long an open question. For the circumstance, that among the papers which Sir William Coventry left behind him, there was one of the no doubt once numerous versions of the first (and MS.) issue, lent force to an identification which Sir William, during his life, had unequivocally (though appreciatively) denied. It thus happened that the three earliest *printed* editions (1688–9) appeared with an ascription to 'The honourable Sir W. C.'.

Evidence, however, first adduced by the present writer in the *English Historical Review* of October 1896, and amplified in the second volume of the *Life and Works of Lord Halifax* by the same author (1898), proves that it was composed by Lord Halifax; and was circulated *anonymously*, in MS., '*to the King*' and other influential persons between 5 December 1684 and 16/26 January 1684/5. It was subsequently (though privately) owned (and revised) by Halifax for another, also anonymous edition; and was eventually included in his acknowledged, though posthumous, *Miscellanies*.

The exciting cause was evidently a violent political diatribe which appeared on 6 December 1684 in L'Estrange's *Observator*; wherein under its current nickname, and from an extreme 'Tory' standpoint, the policy of moderation was satirized with all the flippant virulence characteristic of L'Estrange. His status, as practically responsible for the censorship of the Press, may account, in part at least, for the anonymous, and originally MS., character of the Halifax retort.

But the intention of the piece was far more serious than could have been anticipated from so ephemeral an occasion. In motive perhaps, though neither in aim nor in attitude, it may best be compared with Bolingbroke's *Patriot King*. Its objects, in fact, are many sided. It is a vindication of the statesman's own policy, and it embodies a political programme primarily destined for the Royal eye. It is a defence of limited monarchy, as opposed to autocracy. It includes a severe censure of recent Government policy, especially in foreign affairs. In fine, it is the expression of a general political outlook essentially English and essentially sane, equally remote from the dogmatism of the partisan, and the crude ideals of mere theory.

The immediate aim of the pamphlet detracts in some degree from its value as an exposition of personal opinion. It is tinged rather too much with the courtly rhetoric appropriate to a Royal ear. In the *Character* and the *New Model at Sea*, for instance (though the conclusions may be the same), the relative merits of a Republican and a Monarchic constitution are very differently staged. Again, the panegyric on Charles II, with which the *Character* concludes, affords an amusing contrast to the posthumous portrait by our author. For if the same features are suggested, the *Trimmer* lays on the colouring with a brush judiciously liberal.

The 'occasional' motive, on the other hand, lends the work both coherence and significance. The initial attack on pamphleteers is suitable enough in a retort. The invections against judicial profligacy gain significance when we remember that Jeffreys was Chief Justice. The sarcastic references to the holders of reversionary rights take a new emphasis, when we apply them to the ascendancy of the Duke of York; and the Grand Monarque is readily recognized in the ideal tyrant of the author's abhorrence. The prophecies of a political judgment (looming, though not apparent) can be easily interpreted in the light of existing anticipations; while we can without difficulty identify the politicians who 'fear to throw themselves on their country'. And well indeed had it been for James II had he digested the remarkable passage which warned him that 'There is a soul in the great body of the people'.

It is, however, as the embodiment of a policy that we are here mainly concerned with the pamphlet under discussion. As regards the religious question, we see that while Halifax *strenuously upheld the principles of the Test Act and the exclusion of Papists from political life*, while he condemned with equal vigour *any attempt to abrogate by proclamation the so-called penal statutes*, he had now withdrawn his assent from the 'Popish Plot' revelations, and deprecated the violent policy to which they had given rise; that in relation to both Papist and Protestant Dissenters he favoured the mildest possible construction of the existing Recusancy laws; and anticipated their eventual repeal by statute, and a Parliamentary toleration. The section which relates to Foreign Affairs is, however, from our point of view perhaps the most important. We mark with keen appreciation its attitude of uncompromising hostility to the progress of French ambition, its daring allusions to the Dover Treaty in its political aspect, its bold and statesmanlike strictures upon the foreign policy which had been pursued by the Administration, in despite of the Marquis, during the three preceding years; and the urgency, the almost despairing urgency, with which it advocates a return to the principles of the Triple Alliance. The author deprecates, indeed, the impression that he would sacrifice the domestic interests of England to the exigencies of Continental policy; but he suggests the possibility of a *via media* between the extremes of bravado and subservience. The topic evokes, in fact, the one note of passion whose vibrations disturb the serene intellectual atmosphere of the later Halifax pamphlets; and in an access of indignant patriotism the Minister protests that when he beholds the 'Roses blasted and discoloured whilst the Lilies triumph and grow insolent upon the comparison; when he considereth our own once flourishing Laurel, now withered and dying and nothing left us but the remembrance of a better part in History than we shall make for the next age', he is 'tempted to go out of the world like a Roman philosopher, rather than endure the burden of life under such a discouraging prospect'.

On the literary merits of this remarkable essay it is needless that we should dilate. It exhibits in a consummate degree the characteristics of its author's style—a style pure, vivid, colloquial—chequered perhaps by a gentlemanly carelessness in the construction of the sentences, but not infrequently rising to a strain of unpremeditated eloquence; the style, in a word, of an orator and of a man of the world. If it lacks the varied vocabulary of the author's favourite Montaigne, it shares his racy vigour, his abhorrence of the pedantic and the formal, his return to those familiar idioms of common life which the Frenchman so admirably describes as the 'subsoil of the language'. In wealth of witty allusion—a wit seldom defaced by the indecency so characteristic of Montaigne's own pages—the Englishman excels; and the father of the modern essay cannot compare with his disciple in the art of a penetrating, yet delicate irony. While those acquainted with Dean Church's great *Essay on Montaigne* or Frederick Denison Maurice's fine passage on that writer in his *Moral and Metaphysical Philosophy* cannot fail to detect analogies yet more significant and extensive.

It is therefore most interesting that at this very moment Lord Halifax may have been renewing his acquaintance with his old favourite. For Charles Cotton, with whom Halifax had a slight acquaintance, had recently completed his translation of Montaigne's Essays, which appeared, with a dedication to the Lord Privy Seal, very early in the following year; and Halifax acknowledged the compliment in a letter which—first printed in his own *Miscellanies*—reappeared in Cotton's fifth edition (1738).

In this appreciation Halifax returns thanks for the

book in the world I am the best entertained with...I have till now thought wit could not be translated...but you have so kept the original strength of his thought, that it almost tempts a man to believe in the transmigration of souls, and that his being used to Hills is come into the moorlands [of Derbyshire] to reward us here in England for doing him more right than his country will afford him.... To translate and make him ours is not only a valuable acquisition to us, but a just censure of the critical impertinence of those French scribblers who have taken pains to make little cavils and exceptions to lessen the reputation of this great man, whom nature hath made too big to confine himself to the Exactness of a studied style. He let his mind have its full flight, and showeth by a generous kind of negligence that he did not write for praise but to give the world a true picture of himself and of mankind. He scorned affected periods, or to please the mistaken reader with an empty chime of words....

So much for *The Character of a Trimmer*.

Meanwhile to this masked assault on the enemy's position, Lord Halifax continued to add more practical though still cautious manœuvres. His correspondence with the Duke of Monmouth, then lingering at The Hague (under the almost ostentatious patronage of the Prince of Orange) was uninterrupted. On 5/15 January 1684/5 the Duke received a letter from the Lord Privy Seal, with a marginal note from the King, telling him, 'that in February' he 'should have leave to return; that matters were concerting towards it; and that [the Duke of York] had no suspicion', notwithstanding his nephew's good reception by the Prince.

On 3 February Monmouth received another letter from the same hand, telling him that his business was almost as well as done, but (the issue) must be so sudden as to leave the Duke of York's party no time to counter-plot. He was further informed that his uncle would probably choose Scotland rather than Flanders for his retreat 'which was all one to the King'.

But a strange reversal of fortune had even then already befallen all the parties concerned in this affair. Halifax had been pursuing the investigation of the Hearth-money frauds as a direct assault on Lord Rochester; and 2 February—the day before the receipt by Monmouth of the above-mentioned letter—had been appointed for an examination by the King. It was commonly expected that Lord Rochester would prove to be implicated, and might even be committed to the Tower.

On that very morning, however, the King fell suddenly ill with the symptoms of an apoplectic seizure. At first he rallied, and hopes were entertained for his recovery; but at midnight two days later his condition appeared desperate. By then the Queen, who had not hitherto left his bedside, had been compelled by sheer exhaustion to retire; but she now entrusted to her Chancellor, Lord Halifax, the expression of her 'heart-felt and painful grief'; withal asking her husband's pardon 'for anything in which she might have displeased him'. Lord Halifax is said to have discharged his mission 'with very great eloquence'. And the King 'with some trouble' returned the well-known answer, that it was not for her to ask his pardon but for him to ask hers, 'which he did from his heart'.

Thirty-six hours later, after the strange reconciliation with Rome, which the Marquis certainly suspected, Charles II breathed his last.

The Duke of York, upon his brother's illness, had immediately stopped the ports; perhaps apprehending the possibility of Monmouth's unbidden return. It was the Marquis, on the other hand, who first despatched to the exile the tidings of his father's death. 'O cruel fate!' runs the record in the diary of the disconsolate son; and the words might as fitly represent the sensations of his Grace's mentor.

For Charles himself, indeed, the Marquis can have entertained but a tepid, half-cynical affection, as the subtle *Character* he has left us sufficiently testifies. A slight though brilliant specimen of intellectual analysis, it differs from other contemporary portraits in that it is neither a eulogy nor a libel, and its cool dispassionate estimate bears on its surface the stamp of an almost scientific impartiality. His portrait, of course, presents to us, not the young, energetic and promising sovereign of the Restoration era, to whom modern admirers confine our attention; but the elderly voluptuary, the dyed-in-the-grain dissembler, with whom alone Halifax had any close contact.

But the great revolution which the Minister had contemplated centred, and centred exclusively, round the person of the departed monarch. And with him passed every political hope the Minister had dared to entertain.

CHAPTER X

IN DISGRACE, 1685–1688

PART I. PRESIDENT OF THE COUNCIL, FEBRUARY TO OCTOBER 1685

THE event, from a Ministerial point of view, was, indeed, catastrophic. Four days had sufficed to obliterate the importance of the Marquis and annihilate his prospects. Nor did King James lose any time in emphasizing the changed situation. Three days after the new King's accession, the Marquis had a 'secret'—this probably means a 'private'—audience, in which, says Burnet, the Minister 'made some excuses to the King for the distance in which he had lived with him of late'. These the King put by 'handsomely enough', telling him that 'he would remember nothing that was past, except his behaviour in the business of the Exclusion'. To this Halifax replied that the King 'knew upon what bottom he stood, and that, so long as the King exacted no other service of him than that which was consistent with the law, no man should serve him with more zeal'.

Despite these preliminary and reciprocal civilities, the King proceeded to warn his Minister of the impending triumph of Rochester, whose appointment to the long-coveted post of Lord Treasurer was announced on the following day. 'My Lord Rochester', says a contemporary letter, 'is the premier Minister now, and the discourse of his...going into Ireland is at an end.'

In effect, Lord Rochester transferred to his brother, Lord Clarendon, the expected reversion of that lucrative, if invidious, office; while Lord Halifax, to his intense disgust, found himself, for that very brother's temporary convenience, 'kicked up' in his turn, from the post of Lord Privy Seal to the discredited dignity of Lord President. Yet even this mortification did not adequately symbolize the change in his prospects. King James, in a frank discourse with the French Ambassador, spoke at length of the reasons which obliged him to continue in office those known to have been 'his most dangerous enemies during the life of the King his brother', explaining the necessity he was under of giving a further proof of his 'moderation' by 'not suffering the Marquis of Halifax to be entirely unemployed'. But he added that he knew him, and could 'never rely upon him; that he had admitted him to no share in the real secret of his affairs, and that his office of President would only show the little credit he was in'.

These expressions convey with perfect accuracy the position of Lord Halifax during the six months for which he continued to hold office. Though Lord Rochester, in apologizing to the French Ambassador for the summons of Parliament, which was necessitated by the lapse of revenue, explained that the King only wished to anticipate the inevitable urgency of Lord Halifax in that direction, the Marquis, during the first Administration of James II, was, in practice, little more than a dignified cypher. Lord Halifax, however, accepted his defeat with polite and courtly resignation, told Reresby that his relations with Rochester continued to be 'kind', and that he himself 'used his constant endeavours to serve the King, and would continue them, hoping his Majesty would put no discouragement upon them by imposing the Popish religion, which he seemed sorrowfully to apprehend'.

His 'services', however, took the form of frequent and unpalatable remonstrance, so outspoken indeed, that Halifax himself in conversation with Reresby, expressed his wonder that the King, considering his 'temper', took it so calmly as he did. In two private audiences which King James vouchsafed him within three months of his accession, he urged upon the King the supreme importance of his preliminary steps. He warned him against the impolicy of his open and unmitigated threats, conveyed through the medium of Chief Justice Jeffreys while on circuit, and directly communicated by the King to the Privy Council, that all attempts at granting the revenue for specific periods would be met by an immediate Dissolution. Such threats Halifax stigmatized as unprecedented, and certain to exasperate Parliament, ever jealous of Royal interference, even when most desirous of propitiating the Sovereign. The pride of a great Assembly, he argued, is a dangerous thing to wound, since injured vanity can lend courage, even to the vacillating and the fearful.

Moreover, Lord Halifax, as we should expect, declined to curry favour with the King by any compliance with the King's ecclesiastical predilections. Barillon has told us, and Lord Macaulay with his usual vividness has pictured, how, when the new King, in state, attended an Easter Mass, Lord Sunderland accompanied him, and Lord Rochester evaded a decision; while Lord Halifax, standing with the staunch old Duke of Ormonde immovable in the ante-room, watched the 'time-servers who had pretended to shudder at the thought of a Popish King, and who had shed without pity the innocent blood of a Popish Peer, now elbow each other to get near a Popish Altar'.

But despite his external equanimity, it is obvious that Lord Halifax resented with poignant mortification the explicit reverse which had befallen him, and anticipated the future with very justifiable misgiving. We find him relating to Reresby 'several passages of the late King's kindness to him'. And Reresby adds, no doubt on the hints thus afforded him, '*certainly no man was in greater favour with him when he unfortunately died*'.

And what of his accomplices, in what we may describe as the 'Bedchamber Plot'? The Stadtholder, with his usual imperturbable fortitude, accepted the changed situation. Faithful as ever to his one political ideal he still hoped, by persevering and respectful assiduity, to detach his exalted kinsman from the trammels of a French Alliance. The military reputation of the new monarch, and the events of 1678, indeed suggested, even to the Prince, that his father-in-law might not be altogether impervious to the motive of international emulation.

This change of policy naturally affected the relations between the Prince and the Duke of Monmouth, his recent ally. On the whole William seems to have extricated himself, as well as circumstances permitted, from a very difficult dilemma. He begged his young cousin to leave The Hague before his extradition should be demanded; and urged that he should enter the service of the Emperor in the capacity of a soldier of fortune. This solution was not without attractions for the disillusioned exile; and, but for the fatal solicitations of the Scottish and English refugees, the Duke might have acquiesced in these well-meant and sensible proposals.

To Halifax, who seems to have shared the hopes of the Stadtholder, these afforded almost the only gleam of light on a darkening horizon. He told Burnet that perhaps 'the King would declare himself against France and for bringing the State of Europe to a righter balance'. The Court of Spain and the States would make, he said, all possible advances to secure this, and thus 'we would be quickly able to judge whether bigotry or a desire of glory wrought most powerfully on the King'.

The anticipations of Halifax derived some plausibility from the attitude of reserve which James, on his accession, affected towards the Court of Versailles, and the apparent cordiality with which he at first responded to the Dutch overtures. These have deceived even some later historians, but their conclusions are certainly erroneous. The foreign policy of James was, in fact, one of weak and blundering oscillation. His sympathies were with France, but, on the other hand, he dreaded above all things the advent of the Great War which loomed so menacingly on the horizon. In such a conflict England could scarce remain neutral, and intervention would involve dependence on Parliamentary support, and the indefinite postponement of the religious revolution. He therefore endeavoured to ward off the threatened evil by balancing the adverse Powers.

Special motives, moreover, steered him, in the case of the Prince of Orange. He was alive to the strength of the Prince's position as a possible centre of disaffection; and believed that it might be possible, by flattering his hopes on the question of foreign policy, to obtain from his son-in-law, the husband of the heiress-presumptive, a measure of co-operation as regards the toleration of the Roman Catholic faith.

Under these circumstances, during the August following, Lords Halifax, Sunderland, Rochester and Middleton were appointed Commissioners, for the renewal and confirmation of the treaties between England and the States. The nomination of Halifax attracted particular attention; he 'is devoted to the Prince of Orange', writes M. d'Avaux from The Hague. Eventually the Treaty of Alliance was signed on 17/27 August 1685, being regarded as a great triumph for the Prince of Orange, and as a decided blow to French interests on the Continent.

But foreign policy was by no means the only issue which excited the anxiety of Halifax. In the hands of a religious bigot, the power of entrusting the government of the country to members of the religious minority was certain (as the crisis of 1674 had clearly testified) to prove a dangerous and powerful instrument; and the Marquis, with his usual sagacity, had always perceived that the real crux of the situation was involved in the question of religious 'Tests'.

In these circumstances, Lord Halifax anticipated with grave anxiety the results of the approaching session. During an interview between himself and Dr Burnet—so the latter assures us in his *contemporary* record—the Marquis expressed hopes that 'the next session of Parliament would be short, since it was to be in summer; and if they did not ru(i)n the nation in a heat, but left their work half done to a winter's session, there would still be hopes. Since after members had been once together "and had considered the interest of the nation, or their own in particular" they would more easily be prevailed on at least...to be so sparing in their bounty, that the Court might have frequent occasions of bringing them together.'

His hopes were, however, entirely frustrated. Parliament met on 17 May, when, despite the warnings already, as we know, received from Lord Halifax, his Majesty again, and publicly, announced that the method of temporary Supply, approved by the Marquis, would be highly resented by the Crown.

The House of Commons, perhaps in part owing to the *Quo Warranto* policy, was still under the spell of that strange spasm of enthusiasm which had greeted the accession of James II. It was now further won over by his Majesty's judicious conduct at his accession, and his insinuation that liberal financial supplies would obviate dependence on extraneous sources, i.e. French subsidies. *It voted the revenue for life, and an extraordinary supply of* £400,000.

During the course of the Session, Lord Halifax was reintroduced, under his new title, by Lord Clarendon, and by his own kinsmen and former ward, the young Duke of Shrewsbury, a recent convert from Romanism; but no speech of his is recorded during this short and too fateful Session, which was brought to an abrupt conclusion through the sudden and unexpected invasion by the Duke of Monmouth.

The letters received by Lord Halifax during this period included many references to the Rebellion. But though his son, Lord Eland, had commanded a troop of horse during the brief campaign (only to resign his commission immediately on its conclusion), no allusion to this extraordinary episode, on the part of Lord Halifax, has been recovered, even in a letter written by him within a fortnight of the Duke's execution. But we can hardly be wrong in surmising that he will have followed, with as much concern as reprobation, the spasmodic successes and terrible catastrophe of his recent associate.

The letter of 23 July (O.S.), to which we refer above, was addressed to Henry Savile (then taking a cure at a watering place), and relates to the anxiety of his own daughter-in-law, Lady Eland, for the safety of her mother, who was seeking a refuge in England. Halifax writes:

...My lady thinketh that if you have health enough to continue the intentions you had of making a step to Paris, any thing from hence in favour of her Mother would be much better transacted, you being upon the place, than it can be without that help. Besides I am of opinion that the next two or three months will be so very critical as to our affairs that it will be seen within that compass of time whether England can in any degree be a sanctuary for distressed Protestants...so I recommend you to your waters, and wish they may do better with you than my skill in physic would allow me to expect.

The national crisis did not materialize quite so soon as Lord Halifax expected; but his own fate was fixed within the term suggested.

The Rebellion had necessitated a large increase in the military establishment, which by this time amounted to 20,000 men. These forces James, in defiance of public opinion, had determined to maintain; and the first intimation of his fixed resolve to free himself and his co-religionists from the trammels of the law, had been symbolized by the military commissions now illegally conferred upon Papist officers. At Council, James went further, and expressed a hope of seeing Papists once more in the Upper House. Halifax called attention to the Test Acts, and their incompatibility with the policy in question. James retorted that the supply of Protestant officers had fallen short in the recent crisis, that he intended to support his nominees, and that he expected from his Ministers, not opposition, but advice as to methods.

Hereupon, several interviews took place between the King and the Lord President of the Council; 'the man [it was said] of the greatest weight that was likely to be on the contrary side'. In these 'his Majesty expressed himself with kindness', but the Minister showed no sign of submission.

The King then allowed it to be known 'that he would be served by none but those that would be for the repeal of the Tests'.

The situation thus became critical, and on the Sunday previous to 19/29 October, the King received Halifax in a final audience, and asked him how he intended to vote. 'He very frankly answered he would never consent to it; he thought the keeping up those laws was necessary even for the King's service, since the nation trusted so much to them, that the public quiet was chiefly preserved by that means. Upon this the King told him that though he would never forget past services, yet since he would not be prevailed on in that particular he was resolved to have all of a piece.'

On the following day M. Barillon wrote as follows to his Government:

London, 19/29 *October* 1685

Yesterday morning [the King of England] took me into his closet, and told me, he had several things to communicate to me, in order that I might acquaint your Majesty with them, as he did not wish to do anything important or of consequence without imparting it to you; that the first was, the resolution he had taken not to suffer the Marquis of Halifax to continue any longer in office, and that he should deprive him of the Presidency of the Council; that I knew that, during the reign of the late King, his brother, he had had a bad opinion of the Marquis's sentiments and conduct, and did not think him sufficiently attached to monarchy; that since his accession to the crown he had endeavoured to inspire him with better sentiments, and to induce him to follow maxims conformable to those which were becoming the Minister of a King, and even a good subject; that he had seen that his principles were unchangeable, and that, therefore, he was determined no longer to employ him; that there had been a wish to divert him from doing this, previous to the meeting of Parliament; and to induce him rather to make use of the Marquis of Halifax in that assembly, for the purpose of obtaining with greater ease those things which he might desire; but that it was for this very reason he wished to dismiss him from his councils; that his example might infect many persons, and strengthen the party who might wish to resist him; that he knew the inconveniences of a divided Council, and of suffering his Ministers to entertain sentiments contrary to his own; that his late brother experienced its ill effects, and that he would pursue a different conduct. He added that he designed to obtain from the Parliament a repeal of the Test and Habeas Corpus Acts, the first of which is the destruction of the Catholic religion, and the other of the royal authority; that he hopes to accomplish it, and that the Marquis of Halifax would not have had courage and firmness enough to support the good cause, and that he would do the less harm by having no connection with affairs, and being in disgrace. [Barillon made a suitable compliment.] His Majesty replied with a smile, 'I do not think the King your master will be displeased with the removal of Lord Halifax from my councels. I know, however, that the Ministers of the confederates will be mortified at it, and that they had a high opinion of his power.' I answered [says Barillon] that I had acted in concert with His Majesty in the time of the late King his brother to procure the dismissal of my Lord Halifax from office; but that I never thought he possessed the least power since the King's decease; that I agreed, however, that his removal would be productive of good effects in England, and abroad, by destroying the opinion which the Ministers of the House of Austria endeavour to establish on the continent, that the friendship and good understanding subsisting between Your Majesty and [the King of England] is greatly diminished; that I knew even that the Dutch Ambassadors had left England two days since, fully persuaded that the Marquis of Halifax was one of the most accredited of the Ministers, and one on whose friendship the Prince of Orange could place the most reliance....

Two days later (21 October), at a meeting of the Privy Council, the absence of the Lord President occasioned general remark. The King explained 'that he had reason to be dissatisfied with the Marquis of Halifax and thought it fit to continue him no longer in the place of Lord President of the Council'. He then gave orders 'that his name should be eliminated from the list of Privy Councillors'; and Lord Halifax, having within 24 hours resigned his appointment as Chancellor to the Queen Dowager, his fall was complete.

He remained, however, on good terms with Her Majesty, and thus was able to procure for his cousin, Mr Thynne, the office of Treasurer of her household.

PART II. OUT OF OFFICE, OCTOBER 1685 TO OCTOBER 1688

The dismissal of Lord Halifax naturally attracted general attention. The Spanish and Dutch Ambassadors and the Chargé d'Affaires of the Imperial legation were outspoken in their comments, and it proved a theme well-nigh inexhaustible for the pen of the French Ambassador. To his first dispatch on the subject Louis XIV had replied that 'the King of England is justified in believing, that since Lord Halifax has no religion he cannot be a very faithful Minister, or one much disposed towards the maintenance of the Royal Authority', and in reference to a second he wrote 'Monsieur Barillon, your letter of the 5th of this month informs me of the different opinions that are entertained where you are on the disgrace of the Marquis of Halifax, but whatever effect it may produce, you are well aware that it cannot but be very advantageous to my interests that a Minister so devoted to Spain and so inimical to the Catholic religion, has been removed from the councils of the King of England; and I assure myself moreover that this act of firmness will still further augment the authority of the King, and even make the Parliament yield more readily to what he may desire of it. I leave it to your prudence to inform him of my sentiments on this subject if you think proper.'

At home, of course, public opinion was deeply stirred. Reresby bewailed the news, regretting the loss of a 'true and kind patron', and fearing 'that the public might suffer as well as his friends' from the disappearance of 'a man of extraordinary parts' and 'so able a person in all business', one 'so generally looked upon as a wise man and a good subject, that the removal of him, especially at the beginning of Parliament, astonished a great many and made them fear...a change of Councils as well as Councillors'.

And what meanwhile was the attitude of Halifax himself?

When Reresby arrived in town for the Session, he heard from the statesman's own lips the particulars of his dismissal. Halifax said 'he might have continued with greater advantages than ever, if he would have joined in some things which he saw were contriving,...which he could not agree to; that the King parted with him with kind expressions; did assign [publicly] no cause for his dismissal, nor would put any person in his place'.

But Lord Halifax explained himself most fully by two long letters to his friend Lord Chesterfield; who, in a very eulogistic epistle, had desired him to further the Earl's intended resignation of the Justiceship in Eyre, to which office Chesterfield, for reasons of health, felt himself unequal:

THE MARQUIS OF HALIFAX *to* THE EARL OF CHESTERFIELD

October 1685

My Lord,—Depending upon the same hand, that brought mee your letter, for the returning my answer to it,* it was not in my power to send it sooner than he called for it, which he did this very moment, giving mee notice he will go with it tomorrow morning. I must now first tell your lordship, that I should have demurred to your commands, tho' they had found mee in a condition to obey them, from the belief I have, that my observing them in this case had not been at all for your service. I consider first, that both the thing itselfe, and the manner of your resigning, let it have been never so well cloathed with all the appearance imaginable of respect and duty, would have been as deeply resented and produced as much anger, as the most eminent act of opposition to the king's will in relation to the publique; so that your lordship had marqued yourself to receive, upon any occasion, the utmost effects of his displeasure, without the satisfaction of contributing any thing to the preservation of those things for which all good men may be allowed to contend, within the termes of decency. I will not alleadge my example as an argument to persuade one, who can judge better; but, I am very well satisfied with my own method of not turning away my master; but rather chose to

* This shows the general reluctance to entrust important letters to the post.

receive his commands for my dismission, which I did, after two severall audiences I had upon that subject, in which I received a great many kind words and took leave of him very well satisfied in these two respects; that I neither had any thing layd to my charge, nor so much as any hard words to mortify me, nor any obligations layd upon mee, to lay any greater restraint upon mee than that which shall arise from my duty. The particulars of the discourse I had with his majesty are worth your knowing, but to long to entertaine you with by letter. I will onely tell you in short, that I have a fayre fall, and am turned away, because I could not prevayle with myselfe to promise before hand, to bee for taking away the Test and the bill of Habeas Corpus. I need say no more to convince my Lord of Chesterfield of the necessity of his comming up; and, as I have taken measures with your lordship more than with any man living, and that you have had a confidence in mee, that I never did nor will abuse, I doe, from the kindest thoughts I can have for you, summon you to execute the promise you made mee to come up, if I thought it fit for you; and, that I may not be so arrogant as to expect, that so much better a judge than I should have implicite faith in this case, I will offer you these reasons: (1) My Lord Fauconbridge and others make it their business to spred it abroad, that you will not come up; which giveth discouragement as well as dissatisfaction to those, whose opinion you value, and who have a true friendship and esteem for you. (2) If you should not come up, you will send your proxey, which you will not put in an ill hand; and, if you place it in a good one, you will have his guilt as sure as hee hath your vote. (3) There can not be so good an opportunity for your being eased of your place, as to have it taken away; which it certainly will be for your voting in these matters against the court. (4) To show you that it is neither out of any eagernesse of my own, nor out of a desire to engage so noble a friend to take part in my danger, I doe solemnly protest to you, upon my faith, that by the best calculations I can hitherto make of a thing of this nature, which must be lyable to uncertainty, I beleive these two things probable; either, that upon sounding men they will be so discoraged as not to attempt these things; or, if they doe, that they will fayle in them. Your lordship would wonder what kind of men are resty in this case; men that wear red coats, that have lept hedge and ditch in everything else, but swear they will never give up these bills. I may bee mistaken, but I would not for the world make use knowingly of a false argument to mislead your lordship, and it would therefore trouble mee that such a criticall thing as this should either be prevented or baffled without your having a part in it, as you have hitherto had in everything that was just and honourable for you to appeare in. Lord Nottingham, Bishop of London, Lord Bridgwater, all the Bishops, Lord Danby—nay even my Lord Culpeper, if he may be relyed upon, many of those who are called Court lords, talke freely in this case. In the house of Commons the Sollicitour Generall resolved to lay himself out in it; those who are managers for the court there do, to my knowledge, swear they will oppose earnestly. The officers in the army begin to think the repealing the Test will be voting themselves out of their places; in short, I doe againe repeat it that I am extreamly persuaded these things will not be carried. There is another thing which, I imagine, may chiefly discorage your lordship from a journey at this time, that is the tryals; to this I offer, that, first, it is pretty sure all the lords* will be summoned upon such an occasion, and you would bee less willing to disobey their summons in this than in most cases. If any thing under heaven concerneth the lords and their posterity, it is that they should be judged by a great number rather than by a small one. The imployment, no doubt, is unpleasant, but the consequence of declining it might be much more so; besides, in your case, if you have a particular tenderness, I engage myself so farre to comply with it, as to contrive wayes to excuse your lordship, when I will not go about to do it for myselfe. And a great deale will be allowed by your friends to a man of your importance, provided they may have your countenance and assistance, if there should be occation, in defending those bills which are the strongest bulwarks of all that is left us.

This session will either produce moderation of one side, or else, after men have done their duty, give them ease for ever hereafter from contending to no purpose. Upon these reasons, I conjure you, for your own sake as well as ours, to come up; but, at the same time I must assure you, that let your resolutions be what you please, mine shall ever bee to bee,

My dear Lord,

Your most faithfull, humble and obedient servant,

HALIFAX

In return, Lord Chesterfield expressed an opinion that a studied seclusion in the country must procure him the desired dismissal, which could scarcely follow from action on his part in the House of Lords without a violation of Parliamentary privilege. He further expressed his great objection to taking part in the trials of the lords accused of complicity in Monmouth's rising. The evidence, he submits, is not likely to be more trustworthy than that against Stafford, yet a vote in their favour would be construed as disloyalty. As a compromise he offers Halifax his proxy, and chides him for supposing that his friend could be influenced by fear of personal consequences.

Lord Halifax responded as follows:

THE MARQUIS OF HALIFAX *to* THE EARL OF CHESTERFIELD

10 *November* 1685

My Lord—Upon the best consideration I am capable of, I doe still persist in my opinion, that this is not a seasonable time for your lordship to surrender your office; and, that by staying a little longer, you may chuse a time, in which it will bee lesse ill taken that it would be at present.

* I.e. of the Lords implicated in the Monmouth rebellion.

As to your coming up, I am to tell your lordship, the house is to bee called within a week; and, I could wish with all my heart, that you would over-rule your aversion to the journy, since I make very much difference between my Lord of Chesterfield and his proxy. I know of what weight your assistance is in speaking, as well as your countenance in being present; and as for the tryals, your friends would so order it, that wee could get you excused one way or other, tho' you were in town, provided wee might reserve you for some of those criticall debates upon which, to our thinking, every thing dependeth. I have perswaded my Lord Way-moth to come up, who had taken other resolutions; but after all, if your lordship can not comply with the wishes of your freinds in this particular without doing too great a violence upon your inclination, I shall not bee less zealous to serve you in your own way, than I have appeared to be in pressing you to agree with mine; and, therefore, in that case, I shall propose to you, that you will immediately give order that I may have your proxie; then upon caling the house the next week, when your lord-ship is named, I will say you have acquainted mee, you are at present very much indisposed, but that you intend, as soon as you can do it with any safety, which you hope may be in a little time, to come up and attend the house; and, in the mean time, that you will put your proxie into my hands. This, I suppose, may bee better than an excuse for your absence during the whole session; by this way, if you continu (sic) to be of the same mind, you may attaine your end without being put to send up affidavits of the condition of your health, which some lords talke of, and as it hath been sometimes practised, if your lordship remember it. The king's speech this day, in which hee asketh mony for his army, and telleth us, hee in-tendeth to keep the popish officers, hath put the commons into so ill humour, that tho' they were pressed to vote a supply immediately, they have put of the consideration of the whole speech till Thursday, at which the court is not at all satisfyed. I need not make any apology for that, which your lordship sayeth looketh less kind than you might expect from mee; since my meaning in this and all other things relating to you shall be such, as shall suffitiently justify me, that I cannot have a thought disagreeing from the professions I have made of being ever,

My Lord, Your lordship's most humble
and most obedient servant,
HALIFAX

Parliament had met under the gloomy shadow of the Revocation of the Edict of Nantes which had just taken place; and grim notice was taken of the sinister comments of the Bishop of Valence, who, in the name of the French clergy, had publicly congratulated Louis XIV on setting so excellent an example to the King of England and his heretical subjects. In the opening speech of King James to which Halifax refers, the King had publicly announced his intention of retaining a standing army, and of including, in defiance of the Test Act, the recently appointed Papist officers; and had had the effrontery to demand an additional Supply for these unpopular purposes. The Lords had voted, as usual, their formal thanks; the Lower House, hitherto so complacent, showed strong symptoms of discontent. It voted that the efficiency of the *Militia*, the legal and popular branch of the forces, should be further secured; reduced the subsidy demanded by nearly half; and while offering to *indemnify* the illegally appointed officers, respectfully vetoed their retention. And on the 19th, in the House of Lords, the new Lord Devonshire—the Lord Cavendish of the Russell episode—moved, in the very presence of James, that their Lordships should *reconsider* the speech.

The reports of the ensuing debate are singularly conflicting, but it must have been Halifax who was responsible for the sarcastic hit that while thanks were due for any speech of His Majesty, thanks were doubly so due 'when he spoke plainly'. The Government dared not take a division, and the desired debate was unanimously fixed for the following Monday. But James had seen enough. Within twenty-four hours he prorogued, till the following February, after only a ten days' session, a Parliament which never sat again. Moreover, on 4 December—contrary to the promise which Lord Halifax had received—Lord Sunderland, without resigning the Seals, took his brother-in-law's former place as President of the Council.

The appointment was extremely significant. Jealous of the Hyde brothers, Sunderland had determined to outstrip them by unscrupulous complaisance. Adroit, obsequious, unprincipled, he insinuated himself into the confidence of the Queen, the Jesuits and the French Court, from which last he drew a pension. He thus remained, in effect, Prime Minister from 1685 to 1688; monopolizing, with a knot of extreme and totally inexperienced Papists, the confidence of the infatuated Master, whose Exclusion he had so violently advocated.

The contemporary despatches of the Nuncio Adda—who, to the alarm and disgust of Englishmen, had recently arrived from Rome—give a curious and interesting view of the light in which Lord Halifax was regarded by the more moderate of the Papist community:

> I have opportunities of learning [he writes] from various persons, that many of these Lords, who are rich in Church property, among them My lord Alifax, who possesses not a little, fear, or pretend to fear, lest they

should lose them upon a reconciliation with the Church; and this fear, whether real or pretended, is in their case a motive for opposing, and impeding whatever can advantage religion. [Again, he understands] that certain proposals have been secretly made, by a favorite of the King's, who is a friend of Lord Alifax, to restore him to the favour of his Majesty, and induce him to concur with the King's designs, but the desired result has not been attained; for Alifax having observed to this individual, that he had never endorsed the King's design of removing the Test, and of upholding, in general, the Catholics employed, added, however, that some compromise (little, I fancy, agreeable to the King's dignity, and to the weal of religion) might be easily arranged; and these opinions having been reported to his Majesty, he dilated upon the fact, that Alifax was the relentless foe, both of himself and of the Catholics. Wherefore from this man, who has great credit in the Parliament, and great eloquence, we can only expect the most uncompromising hostility; and the most important feature is, that in the Royal party there is not a man who can counterbalance him, either as regards learning, or the name he has among the members.

A few days later the Nuncio adds that, in the event of another session, great opposition to the dispensing power is expected in the Upper House; the Peers maintaining that at the present rate there will soon be no laws left in the kingdom.

'I know', he proceeds, 'that yesterday lord Alifax said plainly to a person, from whom I had it, that the King had no such absolute power, quoting many Acts to prove his contention; *adding that if the King had desired (?) to remove the penal laws, he might have probably succeeded; and even if his Majesty had wished for many more Catholic officers in the army, than he now employs, Parliament would have granted this*; so that your Excellency's supreme wisdom will perceive that it is not these individual officers who occasion these contests, but it is the power of the King, which they desire to question, and to see lessened.'

These very explicit admissions on the part of a leading antagonist effectually disposed of the plea that the rupture between Crown and people was due to the unyielding bigotry of the Protestant rather than to the domineering attitude of the King.

Warned by such indications, the King on 8 January again prorogued Parliament till May.

By 13 February it was known that Lord Halifax had resolved to 'turn country gentleman', as Chesterfield put it, and to set out for Rufford in a month's time. His journey was, however, delayed by the arrival of his son's mother-in-law, a fugitive from the Revocation of the Edict. But he was able, none the less, to start on 22 March.

'The Lord Marquis of Halifax', so the Dutch despatches record, 'left yesterday for his Yorkshire estates with the intention of not returning except for the Session of Parliament; he did not see their Majesties before starting, being of opinion it had been too great boldness to enter their presence, having been relieved of all his charges; but he took leave of the Queen Dowager, who honoured the Lady Marchioness, on her departure, with a beautiful diamond ring'—worth it was said more than £1300—'which she drew from her finger, begging her to wear it as a remembrance.'

She seems also to have obtained his Lordship's services in the capacity of a match-maker, hoping to secure a wealthy heiress for her Chamberlain, Lord Feversham; but in this negotiation he appears to have been unsuccessful.

Lord Halifax remained in the country more than three months, and this seems to have been the last visit (in any case the last visit of considerable length) which he paid to Rufford. It is possible that he employed this period of comparative idleness in preparing that slight but remarkable *Character* of Charles II to which we have previously referred; which may possibly have formed part of the now destroyed *Memoirs*, and which is one of his most finished productions.

His friends in town meanwhile kept the retired statesman well abreast with news. Nor was he without visitors. In May, his brother escorted Madame de Gouvernet and a daughter to Rufford —a visit which, for some reason unknown, occasioned much comment. In effect the attitude of the disgraced Minister, even in his retirement, aroused extreme curiosity, and Roman Catholics began to talk of suspicious converse at Rufford.

The family party was increased early in June by the arrival of Lord William, the second son, whose time since leaving Oxford had been spent in foreign travel. While passing through London, he had made the most favourable impression on his curiously assorted uncles, Sir William Coventry, Lord Sunderland, and Henry Savile. The solicitude on his behalf displayed by the last named has in it something pathetic. He knew that Lord Eland, by a long course of reckless dissipation, had alienated father and friends, and brought himself to death's door; and that Lord George, the youngest son—at this time serving as a volunteer in the Imperial army against the Turks—was suffering severe privation on account of difficulties in the exchange, aggravated by his inexperience. An excellent youth, but as his letters testify, no scholar, he stood much in awe of his brilliant father; and the good uncle now implores the Marquis to use his second son, at any rate, more like a man than a boy; and to show 'a good deal of friendly familiarity; which is the best method to prevent his rebelling like one brother, and being cowed like the other'. The hopes and advice of the warm-hearted courtier were apparently answered; and Lord William, who, though not brilliant, appears to have been considered both sensible and steady, soon gained and preserved his father's entire affection.

But over that father at this moment impended a fresh and cruel family bereavement. He had already lost, two years earlier, his old friend and mother-in-law, the elder Lady Sunderland. Now on 28 May 1686, Sir William Coventry, who had long suffered under a complication of disorders, went down to Tunbridge Wells, which he regarded as a desperate resource. 'If the waters', he wrote, 'do not cure me, the earth must.' The treatment, however, only aggravated his sufferings, and on 23 June he died. 'His dying', wrote the Vice-Chamberlain who had attended him to the last '...was as regular and exemplary as his living; he had his senses to the last moment and recommended himself kindly to you.' Apart from a few testamentary gifts (among them £50 to Lord Halifax for the purchase of a mourning ring), Sir William left, besides munificent bequests to the French refugees and for the redemption of slaves at Algiers (of whom sixty had already owed him their freedom), a very handsome legacy to Henry Savile. 'God comfort you for the loss of our dearest uncle', wrote the kindly sorrowful legatee, 'upon my salvation, all he has left me does not comfort me.'

Business connected with this melancholy event probably accounts for the journey to town which, in July, brought the retirement of Lord Halifax to a sudden termination. But, as was natural, political motives were conjectured, and Lord Chesterfield was much alarmed by a rumour that his lordship went up to accept the Treasury. 'The eyes of the whole kingdom', he writes, 'are so fixed upon your Lordship that you must permit mee to comment on the least of your actions...the sober and honest party do think that next to his Majesty, their happiness or misery doth more depend on your Lordship than on any man in England...you cannot blame the fears or jealousies of those who in a desperate condition do value your lordship as their last hope.'

This letter seems to have crossed the following one from Lord Halifax:

THE MARQUIS OF HALIFAX *to* THE EARL OF CHESTERFIELD

London, 20 July 1686

My Lord—My hasty comming up to town was unseasonable in this respect, that, in a very few dayes, I had resolved to have given myself the satisfaction of waiting on your lordship at Bretby, where, no doubt, you have heard that I came up for a place at court; a report I met with here, at my arrivall, and heard it againe out of the country, at the rebound. I doe not find the measures now taken are such as would incourage a man to bee a gamester, after hee hath been turned out for a wrangler;* except one could divest one's selfe of those foolish things called principles, which I find the wiser sort of men use like their cloths, and make them yeeld to the fashion, what ever it is; which is a pitch of understanding I can not yet come up to, and, consequently, am too dull to meddle with so nimble a trade as that of the politiques is grown of late in the world. I am too slow a beast to keep pace with them, now that they are upon the gallop. The four new privy councellours, the commission of supremacy, and severall other things said to bee intended, give a pretty fair prospect of what is reasonably to bee expected; and every thing seemeth to be now so layed open and so playne, that there is but one thing that looketh like a mystery, and that is the giving it out with the greatest assurance imaginable that the parliament shall sit at the time appointed; which is so strange a piece of councell, considering the preliminaries which are made and still making that it is not easy, by what appeareth, to reconcile it to any degree of good sense. However, it is good to prepare against every thing that may happen, though never so unlikely, and especially in a thing of this nature, upon which so very much will depend; so that I hope your lordship will resolve to bee in town in winter; or if you have taken a resolution in generall against coming up so soon, I beg you will so farre make an exception to the rule, as to attend the parliament, if it meeteth, and to give that very great satisfaction to your friends here, as to allow us to depend on it. It is supposed the Bishop of London will be made one of the first instances of the ecclesiasticall authority lodged in the seven appointed by the late commission, though hee is not conscious to him selfe of any act done, that can give them any legall hold of him. It is believed, too, that the whole clergy will feel the effects of their power; and some go so farre as to suppose there may be an universall inhibition of preaching, which will be a great step, and a severe tryall upon the people; who generally place their religion in the pulpit, as the papists do theirs upon the altar. I came up with full resolution of staying but a week, yet am not onley detained longer, but business doth grow upon me in this place, that I am some times in doubt whether I shall not bee forced to send up for my family, without returning to it, which is

* 'Wrangler—a perverse, peevish, disputative man' (Johnson).

no very pleasant speculation at this time of the year, and when the town is more desolate and dismal than I yet ever saw it, in a long vacation. All the entertainment and the plenty is at the camp, where there is such feasting as hath not been known in England; especially by your friend my Lord Dunbarton (sic), who may be presumed not to defray such an extravagant expense out of his own revenues. My Lord Weymouth is so slow in his motion towards forreigne parts that it is to be hoped he will lay aside the thoughts of rambling, at least for the present. My opinion, as things now stand, is to goe alone with the fate of a nation, as far as one may do it with any tolerable prudence. Perhaps there are few men of my small value in the world, that have more reasons to take their precautions against a storme; and yet I cannot prevayle with my selfe to bee wise at too remote a distance, especially whilst I think there is any room left for to doe my duty, and to follow men of more weight in anything that may conduce to a publick service. Of this I am sure, that in all capacities, places, revolutions, and times, I must ever bee

My dear Lord's

Most faithfull and obedient servant,

HALIFAX

This remarkable letter deserves close scrutiny. We must in the first place remember that the political correspondence of the time lay always open to official examination, and is therefore ambiguously phrased. The writer's object in this case is clear. He wishes to reassure his correspondent as regards a rumour of his own apostasy, and to secure his attendance at the next Session of Parliament. He deprecates Lord Weymouth's reported intention of avoiding such attendance by means of absence abroad. This policy Lord Halifax implicitly condemns. He intends to continue his own opposition in the Upper House '*as far as one can do it with any tolerable prudence*'.

What, we ask, did Lord Halifax regard as the limits of 'tolerable prudence', and what were his special reasons for 'taking precautions against a storm'? What were the conditions under which he would consider there was no room left for doing his duty in the public service? We can only conjecture, but this we may reasonably do.

First we gather that he proposed to continue the struggle to the very verge of constitutional resistance.

Secondly, he cannot have failed to recognize that the fortunes of the national majority, and in especial of its leaders, hinged upon the retention of the Test and Habeas Corpus Acts. The leaders, in fact, to transfer a saying of Halifax, 'could not be hanged so long as there was law in England'. The repeal of these Acts presupposed the connivance of Parliament; and this—or the actual or practical supersession of such Acts by an exertion of the prerogative—would place the leading Parliamentarians in general, and Lord Halifax, as the most conspicuous, in particular, at the mercy of the Crown. Under such circumstances, Lord Halifax would appear to have contemplated, at any rate, a presumably temporary retirement to the Continent—and we may surmise, to Holland. How shall we judge him?

As regards matters political no less than judicial, there arise conjunctures, in which, to quote Halifax himself, 'there is no room for prudence'. But our age, no less than his own, has unhappily seen too many examples of patriots threatened by triumphant tyranny; and forced to choose between an heroic 'death in the last ditch', and a strategic withdrawal from the last tenable position. Dare we pass judgment on those faced by that grim alternative, whatever their decision? I think not. In the present instance it is enough for us to recognize that Halifax never admitted that the hour had arrived for so drastic a dilemma; since even the abrogation of the Test Act by an act of prerogative, and the prosecution of the Bishops, were to find him still at his post, as leader of the Opposition.

And when, in August 1686—about a month after the date of the last letter—he approached (so the King's biographer informs us) King James himself with a request for an audience, this implied no hint of surrender, but rather the hint of a statesmanlike *via media*. 'He was ready', he said, 'to serve the King', but, 'in his own way, by endeavouring' in Parliament 'to repeal the *penal statutes'* against Romanism. The King refused to see him in public, but would have conceded a private interview; which suggestion, however, fell through; because when sounded as to the *Test*, Halifax rejoined that there was no need to take that away *as the judges had declared that his Majesty could dispense with it.*

This touch of true Savilian sarcasm was not the only specimen of his sardonic wit current at the time, for instance:

(1) Lord Perth, Chancellor of Scotland, anxious to eclipse Lord Queensberry in the Royal favour, apostatized to Rome. While his retention of office was in the balance, he met Lord Halifax 'and made him a compliment' that they two would soon be fellow-sufferers. The retort of Halifax has been given in two forms: 'You will certainly be saved by faith though not by merit', or in the

more epigrammatic and probable version, 'Not so, my Lord, your faith will make you whole.'

(2) The King himself was at one period urging upon Halifax a change of religion; Halifax reminded him that in the parable the same consideration was paid to those who came late into the vineyard as to those who came early.

(3) Lord Halifax told his lady he was sorry he must part with her, but he designed to turn Papist. She said she hoped he would think better of it, but if so, why part from her? He said, 'because he was resolved to be a priest; since, having considered the matter fully, he thought it much better to be a coachman than a coach-horse'.

Meanwhile, just at this time of crisis, Lord Halifax was a prey to fresh domestic anxieties. On 25 July he wrote as follows, from London, to his brother, then taking the waters at Tunbridge Wells:

It belongeth generally to those who are in town to write to their friends in the country; but considering what a place the town is now, and how ill qualified I am at present to inform myself of anything worth knowing, it is much more indifferent, whether or no I acquit myself of this piece of duty. Only the last news from Buda giveth me some grounds to write to you, that, if you hear your nephew is shot through the belly, you may know at the same time that his bowells are not touch'd, and, by a letter written four days after the action, he was said to be in a hopefull way of recovery; this doth in a great measure allay my disquiets for him, though some fears will remain with me till I hear again, which I suppose will be in a little time. If he have the good fortune to escape this danger, such an honourable wound will be an ornament at least to him, and in another time might be of some use to him for the better introducing him into the world. Mr [Harbord] hath been very kind to him, as he seemeth to express in a letter he sent to Mr Fisher, his agent here in town, in which he sayeth he will not leave Buda till he seeth what will become of your nephew. I begin to doubt that my small affairs will detain me so much longer here than I intended, as to make me send up for my family instead of going down to it, but of this I am not yet resolved. Yours.

This letter crossed one of anxious inquiry from the affectionate uncle, in acknowledging which Lord Halifax writes: 'I forgive all Mr Harbord's irregularities in friendship' (he had been active against Halifax in 1680), 'for his kindness to your nephew, which is so seasonable that I am very thankful for it. Since you find some beginnings of amendment in your health, you are to continue the means of increasing it, though I confess I have a lower opinion of the virtue of waters than is fashionable for a man to have, the doctors in vogue having declared so much for them. I begin to be of opinion you may find me in town at your return though I am as yet unfixed in that matter.' In fact, Lord Halifax (who, as an old servant subsequently recalled with tears, had promised him to return in three weeks) not only remained on in town, but appears to have made, during the course of the autumn, a purchase which eclipsed Rufford in his attentions, if not in his regard. Tempted no doubt by its proximity to London, he settled at Berry Mead Priory, a 'villa' with attractive gardens, situated in Acton, then a country village five miles from town; and it is more than doubtful whether he ever saw Rufford again.

Meanwhile the political situation rapidly developed. On 6 December the new Ecclesiastical Commission suspended the Bishop of London, who had refused to inhibit a clergyman for a so-called seditious sermon. Ecclesiastical law required a submission within six months, in order to obviate further proceedings against him. The Bishop, about 22 October, seems to have submitted to Halifax, for criticism, some form of petition or appeal. Lord Halifax deprecated this proceeding in terms so extremely cryptic that they throw no light on the matter. It is clear, however, that he urged the Bishop to refrain from any course of action until he had seen Lord Nottingham 'and that other friend where [i.e. at whose house] I saw you in Westminster'.

Actually, six months later the Bishop presented a non-committal petition, which stopped further proceedings, but did not remove the suspension.

Meanwhile a further centre of interest was developing at The Hague, where Lord Halifax had been fortunate enough to secure an unexceptionable agent. Lord William Savile had returned to the Continent in September. He had soon made his way to The Hague; and Lord Halifax seized—if he had not made—the opportunity of renewing, through this trustworthy channel, his correspondence with the Stadtholder.

After so long respite, your Highnesse will allow me to make use of the priviledge of presenting my duty to you, and to put you in mind that my conjectures concerning the parliament have proved true; and if you will give me leave to make my guesses of what is to come, I am of opinion that the meeting appointed in February will not hold, there being no steps made to make it more advisable at that time than it was last month. Besides, the condition the King of France is in,* which is looked upon here

* He had had several surgical operations and it was believed he could not live two years.

as desperate, is a circumstance of that weight, that it must probably either produce a new scheme, or make very great alterations in the old one. Your Highnesse seeth of what use it is to stand firm and quiet, neither to yield nor to give advantage by acting unseasonably. Accidents come that either relieve, or at least help to keep off the things we fear for a longer time, and that is no small matter in the affairs of this world. I must give (you) my most humble thanks for your Highnesses favours to my son, who is, as becometh him, extremely proud of them, and will I hope make it his ambition, as well as it is his duty, to deserve them; if hee should not, hee must renounce the rest of his family, and particularly your Highnesses eternally devoted servant.

London, 7 *December* 1686

A second letter dated 18 January (N.S.) is mainly occupied with expression of thanks for the favourable reception of Lord William, but it concludes with the following words:

the motion of publique things, at present, hath not only variety, but some kind of contradiction in it. It is very rapid, if looked upon on one side, if on the other, it is as slow; for though there appeareth the utmost vigour to pursue the designe which hath been so long laid, there seemeth to bee no less firmenesse in the nation, and aversion to change; so that conversions are so thin, and those which are, so little fit to be examples, that the prevayling party is not a little discountenanced by making no quicker progress; for that reason it is beleved they will mend their pace; and if so, every day will give more light to what is intended, though it is already no more a mystery. Whatever happeneth, nothing must ever alter my resolutions of being devoted to your Highness's service.

London, 18 *January* 1686/7 s.v.

These letters serve as an introduction to a new and important episode of the great political drama which was now so rapidly developing on the European stage. We have already touched on the political motives which appeared at this moment to be drawing the King and the Prince of Orange towards a more or less possible compromise. Now, during the month of November, James II sent the celebrated William Penn—no Papist, but a Quaker, and a philosopher—on an important mission to Holland.

Burnet, then at The Hague, and in some degree at least in the confidence of the Prince, says that James engaged to join forces with the States in a coalition against France, in return for the Prince's support as regards a repeal of the Test and Penal Statutes. The temptation was certainly strong, but the Prince, well aware of English feeling on the subject, dared not acquiesce; and replied, in words which Halifax might have dictated, that 'he readily consented to a toleration of popery, as well as of the dissenters, *provided it were proposed and passed in parliament*, and he promised his assistance, if there was need of it, to get it to pass...but *he looked on the Tests as such a real security and indeed the only one, where the King was of another religion*, that he would join in no counsels with those that intended to repeal those laws...'.

A prudent statesman, even though a Roman Catholic, would surely have grasped at so liberal a compromise; but, as Penn told the Prince, 'the King would have all or nothing'; so the scheme fell through.

This 'thorough' policy King James proceeded to carry out.

Severe pressure upon the point at issue was now applied to Ministers, courtiers and Members of Parliament. About January 1687/8, the Hydes, who, though compliant to an excessive degree, yet refused to apostatize, were dismissed; and their appointments (the Treasury, the Privy Seal, and Ireland) were given, in defiance of the Test Acts, to Popish successors. Meanwhile ordinary Members of Parliament were 'closeted' or personally examined by their Sovereign as to their views; while Members of Parliament, such as Harry Savile, who were also Officers of the Household, received warning as to the certain results of obduracy.

Under the circumstances, the uneasiness of William became urgent. No whisper as to a possible male heir to the throne arose till many months later, but there were rumours, fostered by France, that the Protestant convictions of the King's son-in-law, Prince George, might not prove impregnable; and French agents were hinting that an attempt might be made to supersede the claims of the Princess of Orange by those of her younger sister.[18]

Under these circumstances the Stadtholder, in February 1686/7, entrusted M. Dykvelt, envoy extraordinary from the States to the King of England, with a 'covering' letter to Lord Halifax. This contained the Envoy's credentials for entering into the closest personal relations that prudence and diplomatic decency might permit, with the heads of the Opposition.

Initial difficulties supervened, since Lord Halifax was in disgrace with the Court, to which Dykvelt was formally accredited. Harry Savile indeed, who, though in daily expectation of losing his place, had not yet received his dismissal, might have served as a convenient intermediary, but he happened to be out of town. The Marquis therefore sent his respects to Dykvelt through Lord

Mordaunt, intimating that he did not intend to wait on the Envoy unless he should consider it convenient.

A few days later Harry himself was 'out'; and faced with somewhat rueful courage the loss of an office which had so long been the goal of a modest ambition, and a stipend which formed no inconsiderable part of a slender income.

Notwithstanding these difficulties, however, and the open suspicions with which the King regarded him, Dykvelt succeeded in arranging (at Lord Shrewsbury's residence) a series of meetings; at which the principal attendants were Halifax, Shrewsbury, Danby, Nottingham, Mordaunt, Lumley, Herbert and Admiral Russell. Of these, four were subsequently to become signatories of the final invitation to William.

At this time, however, no such action was in contemplation. Dykvelt's attitude was one of general propitiation. He assured the Church party of the Prince's fidelity to its interest; but promised the Protestant dissenters (in the event of the Princess's succession) a comprehension (presumably of the Moderate Presbyterians) 'in case they stood firm to the common interest'; and foreshadowed a toleration for the remaining sects. He remonstrated with James in the most open and fearless fashion upon the folly of the policy he was pursuing, and adjured the leading Roman Catholics to be content with a legal toleration.

His efforts, however, proved vain. James, now convinced that he could expect no assistance from either his son-in-law or from a Parliamentary Session, once more prorogued; and announced his intention of abrogating, by his own act, the Test and Penal Laws. Accordingly on 4 April these were virtually annulled by a Declaration of Indulgence.

The Envoy thereupon, in full possession of the facts of the situation, prepared to return; bearing private, though cautious, missives from several of the politicians with whom he had been associating. That of Halifax runs as follows:

THE MARQUIS OF HALIFAX *to* THE PRINCE OF ORANGE

31 *May* 1687

I deferred my thanks for the honour of your Highnesse's letter, till I could pay them by the same hand that brought it. Having had the opportunity of discoursing frequently, and at large, with Monsieur Dickfielt, it would be less proper now to enter into particulars, or to make repetitions of that, which hee will be so much better able to explain. I shall, therefore, onely put your Highnesse in mind, that my conjectures about the meeting of the plt. have not hitherto been disappointed; and if I may be allowed to continue them, I am of opinion there will bee none in November, neither this, nor a new one; though that is threatened, upon a supposition, that it shall be made up of Dissenters, and that they will comply with whatever shall be expected of them. Neither of these will bee found true, in my opinion, if the tryal should be made; there are a great many circumstances which make such a scheme very impracticable, and the more they consider it, the more they will be discouraged from attempting it. Besides, the case, in short, is this; the great design cannot bee carried on without numbers; numbers cannot be had without converts, the old stock not being sufficient; converts will not venture till they have such a law to secure them as hath no exception to it; so that an irregularity, or any degree of violence to the law, would so intirely take away the effect of it, that men would as little run the hazard of changing their religion after the making it, as before. This reason alone fixeth my opinion, though other arguments are not wanting. And upon this foundation I have no kind of apprehension, that the Legislative power can ever be brought to pursue the present designs; But our affairs here depend so much upon what may be done abroad, that our thoughts, though never so reasonable, may be changed by what we may hear by the next post. A war in Germany, and much more if one nearer to us, will have such an influence here, that our councels must be fitted to it; and whether or no we shall have an avowed part in it, it is pretty sure we shall have a leaning to one of the parties; and our resolutions at home are to be suited to the interests abroad, which we shall happen to espouse. Men's jealousies here are so raised, that they can hardly believe the King of France's journey to Luxembourgh to have no more in it than bare curiosity to see it; but your Highness hath your eyes so open, and your thoughts so intent upon everything that moveth, that, no doubt, you either see there is no mystery, or, if there is, you have searched to the bottom of it. Monsieur Dickfielt will entertain your Highnesse with all his observations, which he hath made with great diligence, having conversed with men of all complexions, and by that means he knoweth a great deal of the present state of our affairs. The opportunities he hath had, will make him the more welcome here againe, whenever there shall be a fair occasion of bringing him. His free way of conversing, giveth him an easier admittance than he would have, if hee was too reserved; and his being known to be a creature of your Highnesse, encourageth men to talk to him with less restraint. May your Highness continue well and safe, and may no ill happen to you, till I cease to be the most devoted of your servants.

It is difficult to over-estimate the importance of Dykvelt's mission; whose effort, and its failure, clarified the position, and the views, of the contending parties. He was followed during August by another envoy who carried on the correspondence. The next reply of Halifax was sent through Lord Shrewsbury, who had recently been deprived of his regiment:

THE MARQUIS OF HALIFAX *to* THE PRINCE OF ORANGE

It would be unnecessary to give your Highness a recommending character of my Lord of Shrewsbury, who hath already so good a one established and allowed in the world; I shall only say, in short, that hee is, without any competition, the most considerable man of quality that is growing up amongst us; that he hath right thoughts for the public and a most particular veneration for your Highnesse; he is loose and untyed from any faction that might render him partial, or give a wrong bias to his opinion; and I do not doubt, but upon the first discourse you shall have with him, you will be encouraged to treat him without any manner of reserve. There is so little alteration here since Monsieur Dickfielt left us, that I can hardly acquaint you with any thing of moment which would be new to you.... Your Highnesse seemeth to mee to bee in the best method that can be imagined, in being firme to your true interest, unmooveable in every thing that is essential, and cautious to give no advantage which might, with any colour of reason, bee made use of against you. This conduct being continued, can hardly fayle, there being so many things that concurre to make it succeed.... Wee are full of the news from Hungary,[19] which is not equally welcome to the several princes in Christendome. We think it may have a considerable influence upon this part of the world, and if the season was not too farre advanced, we are apt to beleeve France might this very year give some trouble to its neighbours.

What part we here might have in it, I cannot tell, but suppose we shall bee slow to ingage in a war, which, besides the expense, to which wee cannot furnish, is lyable to so many accidents, that we shall not bee persuaded to runne the hazard of it. Your Highnesse hath your thoughts intent upon every new thing that ariseth in the world, and knoweth better than any body how to improve every conjuncture, and turne it to the advantage of that interest of which you are the chiefe support; and as your care and skill will never be wanting, so, I hope, they will meet with their just reward of good successe, which is the top of my wishes, as it is the utmost of my ambition to be serviceable to a Prince to whom I am eternally devoted.

London, 25 *August* 1687

Meanwhile, ever since the appearance of the Declaration of Indulgence, the main anxiety of all parties had centred upon the attitude of the Protestant Nonconformists. On the one side, great exertions seem to have been made by the Court to procure, from the various dissenting bodies, addresses of thanks and approval. On the other, divers pamphlets urged the Dissenters, in the name of the Church, to reject the proffered alliance of the Papist King.

Of these, the only one now remembered is the famous *Letter to a Dissenter*, which, though signed with the enigmatic initials 'T.W.' ('T[he] W[riter]'?), was certainly written by Lord Halifax. His authorship seems to have been from the first suspected, and significant hints that the tract might be liable to prosecution in 'Westminster Hall' showed that the mask of pseudonymity, though thin, was not altogether superfluous.

Its success was immediate, overwhelming, and, for the day, enormous. At least three editions were published within the year, representing, it was said, 20,000 copies. Later critics have endorsed the verdict of contemporaries. Sir James Mackintosh has described it as perhaps the most perfect example of a political tract; Von Ranke, no friendly witness, considers Lord Halifax one of the finest pamphleteers that have ever lived; and the eulogies of Macaulay are equally impressive.

In its sage and statesmanlike pages, the dangers of an alliance with Rome are forcibly painted: the Nonconformists are exhorted to pause ere they sacrifice, to a momentary and personal relief, the liberties of their country. They are reminded that under the reign of the 'next heir', Princess Mary, their reasonable aspirations bid fair to be abundantly satisfied, in legal fashion. They are assured that the Church of England, convinced of her error, has abandoned the attitude of persecution; and that the Protestants, if they offer an unbroken front to Popery, and remain 'still, quiet and undivided—firm at the same time to [their] Religion, [their] Loyalty, and [their] Laws',—must win at length, if only by sheer force of numbers.

As for its effect upon Nonconformist opinion, we need only quote Baxter; who early recognized its authorship, and testifies that the wiser part of the Dissenters 'waited in expectation of seeing the effects of the Marquis's declaration on behalf of the Church party'.

The remainder of the year, from the political point of view, was chiefly remarkable for the King's endeavours to subvert the constitution of the Charterhouse by the presentation of a Roman Catholic beneficiary; the first attempt of its kind, which was frustrated by the firmness of the governors, of whom Halifax was one.* And further, by those renewed 'Regulations' of the Municipalities, the Lieutenancies, and the County Benches, by which the Court hoped to promote the return of a subservient Parliament.

* Carte's *Ormonde*, IV, 684.

For Lord Halifax, it was again unhappily distinguished by acute domestic trouble. Henry Coventry had survived, by only a few months, his brother William; Henry Savile, the elder, now developed a painful internal malady; and in July, five months after his disgrace, he went to Paris for a surgical operation. A few days before the critical date, he wrote a letter to Lord Halifax which presumably proved the last of the long and affectionate correspondence, to which we owe so much. In it he entrusted some commissions to his brother's care, adding with his usual grace: 'You will pardon all these precise orders, but a sick man is a kind of prince in point of authority, and grows peevish if the whole world does not comply with him; so that, very wisely, we never think ourselves so much masters of the world, as when we are at least in some hazard of leaving it.' The operation, in fact, proved successful, and Lord George, who joined his uncle in Paris, thought him in a fair way of recovery. Complications, however, supervened, and on 6/16 October he breathed his last. 'I think', wrote Lord Weymouth to Lord Halifax, 'the whole nation partakes with you, for never was man more, nor more deservedly, beloved.'

Almost at the same time died, without issue, Henry Savile's eldest nephew, Lord Eland, his brother's son and heir, the victim apparently of unbridled self-indulgence. The breach with his father had long since reached such a point that Lord Halifax, a year earlier, with a severity deprecated by Henry Savile, had forbidden Lord William to visit his brother, even then dangerously ill. Lord Weymouth, however, in condoling with Lord Halifax, declares that the tenderness he had displayed towards his disobedient son had justly acquired for him the reputation of the best father in the world.

Lord Halifax now seems to have retained few of the friends of his own youth save this same Lord Weymouth. His affections appear to have henceforth centred completely on the son who had become his heir; and whom the elder Henry, in his last letter, had described as the 'second half' of his father. His marriage with a great heiress, a niece of Lord Nottingham, which took place in the following November, seems to have been the one bright spot in the family prospect.

To his young daughter again, the only surviving child of his second marriage, Lord Halifax appears to have been greatly devoted; and for her (not improbably at this very time) he wrote his *Advice to a Daughter*. This, through the treachery of a scrivener, to whom the manuscript had been entrusted for transcription, was published anonymously and, it is said, inaccurately about the beginning of 1687.[20] This little work, of which the authorship soon became known, attained immense popularity; it ran through between twenty and thirty editions, was translated into both French and Italian; and remained until the advent of Gregory's 'Father's Legacy', a hundred years later, the orthodox manual for the benefit of young girls. It is probable, indeed, that Lord Halifax shared in this respect the fate of his grandson Lord Chesterfield, and was less remembered during a century for his political gifts, than by the instructions he had formulated for a favourite child. A further parallel may be traced; since the father-in-law of Lady Elizabeth Savile has unkindly recorded his opinion that the parental solicitude of Halifax had been 'labour in vain'.

In style, this little treatise is even more finished than the occasional pamphlets of our author. The chapter on *Religion* affords a curious contrast to the opinions so generally imputed to the Marquis; while that on *Marriage* is singularly repellent to modern taste. The later seventeenth century was not an age of sentiment; and the purely business standpoint, from which the marriage contract was usually regarded, is more than faithfully mirrored in the serene cynicism of Lord Halifax. The alternative of a union founded upon mutual attachment is calmly set aside; and it is regarded as practically inevitable that a woman should begin her married life with at least 'a little aversion'. So marked is this insistence that we incline to the surmise that the marriage of his elder daughter had proved unsatisfactory, and that Lady Carberry had not been able to accommodate herself to the situation. Nothing else would seem to explain the almost brutal frankness with which her probable future is pictured to this child of twelve. Nor are the cold-blooded consolations proposed to the wives of unfaithful or intemperate husbands very compatible with warmth of feeling or even with a sense of delicacy on the part of the lady; while even the chapter on *Friendship* is singularly cool.

The sections, however, which turn upon the management of house, family, and servants; on behaviour and conversation; on censure, vanity and affectation; on pride, diversions and dancing, are nearly perfect in their kind, and delight us as much by their witty vivacity as by their shrewd Baconian good sense. The admonitions of Lord Halifax, though addressed to that part of mankind in whose education external graces have ever played so natural a part, show hardly a trace of the foppery—intellectual, social, and moral—to which the virile understanding of Lord Chesterfield too often stooped. Nor can they be reproached with the laxity of morals which has been made a charge against the celebrated *Letters*; though a captious critic might even insinuate that the Marquis (like some other moralists), while arrogating to his own sex a monopoly of intellectual superiority, liberally abandons in favour of a weaker, the entire field of the moral virtues.

We must now however return to public affairs, which were slowly approaching their great crisis; and in especial to the course of that political correspondence between the Prince of Orange and the Protestant leaders, which had been initiated by Dykvelt, and maintained, with some affectation of secrecy, during the remainder of the year 1687. In its origin purely constitutional, this character, in the case of Lord Halifax, it retained to the last. How soon it passed, in other hands, into the category of intrigue we do not know. But we must always remember that the Prince's interest in English affairs was primarily neither dynastic, political, nor ecclesiastical. His attention, as that of all continental observers, was at this time focused on the impending resumption of the titanic struggle between France and the rest of Europe; his object being to ensure that our weight should be thrown into the anti-Gallican scale.

Lord Shrewsbury, one of those who eventually signed the invitation to William, once told Halifax that the Prince would have invaded England had the Prince of Wales never been born. It is in fact believed that the dying Elector of Brandenburg had in August 1686 repeated to the Prince of Orange advice—first suggested by him on the death of Charles II—that the Prince should land in England with 10,000 men.[21] He had naturally preferred more peaceful methods of persuasion; but he had been countered by the obstinacy of his father-in-law, and was therefore now open to more extreme suggestions on the part of his English correspondents.

When, by whom, and in what terms the suggestion of an armed descent first emanated from *Englishmen* we cannot say. We only know that early in 1687, Henry Sidney (who had converted William to the Exclusion policy in 1680) came to The Hague; that in June 1687 Danby (emulating as he says the caution of Halifax) entrusted Dykvelt with a letter to the Prince, containing an enigmatic reference to some 'overture' or proposal, unspecified; that a passage in Burnet's original memoirs, written on or immediately before 26 December 1687, explicitly suggests that the Prince may find himself compelled to intervene in the affairs of Britain, since a rebellion of which he should not retain control must certainly entail a Republic; and that only after this statement does Burnet mention the Royal Proclamation which announced the pregnancy of the Queen. But it was not till April 1688 that Admiral Russell 'positively' asked the Prince 'What might be expected of him?' and received the answer that, if asked by responsible persons, he might be able to 'come over' by the end of September.

In these subterraneous consultations Halifax had no part. It is certain, however, that the conspirators, at some period of their long-drawn-out discussions, made some approaches to Halifax, but at what stage and in what manner is never clear. Henry Sidney, we know, was the go-between; but Burnet's own accounts of the matter are not identical. In his contemporary Memoirs, he states that Halifax was 'tried at a distance,* but he did not encourage a further freedom; and upon a general discourse he expressed his dislike of the design as unpracticable, and depending upon so many accidents† that he thought it a needless putting of all things upon so dangerous an issue'. If we combine Burnet's original 'distance' and 'general discourse' we must presume that Sidney never broached the project as an *actual* but as a mere *speculative* possibility; but it is impossible to reconcile the 'great distance' of Burnet's *final* version with its 'would advise the Prince's coming over'—than which we can conceive nothing more explicit.

But whatever the nature of Sidney's hints it is clear that the 'possibility' never evoked from Lord Halifax the slightest sign of acquiescence. That he may, however, have *suspected* where he *knew* nothing, seems quite probable from the following important letter, dated 12 April 1688. The date, we see, almost coincides with Russell's fateful query. The italics are our own:

THE MARQUIS OF HALIFAX *to* THE PRINCE OF ORANGE

I avoid giving your Highnesse unnecessary trouble, and though this hath a good conveyance, yet it may, perhaps, bee so long in its way to you, that it will not bee pertinent to repeat what you will have had from other hands....In some particulars, to men at a distance, the engine

* The final recession of his History says 'at a great distance', and adds 'if he would advise the Prince's coming over'.

† The final version of the History reads 'of seas and winds'.

seemeth to moove fast, but by looking neerer, one may see it doth not stirre upon the whole matter, so that *here is a rapid motion without advancing a step, which is the onely miracle that church hath yet shewed to us. Every attempt turneth back upon them. They change the magistracy in the corporations, and still for the worse, as to their own designs. The irregular methods have spent themselves without effect; they have runne so fast that they begin to bee out of breath, and the exercise of extraordinary powers, both ecclesiastical and civill, is so farre from fixing the right of them, that men are more united in objecting to them. The world is still where it was, with this onely difference, that it groweth every day more averse to that which is endeavoured to bee imposed upon them.* The very Papists who have estates act unwillingly like pressed men, and have such an eye to what may happen in a revolution, that their present advantages hardly make amends for their fears; upon the whole, they are so divided between the fear of losing their opportunity by delay, or spoyling it with too much haste, that their steps are wavering and uncertaine, and distrusting the very instruments they use, they are under great mortifications, notwithstanding the appearance of carrying everything without opposition. Being thus discouraged by their ill successe in their attempts, some say they are altering their scheme, and not finding their expectations answered by the Dissenters, they have thoughts of returning to their old friends, the high Church men. But the truth is, the Papists have of late been so hard and fierce upon them, that the very species of those formerly mistaken men is destroyed; they have so broken that loom in pieces, that they cannot now set it up againe to work upon it. *In the mean time the men at the helme are certainly divided amongst themselves, which will produce great effects, if men will let it work, and not prevent the advantages that may bee expected, by being too unquiet, or doing things out of season; the great thing to bee done now, is to do nothing, but wait for the good consequences of their divisions and mistakes. Unseasonable stirrings, or anything that looketh like the Protestants being the Aggressors, will tend to unite them, and by that means will bee a disappointment to those hopes, which otherwise can hardly fayle: Nothing, therefore, in the present conjuncture can bee more dangerous than unskilful Agitators, warm men who would bee active at a wrong time, and want patience to keep their zele from running away with them.* It is said by some, that there is an intention of making a new attempt to beget a better understanding with your Highnesse; that in order to it, the present Envoy, as lesse acceptable, is to bee removed, and another sent, who, if he should bee less known, may, perhaps, for that very reason, bee the more dangerous; If this should be true, and that softer proposals should bee made from hence, it will deserve all your caution to receave them so as neither to give advantage by rejecting them too roughly on one side, or on the other, by giving any colour for them to pretend there is a consent given to any thing that may be inconvenient. After the reports raised here, without any manner of ground, first of your Highnesse being a Papist, then of your being desirous to have the Test repealed, there is nothing of that kind which may not be thought possible; so that if there should now bee any neerer treaty, it might, perhaps, bee made use of with more advantage by them, to mislead men at a distance into a wrong beliefe. In lower instances,* it hath not been unusuall, in such cases, to set proposals on foot, of which no other effect is expected, than to bring men under doubts and suspicions from their own friends. The instruments that shall be made use of, their interests and dependencies being well considered and examined, will give a great deal of light, if anything of this kind should bee attempted; and *it happeneth well, that they will have to do with one who knoweth so well how to judge of men and things, as not to be within the danger of being easily surprized, neither by any upon this occasion, nor by any other of our countrymen who speak what is dictated to them by men of severall interests; or endeavour to value themselves upon their correspondencies and influences here, which, I doubt, have seldome foundation strong enough for your Highness to build upon. There can be nothing better recommended to you, than the continuance of the method which you practise; neither to comply in anything that it unfit, nor to provoke further anger by any act that is unnecessary.* This will not, perhaps, bee sufficient to prevent ill-will, but it will, in a great measure, secure you from the ill effects of it. Your Highnesse must allow mee to applaud my good fortune in not having hitherto made a wrong conjecture about the sitting of the parliament....The other great point which at present maketh the discourse is, whether England will have a warre with the States; in this, the more thinking sort of men are of opinion there will be none. There is disposition enough for it, for reasons which need not to bee explained; but there are so many discouraging circumstances, and the prejudice from ill success would bee so much greater than the utmost which can bee hoped in case of prospering, that the men in power must go against all the common methods of arguing, if they venture upon an experiment which may be so destructive to them. I have tired your Highnesse so long, that it is time for mee to close with my wishes for your own and the Princesse's health, which are of that consequence to the world, that nothing can bee desperate whilst you are well and safe. For my selfe, I must ever be unalterably devoted to you.

London, 12 *April* 1888

The 'wait and see' attitude of Lord Halifax at this crucial moment (which runs curiously parallel to that of Clarendon during the period immediately preceding the Restoration) has been severely criticized, not to say satirized, by eminent historians, such as Macaulay; who in their own enthusiasm for the Revolution of 1688 presuppose that Halifax *must* have sympathized with designs for which he refused to compromise his own safety. As a matter of fact, the line really taken by Lord Halifax was entirely in accordance with his own previous history. In a similar though undoubtedly less urgent crisis he had opposed the Exclusion project, largely because it might possibly occasion a civil war; and the bloodless

* He probably hints at himself.

issue of William III's expedition cannot blind us to the fact that it must have appeared beforehand as rendering a civil war inevitable. Lord Halifax, in the letter just given, shows clearly his belief, that the state of feeling in the country was such as to preclude any Parliamentary sanction to the King's designs; and that without such sanction, any success he might attain would be merely apparent and evanescent. He believed in fact that the country could be saved by purely passive resistance.

Undoubtedly too, he could then have laid stress on arguments which the efflux of time has finally exploded. King James II, who actually survived his deposition thirteen years, was in 1688 an elderly man of impaired constitution; and there was a strong and in some respects reasoned belief in a fatality attending his offspring. His hopes presupposed, not only the birth of a son, healthy enough to evade the fate which had already overtaken six out of the King's eight children, but also able to survive, until the date of his own majority; and this, in 1688, seemed extremely improbable.

Nor is it open to dispute that the attitude of purely constitutional opposition, so long as it offered any prospect of success, was strongly preferable from a national point of view. To defend a legal position by expedients which are entirely illegal is a policy which must be reserved for the last resort; and men will always dispute as to when that final stage has been reached.

On the other hand, Halifax seems to have minimized certain possibilities which doubtless weighed heavily with the conspirators. The Prince himself, of course, was entirely actuated by the urgency of the Continental situation and the desire of engaging this country in the great coalition against France. More strictly national interests no doubt appealed to the Englishmen concerned. The manipulation of the Corporations, even though so far, according to the belief of Halifax, it had proved unsuccessful, might, if steadily pursued and reinforced by the creation of Peers, which the King was understood to contemplate, have finally produced a subservient Parliament. And in the second place, the existence of the standing army was a very ominous factor. For if, so far, it were imbued by a National spirit, a sufficient infiltration of Popish officers, and the introduction of foreign or Irish mercenaries, might have produced a force dependent on, and therefore devoted to, the prerogative. A third argument would not have appealed to Lord Halifax; who never affected to doubt the legitimacy of the Prince of Wales.

But while we point out the weak points in the 'wait and see' attitude adopted by Lord Halifax, it is necessary to combat with some energy the animadversions which Macaulay, so enthusiastic an admirer of his writings, passes on the character of their author. We grant, that even in his early youth, his prudent Coventry blood may have disinclined him for the 'insecure and agitated life of a conspirator' in which others at that time apparently would have involved him. A 'sceptic' in the original sense of the word he undoubtedly was; but to stigmatize as a voluptuary the man at whom lampooners sneered as

losing all soft days and sensual nights

in the unnecessary pursuit of business;—who was notoriously indifferent to foppery and abstemious in his habits; who only made merry once a year with the old Duke of Ormonde over a bottle apiece and was heartily contemptuous of the prevalent vices of the day—is wide of the mark indeed. He was not, says Macaulay, a man to die a martyr in any cause. Most certainly he was not the man to risk life, the family fortunes, and the future of his favourite son, in an undertaking of which he did not approve. But it would be gross injustice to presume that if offered his life—say, as the price of a feigned conversion to the Roman faith, or of complicity in the unconstitutional designs of King James—he would not have faced the grim alternative with cool and philosophic fortitude.

We must now, however, return to the general course of public affairs, where a sudden crisis was at hand; one not anticipated, it is clear, by any of the parties concerned.

On 27 April, about a fortnight after the date of Lord Halifax's last-quoted letter, appeared a *second* Declaration of Indulgence, of which, as it was a mere recapitulation of the first, the motive is not very clear. A few days later, however, it was followed by an order in Council, directing it to be read on two successive Sundays in the churches and chapels of the Kingdom.

The London clergy at once determined to disobey the Order, and seven Bishops at ten o'clock on the evening of 18 May presented a petition to the King defending a definite refusal. The bitterly mortified Monarch is said to have frequently adverted next morning to a warning once uttered by Lord Halifax: 'Your Father suffered for the church [and] not the church for [your Father].'

Lord Halifax had not been consulted by the Bishops, but he and Lord Nottingham—the oracle of the Moderate High Churchmen—

when approached by some of the beneficed clergy, had opined that no time remained for concerted action, and that spasmodic refusals would only ruin those who disobeyed.

Their anticipations were, however, refuted, for in the event only 4 per cent. of the London clergy read the Declaration. Foiled and exasperated, James formed the fatal resolution of indicting the seven Bishops (as instigators) for libel. They appeared before the Council on 8 June; upon their refusal to enter into recognizances were committed to the Tower; and a few hours after this incarceration the usual ceremonies announced to the world that the King had a son and heir.

Within a few days, Lord Halifax called at the Tower and advised each of the Prelates to secure three Peers to be bail for him on their next appearance in Court, a policy to which they then demurred; and he then probably laid before them the draft of a very lengthy and politely exasperating petition (possibly intended for eventual publication), which, however, the Bishops seem to have had the wisdom to decline. We quote a few paragraphs. After appropriate preliminary reference to the issues of duty and conscience, the appeal continues:

Besides other arguments, we considered what hath been declared upon this subject...in Parliament. First his late Majesty's solemn assurances to both houses that the Declaration for liberty of conscience should not be drawn into consequence or example;...(and) that the said Declaration was cancelled; and...the thanks of the house voted as for a full and entire answer. [Also] we remembered the votes and addresses of the last House of Commons, and...in the House of Lords, of which we have the honour to be Members; where the sense of the House appeared so visibly, that your Majesty did not think it necessary to stay for...a vote, having been pleased to prorogue the Parliament, before the day to which the debate was adjourned....As Bishops it is not justifiable for us to venture upon doing any act [which] may be in any degree a prejudice to the Church....As Peers of Parliament it is a tender thing for us to do anything which may give the House of Peers...matter of objection to us. [As subjects] we think ourselves obliged to suit our behaviour to your Majesty's promise that you will support the Church of England, *as it is by Law Established*....We presume that your Majesty, by your discerning judgment, and...the means used [to test public opinion] must be sensible that we are not singular in this opinion which is now imputed as a crime to us; and we assure ourselves that you will yet be more convinced of it, at the [promised] meeting of Parliament....It is there your Majesty will have the truest information, how far the proceedings against us have been regularly pursued; and there also we shall have the opportunity of showing how far we are from being averse to a fair liberty of conscience for Protestant Dissenters, etc.

Despite the passages of elaborate respect with which this exasperating retort was liberally garnished, we think that in declining to employ it, the Bishops showed more sagacity than the Peer.

Eventually, on the first day of term the Bishops were brought before the Court of King's Bench, which then sat in Westminster Hall. The prelates had apparently reconsidered the suggestion of Halifax, and three Peers were at hand as security for each Bishop; Halifax with his son-in-law Carberry being two of the three held in readiness for the Bishop of St Asaph's; but the Bishops' own recognizances were in fact deemed sufficient.

The trial which took place on 29–30 June, under circumstances of great excitement, has been described in Macaulay's most brilliant manner. The Marquis seems to have headed the twenty-nine Peers who lent the support of their sympathy to the defendants; while in dramatic contrast, his brother-in-law, Lord President Sunderland—who, a few days earlier had professed his adhesion to the Roman communion—appeared as the reluctant witness for a prosecution which his shrewdness had deprecated in vain. The critical moment came at last; and a contemporary records how, as the words '*not guilty*' passed the lips of the foreman of the Jury 'the Marquis of Halifax waving his hat above his head, cried Huzzah. The Lords and Gentlemen took the shout from him. It in an instant filled the whole Hall with the loudest acclamations of joy, which were immediately taken again by the crowds waiting in Palace Yard and in Westminster; from whence like a roll and roar of thunder it was carried in and through the City of London and spread over the parts adjacent, and as fast as it could fly, over the whole Kingdom.'

To Lord Halifax it must have seemed that the policy of passive resistance, which he was championing, had secured another and a magnificent victory. But some of his former friends thought otherwise or had gone too far to retreat.

For that night, while the nation was still in a ferment of delight at the result, seven men assembled—probably at Lord Shrewsbury's. And there Henry Sidney, the brother-in-law of Halifax, Shrewsbury, his kinsman and former Ward, Compton, Bishop of London, whom he had counselled, Danby, his life-long rival, Lord Devonshire and Admiral Russell of the old Exclusion party, and

Lumley, hitherto ranked among the assertors of prerogative, set their cyphers to the celebrated 'Invitation'. In this, without defining the object of their manœuvres, or the capacity in which the Prince of Orange is to act—but with the assertion that nineteen-twentieths of the people desire 'a change'—they request the Prince to give, by an armed descent, such assistance as Russell and Zulestein had declared him ready and willing to concede.

Lord Halifax of course was entirely ignorant of the momentous step; though Nottingham, at this time his close associate, had been actually initiated, but had, on conscientious scruples, withdrawn at the last moment—a perilous proceeding.

Three weeks later, indeed, we find Halifax still writing to the Prince as follows:

THE MARQUIS OF HALIFAX *to* THE PRINCE OF ORANGE

So many things have happened of late, that it is reasonable enough to conclude, upon the first apprehension of them, that they should produce great alterations in reference to the publique, and yet with all this, upon a strict observation of all circumstances, I see nothing to raise more hopes on one side, or to incline the other to despayre....The several parties though differing never so much in other things, seem to agree in their resolution of preserving, by all legall means, the securityes of their Religion and their Laws. The last businesse concerning the bishops hath had such an effect, that it is hardly to bee imagined; the consequences are not seen to their full extent by the men in power though they are not a little mortified by the ill successe of it. I look upon it as that which hath brought all the Protestants [together], and bound them up into a knot, that cannot easily be untyed. It is one of those kind of faults that can never bee repayred. All that can bee done to mend it will probably make it worse, as is seen already by every step that hath been since made to recover the reputation they have lost by it. It is given out, that there will bee yet some further proceedings against the bishops; but in that I am an unbeliever, as well as concerning the meeting of the Plt;...In short, I still remaine persuaded that there is no effectuall progresse made towards the great designe; and even the thing that party relyeth upon, is subject to so many accidents and uncertainties, that according to humane probability wee are secure, notwithstanding the ill appearances which fright most, when they are least examined. I wish your Highnesse all happiness, and to myself the continuance of your good opinion, which cannot be more valued by any man living, than it is by your most devoted servant.

London, 25 *July* 1888

The last sentence but one probably refers to the precarious state of the new born Prince's health.

CHAPTER XI

THE REVOLUTION

THE twenty-four hours which included the acquittal of the Bishops, and the secret signing of the Appeal to the Prince of Orange, had left Halifax, as far as public opinion was concerned, at the acme of his reputation. He stood forth as the representative of the Constitutional Opposition, to which the mass of the population no doubt inclined; and, incidentally, his actions had conciliated—in all but their extreme sections—both the 'Court' and 'Country' parties; with one or other of which he had always hitherto found himself at variance.

Meanwhile, between the events of 29 June and the actual sailing of the Prince of Orange's expedition on 27 September, there intervened a strange interval. On the Prince's side this was employed in those vast and semi-clandestine preparations, that network of complicated diplomacy, by which the Stadtholder, dexterously availing himself of a well-justified alarm at the French King's military preparations, secured the acquiescence of the Continental Confederates in his daring adventure.

Parallel to these elaborate and successful intrigues there ran the vain attempts of Louis XIV to rouse the infatuated James to a sense of his danger; the secret organization of Yorkshire, where the Prince should originally have landed, by Danby and his friends;* and the extraordinary passivity with which the mass of the English people, and Lord Halifax at their head, apparently regarded the great prologue which was slowly evolving.

Lord Halifax himself had in fact attained a position of complete independence. He had evaded on the one hand all possible complicity with the conspirators, and he now continued to obviate all overtures which might emanate from the Court.

These took their rise from the fears of Lord Sunderland. That astute time-server was in fact the only man who seems to have recognized, in some measure at least, the danger of the situation. He was shrewd enough to realize the odium excited by the prosecution of the Bishops; and had become aware to some extent, through his wife's intimacy with Henry Sidney, of the intrigues

* Browning's *Danby*, p. 89.

between his associates and the Stadtholder. He was now all for that form of conciliation, which we of to-day call 'appeasement'. For Lord Halifax was undoubtedly the 'one very eminent member of the Country [interest] who I would have persuaded to come into business, which he might have done, to resist the violence of those in power'; but who 'despair[ing] of being able to do any good... would not engage'. More curtly, Lord Halifax himself records that Sunderland 'would have spoken to me before he left his place but I declined'. The Marquis was indeed persuaded to meet James II at the house of a well-known and 'very cunning' intriguer, one Lady Oglethorpe, once a favourite waiting woman of the Duchess of Portsmouth; but the conference proved entirely abortive. A rumour that his son, the new Lord Eland, eventually joined the Prince's expedition, appears for the first time fourteen years after the event, and two years after Lord Eland's death (as second Marquis); and it may be confidently dismissed as erroneously founded on the visit to The Hague to which we have already referred.

James II, meanwhile, remained ostensibly[22] unmoved by the signs of impending disaster; but having at length made up his mind to face a session of Parliament, he, on 20 or 21 September, issued a Proclamation to that effect. This contained a celebrated and very ambiguous clause, which appeared to offer some 'Equivalent' security in return for the repeal of the Test and Penal Laws. This suggestion had long been current in Roman Catholic circles, and had already evoked the sarcasms of the Marquis. Months before he had replied to a friend who argued for such an 'Equivalent': 'Look at my nose, it is a very ugly one, but I would not take one five hundred times better as an equivalent, because my own is fast to my face.' He now prepared and issued anonymously, early in October, his *Anatomy of an Equivalent*.

Less rhetorical than the *Character of a Trimmer*, less popular in its arguments than the *Letter to a Dissenter*, the *Anatomy of an Equivalent* is perhaps, on the whole, as a literary production, the ablest and the most characteristic of the shorter Halifax pamphlets. Occasional in its origin, it is particularly remarkable for its abstract —we may almost say its scientific—treatment of a burning contemporary theme. The phenomena of the actual situation are indicated, slightly indeed, but with a discriminating accuracy; the laws of which they are the expression are developed with an admirable discernment. Our author takes his stand neither upon

Constitutional precedent, nor upon logical formulae, but upon the broad facts of human nature and actual experience; clothing his nervous argument with the ornaments of a quiet and finished satire, exquisitely grateful to the weary student of polemical literature. It attracted, however, far less attention than the *Letter to a Dissenter*; and though subsequently republished in several collections and included in the Halifax Miscellanies, it never reached a second edition.[23] The juncture for which it was written was evanescent, being almost at once superseded by more startling developments.

By 30 August/9 September 1688, the imminence of the impending invasion was realized by the French Ambassador at The Hague, whose reports reached James, through M. Barillon, on 4/14 September. But, astonishing to relate, it was not till six days later that His Majesty could be compelled to admit even the possibility of an actual descent, nor would he even then confess to the slightest uneasiness. He merely announced to Barillon the military measures which, under such problematical circumstances, he proposed to adopt; with the addition that on the first news of a landing, Halifax, Danby, Shrewsbury and Nottingham, with such other Lords as might be suspected of complicity, should be immediately arrested.

A week later the King received intelligence that the Dutch fleet had actually weighed anchor. Thereupon, on the plea that all the energies of the country must be concentrated on the repulse of the invader, he took the very unpopular step of cancelling the Parliamentary writs.

By this time, however, he found himself pursued by the urgent remonstrances of Sunderland, whom terror had finally persuaded that public opinion must be appeased at any and every cost. It was upon his representation (or so at least Lord Sunderland avers) that the design of widespread arrests on suspicion was abandoned. Lord Delamere dilates on the folly shown by the Government in pretermitting this precaution; and as he would certainly have been one of the first—and most justly—suspected, his opinion has at least the merit of impartiality.

But this was only one of the concessions upon which the agitated Sunderland insisted. Such of the Bishops as had been in the Tower, and were now available, were ostentatiously consulted, and the suspension of the Bishop of London was removed. Disgraced Justices and Deputy Lieutenants had their commissions renewed, the City Charter and a large number of provincial charters were restored. The hated Ecclesiastical Commission received its death blow; orders were issued for the re-establishment of the Magdalen Fellows; Roman Catholic schools and chapels were closed, and an amnesty declared. Sweeping, however, as these concessions appear, they shared the usual fate of favours obviously extorted; and men realized fully (as Mazure wittily observes) that their obligation was to the Prince and not to the King.

These steps, however, evoked a transient flutter of loyalty in high circles; Nottingham, and it is said Danby, kissed hands. Lord Halifax, as Mazure remarks, showed a greater sense of decency; he awaited an invitation from the Court, but said openly that he had no share in the Prince's enterprise.

He was not, however, approached by the Government till 21 October, when he was summoned, with the other members of the House of Lords, for some purpose unspecified, and the nature of which, as Halifax confessed, he could not imagine. In fact, the King, alarmed by a pamphlet from Holland in which the story of a supposititious birth was boldly affirmed, had ordered witnesses to the circumstances of the Queen's delivery to be examined before the Council. He even proposed that the evidence should be printed; but Lord Halifax energetically replied that if this precaution was necessary for the rabble, persons of honour did not *require* it. 'The Marquis of Halifax', writes Penn, 'kissed the King's hand; this fills all places at present.' But, as Charles Bertie adds, 'little conversation passed between them'.

Sunderland, in these conciliatory measures, had, however, overreached himself, for they had embittered the ultra-Roman party, to which he had so long allied himself. Their invectives visibly affected the King; and when on 25 October news arrived of the postponement of the descent, by reason of a violent storm, the Lord President found himself summarily cashiered. After two vain attempts to re-establish his influence, he at length, six weeks after his fall, fled, strange to say, to *Amsterdam*. Two letters which he addressed to his brother-in-law Halifax, one before and one after his flight, are among the most abject exhibitions of grovelling servility which it is possible to conceive.

On 1 November the Prince resumed his interrupted voyage, and the same day his Declaration circulated in London. This manifesto, as is well known, recapitulated the extra-legal proceedings of the King, cast doubts upon the legitimacy of the Prince of Wales, referred the questions at issue to the decision of a free and legal

Parliament, and asserted that the Prince of Orange had undertaken his expedition *upon the invitation of many lords spiritual and temporal.*

Thereupon the King, whose state of indecision had become pitiable, summoned for interrogation all available Peers. Nottingham and Halifax were examined together on the evening of Sunday, 4 November, at Colchester, where James was reviewing troops. 'Halifax', says Macaulay, quoting a despatch of the Spanish Ambassador, 'though conscious of innocence, refused at first to make any answer. "Your Majesty asks me", said he, "whether I have committed High Treason. If I am suspected, let me be brought before my Peers. And how can your Majesty place any dependence on the answer of a culprit whose life is at stake? Even if I had invited His Highness over, I should without scruple plead Not Guilty."'

The response has at first a melodramatic flavour very inappropriate to Lord Halifax. But rumours of an intention to commit him to the Tower were current, and may very possibly have reached the Marquis himself. James, however, reassured his former Minister, declaring 'he did not at all consider Halifax as a culprit and that he had asked the question as one gentleman asks another who had been calumniated whether there be any foundation for the calumny'. 'In that case', said Halifax, 'I have no objection to aver as a gentleman to a gentleman, on my honour, which is as sacred as my oath, that I have not invited the Prince of Orange over.' 'The answers', added the Spaniard, 'are certain, though questioned at Court.'

Here, however, the complacence of Halifax and his fellows reached its bound. None was prepared to produce, for publication, a formal repudiation of the expedition; and despite the urgent appeals of the Monarch 'no one of the Lords', say the Dutch despatches, 'deigned to offer his service or assistance, but only observed how distressed they were to see that His Majesty's affairs had reached so unhappy a condition'. That James dismissed these discouraging counsellors 'with much displeasure', is not perhaps surprising.

Within twenty-four hours of this audience the Prince landed at Torbay, by the 8th he had reached Exeter, unopposed, and there he remained till the 21st awaiting those English reinforcements which at first came in so tardily.

But if the Prince's reception by no means answered his expectations, the temper evinced by those who still remained ostensibly loyal proved equally disquieting to the Court. 'The People', as Halifax had shrewdly hinted four years earlier in his *Character of a Trimmer*, 'can seldom agree to move together against a Government, but they can, to sit still and let it be undone.' This phrase describes with admirable force the state of public opinion at the epoch of the Revolution. For the Prince himself, who was personally unknown to the populace, and whose action was tacitly condemned by a large proportion of the upper classes, very little enthusiasm existed; but for the King there was none. Every Protestant of distinction, with few exceptions, resented personal injuries at His Majesty's hands; those by whom the intervention of the Prince was least approved, sympathized at least with its professed objects; and his denunciation of the King's measures evoked an echo as sincere as did his prescription of a Parliamentary remedy. Reasons political, conscientious, or prudential restrained many from drawing their swords in favour of the Prince, but they were equally unprepared to draw them against him; and in minds thus paralysed by conflicting motives, the irresolution of the Court acted as a damper to the last flickerings of zeal. The majority were, in fact, 'trimmers' through force of circumstances; and it is to this fact—which has never, we believe, received the attention it deserves—that the bloodless character of the great change must be in large measure ascribed.

The natural outcome of all this was a desire for accommodation between the parties. The expedient of a 'free Parliament' seemed the most likely basis for an understanding; and on 8 November, two days after the news of the Prince's landing, the brothers-in-law of the King, Lords Clarendon and Rochester, with certain of the High Church Bishops, consulted on the propriety of an address to the King. This was to urge that in order to prevent the effusion of blood, a Parliament might be summoned.

It was decided to sound Lord Halifax; but when Lord Clarendon waited on him (10 November) he found that the Marquis had been already approached by the Bishop of Peterborough, and was himself proposing a consultation with the Archbishop in order to construct a similar memorial. He had, indeed, arranged a meeting at Dr Sherlock's with certain other bishops for seven o'clock the same evening, 'to see what they would make of it'. 'But', said his Lordship, 'when we have done, I know not who will join in it; if we cannot make a number, the going with a few will disparage the thing.' Moreover, 'it would not be proper for all the Lords to join in the address'. After a certain amount of shilly-shallying the objections of the Marquis became apparent. Could Lord Clarendon, he asked on the following day, 'think it fit that my Lord Chancellor (Jeffreys) should sign the petition?' Clarendon professed his perfect indifference. 'Then', said my Lord, 'I will not join with any who have sat in the ecclesiastical commission. I have no exceptions to my Lord Rochester, but he has sat in that court. Those proceedings must be questioned and therefore it is not fit that any in that commission should sign this petition.' He was strongly, but vainly, supported by Lord Nottingham; and when, on the evening of the 16th, another meeting of the proposed signatories took place, a member of that very same Commission took the chair. Some maintained that Lord Halifax attended, and moved that those Lords who had joined the Prince should take their seats in the proposed Parliament; and that upon the rejection of his motion he left the room. In any case his signature was not appended to the Address, which was presented to the King as he was about to leave London for the Army headquarters. His Majesty, who had from the first energetically repudiated the idea of accommodation, rejected it, in somewhat abrupt fashion, on the plea that no Parliament could be independent whilst menaced by a foreign force.

But while the Lords dallied, and the King procrastinated, others were acting. Events in the provinces were moving faster. Persons of consideration, both Whig and Tory, in the West of England, were joining the Prince's standard; the North, tardily enough, was beginning to rise. Danby, despite the opposition of Reresby, the former confidant of Halifax, was seizing York. Lord Delamere was 'up' in Chester. Devonshire headed the malcontents in Derby and Nottinghamshire, while Colonel Lord Cornbury, son and heir of Lord Clarendon and nephew by marriage to the King, was stirring up military unrest. The King himself, bewildered by all these untoward tidings, had no sooner reached headquarters than he decided on retreating upon London. The defection of his nephew, the Duke of Grafton, of his own favourite Churchill, of his son-in-law Prince George, and of his daughter Princess Anne, proved the culumating point; and clinched his determination to take the fatal step whereto he had for some time been urged by the emissaries of Louis XIV. That England should be forced into the obviously impending Continental struggle had long been the French aim; and he was now manœuvring to secure the King, his wife and heir, as hostages for her fidelity. To this end financial aid was being liberally supplied, and the agent of Modena and France, Rizzini, had not ceased to urge—with success—the immediate despatch of the Queen and little Prince to the nearest Continental port.[24]

Meanwhile, it was obviously essential that steps for this purpose should be very carefully masked. James therefore on 27 November—basing his action on the petition so peremptorily dismissed ten days earlier—summoned a conference of the Peers then in town. Nine Bishops attended, with between thirty and forty temporal Peers, among whom was Lord Halifax. The King announced himself ready to acquiesce in the re-issue of Parliamentary writs, and asked further advice of the meeting.

A cleavage between the Moderate opposition and the former Court party became immediately obvious. One of the former, who had refused to subscribe to the memorial, asked the subscribers to explain themselves. Several defended their action, including Lord Rochester, who directly suggested a negotiation with the Prince. Lord Clarendon—irritated perhaps by the earlier rejection of the memorial, spoke with a violence which was said to be too much like a pedagogue addressing a pupil. Lord Halifax, who followed, was evidently anxious to dissociate himself from the Hydes. His language was described by a contemporary as 'tender and obliging' in the extreme, by James himself as marked by 'great respect and seeming concern', and by Lord Clarendon as 'flattering'. Macaulay reminds us that what might be flattery to the powerful is a debt of humanity to the fallen; but Savile's opening sentence—*at least as Clarendon has reported it*—was certainly disingenuous. He said he had not joined in the petition 'because he believed it would displease the King, and he should always be very tender of doing that'. He admitted that 'he thought the meeting of a Parliament at this time very impracticable, though he must own he would never at any time advise against the calling of a Parliament; that the sending commissioners to the Prince of Orange might do well, if the King would make some concessions by way of preliminaries, and would make all things more easy; that the doing of some things at one time might be interpreted to be prudent, which at another time might be thought too complying'. Fully seconded by Lord Nottingham he politely, but significantly, intimated that, while a negotiation appeared the only possible remedy, he was 'sensible it would prove a bitter draught to His Majesty, who must swallow many disagreeable propositions and yield to such conditions as would be exceeding grievous to him'.

Indeed, neither Halifax nor Nottingham failed, as even Clarendon confesses, to lay all miscarriages 'open; though in smoother words than I had done'. In fine, according to Cunningham.[25] Halifax declined to offer specific advice, saying that Counsel was to 'be sought for of God who alone knew what every man ought to avoid and what to follow in particular cases'. Other suggestions, however, do seem to have been offered to the meeting by Halifax himself and others; and Nottingham appears to have put forward, as acceptable preliminaries, (1) the dismissal of all Roman Catholic officials, (2) an entire separation from the interests of France, and (3) a general amnesty. To this last proposition James showed special reluctance, and though the meeting favoured, in general, the idea of a negotiation, when it broke up the reissue of writs seemed the only point really settled.

This mattered the less, since the whole conference had been, in fact, called merely as a blind. For, as we now know, these consultations could have had no influence on the ultimate issue; since James had already taken the fatal resolution of throwing himself and his family into the arms of France. To continue the deception, none the less, it was necessary to select Commissioners for the proposed negotiation. The list originally drawn up seems to have included Lords Halifax and Rochester, with Godolphin and two Bishops. The spiritual Peers, however, were soon omitted. Halifax refused to serve with Rochester; and Lord Nottingham—probably on the motion of Halifax—replaced him.

Several interviews took place between the King and Halifax, who was also received by the Queen. At their first meeting on 28 November, Halifax by his own account spoke more 'home' to the King than even Clarendon had ventured to do. At another audience Nottingham was also present. In the course of these discussions, according to Halifax, the King was bluntly informed that there were only two alternatives; 'either to make a great condescension without reserve, or to venture at the head of those troops that had not revolted'. To this second suggestion the King replied 'that the last was not to be done, for no man would engage against all reason'; while Halifax adds the sarcastic note 'he would not do the first neither'. It is certain that the two noblemen were offered, and refused, the highest posts in the kingdom. Both, however, definitely accepted a place on the conciliatory mission, and their credentials were at once drawn up. As Godolphin, the third Commissioner, was generally regarded as a 'persona' peculiarly 'grata' to the Prince of Orange, the composition of the Commission was generally considered as appropriate to its purpose. Why Clarendon chose this moment for joining the Prince is not clear, unless it was due to jealousy.

The exact terms of the Commission have not been recovered. Halifax, by his own account, had clearly warned James that his Highness would certainly decline any arrangement which should render it possible for His Majesty to do such things as he had done 'heretofore against the laws'. James, on his part, had assured Halifax that 'he was willing to make large concessions for peace'. The *Gazette* of 30 November, in reporting the appointment of the Commission, proclaimed a general pardon, and a summons of Parliament, with the express proviso that persons in arms with the Prince were qualified to attend its deliberations. So far, therefore, the policy of Halifax had prevailed; but he can hardly have inspired the clause which retained Roman Catholics, actually in office, until the meeting of Parliament.

The Commissioners confronted their decidedly distasteful errand with considerable misgivings, and little expectation of a favourable result; for, as Lord Nottingham shrewdly comments, the affairs of the Prince admitted of little delay, '*especially since the King of France's troops have...advanced to Boisleduc and burnt twelve villages thereabout*'. Halifax on his part must have found himself in a peculiarly invidious position, as representing a monarch under whom he had indeed served, but who had, until this crisis, throughout rejected his counsels; and whose invidious policies he might by this step appear to condone. Indeed, among the more advanced Whigs generally—in the Prince's camp more particularly, and in the breast of the Stadtholder especially—his mere acceptance had already excited a jealous resentment, which time was to intensify.

Meanwhile, the advice which Lord Halifax was at this moment urging upon James seems sufficient proof both of his sincerity and of his forebodings. Though not in the King's confidence, or aware of his actual intentions to quit the country, he clearly realized that the ultra-Roman faction, fearful lest the King should come to terms with their opponents, were advocating a policy of flight. Seconded by the more moderate wing of the Court section, which included Lord Bellasis, a Roman Catholic, the Secretaries, and Godolphin, Lord Halifax continued to remonstrate (*as Barillon himself tells us*) in very forcible terms. Retirement, he warned him, must prove absolutely fatal, while if His Majesty could but resolve to satisfy the country, both with regard to its laws and the Protestant religion, he would secure a widespread support and complete immunity from personal risk; and he insisted that Parliament alone must govern English affairs and give shape to the Government.

Meanwhile, as a negotiator, or mediator, Halifax must have been anxious to obtain some insight into the views of the other side. Hence the visit which, either just before, or just after, the above audience, Lord Halifax paid to Sir Robert Howard. Politician and play-wright, the latter, who had become an ardent partizan of the Prince, had been detained in London by a fit of the gout. In an account of the interview, he described Lord Halifax as discussing the situation 'with some trouble', which Sir Robert, by his own account, tried to intensify; remarking that the Marquis would 'give very unhappy suspicions that he was engaged in a design to give a stop to [the Prince's] advancing [upon the capital] by the delays of a treaty and the mistaken notion of an accommodation; for I plainly told him that nothing of the sort would be endured, for there was no room left for trust, and everything must be built upon new foundations. [The Marquis] seemed then fully to agree with me and assured me he would not act so as to deserve the least censure of this nature.'

Some historians—even including one so pre-eminent as Von Ranke—have adduced these passages as evidence that Lord Halifax undertook the embassy with perfidious intentions. To us, it seems that Halifax disclaimed any intention of impeding the Prince by purely procrastinating tactics.

The Commission now received its formal instructions, which, as both Godolphin and James II's biographer agree, proved meagre, diffuse, and limited. They were directed to inform the Prince of the intended Session, and assure security to all entitled to attend; and also to remind his Highness that such a free Parliament had been the ostensible object of his expedition. His Majesty therefore proposed a treaty for that purpose, but insisted as its indispensable preliminary that the respective armies should be stationed out of London, until the conclusion of the Session.

Starting on the 2nd, the Commissioners slept the first night at Windsor, and the next at Reading; where, finding the emissary they had despatched as their forerunner dead drunk, they were forced to await the return of a second and more trustworthy messenger, thence despatched. He is said to have reached the Prince's force at Edington, apparently on the way to Oxford; but on receiving this intimation, William forthwith turned in the direction of the capital. The requisite passes reached the Commissioners on the 5th, and their next stages were Andover and Ramsbury, where they took up their quarters. The Prince next day reached Hungerford, where on the following morning (8 December) he received the Commissioners.

The Commissioners had arranged a regular service of couriers by which, the same day, they despatched the following report to Lord Middleton, Secretary of State. Godolphin's writing seems to be recognizable in the body of the letter, that of Halifax in the postscript.

Ramesbury-House, 8 *December* 1688

My Lord,—We were last night appointed to wait of the Prince at 10 a clock this morning at Hungerford; when we came thither We found the Prince with severall Lords about him, and having delivered him his Maties. Letter, We asked him, if We should say to him what we had in command, there; or if he would hear Us elsewhere? hee replied, there; And then I, the M. of Hallifax, delivered him what we had aggreed should be said; a Copy whereof goeth herewith inclosed. The Prince said he did not doubt but We had seen his Declaration and he had little more to say, than what was therein expressed, touching the Grounds and reasons, of his coming into England, which was to maintain the Protestant Religion, and to preserve the Lawes, and liberties of the people; But that those Lords who had joined with him, being concerned in the matter, he would send some of them to speak with us further about it.

Being retired into another Room, there came to Us presently after, the Mal. de Schomberg, and ye Earles of Oxford and Clarendon, who from ye Prince, desired Us to putt into Writing what had been said, and to signe it, that the Lords might consider of it; which We did and delivered it to them; who Carried it back to the Prince; and in a little while after Mor. Benting came to Us, and told us from the Prince, he would give Us an Answer to morrow; and We intend accordingly to go and receive it at Littlecott, whither ye Prince is removed this night, by reason of the straitnesse and inconveniencie of his Quarters at Hungerford. We observed that there was particular care taken, that none of the English should speake to Us, the Reason for it being given Us, that it was to avoyd giving any Cause of Jealousy to any of ye Lords who might be disposed to it; and it was hinted to Us, that many of the Lords are very suspicious, least an Accommodation should be made which might not provide so largely for their Security as they expected.

Mor. Benting came from ye Prince and invited us to dinner, and nothing passed but indifferent things; After dinner We had promiscuous discourse with severall of the English who came into the Room where the Prince had dined, and by that means and by putting together severall things that were sayd to Us there, we cannot but forme some kind of Conjecture; tho

We are not able to determine anything positively, till we receive an Answer to what We delivered.

That which We apprehend At present is, yt. there is no kind of Disposition to stopp the march of their Army; the Generall opinion of the Lords and other English being so much against it, that there is little grounds to hope, that the Prince will go about to Over-rule it.

Some of the particulars which We can gather by common discourse, they may probably insist upon, are these: That all Papists be removed out of all offices and Trusts, Military as well as Civill, for while any of that party have armes in their hands, they cannot think their sitting in Parliament sufficiently secured. That they cannot accept of any Pardons, for that they will thereby own themselves to be Criminalls; But expect to have some Declaration that what they have done, in defence of the Lawes, needs no Pardon.

It is also sayd by some, that tho' they could be secure in coming to Parliament, yet if the King should bee perswaded to Dissolve it, before their Grievances bee redressed, and their Libertyes secured, it would bee a certaine Delay, and very much hazzard their dessein for the Good of the Publick, which by the methods they are now in, they think, they shall quickly obtaine;

These things We desire your Ldp. to lay before his Matie. as Our Conjectures onely; which Wee thought our duty to send by Expresse, that We might give his Maiestie. all the Light we can as soon as may be.

We remaine, My Lord,

Your Lordps. most faithfull Servants,

HALIFAX, NOTTINGHAM, GODOLPHIN

We must not Omitt to tell yor. Ldp. that ye Association which was begun in Devonshire is signed by all Noblemen and Gent. whatsoever that come in to ye Prince as he marcheth.

The paper handed by the Commissioners is merely a brief rescript of their instructions, but is in the style of Halifax.

The despatch was of course by no means reassuring to its unfortunate recipient. He at once advised the Nuncio to embark, and subsequently told Barillon that the despatch had occasioned his final resolution of sending his wife and child to France. This he carried into effect the same night, having secretly promised the Queen that he would follow within twenty-four hours.

But while the report certainly conduced to this event, there is no reason whatever to suppose that it was sent with this intention, or was accompanied by a letter from Halifax or Godolphin urging such a step. This was subsequently maintained by some of his

Lordship's ill-wishers, but never by James II himself, whose silence on the point is conclusive. Indeed, as we have seen already, Lord Halifax, on the contrary, had, on the quite indisputable evidence of Barillon, strongly warned the King against taking such a step. Moreover, Halifax, despite the Prince's embargo, had, in conversation between the parties, contrived to elicit from the incautious Burnet that the invaders had no desire to have the King in their hands and that there was nothing so much to be wished for by them as his voluntary flight.

The Prince's answer to the King 'with the advice of the Lords and Gentlemen assembled with us' was returned to the Commissioners at Littlecote on 10 December. It demanded: the disarmament, disbanding and removal from employment of all Papists; that all proclamations reflecting upon the Prince and the invading force should be recalled; that to prevent the landing of French or other foreign troops, the Tower and Tilbury Fort should be entrusted to the custody of the City and that Portsmouth,* for the same reason, should be entrusted to such hands as should be agreeable to both parties; that if the King should remain in London for the Session, the Prince should remove there also, with an equivalent number of guards; that the armies also should remain equidistant from London, and that no further forces should be brought into the kingdom; and, finally, that the Prince's army, until the meeting of Parliament, should be maintained out of the public revenue.

To these demands the Commissioners answered that they had power to agree to some but not all of them, and proposed a return for his Majesty's further instructions; the Prince having agreed that his troops, meanwhile, should not, within three days, approach London by a greater advance than thirty miles.

Some authorities, including Godolphin himself, suggest that the Commissioners were agreeably surprised by the comparative moderation of the Prince's demands, which in truth approximated very nearly to the preliminaries recommended by Halifax. And an authority which we may presume to be Barillon tells us that these facts were reported by the Commissioners to the King; with the additional suggestion that during the proposed interval, arrangements for the meeting of Parliament could be made by mutual consent, and the expression of an opinion that, as far as could be judged, a settlement appeared possible.

* All these strongholds, it must be noted, being at this moment in Papist hands.

The Commissioners, having despatched their report by express, duly started themselves.

But at Whitehall, meanwhile, a dramatic transformation had taken place.[26] That very morning a startled Court had risen to learn that at the preceding midnight the Queen and Prince of Wales had been covertly despatched to France; while it was shrewdly suspected by all (save the moderate Papists, such as Dumbarton, who could not credit the possibility of such a desertion) that the King intended to follow them.

All that momentous day His Majesty had been engaged in a variety of public interviews; and at a Council held that evening he had assured those present that he had no intention of leaving the country. Nevertheless, about midnight Lord Ailesbury, a Gentleman of the Bedchamber, unconvinced by these protestations, had obtained an audience; and taxing His Majesty with an unavowed intention of flight, had implored him, in moving terms, to rescind so fatal a resolution. He prayed him with passionate vehemence to march upon Nottingham, pressed on him the protestations of fidelity, which he had been charged to deliver from the remaining officers, and when argument appeared useless, besought his Sovereign to await, at least, the return of the Commissioners.

On retiring from the Presence Ailesbury had encountered Lord Middleton, bringing the Commissioners' despatches, which had apparently just arrived. Ailesbury had asked him, what news they contained. 'As far as I can remember', says Ailesbury, 'his answer was neither good nor bad.'

James, however, seems to have gathered either from Middleton's reply, or from some talk in the Ante-Chamber, 'that they expressed his Highness's inclination to treat, and gave more hope of the situation'. James then said aloud to Middleton: 'That is very good, my lord; to-morrow at nine o'clock, I will return an answer to your Office.' Within a few minutes he retired, and as he stepped into bed, whispered to Lord Mulgrave 'that his Commissioners had newly sent him a very hopeful account of some good accommodation with the Prince of Orange', though he admitted that the Prince still approached London.

A few minutes later the King had silently risen, and having cancelled the writs for the Parliament, despatched a letter to the Earl of Feversham, Commander-in-chief, which that officer interpreted as a direction to disband the army. About three o'clock in the morning His Majesty had left the palace by a secret door, and carrying with him, with the avowed intention that anarchy might succeed him, the Great Seal, he had taken the road to Sheerness.

The Commissioners reached London the afternoon of the same day, to find the country without a Government; and, according to one report, it was a communication from these three which compelled the Prince to believe a rumour which had previously seemed incredible.

The awful moments of suspense which had followed the discovery of the King's flight had already brought into play, after a sufficiently striking fashion, the political instinct so characteristic of Englishmen. It chanced that the Peers then in town had previously received the King's summons to assemble that morning, and assist the Privy Council. They had met accordingly at the Guildhall, Archbishop Sancroft taking the Chair, and had forthwith assumed the task of maintaining order, and the authority of a Provisional Government. As such, though without inviting the Prince to London, they had issued a declaration laudatory of his undertaking, drafted by four High Churchmen; and promised to co-operate with him in obtaining, by means of a free Parliament, a settlement. They had given orders to the military authorities to remove their forces to distant quarters, and to the fleet to avoid collision with the Dutch.

The night was one of riot and terror; the *mobile vulgus*, only just degraded to the then cant appellation of 'mob', felt the reins were loose, and amid scenes of great excitement proceeded to sack or burn the houses of several foreign Ministers. St James's Square was saved; M. Barillon, who lived there, was not personally unpopular; and, like Lord Halifax and other men of rank in the Square, had asked for a guard.

When, on the following morning, the Lords reassembled (this time in the Council Chamber at Whitehall), the Archbishop did not appear. Lord Halifax, alone of the newly returned Commissioners, attended, and was voted into the Chair. Having passed an order which threatened with the rigour of the law all such as attacked houses in general, and the Embassies in particular, the Assembly called on all Protestant officials to exercise their functions and to call out the Militia.

On the following night, however, intensified by a rumour that the disbanded Irish regiments were marching on London, the disorders revived; and next morning the Lords, still under the presidency of Halifax, issued instructions to the Trained Bands to fire on the rioters, if necessary, with bullet; gave orders that 'cannon should be planted in the Park, Charing Cross, at the entrance into Piccadilly from Hyde Park side, and other places; that the footguards should stand to their arms in St James's Park, and the Horse Guards the same, with other necessary orders'.

While they were thus deliberating, a countryman arrived bearing a letter, without address, but in the hand of King James, intimating that he had fallen into the hands of the mob at Faversham and imploring assistance. The messenger lingered unnoticed by the Council door till Lord Mulgrave indignantly called the attention of the Assembly to this neglect. Lord Halifax attempted to adjourn, but Mulgrave was insistent, and the letter was read.

From the accounts of foreign diplomatists[27] it would appear that a deputation of the Peers most in favour with the King was despatched to beg the King's return and assure him of safety, but without impeding his departure. The deputation found the crowd in a rather truculent mood. Its spokesman declared it would not suffer the King to go to France and return with foreign troops to seize and waste the country. The Lords, realizing in the course of the day, that an armed escort was urgently required, despatched Lord Feversham on the following night with a party of the guards. He insisted that the words 'to receive His Majesty's orders and protect his person' should be added to his instructions, and forthwith started on his errand.

A few hours later, the Assembly received a message from the Prince of Orange. This accepted the invitation to London which the City—more forward than the Peers—had already despatched. He had already on his own responsibility required the officers of the King's army to recall their disbanded men to the colours. Whether they did or did not know this, the Peers now issued such orders to Irish officers and soldiers, with promises of subsistence to the compliant and threats of arrest in cases of contumacy. Next day (15 December) was occupied by an examination of Lord Jeffreys, as to the Writs and Great Seal; and on the 16th James reached London.

The Imperial representative Hoffmann[28] lays stress on the warm welcome he received, and the general relief expressed; in which, however, he explains, there was nothing personal. The country as a whole, he says, dreaded nothing so much as that its own Sovereign should be a hostage in the hands of France. He even suggests that it was hoped the Prince of Orange might be declared Commander-in-chief of the English forces, in an anti-French campaign.

But on one outstanding personality the King's return made a very different impression. Lord Halifax at once left London, and joined the Prince of Orange, who by then had reached Windsor.

His dilemma, indeed, was one of extreme difficulty. It was obviously impossible for him to resume relations with the returning monarch. Assuming, as we must do, that Halifax had throughout acted in good faith, James II had, by his flight, inflicted an undeserved and humiliating slight upon the head of his Commission; and what was far more serious, had seemed to justify the very invidious charge of complicity in an attempt to delay the Prince's march by a purely delusive negotiation. The King had thus, in response to the panic-stricken exhortation of an ultra-Papist Knot, deliberately taken the step against which Lord Halifax had most strenuously advised him, and which, as the Marquis knew, was the one most desired by his adversaries. He had thrown himself and his family into the arms of France, the great enemy, according to Lord Halifax, of all English interests. Moreover, as President of the self-constituted Provisional Government, Lord Halifax stood obnoxious to the wrath of one who had already expressed 'much dissatisfaction' with the patriotic energy, which had dared to save from disaster the capital he had so deliberately abandoned. Resentment and apprehension will have but intensified his conviction that, since James had thus become impossible, his rival alone could now secure the safety of the country.

The Prince, with whose fortunes Halifax had thus definitely identified himself, had, almost simultaneously, taken on his own part a decisive step. The flight of the Royal family and the subsequent disbanding of the Royal forces had placed the ball at the Stadtholder's foot; and perhaps inspired him, for the first time, with the idea of actually supplanting his father-in-law. Only thus could he counterbalance the advantage which the policy of Louis XIV must derive while he held the King of England and his heir as a symbol of their country's alliance. To William, therefore, the unexpected and involuntary return of James to his capital must have appeared a bitter blow.

He had made no attempt to conceal his own mortification; had curtly refused the invitation to St James's Palace which the King, while on his way to London, had sent him; had arrested on a technical, but so Lord Wolseley maintains, a perfectly valid pretext, Lord Feversham its bearer; and had intimated, through his favourite, Count Zulestein, that His Majesty would do well to remain at Rochester, from which place his letter had been despatched. It was the letter of a victorious general to his opponent; a position in which, as a contemporary Whig pamphlet shrewdly remarks, *William now stood in relation to his father-in-law, though not to the nation*.

His next move is described by Lord Clarendon, then lodging at Windsor, who on the following day was summoned to the Castle. In an inner room, he says:

> I found...several Lords—and Lord Halifax in the midst of them; who presently turned to me, and said the Prince had sent for all the peers who were at Windsor, to advise with them about what was fit to be done upon the King's being come to Whitehall; and that as I came late, he would tell me what they had resolved upon. I said if the resolution was taken, there was no need of informing me of anything; but he went on and said, that Monsieur Zulestein had missed the King on the road and that his Majesty was come the last night to Whitehall; that he had written to the Prince, and invited him to St. James, and to send what forces he pleased to town; but the Lords were of opinion the King should be advised to leave Whitehall, and to go to Ham [where was a villa on the river once belonging to Lord Lauderdale and by him magnificently adorned]. I asked why the King must leave Whitehall. It was answered, the Prince did not believe he could be safe there. I then asked 'Why must he go to Ham?' Lord Halifax answered, the Lords are agreed, and have sent to desire the Prince to come to them; and while he was yet speaking, the Prince came into the room. My Lord Halifax gave him an account of the resolution the Lords were come to, which was drawn up in writing.

Some further debate then took place, during which (by Clarendon's own account) that Lord again remonstrated and suggested he should retire to one of his own palaces, under protection of his own guards; but he says that Lord Delamere retorted '*he no longer considered him as King*'. The Prince having approved the paper, Lord Halifax said 'there had been very free debates which would not be very fit to be talked of', alluding apparently to some violent proposals made by an extremist minority; and the Prince thereupon enjoined secrecy on all present.

'The Prince then said,' continues Clarendon, 'Now we must consider who shall carry this message to the King.' Lord Halifax said he thought it were best to be sent by some of the Prince's officers, and Clarendon thought he named 'Count Solmes', but the Prince replied, 'By your favour, my Lord, it is the advice of the Peers here, and some of you shall carry it', and so in the same breath he named the Lords Halifax, Shrewsbury and Delamere. Lord Mulgrave, who was not present, and who was no friend to Halifax, declares that the Prince as he owned afterwards, 'could not help smiling' to see the former Commissioner 'accept to act so low a part so very willingly'.

The three Lords received instructions to tell the King 'that it is thought convenient, that for the greater quiet of the City and for the safety of his Person, that he do remove to Ham, where he shall be attended by [his]* guards who will be ready to preserve him from any disturbance'.

So far the decision to require the King's departure from London—a step on which Jacobite propaganda was subsequently to lay such ferocious stress, and which, indeed, unless it was intended that William should remain at an equal distance from London, seems singularly injudicious—had rested on the shoulders of the Windsor meeting in general and of Lord Halifax in particular. But for a subsequent and far grosser want of tact and even of decency, which produced a still greater effect in the same direction, William alone can be held responsible. Even before the Lords could reach London, Count Solmes received orders to replace the English sentries at Whitehall by the *Dutch* guards.

During the next few hours the Prince advanced his quarters to Sion House, a few miles out of town, and about ten in the evening Count Solmes and his troops, who had been delayed in transit, and who amounted, it is said, to 1300 men, entered London. Having invested St James's Palace, they marched, with matches lit for action, upon Whitehall. The rumour of their approach reached King James who saw in it only an incorrect report of the Prince's arrival in London. About eleven o'clock, however, as the King was retiring, Lord Ailesbury informed him that Count Solmes was without, with a message from the Prince of Orange. James having sent for Solmes, who explained his errand, at first expostulated with the Dutchman, as having mistaken his orders, but Solmes produced written instructions. The gallant old Lord Craven, Colonel of the 2nd Foot Guards, who was in command at the Palace, would have offered a forcible resistance. Two at least of the Lords sent by the Prince had by this time arrived, namely, Shrewsbury and Delamere; and the latter declares that if James had had the slightest grain of courage

* This seems the most probable reading; an omission of the word 'his' in Burnet's *Reflections* seems a misprint.

he could have arrested them and cut in pieces the forces that came with Solmes; which might have turned the odds on his side. James, however, knew what Delamere (magnifying his own danger) overlooks, that so far as his own previous orders had been obeyed, the King's army no longer existed. He sent orders that the Royal guards should withdraw.

By one o'clock, therefore, under the supervision of Shrewsbury and Delamere, the Dutch guards were posted. Some half-hour later Middleton received a billet over the signature of the three Deputies (Halifax having apparently arrived after the others). It informed James that they were the bearers of a message from the Prince to the King 'of so great an importance that they desired' immediate admittance to the Presence.

Lord Middleton having in vain requested a few hours' delay 'told the messenger he would be ready at the stairs of the Guard Chamber to carry the Lords to the King'. He seems to have waked his master, who had fallen asleep, by warning him of the impending interview. He did not rise from his bed, and apparently about two o'clock the deputation was admitted to the bedchamber; where 'after an apology for coming at an hour which might give him disturbance, the Prince's message was delivered him'. The King appears to have signified his compliance, but asked 'whether he might not appoint what servants should attend him'. Lord Halifax answered, 'That it was left to him to give orders in that as he pleased', but 'that he would be pleased to remove so early, as to be at Ham by noon, by this means to prevent the meeting the Prince on his way to London, where he was to come the same day'; and that 'the Prince of Orange would take care to appoint a suitable guard to attend him there, to secure him from any harm'. The King, to use his own words, 'seeing there was no remedy, being absolutely in their power, told them, he was content to go out of town, but that Ham was a very ill winter house and unfurnished' (i.e. probably, unprepared for immediate occupation). My Lord Halifax replied that his Majesty's 'officers might soon do that'. The deputation, it would appear, then took its leave, but no sooner had they left the bedchamber than the King sent for them again, and told them (as Burnet records) 'that he had forgot to acquaint them with his Resolution before the Message came, to send my Lord Godolphin next morning to the Prince to propose his going back to Rochester; he finding by the message that Monsieur Zulestein was charged with, that the Prince had no mind he should be in

London; and therefore he now desired that he might rather return to Rochester than go to any other place'. He laid special stress on the fact that Lord Feversham's guards were there. The Lords replied that they would immediately send an account to the Prince, of what his Majesty desired, 'and did not doubt of such an answer as would be to his satisfaction'. The reply they undertook should be returned before nine in the morning, but his Majesty 'must be then ready to be gone'. The answer arrived before eight next morning in a letter from the King's familiar, Bentinck; by which the Prince agreed to the Rochester proposal, provided the Dutch guards should attend the King.

'The King's Barge with the coaches and pads being ready,' writes the biographer of James, 'he ordered them with the Prince of Orange's guards to go over the bridge and meet him at Gravesend, but my Lord Halifax opposed it, saying their going through the City might cause disorder and move compassion, and was for their going over at Lambeth ferry.' James replied that this might delay their arrival at Gravesend, 'but that Lord', he says, 'nothing moved with this, pressed earnestly their going by Lambeth and was very unreasonable in his arguing, not to give it a worse name, but my Lord Shrewsbury was fair and civil and agreed to what his Majesty said'. Eventually, amid many tears from the gentlemen of the Court, James embarked, reaching Gravesend the same night and Rochester the following day.

The harshness displayed by the Marquis on this occasion has been severely stigmatized, by some, as a piece of time service, designed to propitiate the Prince of Orange; we may more probably ascribe it to the fear of an attempt at rescue, or, with Macaulay, to the irritating remembrance of the mock embassy.

It was reported in some quarters that on the evening of the same day, a few hours after the Prince had taken up his quarters at St James's, 'the Marquis of Halifax told the Prince he might be what he pleased himself...for as nobody knew what to do with him, so nobody knew what to do without him'. The epigram is very much in the vein of Halifax, but is more likely to have been said *of* the Prince than *to* him.

Two days later (20 December) the Prince summoned to St James's Palace the Peers then in town. They met the next morning, when the Prince informed them that he should reserve to himself the direction of military affairs, leaving to them the civil administration, and the arrangements for a free Parliament.

Next day the Peers met again in the House of Lords, as the most convenient centre, when Halifax was voted into the Chair. An anonymous contemporary distinguished three parties in the assembly, a so-called 'Commonwealth' (or Radical) party, desirous of a Stadtholder rather than a King; a party that would depose the King in favour of his nephew; and a party that 'would make all the offers in the world' to James, in order to induce his return. 'My Lord Delamere', adds our informant, 'appears like a fury, and my Lord Halifax trims it like himself.' A very extreme Whig, however, bears witness to 'the great wisdom, courage and zeal for the good of the Commonwealth' which Halifax, he says, displayed. The meeting, on the motion, it is said, of Lord Halifax (but from which the Prince, having his eyes on the Empire and Spain, strongly dissented), voted that Papists, though with numerous exceptions, should be banished from London. It further ordered the arrest of Irish officers, as hostages for their Protestant compatriots; and voted that the King should be desired to concur in calling a new Parliament. When, however, after a Sunday's adjournment, the House came together again, it was met by the news that James, on the preceding day, strongly urged thereto by the French agent, Rizzini,[29] had left Rochester for France.

This step for the moment proved a death blow to the energy of his supporters. The Lords refused to send for an explanatory letter left by the King; and after a lively and exciting debate, resolved that since, owing to the absence of the King and the Great Seal, a legal Parliament had become impossible, the Prince should be asked to send a circular letter to all constituent bodies, desiring them to elect representatives for a Convention; and should himself meanwhile assume the Administration. This was seconded by a meeting of surviving members of the Parliaments of Charles II, and as respects Scotland by a meeting of Scottish Lords and gentlemen then in London.

During the three weeks which ensued, the Prince studiously refrained from all interference with the business of the elections. The impassive and enigmatic reserve which he maintained has been often noted; but to one Englishman, at least, his intentions were, from the first, laid open.

Two days after the Prince had accepted the Administration, Lord Halifax began taking, on loose sheets, brief notes of their intercourse together. These still remain, although the *Memoirs* which were presumably founded on them, and on other similar memoranda, have been destroyed. Those relating to the first year after the Revolution are of peculiar interest, though rather as throwing light on the personality of King William than on that of Halifax.

In the earliest interview, a private one, which took place 30 December 1688, his Highness seems to have discussed, with remarkable frankness, the existing situation. He showed implicitly that he regarded his own elevation to the throne as practically assured, and contemplated the postponement of the Princess Anne's interest to his own. He evinced a strong jealousy of the 'Commonwealth' party, in which he probably included the extreme Whigs; said that at the best they wanted to have a Duke of Venice, and that he had not come over to establish a Commonwealth. He observed that he was sure of one thing—he would not stay in England if the King returned; and added, 'with the strongest asseverations', that he should withdraw if they attempted to make him Regent. He had at any rate secured a trustworthy confidant; for it is certain that Halifax himself, during the momentous interval which followed, maintained, on his part also, a studied reticence.

The Convention met on 22 January; Lord Eland represented Newark. As no Lord Chancellor could be acknowledged, the Lords were compelled to *elect* a speaker. It is said that Lords Halifax and Danby were rival candidates for the post; the first symptom of a revived and ancient jealousy, which became a determining factor in our statesman's later career. The choice of the House fell on Halifax.

A letter from the Prince was read, recommending to the Convention the consideration of the entire political situation, exhorting them to unity, and to the rapidity of decision which the state of Ireland and the Continent demanded; and intimating a hope that England, in return for the assistance lent by the States, which had already declared war on France, would herself declare war on the latter power.

The House returned thanks for the Prince's care of the State, and recommended to his charge the State of Ireland, but left the final admonition of the Prince unanswered.

It was believed that the Upper House favoured a Regency, the Lower more stringent measures; but that the first vote on the question, from wherever emanating, would carry weight. Lord Halifax, from the beginning showed his determination that the Commons should take the initiative; and this appears to have been the earliest intimation received by the more Conservative faction that the erstwhile champion of the anti-exclusionists had abandoned his former standpoint.

The crucial debate took place in the House of Commons on 28 January, and on the 29th that House acquainted the Lords with two formal resolutions: one (eventually passed nem. con. in both Houses) to the effect that a Popish King had been found by experience inconsistent with a Protestant Government; the other, the famous vote which implied that James II had *abdicated* the Government, and that the throne was vacant. On this vote Lord Eland, influenced no doubt through his kinsman by marriage, Lord Nottingham, seems to have voted with the *Regency* minority.

In the Upper House, after a long debate in Committee, a resolution inferentially favouring a Regency was proposed, and supported by Nottingham, Weymouth and Chesterfield, all friends of Halifax. It was lost by two votes; Lord Halifax and Lord Danby voting with the 'vacancy' majority, for whose success, it was believed by some, their exertions were mainly responsible.

But if the apparently unexpected defection of Halifax proved fatal to the Regency party, it proved no less destructive to the widespread authority and reputation which, ever since his dismissal from office by James II, he had certainly enjoyed. He lost thus, not only the confidence which he had gained from the Tories, by the defence of the Limitation and Regency expedients in 1680, but also the confidence and respect his whole conduct so far had secured from the Moderates. And this, without in the smallest degree conciliating the hatred of the exclusionist Whigs, of which he was soon to experience the undiminished virulence. His action was very generally ascribed to a personal and unscrupulous ambition; in fact, to the desire of conciliating the Coming Man to whom he had given so tardy an adhesion.

But these harsh criticisms overlooked the crucial facts. The opposition of Lord Halifax to the Bill of Exclusion had been based upon opportunist principles, and upon contingencies which had ceased to exist. Lord Halifax had never before shown himself a worshipper of the rising, or even the risen, sun; his relations with James as heir-presumptive had been only one degree less strained than they became after his accession. And though undoubtedly fond of power, the Marquis had shown no desire to grasp it at the expense either of his principles or safety. The greater part of his life had been spent in Opposition and his talents and disposition rendered the rank and importance of an Opposition leader little if any less acceptable than Ministerial pre-eminence. At this moment he was expressing the gravest doubts as to the permanence of the new settlement, and made a point of accepting as few as possible of the compromising honours within his reach. These considerations point to the conclusion that Halifax, in forwarding by every means in his power the elevation of William to the throne of England, was actuated by the following motives:

I. The actual situation of England at this moment was almost unprecedented. No legal Government existed, yet the most perfect order prevailed throughout the kingdom. This strange position of affairs was in its nature temporary and precarious, and depended wholly on the confidence inspired by the presence of the Prince of Orange. He had gained rapidly in popularity, and was at the moment obviously master of the situation. He formed the central pivot round which all revolved; and his withdrawal from the scene must have involved a political anarchy, leading perhaps to the triumphant return of James at the head of a French army. The elevation of the Stadtholder to the Regency of England would no doubt have conciliated the great bulk of English opinion, and would have been no less consonant with his original Declaration, than with the views advocated by Halifax in 1679–81. But to such a course there existed in 1688/9 a final objection; Lord Halifax was aware that the Prince had determined to decline the Regency. That his determination could be shaken was a known impossibility; his assistance would be available upon his own terms, or not at all. Well has Saint-Beuve defined 'la toute-puissance de l'homme dont la caractère est avant tout une *volonté invincible*'.

II. To this supreme argument a second one may be added. The Acts of the Convention, which was not acknowledged by James, were, from the narrow standpoint of the Constitutional lawyer, Acts of *Treason*. In the event of a counter-revolution its members would have lain at the mercy of James, and could have been carried at once to the Bar. Nor could they under a Regency have appealed to the well-known statute of Henry VII (under which obedience to a King *de facto* cannot be punished as rebellion) or to such a Parliamentary amnesty as had been proposed in 1680/1. Those who had seen the statute of Henry VII pleaded—*and pleaded in vain*—by Sir Harry Vane and Henry Martin, *because the Government they had obeyed was not a legal one*, had reason to consider the point one of practical importance. This fact, indeed, is admitted by writers as far apart as Von Ranke and Swift, Mazure and Hallam.

The critical vote once passed, matters proceeded rapidly. On 30 January the Lords endorsed that part of the Commons vote which imported that James had abdicated, or, as they preferred to express it, had *deserted* the throne.

On 31 January the clause which announced that the throne was therefore vacant was rejected by 52 to 47, having been strenuously opposed (*a*) by the Regency party, (*b*) by those who, with Danby, maintained that the Crown had *already devolved on the Princess Mary*. Against this rejection, Lord Halifax and thirty-five others of the 'vacancy' minority protested.

Matters had thus reached a deadlock. During the two days which followed Sir John Reresby, who had just come up to London, twice met Lord Halifax. The first occasion was at an 'assembly' where discussions were going on between the supporters of the Prince and those of his wife. Perhaps this may have been the meeting at Devonshire House, where, Danby declaring for the Princess, Halifax for the Prince, the latter turned to a Dutch confidant of the Prince and said he thought it would be very proper to know the Prince's own sentiments. The Dutchman, with real or pretended hesitation, opined that the Prince would not like to be his wife's gentleman usher.

> My Lord Halifax told me that night [says Reresby] that he was not privy to this design of the prince's coming at the first; but now that he was here, and upon so good an occasion, we were obliged to defend him. I acquainted him with what I heard, that Lord Danby expected preference before him in the prince's favour. He gave me some reasons which satisfied me to the contrary, and that his lordship began to lag in his zeal for the prince's interest in the House of Lords. One was, that he was never to hope to be Lord Treasurer, the prince having declared he would manage it by commissioners. My Lord Halifax spoke further that himself should be employed and used some arguments to me to prove the legality of accepting to be so. One was, that the King having relinquished the government, it was not for that to be let fall, and it could not be supported if men did not act under those on whom it was conferred, and that as things stood now *salus populi* was *suprema lex*. His lordship said further that there were so many declined to serve, and there were so few fit for it.

On the second occasion he found Halifax closeted with the Prince in his bedchamber; 'coming out to me', says Reresby, 'he said the Prince could not be publicly seen of two hours'. It was a sign of his own rising importance.

The struggle was now drawing to an and. On 2 February, indeed, the two Houses practically declined to receive letters from King James, offering to return and hold a free Parliament; but the Commons resolved to maintain their own original resolution, *Lord Eland again voting with the minority*. While on the 4th, the *Lords* reiterated their own amendment (thirty-nine dissentients, *Lord Halifax included*, entering their protests), and on the 5th the Commons retorted with a resolution to insist.

The Lower House appears to have sat late, for Lord Clarendon bitterly complains that Lord Halifax, awaiting its decision, refused to adjourn till half-past three, and then did so under pressure. 'So unfair he was in the Chair that he would do nothing but what he had a mind to'; and 'so much haste was his Lordship and some others in, to overturn the Government'.

A few hours later, however, 5/15 February the Stadtholder at last showed his hand. In presence of Halifax, Danby, Shrewsbury and some others ('those he most trusted', says Burnet's original *Memoirs*), he publicly expressed his unalterable determination to refuse any share in the administration, unless offered the rank of King Regnant for life.

Under these circumstances took place on 6 February the decisive conference between the Houses. Therein, after a debate in which 'the great argument', says Clarendon, 'used by my Lord Halifax (who was at the head of the prevailing faction and drove furiously) was necessity, and that the throne was only made elective *pro hac vice* and then reverted to its hereditary channel again', the Lords representing the Regency interest, by 65 to 45, surrendered the point at issue. Lord Nottingham voted with the minority; Chesterfield and Weymouth abstained.

It was probably after this vote that Halifax declared in favour of postponing Mary entirely to her husband, and giving her, during his life, the title of Queen Consort only; being, so Burnet says, supported by one Peer alone, the 'vicious and corrupt' Lord Culpepper. Burnet himself, who opposed the idea as most ungenerous and unwise (since it 'would engage the one sex generally against the Prince, and in time they might find the effects of it very sensibly'), declares that Halifax was merely moved by the desire of flattering the Prince; and he has been followed by modern historians of repute. But we must remember the dislike he had expressed in the *Character of a Trimmer* for 'double-bottomed monarchies'. He had never shown special respect for feminine politicians. Moreover, Mary, who was perfectly willing to be superseded by her husband, was at this time an unknown quantity—or shall we say 'quality'?—even to her husband, and, we may add, even to herself.

A doubt exists whether the vote actually adopted—That the Prince and Princess of Orange be declared King and Queen—was proposed by Halifax or Danby. Lord Nottingham then solicited a vote that the Oaths of Allegiance and Supremacy might be modified in favour of those who were ready, even willing, to accept *de facto* those whom they were unable to acknowledge *de jure*. He was seconded by Danby, 'but my Lord Halifax', observes a contemporary report, 'said it would be to ridicule their title and much to the like purpose'. Sharp words passed between him and Danby, whose bitter resentment over the episode is recorded by Reresby.

The famous Declaration of Right now occupied Parliament. While the debate was in progress, a two hours' conversation seems to have taken place at Reresby's lodging, between Lord Halifax and Lady Oglethorpe, an interview for which she had pleaded, and which Halifax had only at long length conceded: 'For he told me', says Reresby, 'it was not amiss to hear what everybody had to say.' In this, according to her own account, she had upbraided him with his conduct to King James; warned him that Sunderland would supplant him as before; predicted that the settlement would not last, that Scotland and Ireland would reject it; and reminded him that even England was by no means unanimous. 'His Lordship', so she told Reresby, 'said there was no great hopes of a lasting peace from this settlement. However, it was the best that could be made at this time of day; that he knew what interest she had with the King, and in case anything happened, desired she would be his friend and he would be hers in another place.'

We must not over-estimate the rather dubious accuracy of a report made by a Jacobite, and a well-known intriguer, to a non-juror, for such was Reresby; but if there is any substratum of truth in her representations, as to the apprehensions entertained by his Lordship, we do not wonder he had appreciated the importance of the Statute Henry VII.

Shortly after this, on 11 February 1688/9, the Princess Mary arrived from Holland. By the 12th the Declaration of Right was completed; and on the 13th, in the Banqueting Chamber at Whitehall, in the presence of the Assembled Convention, the Marquis of Halifax, as Speaker of the House of Lords, proffered the Crown of England to William and Mary.

After the acceptance of this magnificent gift, his Lordship conducted in person the solemn Proclamation in the City.

CHAPTER XII

IN OFFICE FEBRUARY 1688/89 TO FEBRUARY 1689/90

'LE mariage', says Legouvé, 'devient le ménage.' The parties in this strange political contract had now to be tested by the daily prosaic relationships of administrative and legislative routine. If these relations were throughout marked by very fluctuating cordiality, the blame must be equally distributed; since virulent party dissensions, on the one hand, were to be balanced by grave errors of tact and judgment on the part of the new King.

That he began with the best intentions we learn from Lord Halifax himself, who of all men was in a position to know the facts. For throughout the brief period during which Lord Halifax held office under William III, he was undoubtedly, among English politicians, His Majesty's only confidant.

That he should rank high in the new political hierarchy was a foregone conclusion, for his accession to the Prince's party, though tardy, had been invaluable. On the other hand, the claims of Lord Danby were almost equally great, and he had been among the first in the field. Their long drawn rivalry, though not at first openly flaunted, had already shown itself and soon revived in full force; and 'the great question', observes Reresby, was this: which of the two would gain the mastery?

That question was at once, though but temporarily, decided. For within twenty-four hours of the Proclamation, three first-rate political appointments were gazetted. Danby had refused the Seals, and had hoped for the Treasury; but (as Halifax himself told Reresby) he was 'forced to take up' (we should say 'put up') with the Presidency of the Council.

The Marquis meanwhile resumed, by his own desire, his original office of Lord Privy Seal; and since the Great Seal, which some said he had himself declined, was placed in Commission, he continued to officiate as Speaker of the House of Lords.

Lord Danby, for his part, did not attempt to conceal his mortification at this rebuff, and the more freely, as he ascribed his disappointment to the direct influence of his rival. As that rival told his confidant Reresby, Danby was 'down in the mouth and would now let his neighbours be quiet about him'. Lord Halifax added that 'as they stood yet seemingly fair' he had intended to give the Lord President 'no just occasion of difference'. Indeed he adduced the testimony of the new King to the fact that he had so far kept his resolution. For William had admitted that, though it was an inconvenience that the two Ministers 'were not better together', it was no fault of Halifax.

The preference thus shown by William at this juncture is not surprising. For while Halifax was both intellectually and morally greatly the superior, both his policy and his temperament recommended him particularly to the new King. William was aware that from 1672 onwards, and, indeed, from an earlier date, they had always agreed on the one political topic which really appealed to William; i.e. opposition to French ascendancy. And though William, a man essentially of one idea, hardly even affected an interest in our domestic politics—save as they subserved the cause which was his sole preoccupation—yet his views on many insular questions necessarily coincided with those of Halifax. If he urged indemnity for the past, toleration for the future, merely because internal recrimination must weaken energy for the Continental crusade, this necessarily brought him into line with Halifax. If in the strife of parties he was, as he frequently told Halifax, essentially 'a Trimmer', it was only because he hoped thus to consolidate the nation in the face of the common foe. But this again attracted his sympathy to the great 'Trimmer' himself.

Moreover, certain personal characteristics of Halifax at first strengthened the bond. The new King found him greedy neither of money nor patronage. He said, so Halifax himself records, 'he would be my witness I did not recommend men partially.' Nor till exasperated beyond endurance by the unscrupulous attacks of political extremists did Halifax show a trace of the bitter political rancour which was the political curse of the time.

The intimacy between them was at first extremely close. This is clearly reflected in the invaluable journals we have already described. It was to Halifax that the self-contained Dutchman betrayed the sinking of heart which fell upon him with an actual realization of the responsibilities he had so ardently coveted. 'He was desirous to be King', writes Halifax, 'yet really shrank at the burthen, at the very first putting on of his crown....He said, "I saw a young King...and that he required my help....He fancied he was like a King in a play".'

To the Marquis meanwhile the character of the new Sovereign offered, it is clear, an inexhaustible field of observation; and his comments are conceived in the same spirit of almost scientific candour which distinguishes his character of Charles II; to which, indeed, he may have been meditating a companion portrait. The note of respect and admiration is clearly discernible, but criticism is by no means absent. Lord Halifax remarks, though with but a spice of disapproval, the domineering spirit which neither a Republican breeding nor a sense of public duty had ever been able to eradicate; discusses with philosophic freedom the errors of the new Monarch's domestic policy, in particular his want of tact and lack of rapidity in decision; and emphasizes again and again that passionate hatred for France which the shrewd Englishman fully recognized as the real, and indeed the sole motive for his invasion of Britain.

As was only natural, his new master consulted Halifax, almost exclusively, as to the higher political appointments. The two Secretaries of State—Shrewsbury and Nottingham—were chosen at his suggestion. Shrewsbury, despite his charm and ability, proved something of a broken reed. But as regards Nottingham, Bishop Burnet *in his contemporary record*, maintains that 'Nottingham being in the Ministry...first preserved the Church and then the Crown'. For while Shrewsbury—definitely connected with the Whig party—had, as we know, signed the invitation to the Stadtholder, Nottingham, a steady supporter of the 'Church' interest in its least extreme form, had drawn back from signature at the last moment, upon a religious scruple. His inclusion in the Ministry was therefore a pledge of William's intention to 'trim' in the Savilian sense, and base his throne on a National, not a Party, foundation.

Again when, early in May, the new King took his first, and decisive, step in foreign affairs, he was assured of his Minister's support. Under urgent pressure from William, war was declared by this country upon France, on the ground of the assistance it was affording to the exiled King. We thus found ourselves at last involved in the great Continental confederacy against Louis XIV, which already practically included Spain and the Empire, with the United Provinces. How long Lord Halifax had contemplated such a solution of the European situation we already know; we know also that he clearly recognized how fully it had supplied William's one real motive for the invasion of Britain; and his contemporary comment has a touch of the acerbity with which he was subsequently to envisage William's absorption in the anti-French crusade. 'He hath such a mind to France', he wrote in his diary, 'that it would incline one to think he took England only in his way.'

The Commission appointed to draw up the consequent treaty between this country and the States included Lord Halifax, Lord Nottingham, Lord Shrewsbury and Lord Danby; the last-named newly raised (as a sop perhaps for injured feeling) to the Marquisate of Carmarthen. The negotiations were lengthy, lasting from the middle of May to the end of August, and the details remind us that human nature does not alter much from century to century. We find the English insisting on stipulations against a separate peace; and the Dutch criticizing the attempts of interested parties to sow discord between the Allies. Each side objects to submitting its interests, whatever the circumstances, to foreign jurisdiction; the Dutch complain of the Navigation Act, and the King warns them against demanding its repeal. The English are indisposed to promise any specific quota of assistance, while the Dutch desire that the quota should be definite, etc., etc.

The actual signature took place on 24 August/3 September 1689, and it is not without interest—and perhaps of some importance—that the ceremony had been delayed, among other causes, by *indisposition* on the part of Lord Halifax.

Of less, and yet of some, consequence was the concurrence of King and Minister in support of a clause in the original Bill of Rights; which—even thus early in the day—would have settled the ultimate succession to the Crown on the House of Hanover. It was rejected; but the disappointment of its promoters was offset by the opportune birth of a son to the then childless Princess Anne.

The Princess Sophia, as representing the interests of Hanover, despatched a graceful letter of thanks to Lord Halifax, with the tactful expression of satisfaction that a more direct succession seemed ensured, by the recent happy event. Lord Halifax responded as follows:

THE MARQUIS OF HALIFAX *to* PRINCESS SOPHIA

Madame,—C'est une generosité qui n'appartient qu'à S.A. de recevoir les services qu'on tasche de luy rendre, d'une maniere, comme s'ils ne luy estoient pas dus, par la consideration de nos interests, aussi bien que du respect que l'on doit a sa personne, et à l'illustre famille qu'elle a honorée de son alliance; Assurement, Madame, la veneration qu'on a pour S.A. nous inspire l'ambition de luy en pouvoir donner des marques, dans toutes les occasions qui se presentent; et ces sentiments sont si universels, que cela oste entierement la pretention de merite à son egard. Je croy sans difficulté que S.A. n'est pas dans l'impatience de iouir de l'effet de la bonne volonté ou plus tost de la iustice du Parlement quand je considere que sa haute naissance fait la moindre partie de sa figure; qu'elle regne a present par sa reputation tous les estats dans L'Europe, de sorte que par son merite distingué, et par ses qualités elevées, elle a un empire plus estendu qu'une courronne luy pourroit donner. Elle a par tout des Vassaux et des Admirateurs, et dans le grand nombre de ceux qui font gloire de l'estre, je le supplie de croire, qu'il n'y a personne qui puisse estre avec plus de zele, de soumission et de respect que je suis,

Madame,

de S.A.

le tres humble et tres obeissant serviteur,

HALIFAX

Returning from this general to minor domestic issues, we find Lord Halifax warning the new King against the issue of general warrants, and favouring a development of the Cabinet system.

But it is in matters ecclesiastical that we have fullest insight into his views. We see him supporting the interest of the Protestant Dissenters as against the High Church party; and William III, indeed, hinted they would have been ready to accept the Marquis as their acknowledged leader. Sharing as he did the new King's views on Toleration, he no doubt voted for the Bill which secured to the Nonconformists liberty of worship; and both he and the King lost some popularity by fruitless efforts to abolish the Sacramental Test, as applied to the Protestants.

Above all things, however, the Lord Privy Seal was interested in the fate of his friend Lord Nottingham's *Comprehension Bill*, which was designed to reunite the Moderate Presbyterians to the Established Church. Report has it that when one of the Spiritual Peers, rising to support the Bill, hesitated on a point of order, Lord Halifax, from the chair, exclaimed that no orders ought to restrain a Bishop when speaking for Comprehension.

The Bill failed to pass, and in this connection, when talking with his confidant Reresby, Lord Halifax inveighed bitterly against 'the stiffness' of the Anglican clergy; saying if the Church suffered 'it would be by their pretending' (i.e. claiming) 'to have too much'. He described the obstruction of the Bill in the House of

Commons as purely Jacobite in its aims, and fostered by those 'who hated the Dutch and had rather turn Papists than take in the Presbyterians amongst them'; and he correctly apprehended that the Appeal to Convocation, recommended by the Commons, would seal the fate of the Bill.

Nor did he spare the Dissenters in his censure. 'The Presbyterians', he said, 'hated the Church of England men as much, and spoilt their own business by the ill preparing of their Bill of Comprehension', not to mention their favouring of bills, in both Houses, which were obnoxious to the very interest from which they looked for indulgence.

The scanty success of these attempts to unite the various Protestant bodies in face of a common foe was accompanied by other factors of an alarming nature. The mutiny of Dumbarton's regiment, against which Dutch reinforcements had to be despatched, and which occasioned the first Mutiny Bill, gave Halifax some concern; as, if supported by other units, it might have had dangerous consequences. The procrastination of the Commons disturbed him; they acted, he said, 'very slowly and as if the whole world were no more than Westminster'. The King, too, was 'very dilatory in his resolutions, which was a great prejudice to business at a time when it so much required dispatch'. And finally, 'there was a necessity of acting with so many fools, that they were only wise who had nothing to do' (with public affairs).

All these considerations no doubt contributed to the very pessimistic views of the general situation, to which he gave expression, in confidential talks with Reresby. Even before the Proclamation of the new Monarch, his language had been anything but reassuring, and his depression of spirits increased as time went on. He realized, none better, the strength and sullen resentment of the extreme element in the defeated Regency party. He told Reresby on one occasion that 'as the nation now stood, if King (James) were a Protestant he could not be kept out four months'. The chronic ill-health of the new Monarch, and the possibility that he (like his great ancestor) might fall a victim to the hand of an assassin, caused him perpetual anxiety. On hearing that King James had left France for Ireland he expressed his fears that the Papists might now succeed in effecting the death of the new King 'knowing what a task we should have on our hands to defend the crown on the head of a woman'. He considered, however, that the danger of King William's cough 'which increased upon him' an even stronger menace. Four weeks later, however, we find that his spirits had at least temporarily risen; for he told Reresby that if the King outlived this summer, 'which he thought he might... the Government would scarce be shaken though it should devolve on the Queen singly'.

His gloomy prognostications included the fortunes of himself and his family. He presumed indeed that 'whenever' (he no doubt means '*if* ever') a change happened 'there would be a general pardon'; but a rumour, erroneous as it happened, had reached him that such an amnesty 'crept up and down in the world' and that he was excepted in it.

Under these circumstances, so he told Reresby, the concerns of his family would compel him to act with as much moderation as was possible, and therefore he took no great nor additional places, no honours or blue ribbons as others had done. 'Come, Sir John', he exclaimed on another occasion, 'we have wives and children, and we must consider them and not venture too far.'

His maintenance of relations with Reresby himself was part of the same prudent policy; for Reresby, though ready to acknowledge and even serve the Government *de facto*, was himself a non-juror and retained many friends in the ranks of avowed Jacobitism; and Halifax evidently looked for his assistance in case of a counter-revolution. 'As you know', the Marquis once told his ally, 'I gave you some little hints of this change before you went down last' (to the country), 'so you must tell me what you hear on the other side.' For, so Halifax considered, if the danger from Ireland were as real as he feared it was, it was safe to carry fair to those of that party, and to let some know that he spoke always very respectfully of King James, for it might come to blows'. We find, however, that the cool theoretic prudence of Lord Halifax failed him, as usual, completely, when occasions occurred for a tempting and bitter sarcasm; since we have it on the authority of William himself that 'the Marquis of Halifax had lost all credit with Queen Mary' on account of some 'unseasonable jests' he had made, in her presence, with regard to her father.

Lord Halifax meanwhile carried his complaisance so far as to meet a Jacobite lady—probably either Lady Dorchester (the former mistress of King James) or Lady Oglethorpe*—at Reresby's lodgings. She had professed herself ready to inform him 'of some-

* If it was Lady Oglethorpe it is interesting to note she was arrested on the following day on her way to Ireland with compromising papers in her possession.

thing that might be for his own [and] the public service'. The lady, according to Reresby, 'dealt very frankly' with his Lordship 'but durst not say all she knew'. We hear no details, but at the conclusion of the interview Lord Halifax desired her 'in case of any alteration' to 'stand her friend'.

There is something repellant in this readiness to 'serve the time', to 'make the best of two possible worlds'. Such conduct was only too common in the post-Revolution period—as is testified by a curious story current in the writer's family.[30] But Halifax was too big a man—he had been too far responsible for the New Settlement—he had seen too clearly the 'impossibility' of James II as an English King—to make such an 'insurance policy' either dignified or decent. But he was hampered by a weight which, as we are told on the highest authority, so often clogs the attainment of the highest virtue. He, too, had 'great possessions'.

But in the case of Halifax we must distinguish. Here is no suspicion of treachery. The steward of our parable is neither unjust, unfaithful nor disloyal. He does not ingratiate himself elsewhere at the expense of his master's interests; though, apprehending—not, we observe, desiring—a possible reversal, on appeal, of the verdict which has placed his lord in possession, he is careful to retain an interest in the household of the rival claimant. For nothing is more certain—though assertions have been made to the contrary—than that Halifax, during his tenure of office under King William, served that monarch with absolute fidelity. This is proved to the hilt by a statement of James II, quoted by his biographer.

If further evidence were needed, we may note the indirect evidence of Reresby, who always regarded the Marquis as a zealous and sincere Revolution official. He even confesses that he 'temporized a little' with his powerful friend, for it was not, he felt, 'convenient to be too open with a Privy Councillor, and so great a Minister'; although, as he himself puts it, 'I loved him so well that I was ready enough to inform him of what related to the public for his private service, provided it was said in general, and not to the prejudice of any particular person, or a confidence reposed on me'. Again, in all their conversations the Minister, however painfully impressed by the seriousness of the crisis, never failed to lay stress on the magnitude of the efforts which were being made, to repel expected attack. 'All the care that could be taken would be. An army would be presently' (i.e. immediately) 'raised of 20,000 men. All suspicious persons would be secured, for the

Parliament would give the King power to imprison whom he pleased and to keep them secure till they could come to trial. And they would plentifully furnish him for the war.'

Here we must note that these interesting conversations were to be the last which ever passed between the two friends. During the spring, after an interview in which Reresby had consulted the Marquis concerning his own private affairs, Sir John, very suddenly, died; and we thus lose one of our most valuable sources of information concerning Lord Halifax.

The fears of Halifax as to the stability of the Revolution settlement were not, as we know, justified by the event. He was equally mistaken as to the quarter from which danger menaced his own fortunes.

The Tories, it is true, he had indeed, to use Burnet's language, 'totally lost'. His abandonment of the Regency principle they regarded as an act of unprincipled time-service; and his support of the dissenting interest had naturally increased their resentment.

But, in fact, the fierce Parliamentary attacks, which distracted the whole remainder of his official career, and finally, though indirectly, brought it to an abrupt close, came from the extremist section of the Whig party. To these men, Lord Halifax was, from every point of view, anathema. The sources of their hatred dated from 1680. There was Bolton who would willingly have 'stabbed him the first' on a memorable November evening. There was Montague, the unscrupulous brother-in-law of the great-hearted Russell; there was Capel, the embittered brother of Essex; Delamere, the resentful friend of Monmouth; Hampden, the prisoner of 1684; all frantic to revenge the sufferings of 1683–5 on the Chief Minister of that dismal period.

Worse than the past, however, there loomed the intolerable present. The Marquis, who had evaded all the risks of the Great Enterprise, had now none the less attained to the pinnacle of power. He ranked high in the Ministry and he had the King's ear. Moreover, he displayed his influence by the appointment to official vacancies of moderate men, to the exclusion of many staunch Whigs whose services to the Revolution remained, in their own eyes, ill rewarded. 'It was these chiefly', says Burnet, 'that followed and persuaded his impeachment.'

For impeachment was, indeed, the goal of his adversaries, and circumstances favoured their aim. The Bill of Indemnity, despite the urgency of William, had not yet been passed; its list of those offences which were to be regarded as a bar to the benefits of the amnesty was not yet complete. Moreover, the Whig Lords, in the concurrent debates on the Bill of Rights, were striving to wrest from the Crown, in all cases of impeachment, the prerogative of pardon. And, in default of such success, the faction resolved, at any rate, to drive the King into an act of dismissal, or Halifax himself into a forced retirement.

The mutterings of the storm began early. Reflection on 'ill Ministers' and 'the higher end of the Council table' were from the first frequent, though vague, and became specific by degrees. On 5 March the Commons had appointed a committee to consider what persons had been concerned as principals in the Rye House prosecutions, and the attacks on the Charters; both of which charges were soon numbered among the 'crimes' which should exclude the perpetrators from pardon. Lists of the Privy Councillors during the first four years of Charles II's reign were significantly and peremptorily demanded; while, as Macaulay puts it, 'Jack Howe, the Queen's Vice-Chamberlain, on twenty occasions designated Halifax as the cause of all the calamities of the country'.

Lord Halifax, however, faced the prospect before him with commendable coolness. He had already informed Reresby 'that the Commons resolved still to pursue him and my Lord Danby, and that some of them had declared they would give no money to the King till he had laid them and some others...aside'. He did not, however, believe that the King would be 'wrought upon as they thought of'. Indeed, he found the King 'so much his friend that he was only too eager on his lordship's behalf; in so much that he was forced to desire him to be moderate'. Several instances of this are recorded in the Spencer House Journals.

For his own part, so Halifax had continued, he considered himself very capable of defending his own cause, and 'did not value' (i.e. attach any importance to) 'the measures undertaken against him'. If they should succeed, he would not be sorry 'to surrender his place'.

The first serious assault on his position was an attempt to make him responsible for the disasters in Ireland; where, by 19 April, resistance to the Jacobite forces had become almost confined to the cities of Londonderry and Inniskillen.

Lord Danby spread a report (which Burnet says was widely current and generally believed) that Tyrconnell, Lord Lieutenant for King James, would have been ready to surrender upon conditions; but that Lord Halifax had told King William 'if Ireland was quiet, there would be no pretence for keeping up an army, and if there was none, he would be turned out as easily as he had been brought in; for it was impossible to please England long, and he might see they began to be discontented already'.

This story (which may have originated in one of Lord Halifax's irresponsible sarcasms), and a similar rumour that he had disingenuously thwarted the appointment of Clarendon as Viceroy for Ireland, may be safely ignored.

It is, however, certain that at the Committee of Council for Ireland, whereat the attendance of Halifax seems to have been exemplary, considerable friction existed between Halifax (among other members of the board) and the Duke of Schomberg; who had been nominated Commander-in-chief for Ireland, and who was said to be influenced by that bitter enemy to Lord Halifax, Lord Montague. The General accused Halifax of obtaining commissions for incompetent Irish nobles; Halifax charged the Duke with an undue partiality for foreigners and an excessive depreciation of the Irish Protestant guerillas; a charge in which Lord Wolseley concurs.*

But these were purely personal charges and recriminations, and there seems no warrant for fastening upon Lord Halifax any peculiar responsibility for Irish disasters. The utmost endeavours of his adversaries could extract no single compromising circumstance from the minute books of the 'Irish Committee'.

The Irish difficulties and miscarriages were, moreover, of a purely military and administrative nature, and as such could hardly have come within the purview of the Lord Privy Seal. Indeed, we have the high authority of Lord Wolseley for suggesting that the absorption of William in the Continental struggle, his want of interest in what he considered a merely subsidiary conflict, and a tendency to grudge every soldier detached from Continental service, must bear a large proportion of the blame. The attempt to place the burden on the shoulders of Lord Halifax merely proves that Lord Halifax was the best hated member of the Committee; and therefore the one who, as Lord Weymouth wrote to Lord Eland four years later, 'while in play, ever bore the faults of the whole board'.

* This opinion derives support from several passages in the Spencer House Journals and Klopp, *Fall des Hauses Stuart*.

The proceedings on the Irish question began in the House of Commons with the appointment on 1 June of a Committee of Inquiry. A motion obviously directed against Lords Halifax and Carmarthen was immediately tabled, but dropped with an adjournment. Six weeks later the suggestion of a special address against the same lords was only postponed by an equality of votes.

Proceedings in the House of Lords proved equally inconclusive. On 10 July, however, an attempt was made by Montague and others to oust Halifax from the Speaker's Chair. His friends would have evaded the issue, but Halifax insisted on putting the question, which was lost by a large majority.

The vindictive animosity of Lord Montague evidently distressed his sister-in-law, the noble widow of Lord Russell, as we learn from the following correspondence. The troubles of Halifax were being at this time enhanced by family distress; he had lost, within a few days of his taking office, his youngest son, Lord George; and about the period to which we now refer, his eldest daughter, Lady Carberry, died in childbed. Lady Russell, who by a first marriage was Lady Carberry's sister-in-law, appears to have written, on this occasion, a letter of condolence to Lord Halifax, which is now lost, but in which she seems to have expressed her regret at the persecution from which he was suffering. Lord Halifax answered as follows:

Madam,—I must own that my reason is not strong enough to bear with indifference the losses that have lately happened in my family; but, at the same time, I must acknowledge I am not a little supported by the continuance of your Ladyship's favour to me, in the obliging remembrance I have received from you, and in your condoling the affliction of the man in the world that is most devoted to you. I am impatient till I have the honour of an hour's conversation with your Ladyship, to ease my mind of the just complaints I have, that such returns are made to the zeal I have endeavoured to express, in my small capacity, for the good of England. I cannot but think it the fantastical influence of my ill stars, very peculiar to myself, all circumstances considered; but whilst I am under the protection of your Ladyship's better opinion, the malice or mistakes of others can never have the force so much as to discompose,

Madam,

Your Ladyship's most obedient servant,

HALIFAX

London, 23 *July* 1689

Lady Russell's reply has been more than once printed. In it she maintains that she herself has no respect for an affectation of stoical indifference to all that may happen, which seems to her unnatural. 'The Christian religion', she urges, 'has only the power to make a spirit easy under great calamities.' This has been her own experience, as she earnestly desires it may be her correspondent's. 'If I had', she adds, '[a] better or a larger wish to make, your Lordship's constant expressions of esteem for me, and willingness, as I hope, to have me less miserable than I am, *if you had found your power equal to your will** engages me to make it; and that alone would have bound me, though my unworthiness and ill fortune had let you have forgotten me for ever after my sad lot, but since you would not do so, it must deserve a particular acknowledgment for ever, from, etc.'

In view of subsequent events, this pathetic letter is of great importance.

Despite the bitterness he had thus expressed, Lord Halifax faced the situation with unabated coolness. He withstood the King's resolve for a speedy prorogation. 'My desire', he records, 'was [that] they might sit [again] to empty all their shot upon me; quite contrary to the other men of business who were glad to put off the danger.' With characteristic pride he asseverated that he was strong enough to support himself, and had no desire to compromise the King's affairs by leaning on His Majesty.

The assault on him was immediately resumed, and though a motion for a condemnatory address was frustrated, the debate on 'the State of the Nation' which immediately ensued gave ample opportunity for fresh attacks. These culminated in a motion that 'It is inconvenient to His Majesties affairs that the Marquis of Halifax is in His Majesties Council'.

His rivals, however, realizing that they were at the moment in a minority, proceeded to move an adjournment. But the 'judicious and spirited' conduct (to quote Macaulay's words) of his son Lord Eland carried the day. He exclaimed 'that his father was not a man to be trifled with, and that if he should prove guilty the [House] should proceed to punish him; that he had no need to be in office, in order to maintain himself as his rank demanded, since God had already given him more than a sufficiency'. The motion was immediately put, and lost by 90 to 79 votes.

William himself was furious with the promoters of the motion. In private he threatened that they should suffer for their vindictive violence—Henry Capel should not be employed—Leveson Gore

* Italics are our own.

should not have his Peerage, etc.; and he declared that the 'arbitrary speeches' (whatever they may have been) with which Halifax was charged 'were only too gentle'. He carried his resentment against these tactics into action; and less than three weeks later, Lord Halifax was instructed to prorogue the unruly Convention.

Lord Halifax, in this preliminary skirmish, had carried off the honours of war. In the words of the historian Ralph: 'It became evident...that the great end...aimed at of making the Marquis of Halifax accountable for all the [recent] miscarriages...was utterly unattainable.' But the narrowness of the majorities by which he had escaped censure testified to the inveterate hostility of which he was the object; and it is possible that he began tc consider the desirability of a voluntary retirement, so soon as he should have secured his own justification.

From the Speakership of the House of Lords at any rate he had apparently already resolved to resign. Some ascribed his decision to pressure from the King, desirous of placating the Whigs. More probably Halifax himself foresaw the awkwardness of his retaining the Chairmanship, during a session to be presumably occupied by renewed attacks on himself. We know, at any rate, that a fortnight before the end of the recess he received a visit from Lord Clarendon, during which Halifax urged his visitor (who had become a Nonjuror) to attend the approaching debates, and thus 'do much good for the Church of England; which some, he said, considered to be in danger by reason of the King's kindness to some of the Dissenters, though he himself did not share the apprehension'. Clarendon declined, asking only a continuance of the kindness which had allowed him to live undisturbed in the country. Lord Halifax thereupon 'promised me [records Clarendon] to do all that lay in his power, but he said he would not be Speaker'; and therefore would be unable to assist him in case of a 'call of the House'. Whereupon Halifax complained 'what hard measure he had met with in the House of Commons, who had endeavoured to ruin him'; though he fully acknowledged the 'generous behaviour' of Lord Clarendon's son, who had voted in his favour.

In accordance with his above decision Lord Halifax, at the meeting of Council which preceded the meeting of Parliament, gave notice that for several reasons which he forbore to mention he must desire to be excused from doing 'the office of Speaker in the House of Lords'. In this, we find he was succeeded by Chief Baron Atkins.

His anticipations regarding the tenor of the Session were not dispelled; for a new and even more dangerous campaign was at once opened upon him. On 2 November, at the instigation of Lords Montague and Monmouth, the 'mad' Duke of Bolton obtained the appointment of a Committee; 'to consider who were the advisers and prosecutors of the murders of the Lord Russell, Colonel Sidney...and others'; who was responsible for the writs of Quo Warranto against Corporations, and who were the public assertors of the dispensing Power. It was obvious, says Burnet, that the attack was levelled at Lord Halifax, and so he regarded it.

The Committee, usually known as the 'Murder' Committee, originally consisted of thirty-five Peers, including some who were among the bitterest of his enemies; but he himself came in, with the twenty-one subsequently added, of whom the majority seem to have been Tories.

The inquiry lasted from 4 November to 20 December, when the Committee reported; but its real business had begun on 18 November when Dr Tillotson was examined concerning the case of Lord Russell. His evidence (already discussed in a previous chapter) had proved, as we know, entirely favourable to Lord Halifax; having included the testimony of Russell himself, while awaiting execution, on his behalf. The same may be said as regards the trial of Algernon Sidney.

A charge that Halifax had patronized an informer against the accused was countered by him with the explanation; that, while the man, who had revealed the real 'Rye House' (or assassination) conspiracy, had therefore deserved and received some recompense, Halifax himself had had no share in the matter.

The main interest of the inquiry therefore centres for us on the evidence of Mr John Hampden.

This gentleman, generally known as 'the Younger', his father having also played a minor part in the politics of the day, had, as we know, been deeply engaged in the intrigues of 1683. In default of a second witness to a charge of treason, he had stood his trial on a charge of misdemeanour, and had been condemned to an illegal fine of £40,000, i.e. to imprisonment till the death of his father. Nor was that all. After Monmouth's invasion a second witness had become available; and the unhappy man had then been indicted for high treason, *on the same count under which he was even then suffering imprisonment for misdemeanour.* In desperation he had pleaded guilty, making a full and somewhat abject submission, which, reinforced with the powerful advocacy of heavy bribes, had procured his pardon. It seems probable that his sufferings had to some extent impaired his reason, and such was certainly the view of King William.

Lord Halifax, by his own account, had felt some compassion for his wrongs, and had exerted himself to obtain employment for him after the Revolution. Hampden, however, seems to have then made some kind of advances to Halifax, which the latter had rebuffed; and for this or some other reason Hampden had come to regard the Marquis with a rancorous hatred, which he now proceeded to gratify.

His evidence before the Committee, given at great length, was summarized by Lord Halifax in notes which are still extant and may be briefly epitomized thus:

Mr Hampden began by complimenting the Committee upon its action in the matter, and introduced his own evidence by the strange flight that he looked upon himself as murdered, as truly as any of those whose case was under consideration; since few of the Lords, as he maintained, but would have preferred death to such sufferings as he had undergone. The real conspirators, he proceeded, were those by whose instrumentality Russell and the others had been 'murdered'. He then adverted, with peculiar emphasis, to the paper or confession which the Marquis of Halifax had endeavoured to obtain from the Duke of Monmouth; reiterating his former contention that an instrument of that nature was equivalent to his own death-warrant, since documents had been adduced, in lieu of a second witness, to secure the conviction of Sidney. He asserted on the authority of a Mr Waller, who had died in the interim, that the so-called confession of the Duke had determined Charles II against showing mercy to Sidney. He returned with half-crazy vehemence to the details of his own sufferings, which had, he averred, almost cost him his memory; and defended his eventual submission on the ground that no one at that time remained alive who could be injured by the plea of guilty. He boasted, indeed, of its tenor, and declared that, as 'no man may thinke hee ought to be ashamed of that Confession, that thinketh my Ld. Russell was murdered', so the method of revolt was the old English form of protest against tyranny, and the expedition of William but the continuation of the Council of Six. He was compelled to admit that he had applied to Lord Halifax for his intercession, and had sent his wife to thank that lord for his good offices; but he attempted to qualify this by asking to whom, save to enemies, could he have applied on such an occasion.

Among the Halifax MSS. in the possession of the Duke of Devonshire are several loose sheets in the hand of Lord Halifax, which evidently allude to these proceedings. They seem to be notes, presumably for speeches on the Report stage of the Committee, when Lord Halifax, according to a contemporary, 'took occasion to speak somewhat largely...and lashed some members very severely, and took particular notice of Mr Hampden'.

The criticisms applicable to Hampden are as follows:

First. giveth us his Princely approbation of our proceedings. His next businesse was to give evidence that hee was dead: and really he had almost perswaded mee into it, for from a living man I never heard such evidence. Hee said hee was worse than murthered. Hee had raither have been murthered. It was not then his choice. The dead committ no such mistakes, yet etc. Death is looked upon as the worst etc. and hee thought so. Was afraid the paper would hang him. Needed lesse to fear that having such an expedient ready to prevent it. Because a paper was set up for a witnesse! Great difference between the papers; one of moment, if proved! this of none.

2. D. of Monmouth had confessed first of particular men, and of Mr. Hampden himselfe. Before K. [and] the Duke [of York]. That D.M.'s confession of the Plot in Genl. did hurt is no truer, than that his own confession afterwards could do none. Some suffered after. And it was a clear evidence of the plot, and a marque upon a party if there had been any doubt of it. Said hee had almost lost his memory, an inconvenient preface for a Witnesse. I do really beleeve hee suffered a great deal, of which I was sencible, and did my endeavour to prevent them; I [interceded?] for him then, and do now lament the effect they may have had upon him. Hee owned my endeavours to serve him then by his thanks. Since [then] hee sayeth, to whom should hee apply but to his enemies? An extraordinary temper, thanks to his enemies and confessions against his friends, and all this to save a life that was worse than death. Strange! Let him be contented with the honour of a Confessour without pretending to that of a Martyr. Sayeth that the money was taken upon condition that hee would confesse guilty upon the inditement. I do not beleeve that, or that there was any other reason for taking it, than because it was money. I do not think that they valued that confession at a farthing. Sayeth it was onely a compliment, not worth the making it an article. It was not thought that his life would do the Govt. any hurt. From such an exquisite Protestant to have the bringing in the D. of Monmouth to Court obiected is somewhat surprising. Sure I did not recommend my selfe to the other side of the world by it; It looketh as if hee had a hidden remainder of good will for mee, which hee doth not know of, that corrupteth his judgement when it intendeth anything against mee. But this

paper a terrible thing; Overborne and purswaded by a great man. 1. No proofe of that, but dead proofe. 2. No likely hood that any man could have power to overbear if the K. himselfe could not do it. Mr Hampden confesseth hee had heard the D. of Monmouth confessed the plot, so hee needed not have been so allarumed with the paper. 3. The D. of Monmouth was afterwards upon very good termes with mee. 4. The consequence of it certain was nor could bee anything. 5. The K. promised him as the D. told mee that hee should not bee a witnesse.

But now cometh the point. Sydney executed some time after this paper. *ergo* This paper hanged him, and *ergo* Ld. Halifax got this paper on purpose to hang him. Note—The K. balanced till that was don, which is false. Examine what D. of Monmouth said that very night. Ld. Sydney spoke to him. Ay, but old Mr. Waller told him, that the confession of the plot, not of the paper, was the cause of Coll: Sydney's death. 1. Hee doth not say the paper. 2. Mr. Wallers assertion of This was alledged in an unknown country. Sayeth no man will think hee ought to be ashamed of his confession that thinketh Ld. Russell was murthered. I neither reproove him with his Confession nor his evidence, since I think them both insignificant as to any thing but to himselfe, and if hee liketh his own figure the better for it, I am content. Here lyeth a great deal of weight in these words that Ld. Russell was murthered. And hee explaineth his meaning by saying that which seemeth very extraordinary, and deserveth a serious reflection. Being a man of method layeth down his principle. 1. When the Lawes are broke by the Govt. the people hath a right to do themselves justice. 2. The Consequence; hee and 6 more or 16 or what number hee pleaseth may execute that right. 3. From hence, cleer, that the Govrs. are the Conspiratours, and who ever they condemne though by the Lawes in being are murthered because they were on the side of the Lawes. 4. In murther there are no Accessaries; ergo. The whole Nation committed the murther because they stood by and did not hinder it. So not onely the Cabinet Councell, Judges, Councell Jury etc. but all England are impeached by Mr. H. the Atturney Genl. for those few righteous. 'Tis time to look about us. If this witnesse, my Lds. should come to bee your Judge, you are all guilty, and it would bee a question whether you could save yourselves as hee did by your Confession, his Conclusion is very singular. for after having said what a part hee had in the late revolution which is now etc. hee tells us that there was a Chaine in these proceedings which was an evidence of the people's right. That the first plot of Le Rye etc. was an assertion of their right. D. of Monmouth's coming another struggle for liberty. The Kgs. coming [a] continuation, and that hee cometh upon the same foot. In short It is hard that M[r] H[ampden] who maketh so good a complement to K. James in his confession, should make so ill a one to K. William in his evidence.

On 20 November Sir James Forbes, a friend of the Duke of Monmouth, was examined as to the much-debated 'Confession' of His Grace. He described at length how, after the signature had been wrested from the Duke by the importunity of Lord Halifax, Monmouth had despatched his friend to Hampden with the copy of the paper in question, and how Hampden had thereupon exclaimed that he looked upon himself as a dead man. Incidentally, Sir James mentioned that the Duke of Monmouth had distinguished the Duke of York as his implacable enemy, and the author of his existing difficulties, and had complained that he saw he had been brought back to court to do a job on purpose to ruine him. This evidence appears to have elicited from Lord Halifax, on the report of the Committee, a retort scarcely less bitter than the one directed against Mr Hampden.

Sir J. Forbes.

The Scope of Sr. J. his evidence seemeth to bee to shew how intimate hee was with the Duke of Monmouth. Upon which I cannot but observe, that the same D. of Monmouth at this very same time told mee Sr. J. was a very simple fellow. How farre hee hath made good this by an evidence which though it should bee true is of no manner of Signification, must be left etc. Hee was it seemeth as hee sayeth employed to tell this to Mr. Hampbden. Capt. Hampbden out of a desire to reserve himselfe to save the Nation was in that respect very apprehensive, and not from any danger to his own person. In reality this paper would have done more than any thing else to have saved him and the rest. If it had been understood to have been such a piece of killing evidence, It would not have been so easily returned. D. of Monmouth said, hee knew the D. was his implacable enemy and had done all this; Nota. If the D. had done all this, How come I in?

Q. Was the D. so much my friend at that time as that I must ioigne with him in the Contrivance.

Mr. Hampden the aptest in the world to think himselfe a dead man hee said so then and in effect said so at the Committee for he layed his clayme to have those punished that murthered him.

Sir J. Forbes did well to go to somebody else for reasons against the signing the paper; It seemeth hee would not rely upon those of his own growth. [Monmouth] Said hee saw hee was now brought to Court to do a Job on purpose to ruine him. By this, it must be meant that either the K. used this stratagem to destroy him, which is not very supposeable, considering as I may call it, the extravagant kindnesse hee had for him. Or 2ndly that the D. did it, who first knew nothing of his coming in till all had been concerted, and when hee did know it and could not help it was perhaps more troubled at it than at any thing that ever happened to him in his life; or I must endeavour to play this trick of State on pirpose to ruine D. Monmouth, when in reality my part in it to serve him made me runne a hazard of being destroyed by the D.; by whom for this very act I am not perhaps forgiven to this day.

Ld. Halifax perswaded him, but whether it was for his good hee knew not—[*Here notes end abruptly*]

The bitterest invective, however, of which Halifax was master, seems on this occasion to have been reserved for the prime mover in the charges against him, Lord Montague; if, indeed, so scathing a diatribe can actually have been delivered in the House of Lords.

Hee hath an extraordinary way of dead evidence. It hath been of use to him for his profit and now he would have it to be for his Revenge. Hee said Madame owed him so many 1000 pistoles at play, and in Generosity etc. Monsieur payed it. I think living evidence will serve his turne. So farre from a particular animosity, that I take him to bee as much my friend, as hee is any man's in England. Hee hath bin so long my known friend [? and] is now willing to make a sacrifice of his kindnesse to the publique good. To be commended for it. Hee is very fit for businesse, having all the Secrets of the French Embassadour etc. His familiarity with him was onely to get better lights to destroy France. etc. I look with the same eye of charity upon his earnestness to get into K. James his Court. The Appearance was Popish, but the end was Protestant, and so I conclude etc. One thing against his Protestantisme; he was for the Intercession of Saints; hee had that of the K. of France for the blew Ribband.

K. James returned his exclusion to him; Neither his kindnesse to France, nor his Gentlenesse to Popery could reconcile him to him. If it was not a designe for the Protestant Religion his Intimacy with the F. Em: must bee a designe against it. Hee hath been accused of too much opennesse in shewing letters. Perhaps if hee was a Secretary, that place would cure him. Even that iniury to France was not above their Charity to forgive; either it was at first permitted or much must be done to have it pardoned. Hee is so sollicitous to get others out, that it raither seemeth (?) that he meaneth well to himselfe, than ill to any body else.

Chancellour of Scotland told Ld. Preston that my ld. Mountague pressing the K. for his place told him hee would in a very little time give very good evidence of his affection to his Religion.

The Debate in which these speeches appear to have been made was twice adjourned. The Examinations were then communicated to the Commons; and thus—the matter terminated.

'Nothing appeared', says Burnet, 'upon which notes [query votes] or addresses could have been founded.' In plainer English, the Lord Privy Seal had emerged with flying colours. The Duke of Bolton, his inveterate antagonist, upon whose motion the Committee had been appointed, informed the Marquis (as he records in the Devonshire House notebook) that he had become convinced of his Lordship's innocence; and it is no unfair inference of Lord

Macaulay from existing evidence, that Lady Russell had again, and openly, expressed indignation at the part played by her sister's husband.

But the fray was by no means over. The indefatigable Hampden, exasperated rather than chastened by the castigation he had received, was still engineering a fresh and if possible a fiercer onslaught upon the position of the Lord Privy Seal. He accused the Government of employing men of Republican principles—an obvious reference to the reputed sympathies of Lord Halifax—but this charge, coming from the grandson of the great Hampden, could only excite the ribald mirth of the House. He charged the Administration with retaining Ministers who had been voted 'enemies to the King and Kingdom and favourers of Popery'—another unmistakable allusion—and went on to stigmatize those men who, as Commissioners of King James, had endeavoured to oppose the victorious advance of the Prince of Orange. This last charge excited considerable resentment. One old rival of Halifax retorted 'that possibly the best thing they [ever] did was [thus] to mediate peace'; while others asserted that the Commissioners had been selected because 'they had all along disapproved of the King's conduct...had the approbation of the Nation, and were [the] most likely to be agreeable to the Prince'. Others, indeed, repudiated these favourable sentiments with equal indignation; but eventually it was decided that the King should be adjured only to 'find out' the authors of the recent miscarriages, with a view to their punishment; but that no names should be mentioned. An address, ostensibly on these lines, was finally reported on 21 December, by young Hampden.

The report, however, for which no doubt Hampden will have been mainly responsible, proved so violent that his own father disapproved it; and another member exclaimed 'This an address! it is a libel!' It was accordingly recommitted and finally dropped altogether.

But it had done its work; Halifax had finally resolved on abandoning the conflict. Advancing years, domestic calamity, and somewhat impaired health—a motive which he himself avowed—may have had a share in this decision, but the main motive was immediate and political. A considerable proportion of the extraordinary War Supply remained in suspense, and time was running short on the field of military finance.

Halifax therefore, on 24 December, proposed to the King that as a sop to the Opposition, all the three attacked Ministers should 'go off according to the intended Address'. William replied 'that might have very ill consequences, he would see whether the Parliament would give more money before he took his resolution'.

In effect, the King's dilemma was rather a cruel one. It is now clear that on this point the assertions of Burnet, Dalrymple and Macaulay, are erroneous. William III had not tired of his Minister; he deprecated, even to the point of urgency, the retirement of Lord Halifax. Probably at the time he preferred the personality of 'The Trimmer' to that of either Nottingham or Godolphin. But he can hardly have failed to realize, with a latent misgiving, that the withdrawal of the Marquis, while averting much obloquy from the Government, could not disoblige any of the factions on which it depended for support. For if the Whigs abhorred him, the Tories did not love him. Carmarthen, the Tory President of the Council, caballed against the Lord Privy Seal in amicable alliance with Monmouth, the Whig Lord of the Treasury; and the dislike entertained in Whig quarters for his fellow-Commissioners of 1689 was mild compared with their loathing for Lord Halifax. Godolphin, moreover, was probably already contemplating that resolution of retirement which he carried into effect immediately after that of Halifax. Nottingham (who, moreover, steadfastly declined a voluntary retreat) had held office under neither Charles II nor James II; and, furthermore, enjoyed the entire confidence of the staunch, yet more moderate, Churchmen who had rallied to the Revolution settlement. This party William, in his disgust at the unbridled violence of the Whigs, was at the moment specially anxious to conciliate. Moreover, such a policy, if carried into effect, must compel him—though not without some reluctance—to cultivate the good graces of Carmarthen, whose interest with the Tory section was considerable. To do so without exciting the susceptibilities of Halifax was an impossible task. The Marquis is known to have complained 'that there was no competing with the merit of rebellion', i.e. with the signature of the 'Invitation'—to which Carmarthen, and not he, had been accessory; and it is certain that the Dutch Minister saw in the situation only the jealous antagonism of the two inveterate rivals.

A climax was reached on 27 January when the disputes over the Corporation Bill compelled William to end the Session as the prelude to a general election.

If William hoped by this abrupt decision to evade the necessity for any Ministerial resignations, he was mistaken. Four days later Lord Halifax, to use his own words, 'spoke to the King concerning myself. He would not', adds Halifax, 'take any resolution, but agreed to speak further to me concerning it in two or three days'. A week later—the day Parliament was dissolved—he showed Halifax a list of the Cabinet selected to advise the Queen during his own absence, which included Halifax himself. Perhaps he hoped by this renewed proof of continued confidence to shake the resolution of Lord Halifax. His efforts were fruitless, and the same day Lord Halifax wrote to Lord Chesterfield as follows:

London, 6 *February* 1689

The intire friendship and respect I must ever have for my dear lord, maketh me send this advertisement to you, viz. that after having withstood the attempts of my adversaryes in parliament, and out of the annoyance that is naturall to honest men injured defyed their malice instead of courting their friendship, I am apt to think it now (no lesse for the consideration of the publique than for my own ease) may bee fit for me to retire; and, therefore, I am resolved to do it very suddenly. I would not have troubled your lordship with this circumstance concerning myself, but that I heard, upon my place having been offered to you, that you were in some disposition to accept it. This is the occasion of my writing, to desire you would take no resolution of that kind till I have the honour to see you; which will not be long, if the resolution holdeth of calling a new parliament immediately, at which I had much rather have your company than your proxy. The reasons I have to say this are too many to be set down in paper, so that you must give mee so much credit as to believe that, without some reasonable ground to justify me in it, this intimation should not have been given you by,

My dear Lord,

Your, etc.

Pray my lord, let this be burnt, and dispatch my servant back againe.

Two days later, 8 February 1689/90, Lord Halifax formally surrendered the Privy Seal, and the circumstances of the last interview must be given in the words of Halifax himself:

Delivered the seal to [the King]; told him, it was for his service I did it. hee said hee doubted* it was not for his service and that hee did not know where to place them in so good hands etc. I told him I had weighed it etc. and in this hee must give mee leave to overrule him. Hee argued earnestly against mee, and as I was going out, shut the door, and said he would not take the seals, except I promised him I would come into

* I.e. feared.

implyoyment againe when it was for his service: I said, I would, if my health would give mee leave; Tush replyeth hee, you have health enough; I said againe, I must make that exception.

A conversation followed upon impending political appointments and the general situation; in the course of which William clearly announced that no one who had ranked among the persecutors of Halifax should receive preferment. Lord Halifax offered several suggestions, of which one at least was accepted, and so eventually retired from his last official audience.

If we wish for further proof of the King's sincerity in this interview, we have only to turn to a letter which Queen Mary wrote about four months later to King William. She had had, she told him, to reprove Lord Monmouth for his insinuations against certain Ministers. 'I told [him]', writes the Queen, 'that I found it very strange you were not thought fit to choose your own Ministers'; that he and his friends 'had actually removed Lord Halifax', and were now scheming against others.

Probably as a compliment to the retiring statesman, the Privy Seal was placed in Commission.

CHAPTER XIII

IN OPPOSITION TO THE END

THE circumstances of the Lord Privy Seal's retirement were as little understood by contemporaries as by subsequent historians. Some maintained he had been in fact cashiered; others that, despite his apparent retirement, his influence still prevailed.

The violence of the ultra-Whigs, meanwhile, had excited general alarm, and when the new Parliament met, the Tories in the Lower House found themselves possessed of a working majority. This fact further encouraged William in his attempts to conciliate the 'Church' interest, and a situation thus arose which can only be described as paradoxical. For he thus became the patron of a faction which had opposed his pretensions to the Crown, and the opponent of those by whom those pretensions had been forwarded.

The Whigs saw their opportunity, and promptly took advantage of it. They introduced in the House of Lords a Bill which *declared* the legality of all Convention Acts, and *recognized* the reigning Sovereigns as 'rightful and lawful rulers'. This placed a dilemma before the more rigid Tories, who, while willing to *accept* the two as *de facto* occupants of the throne, and to *confirm* their title and the Acts of the Convention, refused to acknowledge either as *de jure*; and they, in fact, opposed the Bill.

The policy of these dissidents received an unexpected reinforcement. Despite the fact that they were led, not only by his friend Nottingham, but by his successful rival Carmarthen, we find Lord Halifax recording his vote in their favour. And when, after long and acrimonious wrangling, the Bill passed all its stages in the Upper House, Lord Halifax, and one other, signed a protest without reasons assigned, while Lord Nottingham, and seventeen more, subscribed another, and a somewhat violent protest, subsequently expunged by the House.

The Whigs, having thus succeeded—though only to a limited degree—in sowing discord between the King and his new allies, next tried to exclude the latter from Parliament by the time-honoured expedient of a 'Test'.

A Bill was introduced in the House of Commons which would have attached to the Oath of Allegiance (upon pain of imprisonment for recusancy), a subsidiary oath expressly 'abjuring' the late King James. This was to be imposed upon all officials, all members of either House, and (at the discretion of a Justice of the Peace) even upon private individuals. It was no less offensive than had been the former Bill to the *de facto* Tories, who were unwilling to swear that the late King retained no 'title' to the Crown. William himself demurred to the severe penalty suggested; and the measure was rejected by the Commons. A modified Bill was therefore introduced in the Upper House, by which the threat of double taxation, with loss of the franchise, replaced the penalty of imprisonment. This seems to have had, originally, the sanction of the King who, however, subsequently withdrew it.

Lord Halifax opposed the measure, and the attempt to interfere with the birthright of the Peers aroused general resentment in their House. The Whigs, foiled in their attempt at 'packing' a Parliament, and satisfied that they had sown sufficient mistrust between the King and the 'Church' party, at length abandoned the Bill.

One Act, however, which was placed on the Statute Book during the Session, must have secured the suffrage of both the King and his former Minister. Party rancour having rendered interminable the proceedings on a 'Bill of Indemnity', William now intervened with an 'Act of Grace'. This protected from recrimination all former agents of James save a specially obnoxious minority, which included Lord Sunderland. Having obtained this long-delayed consummation, together with a substantial Supply, William, on 23 May 1690, rather unexpectedly prorogued.

On the same day Lord Halifax had an audience of the King, at whose instance does not appear; but the colloquy seems to have been amicable. It is clear, however, that despite the resignation of the Minister, William had continued to count on his Parliamentary support; and that the action of the Marquis in regard to the two crucial Bills of the Session had surprised and displeased the King. The following details are given from the contemporary notes of the Marquis:

After the first introduction [says Halifax] I fell upon the Things I heard were objected to me, as first, the Protest [against the] Recognizing Bill. To which I gave my answer, it had been represented to him with the aggravations etc.;* he seemed to be satisfied. Secondly, the Bill of Oaths. He said, Lord Nottingham was always of that opinion viz. of a King *de*

* Probably that he had signed Lord Nottingham's Protest.

facto; said a great many of the clergy had Scruples of that Kind. For that reason I told him it was unseasonable at this time; he seem'd in conclusion to wish it had not come in. He was satisfied I had nothing to do, in the attempt against Lord Carmarthen. He said, Lord Carmarthen was sorry I was out, especially at the last; and that the other Party were mad at themselves for having ever meddl'd with me; Lord Monmouth in particular. He was satisfied I had no part in perswading Lord Shrewsbury to quit.

For the long conversation which followed, on matters of immediate administrative interest, the reader is referred to the original report; but William appears to have spoken with great freedom, requiring on more than one point the advice of his former Minister. Finally, as Lord Halifax tells us, 'The King said, He was still a Trimmer, and would continue so'; and with these words, obviously intended for the conciliation of the Marquis, the *confidential* intercourse of these celebrated men—so far, at least, as we can judge—concludes. They certainly met at least once again, about the affairs of the Queen Dowager.

From this time forth, so far as we can gather, Lord Halifax ceased to attend the meetings of the Privy Council, and appears even to have absented himself from Court functions, at which his wife was still a welcome guest. He declined, however, the 'affectation of a sullen retirement'; and from taste, no doubt, as well as policy, he made no attempt to abandon the political arena. From this indeed, in the seventeenth century, when 'calls of the House' were enforced with some severity, it was, as we have already had occasion to notice, by no means easy for a Peer to withdraw altogether.

From this time therefore we find him an active member of the Parliamentary Opposition.

But we must guard against accepting the acrimonious estimates of his activities, which we find in the pages of his former friend, Bishop Burnet, who was by this time a complete devotee of the Whig party. Not six months after the statesman's retirement, the spiritual Peer was describing him as one who seemed to lean towards the party of King James, and as 'finding fault with everything the Government does'; so that (declares the Bishop) 'he is thought a Jacobite; though', he adds, 'I believe his commerce that way goes no further than that he is laying in, for a pardon and perhaps for favour, if a Revolution should happen, for he is neither a firm nor a stout man. ...I believe he will put nothing to hazard for the interest of

James.' In his published *History*, revised at a later date, when party feelings had become if possible even more embittered, he says that Halifax 'reconciled himself to the *Tories* and became wholly theirs...and did upon all occasions serve the Jacobites, and protect the whole party'. And in his final estimate, written after the death of Savile, he merely says 'he had gone into all the measures of the tories; only he took care to preserve himself from criminal engagements'.

Now, what are the facts? In the first place, it is clear that Halifax never made any advances to the exiled King; and also that no Jacobite emissary ever ventured to approach Halifax till eight months after his resignation. It was then that a Jacobite agent, one Bulkeley, reported to James II a visit he had made to Lord Halifax, and declared that the Marquis had 'received him with open arms [and] promised to do everything in his power to serve the King'. The ardent anticipations and exuberant reports of Jacobite agents, so well described by Winston Churchill in his *Life of Marlborough*, have become almost proverbial; and we may conclude that a few civil replies, a few double-edged compliments, and a few sarcastic evasions from the man who had boasted 'that he always spoke very respectfully of King James' would have sufficed to inflame the susceptible imagination of a Jacobite enthusiast. A kind of insurance against political disaster; to be cheaply purchased at the modest premium of a few equivocal speeches, is the utmost with which we can credit—or discredit—Lord Halifax. Such visits, however, even when from old friends, carried with them an element of danger; and we shall find one of them involving the Marquis in something approaching Misprision of Treason.

Burnet, again, over-simplifies his relationship to the Tories. During the earlier years of William's reign the Tories and the Parliamentary Opposition were not the convertible terms which Burnet—transferring to an earlier period the colouring of a later date—takes for granted. It was not till 1693 that William, on the advice of Sunderland, was to adopt the system of party government. His earlier Ministries were what we should now call Coalitions. Whig and Tory mingled in the Government, and, despite their dissensions, which were perpetual, presented upon occasion a united front to the Parliamentary Opposition. In the ranks of discontent, meanwhile, the disappointed Whigs, to whom the Revolution appeared a measure of insufficient, or even deceptive, scope, coalesced with the more sullen Tories who, though they had rallied to the Revolution settlement, still cast lingering glances towards the pre-Revolution standpoint. Thus the vertical division of parties into 'Whig' and 'Tory' crossed, so to say, the horizontal line, which divided the 'ins' from the 'outs'.

Moreover, at the period when Halifax quitted the Government, the Tory party had actually the preponderance, both in the King's favour and in official position. It was to some extent led by Carmarthen, jealousy of whom had evidently much to do with the acrid tone of our statesman's opposition polemics. It is, indeed, quite clear that Halifax to the last preserved the independent attitude of the 'Trimmer'. His position was rather that of the old Country party, of fifteen years earlier, opposed to the Government of the day but not to the dynasty. To the Opposition as a whole he rendered yeoman and guerrilla service; but he is always mentioned separately in the accounts of contemporary newsmongers; and his last published work was to be severely critical of purely party zeal.

Another criticism made by Burnet—that his intellectual vigour had somewhat abated, that a sensible decline was observable in the quality of his speeches, and that they thenceforth relied more on wit and sarcasm than on sound reasoning—is obviously informed by personal and party spleen, the last charge more especially. For, however much Halifax may have respected Burnet as a Churchman, yet as an active episcopal politician he was notoriously the butt of the statesman's satire. It is no doubt to Burnet that 'Saviliana' refers in a significant passage, which obviously alludes to Burnet's change of views, as regards the doctrine of Non-Resistance.

> When [Halifax], after the Revolution,...saw several papers come out in print justifying what was done, with the names of Divines to them, who not many years before had both writ, and acted quite contrary to their assertions, his Lordship was heard to say to a Divine these remarkeable words. *If you Clergymen minded nothing but to lead good lives yourselves, and to preach good lives to others, your power would be so great by being grounded on vertue, that you could easily prevent misadministration in Kingdoms; you would be a terror to ill princes, and the support of good ones; But your meddling with politicks, and changing opinions to serve your turn, brings a scandal upon your profession; and Religion itself is a sufferer by it.*

And we find his contemporary, Cunningham, relating how on some occasion, when the Bishop had ventured on a rhetorical appeal to the verdict of the Great Assize, Lord Halifax had turned his speech into such exquisite ridicule that the laughter of the whole House, and even of the staid King himself, was directed against him.

But none the less the charge may rest on a basis of truth. Halifax was by this time well over 56, and men aged earlier then than now. He had led a strenuous life; was not, it would appear, blessed with very robust health; and probably had long suffered from the neglected internal injury which, five years later, was to be the cause of his death. It is, however, certain that he retained at least sufficient energy, ability and eloquence to constitute a formidable antagonist, was still foremost in debate, still an authority in Committee, and was not infrequently appointed Speaker *pro tem*.

We must now, however, retrace our steps and take in their chronological order the course of events from the spring of 1690, i.e. from the date of the Minister's retirement.

The recess of this summer overflowed with political excitements. It included the alarms of a possible French invasion, the discovery of Jacobite intrigues, the discreditable and critical defeat of the Allied fleets off Beachy Head, with the ensuing arrest of Admiral Lord Torrington; and it saw the practical conclusion of the Irish campaign at the Battle of the Boyne. Lord Halifax remained throughout all this turmoil quietly settled at Acton, in touch with political issues, but mainly occupied by family correspondence and affairs.

His son seems to have again taken his delicate wife for change of air to the now deserted Rufford, and we find his father writing to him as follows:

THE MARQUIS OF HALIFAX *to* HIS SON WILLIAM LORD ELAND

5 *August* 1690

I have yours and am glad you had so favourable a Journey tho' I could have wish'd you had not had so much rain at your first arrival, I would have nothing to discourage my Daughter from liking Rufford; which I hope will shew the goodness of the Air by not letting her Indisposition stay long with her. As for my Daughter Betty she should not want my consent for a longer time to stay with you, but the truth is, her mother in plain English is not able to bear her absence, and there is no other mistery in it but downright fondness which she cannot resist. You may endeavour to get somebody to keep your wife company whilst you stay in the Country. I believe my cousin Bradshaw and his wife if civilly invited might be so kind as to make such a friendly visit to you. but of that you are to enquire, or to think of somebody else whose Company might be agreable to your wife. I am not sure, but that before the end of the month I may come down myself but it is too uncertain a World to say it positively. Your young woman is very well, and I pretend to be upon very good terms with her. Pray make my Compts. to your Wife, who deserves to be well entertained, and therefore you are to acquit yourself well in it, in the behalf of your affectionate Father

HALIFAX

THE SAME *to* THE SAME

London, 7 *August* 1690

I can say no more concerning Betty than I did in my last, her mothers fondness is above her power to suppress, so that we must all yield to it. In the mean time, for the sake of Rufford, I am much pleas'd with this good weather, which will do it right, and then that Fires are not necessary the whole month of August. That which is to be done in the wilderness for its further improvement is, to strip the hedges, and replant in places that fail, Thin those parts which grow too thick, and cut off the lower branches of the more prosperous trees. You are to tell me your opinion, what you would have done in every thing about the House and Park, since you are likely to be more concern'd in it than I am for the remainder of my Life. Though you have not horses to hunt with your neighbours, I would not have you avoid a fair occasion of inviting them and treating them as well as is to be expected from such a travelling housekeeper; and whatever you lay out in your hospitality shall be allow'd without repining at the reckoning, let your stay be ever so long in the Country. I doubt the Gardens have been neglected which was ill done, since if they had been look'd after you might now at least have had plenty of fruit. Little Nan is growing to be a great Nan with wholesome plump cheeks that I am not displeas'd to look at; I hope her Mother hath by this time lost her headach and that Rufford may brag of improving her health, which I wish for many reasons, but chiefly for her own sake; and pray keep me very well with her, for though I am a Silent Gallant, yet to her, I will be very constant. I have bid Medhurst send you what news there is, every post. Remember me to little Nanny Windsor.—

Young Lady Betty, however, seems to have conquered her mother's reluctance, for we find Lord Eland describing a call paid by himself, 'my Wife and Sister Betty' to the Duke of Newcastle, who showed himself as eccentric and hypochrondriacal as usual. The young man promises to fulfil his Lordship's wishes with regard to the wood, and expresses much solicitude for the improvement of the place. The lodge at the end of the park will soon fall into ruins unless repaired; the great gates in front of the house are dilapidated; the gardens have been neglected; 'but I thinke', adds the young heir, 'the chief blame is to be laid at your Lordship's door, in not visiting 'em oftener'.

The Marquis of Halifax *to* William Lord Eland

14 *August* 1690

I have yours by Betty who is return'd full of yours and your wife's kindness, so that I believe she was not in half so much hast to come up, as her mother was to receive her; I suppose you take care to receive your neighbours kindly, and be sure, whilst you stay, to err on the side of plenty. I find Bird's head did not lye to keep things hansome about the house, which makes the gardens lye neglected, you must observe what is wanting to get it supply'd for another year; for I shall rely upon your information for the putting things in better order. I am sorry to hear your wife has any complaints in point of health; it must be your care to do the honours of Rufford to her and to omit nothing that may contribute to her good humour, whilst I make my interest with Nanny, who I assure you is very prosperous. You will return my Compts. to the Duke of Newcastle when you see him again.

Halifax

Young Lord Eland's letters, for a fortnight, remain very despondent as regards the state of his wife's health. At last, however, she is decidedly better; and his father congratulates him in the following letter, which shows that the statesman was not deficient in the graceful *art d'être grand-père*:

The Marquis of Halifax *to* William Lord Eland

30 *August* 1690

Since my Daughter's illness is worn off you will enjoy the Country with more satisfaction, if the weather does not grow unkind as it has been here to day by continual Rain. But I will not conclude it is so at Rufford, which will be less Solitary whilst my cousin Bradshaws are in the house with you, to help you to pass the evenings which now begin to lengthen. We think your young woman very good Company; she supplys her want of discourse by smiling and staring and is so quiet that I complain of it, having often heard it said that a little vexing and coying is good for childrens health. At present I hear no News from Ireland but if there is any before the Post goes I suppose somebody will send it you; do not forget [to remember] me to your wife.

Your affectionate father

Halifax

The Same *to* The Same

9 *September* (7 *September*?) 1690

I ordered Medhurst by the last post to let you know that it was intended the Parliament should sit the 2nd of next month and though that resolution as to the precise time is interrupted, King's not coming into England yet, it is pretty sure there will be a session as soon as the time for competant notice to the members to come up will admit, so that you are left at liberty to prepare for your return, when you think fit; and I believe the weather has been so little courtly to our southern woman, that she will not be sorry to turn her back upon the North wind that has entertained her so roughly whilst she has been in the Country. I suppose your neighbours will come up too, this being a time that everybodys attendance will be more expected than usual. You will find your small woman in good health and everybody here glad to see you.

Parliament actually met early in October, and during the Session which ensued (October 1690 to January 1690/1) we find Lord Halifax taking a remarkably active part in the business of the Upper House. On three several occasions he was appointed Speaker *pro tem.*; upon two of these the note 'unanimously' is appended in the journal.

Politically, however, his bias can only be traced in the affairs of Lord Torrington, who had been committed to the Tower for supposed treachery and cowardice in the Beachy Head disaster. Public feeling had at first run strongly against him. This bias, however, had soon merged into a belief that he had been sacrificed to the resentment of the Dutch Naval Authorities, whose own fleet had been involved. Attempts were made in the House of Lords to prove the technical invalidity of the procedure against him; and to fix the responsibility for this step on the Committee, which, under the Presidency of Lord Carmarthen, had, during the King's absence, exercised authority. It was Lord Halifax who reported from a select Committee a resolution implying that the commitment was a breach of privilege; and, in fact, the whole affair was regarded by some as a mere episode in the rivalry between 'the two Marquises': the 'white Marquis', Carmarthen (whose pallor was remarkable), and Lord Halifax, who had obviously inherited the 'black' complexion, and nickname, of his uncle Strafford.

Carmarthen, however, had soon an opportunity for reprisals. Bulkeley, though the most exuberant, was not the only Jacobite exile who had called upon Lord Halifax. Somewhat about the same date his old friend Lord Preston, who had remained Jacobite, had arrived in England as the bearer of dispatches from St Germains, and had apparently waited on Lord Halifax. He was almost immediately arrested, tried, and convicted, on a charge of high treason. His fortitude failed him; he saved his life by a written confession, which is not now extant; and Lord Nottingham, on 26 June, informed the King, then in Holland, that while the evidence of Preston, or an associate, implicated several persons in the charge of treason, and Lord Halifax in a charge of Misprision* of Treason, yet neither charge was supported by more than one witness. Halifax, therefore, with the others involved, could only be charged with misdemeanour. The Queen, however, had refused to follow the odious precedent of the Hampden prosecution. It is thus clear that Lord Halifax was only accused of concealing the fact of an old friend's visit, while knowing or suspecting his errand. We may presume that a cryptic letter from Henry Sidney, written to Lord Halifax 27 August 1691, while Sydney was in attendance on the King in Holland, refers to this affair. 'You may', he writes, 'rely upon me for doing you all the service that lies in my power; I told the story I had from you and I think that did you some. I suppose I shall see you before it be long, and in the meantime I am sure that nothing of that matter formerly mentioned to you will be thought of. When I have the happiness to see you I will speak very freely to you, and assure you, as I will do upon all occasions, of being your most humble and faithful servant.'

None the less, when on 16 November the House of Commons demanded—and obtained—the production of the now lost confession, a prominent member of the Opposition wrote that the vote had been 'carried on underhand by the white Marquis's friends, the design being to conciliate himself to the House of Commons and blast the black Marquis and others'. From similar motives, it was supposed, Carmarthen extended a very ill-judged patronage to a scoundrelly and soon disgraced informer, one Fuller, whose circumstances and associates were notorious.

The other business of the Session, in all of which Lord Halifax took an active part, need not detain us. During the following spring, however, the family affairs of Lord Halifax deserve a passing mention.

About the beginning of March 1691/2 the young Lady Elizabeth,† a girl of sixteen, the only remaining child of his second marriage, became the wife of Lord Stanhope, a youth some three years her senior, son and heir of her father's old friend, Lord Chesterfield. It seems doubtful whether the marriage, of which the famous fourth Earl of Chesterfield (rather a Savile than a Stanhope) was the only surviving issue, proved a success. Of Lord Stanhope himself it is said that we know little more concerning him than the fact that he bore the title. We are further assured, however, on the same

* I.e. bare knowledge without assent.

† For whom Halifax had composed four years earlier *The Lady's New Year's Gift*.

authority, that in his youth he was credited with 'strong parts'; that he appeared 'a high Tory, if not a Jacobite'; that his disposition was as morose as his passions were violent; while he 'often thought . . . people behaved ill to him, when they did not in the least intend it'. We confess, on the other hand, to an unkind suspicion that despite the sage though discouraging admonitions of her father, Lady Stanhope, spoilt darling of an adoring mother, was something of a shrew. Scandal maintains that, having subsequently quarrelled with her father-in-law, she declined to drink in his presence, save of her own provision, in ostentatious allusion to the horible legend of his second wife's death by poison.* Not two years after the marriage we find Lord Stanhope complaining bitterly to Lord Halifax. His wife, he declares, when informed that reasons of health and economy must compel her husband, despite her father's expressed wishes, to winter in the country, had retorted, that if he stayed all winter she should repent she had ever married him, intimating, moreover, that if he persisted she should herself remain in town without him. In that case, says the disgusted husband, who can blame him if he go abroad?

The answer of Lord Halifax is remarkable for its moderation, good sense, and kindliness:

THE MARQUIS OF HALIFAX *to* LORD STANHOPE

London, 4 *November* 1693

Nothing ever came to mee, my Ld, more unexpected, than what you tell mee in your letter, and it was the more so, after I had coniured you, before you went, to tell mee, if you had any cause of dissatisfaction; which if you had done, you should have seen, that as I love you equally with my own children, I should not have been partiall to your wife, in any dispute where she was in the wrong. If there is nothing more than that which you mention, that giveth you offence, It will not I hope, upon your second thoughts produce such a resolution as you seem to expresse. If a young Woman, my dear Ld, sayeth a foolish thing, in heat, and as she alleadgeth, in iest too, a husband is not to leave her for it, especially when shee is ready, as it becometh her, to live where ever you think it necessary for your selfe to bee in relation to your health. For as to your wanting money to live in town, it is an argt. that loseth its force by the means you may have of being supplyed, which you might make use of without any scruple. I will promise myselfe, that upon a further consideration, you will suspend at least the putting a thing in practice, agt. which there are too many obiections for one of your Justice and good nature to answer. I am convinced your wife loveth you, and if shee should not, I promise you I will not love her. For my selfe and my wife, I will onely say wee will not yield

* He had suspected her of an intrigue with the Duke of York.

to the nearest of your relations in our reall kindnesse to you; and how wee must bee afflicted to bee so disappointed in our hopes to see you live happily and kindly with your wife you may easily imagine; Therefore let mee earnestly ingage you to make no resolution till wee see you, and let that be as soon as the consideration of your health will allow you. You shall find, you can propose nothing, which you in your deliberate thoughts shall think reasonable, that shall not have our concurrence as well as our endeavour to promote it, and in the mean time, believe it as a truth, that in the relation you have to mee, no man ever had,

A more affectionate humble servant

HALIFAX

I desire you will give my humble service to my Ld. of Chesterfield. I need not tell you how much I desire to heare from you.

This date, however, carries us beyond 1692, to which we must now return.

The public events of that summer had been alarming in the extreme. Scarce had Parliament risen, scarce had William returned after his usual fashion to the Continent, ere it became evident that a French invasion in favour of the exiled James actually impended. A vast army had concentrated upon the coast of Normandy; transports and men of war assembled at La Hogue; while it was known that the three Kingdoms had been denuded of troops, in the interest of the Continental struggle. The consternation in London became intense; among the Jacobites, excitement rose high; 'Everything', writes Lord Wolseley, 'pointed to a counter-revolution.'

The crisis naturally offered fresh and full opportunity for Jacobite intrigue, and for the forgery of imaginary plots, and Lord Halifax soon became a mark for both. Four years later a Jacobite named Cook, of respectable birth and repute, earned his pardon by a confession; in which, among other things, he said that 'several years ago' he had been bidden to see the Marquis of Halifax, as being a man of honour; who received him very civilly. That he communicated to him 'the business of La Hogue' (? of the intended invasion, or the battle which thwarted it) 'whereupon he found him uneasy at his staying longer with him and told him what he had to do', a quite enigmatical sentence. Halifax himself recorded on 17 October 1692, the information given him by one Capell, who told him that a certain Dunbar, a Scotsman, had publicly denounced the Marquis and the Duke of Beaufort, with others, as holding correspondence with King James; and had added 'that I corresponded whilst I was of the Council, and that nothing was done of which I did not give advertisement'. Halifax had, moreover, heard that the said Dunbar 'was preparing his information concerning these things to be presented to the Parliament'.

Meanwhile, an associate of Dunbar was elaborating a more serious charge against Lord Churchill, whose curt and unexplained dismissal earlier in the year had aroused the liveliest excitement; and, as it was largely ascribed to Dutch influence, had also evoked considerable sympathy with the disgraced soldier. Now, on 3 May, at the very crisis of anxiety, a disreputable adventurer named Young accused, upon forged evidence, Lord Marlborough and other prominent men of complicity in a Jacobite conspiracy. The authorities acted with the vigour which the occasion certainly demanded. Two of the accused, Lords Marlborough and Huntingdon, were committed to the Tower by warrant of the Privy Council; which warrant, however, three prominent members (of whom at least two were Whigs) refused to sign. Another of the accused, Dr Sprat, had remained for some days in the custody of the Government messenger. Lord Marlborough and other suspects attempted to sue out their writ of habeas corpus, but the Judges seem to have declared for the legality of a remand.

Three weeks later, however, after the naval victory at La Hogue had annihilated the hopes of the Jacobites, the fraudulent representations of Young were successfully exposed. Lord Marlborough and his companions again demanded the writ; and Marlborough then applied for the services of Lord Halifax and his friends, which were readily accorded. As the writer has never come across any evidence of special intimacy between Halifax and Marlborough, he was probably approached as leader of the Opposition only.

It was no doubt these good offices which drew down on Lords Shrewsbury and Halifax a signal mark of Royal disfavour. For on 23 June 1692, Queen Mary ordered their names to be struck out of the Council 'for that they had forbore to come to Council for some time past'. Yet, strange to say, but three months later, on September 22, the Queen 'did the Marquis of Halifax the honour, to dine with him at Acton'. Was the compliment, we wonder, paid to his Lordship or her Ladyship?

Bishop Sprat speedily published an account of the conspiracy. It extolled highly the fairness and courtesy of the Privy Councillors by whom the investigations had been conducted, but Lord Halifax, in a rather acid series of notes on the narrative which he has left behind him, considers the Bishop 'was full as thankful as was necessary'.

During the following winter session Lords Marlborough and Huntingdon brought before the House the question of their supposed wrongs and found their cause warmly espoused. Most sensible persons were disgusted by the sinister origin of the charges. All Jacobites, or suspected Jacobites, felt the case might have been their own. The extreme Whigs were unanimous in their enthusiasm for the Act of Habeas Corpus, and all the forces of discontent, from pure animus against the Government, rallied in their defence. From none of these was it reasonable to expect a candour capable of admitting that the threat of invasion may justify minor irregularities in practice, though otherwise deserving of censure.

The Judges, when consulted, had maintained that prisoners could be remanded to prison, though only one of the two witnesses required in cases of high treason were a witness *on oath*; but Lord Halifax, in a strong speech, of which he has left notes, retorted that their decisions were liable to revision by the House of Lords. It had been argued that it is hard to compel the Government, in every contingency, to an immediate prosecution. The Marquis, once more intervening, maintained that the hardship inflicted upon accused persons, by the contrary procedure, is even more glaring. Eventually, Lord Halifax reported, from a Select Committee, a resolution reversing the decision of the Judges, for the terms for which he was no doubt largely responsible. A Bill, however, was eventually introduced to indemnify the Ministry, and empower them, in case of invasion, to secure suspected persons who refused to take the oaths or give security.

The Session in which this was an interlude afforded a welcomed vent to much sullen political feeling. The continued financial drain in favour of the Continental War, and especially for the purpose of subsidies to the Allies; the King's Dutch proclivities, and supposed subordination of British interests to the wider issues of the European struggle were all very unpopular. Meanwhile his forbidding lethargic manners, and prolonged absences at the seat of war, continued to support a constant burden of complaint. Raised to the throne by a national revolution, and dependent on the popular will for financial support, no one in fact was less calculated than William III to secure a personal loyalty.

Nor was this all. The unpopularity of both the war and the

King impelled the Government to the discreditable and discredited expedient of political corruption.

All these circumstances had, it is clear, tended to modify the very real admiration with which Lord Halifax, at the first, as the Spencer House Journals show, had certainly regarded the great Dutchman. For it is probably to this Session that we must ascribe a series of acrimonious speeches, notes of which, in the hand of Lord Halifax, were found by the present writer among the Halifax MSS. at Devonshire House.

The first is a speech against the 'Common compliment' of an Address of Thanks in answer to the King's Speech at the opening of Parliament. It is undated, but may be reasonably attributed to this Session.

1. The least things in appearance carry such consequences etc. That there is the most care etc. Where it looketh at first like an affectation to oppose yet very necessary. Good intentions in all. No designe of compliments at the price of hurting the publique. No intention by opposing to do anything either indecent or inconvenient to the Govt.

2. The Liberty of the house is a tender thing. The Freedome of Assemblies is rather insensibly lost by admitting things without taking notice of them, than by any designe to undermine or oppress them. If there is no Love without Jealousy sure no Liberty without it. When a thing is proposed in the shape of respect to the King, though it is sure there is no disguise intended, yet every thing that is done being a Precedent, how a thing well intended may at another time bee ill applyed etc. may bee examined.

3. This matter of thanks hath been debated severall times, and some times with so much heat, That there are instances of its having been layed aside.

4. There was a Remarquable instance of the Inconveniencye some years since; in a very Criticall case. No lesse than the dispensing power was made the consequence of the Question. K. in his speech had told the Plt. hee had imployed men not warranted by the Lawes. The Lds. in the ordinary track of their good manners, gave thanks for the Speech etc. The next day when the severall parts of it were to bee considered, those thanks were made an argt. not to obiect etc. Very hardly recovered.*

5. It came to give thanks onely for the Gracious expressions in his speech This was reducing a Compliment to very little use etc. To bee Considered. That a K's speech in it selfe is neither a Grace nor a disobligation. Hee pronounceth the words, instead of commanding the Ld. upon the Wool sack to deliver his sense. This expedient of Gracious Expressions hath its danger in it. There is not alwayes occasion to use extraordinary expressions of Grace, and according to the Usuall Style it may bee called his Maties. most Gracious Speech, and yet in Strictnesse

* See p. 223.

never a Gracious Expression in it to bee particularly taken notice of. Here then is the Inconvenience. It will bee asked and cannot bee denyed, where are the gracious expressions upon which the thanks are to bee founded? These will bee insisted upon and no doubt allowed etc. but yet really the ransacking a K's speech to find matter for thanks, when there is matter, is an unpleasant undertaking etc. and is yet more so, when it happeneth that there is not a clause which giveth a proper handle for it.

6. Since the debate is arisen: Good either to take such a resolution as shall avoid these difficulties for the future or adjourne the debate and so let it fall gently. A Generall Resolution would take away the obiection of any disrespect to this speech in Particular. In generall, The method inconvenient. That sufficient. In other times Men gave thanks here to receave them againe with interest in another place. The first Moovers of these things did not adde weight to Them. The thankers were knowne for a whole Reigne etc. Then whether the White Staves or the Whole House. In a debate hee that carryeth it for the whole house outvyeth etc. This running of Races who should bee best bred, in this house is very often civility misplaced. It is agt. the dignity of a Great Assembly. Ks. have been upon the Throne to hear such debates which hath not given them the better opinion of this Supream Court.

Perhaps on account of this very speech, the formality of an Address of Thanks was postponed till a later period in the debate, and in the next Session was omitted altogether.

The remainder of this turbulent Session was of a piece with its obstreperous beginning; and His Majesty's formal request for the 'advice' of his Parliament received a most liberal interpretation. Complaints of naval miscarriages and of the asserted preponderance of Dutch officers in the land service—a question which had become acute owing to the very cynical conduct of Solms at Steinkerk—were freely bandied. Indeed (as part of an Address to the King), Lord Halifax, on the motion, it was said, of Marlborough, at length reported a clause demanding that English officers might command foreigners of equal rank, except those employed by Crowned heads.* This very invidious suggestion was adopted.

To this Session also we are now inclined to ascribe a very sharp criticism of Lord Halifax,† concerning the despotic tone of William III's speeches. These, when endorsing the Government's financial demands for the purposes of the war, had always been peremptory; but the circumstances of the moment make the date now given the most probable.

* Thus excepting the forces of the States.

† Ascribed in the present writer's *Life and Works of Halifax* to 1690.

1. Of what use are Prlts. if when there is warre everything that is asked is to be given? When there is no Warre there needeth no great matter. So that a Prince hath by consequence the power of money when hee will, because hee hath warre when he will The Kg having the power to make warre was restrained onely by not having that of taking (?) money but now that is made such a necessary reason for giving all the money that is asked, that the argument turneth the other way, etc. Here hath been too much paines taken lately, onely for the name of liberty. If all is given whilst there is Warre there is nothing left when there is peace. The Jure Divino principle is nothing to this, that is a speculative Notion, controverted too etc. here is a practicall expedient that effectually doth the business. Necessity is alwayes a good argt. if Reall but if hee that createth the necessity hath the benefit of it, the consequences are somewhat inconvenient. When nothing shall be reall but the want of money Engld. hath not its true behaved itselfe very well, but it is most extravagantly fined. The imponents (?) are onely to bee applauded for their confidence etc. but the Swallowers are to bee admired for their easinesse, not to give it a harder word. A Maxime in Law, that no man is to have benefit from his own wrong Act; yet here there is power by declaring warre to provoke a stronger enemy; by which the necessity of self p(re)servation ariseth and that carrieth every thing along with it.

2. If a Prince can first make warre without consent of Plt. (which by the way some thought would have been more throughly considered in the bill of Rights) and then make that warre an argt. agt. the Plts questioning the Proportion or the distribution of what they give these consequences will follow: (1) hee will bee incouraged by his interest to make warre right or wrong when hee is sure to bee over payed for it A Prince must bee very modest that will reiect such a fayre occasion etc. Whatever hee doth with his enemies it is a sure way to subdue his subjects. It must in time make the Govt. so strong that it can not bee resisted and the people so poor that they cannot resist (2) Hee will either keep the Nation alwayes in warre for that reason; It would look Pusillanimity in a Prince not to affect warre, when so encouraged to it. No Prince can bee so chast as that it is advisable to tempt him to committ a rape.

3. When ever the warre is done, Hee hath an Army at his devotion loath to bee disbanded ready to support that power which keepeth them on foot In Ch. 2ds. time there were those that persuaded the Kg. to keep up the Rump Army. Though perhaps att the bottome there is no true reeson in it, yet there is charme in the Musick etc. Such an Argt. as this before hand would have spoyled the Revolution; sure wee are at the Signe of the Labour in Vaine. Venture etc. to root up the tree of Arbitrary power and plant another in the same place; the same leefe, the same fruit onely with another name to it. What will become of the Argt. in other Times; Wee banish L. (?) fears and Jealousies. Whilst the Causes of them are increased. Such uselesse paper as the bill of Rights, and the Reverend Parchment of the Magna Charta will bee the most contemptible piece of Sheepskin So here is a very popular argt. in shew,

that in reality by consequences not at all stretched or affected, is neither more nor lesse than the dissolution of the Govt. The Syllogisme Parlt. must give when the K. will have them; *Ergo etc.* This is extraordinary Logick and somewhat strange that it should begin in Engld. where men have been used to argue in quite another manner. It is not so proper to say the Parlt. will not give money when there is peace, as that they cannot give it after they have parted with all they had during the Warre. Wee have given so much money that France may bee reduced to etc. That must bee a great while of doing, our progresse hath not been great, *ergo* the warre is to last so long that wee must bee undone in the pursuing it or so little a while that it was to no purpose to undertake it. After having said this; It seemeth improper to adde any thing which must bee of lesse weight. Like when the first Reason is impossible; The rest may bee spared. It is no small impudence for such an argt. to walk up and down After having laid down an argt. which if true, no Englishmen can or will give a reply to it; The saying more could not in good sense bee iustified, but that in the particular instance etc. it is not enough to lay down generals, how little so ever to bee controverted, without taking this Argt. in vogue in pieces, and lay open the absurdity of it so plainly that from being dangerous, it may become ridiculous; and to bee smiled at; even by those who let their good manners give it admittance without first asking the advice of their understanding There is a Glibbenesse in some mistakes that maketh them slide into mens beleefe when their Reason which ought to stand sentinelle to our fayth is stept out of the way. There are argts. that surprize the understanding, which afterwards out of Laziness or unthinking forgetteth to throw them out againe. 'Wee must save England' is the introduction of this Argt. though the conclusion of it is, 'wee shall undo it by' etc. 'The thing is grievous but wee must take another time.' Doing a wrong thing at the present to undo it afterwards is such a dangerous experiment that it is not to be tryed without a cleer demonstration which is farre from being here etc. A man that should deal so with a disease in himselfe would let it grow very inconvenient. The taxes are payed in Stirling money The Plt. deserveth argts. of a right allay and not to bee disparaged by having such a thin piece of Sophistry imposed upon it There is not a more unequal kind of trafick or raither a more ungratefull one, than to repay a liberall house of commons with a reason that is an affront to them. It is enough to destroy in the house of Commons the faculty of swallowing which hath been of too good use to the Govt. to bee discouraged etc.

Perhaps we may be tempted to suggest that this speech, of which by the way the whole tendency is purely *Whig*, and shows no trace of Jacobitism, tends somewhat to support Burnet's suggestion that the speeches of Halifax were becoming rather vivacious than sound. The real crux of the situation—whether the continuance of the war was or was *not* imperative in the interest of this country—is left untouched; and the attack revolves entirely around the one assertion—that an unrestrained power of declaring war may become in practice an unrestricted power of taxation.

But over and above all separate causes of complaint the forces of discontent finally rallied for a grand concerted effort against the Government, respecting the character, and future duration, of the existing Parliament.

The report of the Parliamentary Committee for Accounts had thrown into further relief the venality of the existing Parliament, already so notorious. The Revolution Government, as we have seen, was already employing, lavishly, the resources of Parliamentary corruption, so long monopolized by its predecessors; and of which Carmarthen (the Danby of those earlier days) had been largely though not entirely the initiator. The benches of the Lower House swarmed with placemen and dependants.

In consequence of these ominous disclosures, a Bill—commonly known as the 'self-denying' or 'Place' Bill—was introduced in the Lower House.

This provided that no member elected *after January* 1693/4 should accept office from the Crown, on pain of exclusion from the House during the duration of the ensuing Parliament. It found an astonishingly easy passage through the House. The Opposition as a whole desired to weaken the Administration. The ultra-Whigs were specially concerned to minimize the influence of the Crown. The existing place-men—*having so carefully arranged that the Bill should not be retrospective*—were able to claim credit for a virtue, which was entirely vicarious.

In the House of Lords, however (at William's special behest), all the influence of the Court was exerted against the Bill; and it was believed that, should it pass, His Majesty had determined to exert the Royal right of veto.

The Bill, on the other hand, was warmly supported in the Upper House by all the avowed or suspected Jacobites and by all the disgruntled Whigs; who, says Burnet, were joined by 'two able malcontents' 'whose efforts were yet more injurious than theirs—Lords Halifax and Mulgrave'. Attempts were vainly made in Committee to amend the Bill so as to include *pensioners* within its scope, but to admit the retention of *place-men*, after a preliminary vacation of their seats. Finally, however, the Bill itself was rejected by a very narrow majority, on January 4, 1692/3.

A reasoned protest was signed by many of the Whig and Tory Opposition, while Halifax headed a protest without reasons assigned.

During these debates, the Courtiers had very injudiciously argued that the passage of the Bill into law would impel the King to prolong the duration of so largely dependent a Parliament. The Opposition leaders availed themselves of that damaging admission. A week later, Lord Shrewsbury (now formally in Opposition) brought forward in the House of Lords a Bill for the frequent meeting of 'Parliaments', better known by the somewhat ambiguous title of the 'Triennial' Bill. In its original form it was designed to secure Annual Sessions, and *a General Election every year*. The last appalling provision having been speedily negatived, the Bill in its earlier stages aimed at providing for Annual Sessions, triennial elections, and the termination of the existing Parliament on 1 January ensuing—1693/4. This final clause naturally became the battle-ground of parties; and of this debate—or perhaps of his own speech in the debate—Lord Halifax has left a summary, headed N(ew?) P(arliament?):

Con(tra). K. hath taken wrong steps that he must recover etc. before he is in a condition to change the Plt.

Pro. 1. It is a strange remedy to a wrong step to make a wronger. 2. The Contrary is true. this is the onely tolerable remedy. Universall, visible, without it, nothing else will bee beleeved.

Con(tra). It is too deep game to hazard the Crown to the chance of a die.

Pro. The fear of it is a libell upon the Govt. Is this a Plt. or a party? if the first, why fear another? if the last is there anything to bee said for it? Strange to fear that for which the Revolution was principally undertaken. The root of all the ill sendeth out 2 branches. 1. Governing without a Plt, at all. 2. Modelling a Standing Plt. The Triennial Act the onely Remedy for these. If pursuing the intention of the Law is not the surest game a K. can play, where are wee?

Con. Whilst the Warre lasteth; not seasonable to make new experiments.

Pro. Is the true Constitution of Engd. to bee called a new Experiment? Here is a Warre and a Plt. seeme to bee agreed to continue one another. A precedent for any King. Let him but make warre and it giveth him a right to suspend the callinge a New Plt.

Con. Here is a Plt. true to the interest of the Govt. how can it bee justified to change

Pro. 1. It is iustifiable to change it because it is not iustifyable to keep it. 2. Frequent Plts. is a part of the Govt. and therefore the continuance of this Plt. is a Contradiction to an English Govt. If all the Mayors,

Sheriffes etc. of Engd. because true should bee continued during the warre it would bee extraordinary, and yet the same argt. might be alleadged for it.

Con. The Govt. would as faine have a new Plt. as those who presse most for it; but it may endanger All.

Pro. 1. The having a great mind to a thing goeth a great way in most things. Where that, and the Justice of a thing are ioyned men are not apt to see any great danger in doing it.

3. The Govt. would faine have it, and the Nation would faine have it, and yet there is danger in doing it.

4. Where is this danger? If not time enough to call a new Plt. in case of disappointmt. why not call it so much sooner, to give more time. Q[ueen] is a K[ing] too, and may call it before K. cometh over: so there may bee so much time saved. The Govt. whilst it countenanceth the Lawes, and supporteth the Constitution will always have the stronger party. The true Govt. of Engld. is founded in good measure upon a great confidence in the people. It is not very naturall to distrust those, wee intend to bee kind to. Those wee have hurt or intend to hurt naturally raise our suspition. As it is often a necessary thing to suspect, so it is sometimes no very good signe. If the people are to bee trusted with a new election, then the pretended danger is no good argt. If in reason, they are not to bee trusted. (—) It may be a good Argt. but it is no good newes.

Con. It will iustify the suspition of this Plts being corrupted which is a scandall upon men well disposed to the Govt.

Pro. Quite contrary, nothing will confirme it so much as the keeping it. If a standing Plt. is an irregular thing it will bee thought there is some uniustifyable cause for it. It will look like a contract for protection etc. Like Men retained upon condition not to bee put of without very long warning. By many it will be made the onely Reason of keeping this Plt. that the Govt. may not bee put to a repeated expence of making new friends.

The threatened limitation of the Royal prerogative, on so crucial a point, had naturally occasioned the most intense mortification in the mind of William; and Court influence had been strained to the utmost in the House of Lords to obtain its rejection. But the measure—with a clause merely postponing the dissolution till 24 March following—eventually passed both Houses. William, however, remained obdurate; and, despite the remonstrances of Temple, who had been specially consulted in his epicurean retirement, the King on February 14, 1692/3 deliberately refused his consent.

The next move on the part of the Opposition was a vigorous effort to wreck a Money Bill. Such at least was the interpretation placed by the Court on an attempt (said by Burnet to have originated with Halifax and Mulgrave) to amend, in the House of Lords, the Bill imposing the Land Tax. These tactics were duly repelled by the Commons.

Towards the end of the Session the House seems to have found time to discuss the miserable state of Ireland, reduced by the recent war to a state of extreme exhaustion. Under Henry (now Lord) Sidney who had recently accepted the onerous task of Viceroy, for which he seems to have been singularly unfitted, a Parliament had been summoned to Dublin in October 1692. This had disgraced itself by an intemperate Protestantism; but had earned a more creditable reputation by severe reflections on various notorious abuses. It had further put forth a first abortive effort to obtain for the Irish Parliament the same control over finance as was possessed by its English counterpart. A summary prorogation had driven certain indignant members of the Irish Opposition to air their grievances at Westminster. One, Mr Sloan, in particular, urged that 'Poyning's Act' could not deprive the Irish Parliament of all right to *originate* money Bills. This contention seems to have been supported by Halifax in a speech, for which he has left brief and highly technical notes, which will be found in the larger *Life*. The Judges, however, had pronounced adversely on the claim, and the question dropped. But Lord Halifax subsequently ranked among the 'leading members' of his House, who attended the Speaker, when he presented to the King a trenchant address on the general misgovernment of Ireland; which probably occasioned the recall of the incompetent Sydney.

This Session was further remarkable for the origin of the National Debt. This was due to the efforts of Charles Montague, the rising Whig financier, who owed to Halifax his introduction into business, as a Clerk to the Council; and who, after the extinction of the Savile Marquisate, was to assume, to the great confusion of catalogue compilers, the title of Baron and Earl of Halifax. He did this, says Dartmouth, 'in grateful remembrance—as he pretended—of his first benefactor; but [it was] generally thought more out of vanity—of which he had a sufficient share—in hopes of raising it to as high a degree as his benefactor'. He now proposed to raise a million by life annuities at the rate of 10 per cent. interest for ten years and seven afterwards. The scheme became extremely popular, since the difficulty of investing capital other than in land or mortgages was generally acknowledged. The Marquis, whose correspondence bears witness to an extensive traffic in annuities, had hitherto offered one of the few facilities of the kind available. So extensive and well known were his dealings of this sort, that a foreign contemporary wrote: 'Should this arrangement take place, it must ruin the business of the Marquis of Halifax, who for many years has taken up all moneys offered him; but unless the applicants are very aged [caduque] he only gives at the rate of £100 per £1100.'

During this exciting Session we notice one or two further outstanding incidents in which the Marquis was concerned. He ranked among the large majority of Peers who acquitted Lord Mohun of complicity in the murder of Mountford, the actor; a verdict very generally regarded as an instance of gross partiality. But a doubt arises, on reading the evidence, whether a modern jury would have convicted Mohun, a youth not sixteen. The actual murderer had uttered *conditional* threats against the actor, and Mohun had been heard to say that he would stand by his friend. The conditions did *not* occur; and it is therefore possible that Mohun, who entertained a personal liking for Mountford, was not intentionally an accessory to the murder, though it took place while he was talking with the actor.

Wholeheartedly, however, can we understand and approve the action of the Marquis as respects the licensing of books. Lord Halifax joined with other Lords in a protest against the rejection of a proposed amendment to the existing law. This amendment, while asserting a privilege of Peerage, would have excepted from the scope of the Licensing Act all works published with *the names of the author and publisher*. For the system in vogue (so runs the protest) 'subjects all learning and true information to the arbitrary will and pleasure of a mercenary and perhaps ignorant licenser, destroys the properties of authors in their copies, and sets up many monopolies'.

At length, on 14 March 1692/3, Parliament was prorogued. His friend Mr Methuen congratulated Lord Halifax on a brief respite from business; though, as he added, 'in very dangerous weather it is a hard matter for any person whose fortune is engaged on a ship to be satisfied, when any accidents keep the most skilful seaman from the helm'.

The recess, however, proved an anxious one for Halifax in his private capacity. A great fire which at the end of 1692, had already destroyed a large part of Rufford Abbey, was now succeeded by a conflagration, also serious, at his Acton villa. His own state of health seems at one time to have been considered precarious. He appears to have remained in London till late in the season; but Lady Halifax had to leave him, being ordered to drink the waters of a medicinal spring close to Acton, then and subsequently of great repute. Young Lady Eland, on the other hand, whose indisposition seems to have been much more serious, was sent west to 'The Bath'. To these troubles Lord Halifax refers in the following letter to his son.

4 *July* 1693

I received yours last night at my return from Acton, where my wife has been some days, to take the waters, as well as the goodness of that air, being a good deal indisposed. In pursuance of your desires, I sent to know whether the Doctor adhered to his opinion for your wife's longer stay at the Bath and I think it best to send you his answer in his own words, which therefore I have inclos'd. I can say nothing to the visits you intend, since you are the best judge of the necessity of making them; in the meantime the weariness you express of the place where you are, makes me put you in mind of what I told you in our late journey, that without a paradox it is in everybody's power to prevent his being weary in the most unpleasant places, provided there is neither pain nor want to put a mans philosophy to a trial that may be too severe. You have tools to work with, therefore do not let them gather rust for want of their being employ'd. Sir Thomas has your excuse but remember not to give any more occasions for an apology.

A few complimentary letters to Harley, then a rising member of the extreme Whig Opposition, though of no interest in themselves, show a warmer sentiment, for a merely political acquaintance, than we usually find in the correspondence of the Marquis.

To this summer, however, we refer the greater part of a correspondence which displays the Marquis in a decidedly pleasant light.* The Queen Dowager, Catherine, whose residence in England had become embarrassed owing to the Jacobite proclivities of several among her immediate household, had determined, soon after the Revolution, upon returning to the land of her birth. This resolution had been strongly opposed by the Marquis, who appears to have resumed his former post as her Chancellor, and who stood high in her confidence; but the Queen remained firm, and the proposition seems to have been transmitted to the reigning Sovereigns through the Marquis himself. Permission had been with difficulty extorted for the required journey, since the Government obviously

* See 'Sidelights on Catherine of Braganza', *Longman's Magazine*, 1893, by the present author.

disliked the idea that the large sums settled as jointure should be spent out of England; and had further objected to Her Majesty's desire of travelling through France. Eventually, however, the Queen Dowager, after an affecting interview with Queen Mary, left England in March 1692, and reached Lisbon by the year's end.

Lord Halifax, described by her confessor as first in the number of her English friends, remained a faithful guardian of her pecuniary interests, and corresponded with Her Majesty more or less regularly.[31] Long as she had lived in England, she had never learned to write English; but the members of her household, whose letters were supplemented by those of Mr Methuen, our Envoy, supplied this involuntary deficiency and transmitted her kindly messages. The Queen, writes her confessor, 'takes great delight in seeing your expressions...and how carefull you are to putt her in Mind of poore England'. 'If your Lordship', writes her attendant, Lady Tuke, 'did stand now behind the Queen's Chaire at dinner you would see a Little Table suitable to the slender dyet and not be tempted to quarrell with any thing you saw there, but rather advice her Maty. to drink a Little more wine and lesse water.' Gardening, which Lord Halifax had recommended as her pursuit, was carried on under difficulties, and she sent word to the Marquis that, though she had figs of her own, and good ones too, still they wanted the fine flavour of Acton figs, 'which she kindly regrets'. She was unfavourably impressed by her countrywomen, 'whose conversation or chat is so very trifling and different from what the Queen hath been used to in England', and she shocked the King her brother by telling him that English ladies 'talked of news, the success of affairs and what was done or might be expected to be done in the world: the same...as the men'. Eventually, she was to survive Lord Halifax ten years; during the last of which she is said to have displayed, as Regent for her brother, both sense and energy, and to have died respected and lamented.

We must now, however, return to England, and to the date of 1693.

To the events of the preceding session we may ascribe the origin and circulation *in MS. form* of the curious *Maxims of State*; which, though the authorship of Halifax seems to have been from the first generally known or suspected, appeared *anonymously* in a printed sheet during the following year, under the strange heading *Maxims of the great Almansor*, and were subsequently included in all three editions of the Halifax *Miscellanies*. The *title* seems to have been drawn from an astrological work, to which Halifax may have been introduced by the Rosicrucian astrologer Heydon, an acquaintance of his youth. That work had been written in the form of a collection of aphorisms by 'Almansor'* for the instruction of his employer, the Emperor Almamon.

A careful inspection of the *Maxims* of Halifax shows that they constitute a satirical criticism of the political errors, liberally ascribed to William III by the Opposition; namely, an excessive self-will and love of power, a too great indifference to public opinion, want of judgment in the choice of Ministers, etc. But the four bitter epigrams on the employment of political *knaves* are clearly directed against the rising influence of no less a person than *Sunderland.*

For the winter session of 1693–4 found itself transformed by the startling reappearance of that unscrupulous politician in quite a new part.

We last caught sight of the astute intriguer on the day when he had supplicated, in so servile a fashion, the protection of a justly contemptuous kinsman. His serpentine subtlety, however, had lent him an elusive energy—an almost preternatural fascination, which ruder ages might have ascribed to sorcery. Macaulay throws into admirable relief the marvellous address with which—excepted though he was from both Bill of Indemnity and Act of Grace—he had contrived, when the Revolution settlement was barely a year old, to creep out of exile and *kiss hands at Whitehall.* Next, scarce a year later, he had insinuated himself into the good graces of the new King; and by April 1693, had stolen into his seat in the House of Lords. That Sunderland possessed in a high degree the ability and subservience which most recommend a man to the service of a despotic intelligence is true enough; but it is strange that William should have dared to re-employ the most unscrupulous and notorious among the instruments of James II.

Still more remarkable, and if possible more cynical, was the bargain by which Sunderland secured the support of a political party. 'The great news', wrote an anonymous correspondent of Halifax in August 1693, 'is about the meeting of the Great men ...*at Althorpe*, viz. the Lords Shrewsbury, Godolphin and Marlborough, and Messrs Russell, Wharton, etc. Every politic is making his own reflections about it, if you please you may make yours.' A pact between Lord Sunderland and the Whigs had been

* I.e. Jahia Ben Abi Mansur, an Arabian astrologer.

in fact concluded. The Earl bought political immunity and a restoration to political life as the price of his political alliance; and this at the hands of a faction, whose ostentatious horror for a so-called agent of tyranny had rendered it impossible for Lord Halifax to retain a place in the Ministry. Lord Sunderland, for once in his life, certainly fulfilled his professions; and to his influence with William III historians attribute that monarch's final abandonment of the Coalition policy—to which he, like Halifax, had personally inclined—and his conversion to the system of definite party Ministries.

The Whigs thus climbed into power; and at the opening of Parliament the able and conscientious Lord Nottingham—having declined the alternative of a voluntary retirement, which he regarded as implying a confession of incompetence—found himself courteously dismissed from his office as Secretary of State. To this Lord Shrewsbury, after some months vacillation, was compelled to succeed, in an Administration now exclusively Whig.

Parliament met after a season of military and naval disasters; the crushing military defeat of William III at Landen, and the naval catastrophe known as the destruction of the Smyrna fleet. Lord Halifax, however, to the general surprise, for once supported the Government, assisting it in its successful antagonism to a Bill in reform of the Statutes against Treason, which had been twice sent up from the Lower House. Modern opinion would see little in it to condemn; but the Administration urged that it afforded excessive facilities for the acquittal of the guilty; while Lord Halifax—and the House of Lords itself—were probably moved by the absence of any provision for the reform of the Lord Steward's Court, so long a bone of contention between the Houses. This action of Lord Halifax, however, may account for a final rupture between himself and his old friend, Lord Chesterfield; who boasts that during this year 'At dinner I told him before company that I'd rather be a plain honest country gentleman, than a cunning false court knave. After this I never spoke more to his lordship nor he to me'. This break indeed Lord Chesterfield carried so far as to prevent all intercourse between Lady Stanhope and her family.

The Triennial Bill was twice reintroduced, once in each House, but fell through; probably on account of jealousy between the Houses, and evidently to the disgust of the Marquis. The Place Bill, also revived, passed both Houses; but was once more refused the Royal Assent, again to the annoyance of Lord Halifax.

We find him further opposing the Government on the subject of the creation of the Bank of England. Charles Montague, who, as we have seen, had rapidly attained the first rank among contemporary financiers, was desirous of facilitating the raising of Government loans; and appended to a 'Tonnage Bill' a clause which empowered the Government to borrow up to a specific amount. He further arranged for an incorporation of the prospective creditors, on advantageous terms. This excited much criticism in the House of Lords; which, in consequence of a 'call of the House' (with a penalty of £25 on absentees), seems to have been very well attended. The Marquis of Halifax, with the Earls of Nottingham, Rochester and Monmouth, strongly opposed the incorporating clause; they adduced as arguments that in consequence it must become impossible to borrow money upon mortgage, which would diminish the value of land, and disable landowners from raising money in an emergency. They further argued that the accumulation of power in the hands of a private company might become a menace to the King's interest, and even to public liberty; and might impede the free circulation of money. These considerations weighed heavily with many on the Government side; and the Ministerialists, headed by Lord Carmarthen, could only reiterate the urgency of the financial situation, by which alone they had been induced to endorse so unpopular an expedient; with the danger of delay, should a privilege dispute arise over a Money Bill. Admiral Lord Berkeley especially insisted on the necessity of equipping the fleet in time for summer operations; to which Lord Halifax responded, 'that this was not very necessary, since, according to all the information received, it was apparent that the French had no desire to send their fleet to sea'. The argument of expediency however prevailed; and the Revolutionary settlement derived enormous additional stability from an institution which involved so large a proportion of the national savings in its preservation.

The supporters of the Administration now had their reward. Dukedoms were conferred on the great Whig houses of Bedford, Devonshire, and Clare, on Lord Shrewsbury, and lastly on Lord Carmarthen; who thus, as Duke of Leeds, now took triumphant precedence over his early rival, Lord Halifax. 'I will not', wrote his friend Methuen to the latter '...condole with you that by the great honours lately bestowed you have lost so much place.'

During the Session we have just considered Lord Halifax had, on at least one occasion, been obliged to absent himself from the House, on account of a temporary indisposition. But if, as seems possible, he had for a moment contemplated a retirement from public business for reasons of health, the idea soon passed, and Lord Halifax remained to the very end an active Parliamentary politician.

The leisure of the recess was, it would seem, in part devoted to literary effort. In any case, during this year, there appeared the little anonymous tract on naval reorganization—that *Rough Draft of a New Model at Sea* the idea of which we have tentatively traced to the naval crisis of 1667. The anxieties of 1694 were equally acute, and in many respects very similar, especially as regards the vexed questions of discipline and responsibility. These had, since the Revolution, frequently engaged the attention of the Parliamentary Opposition; anxious to represent the fleet, rather than the army, as the appropriate national weapon. In these debates Lord Halifax, we find, had played a conspicuous part, and in the exordium to this tract—added perhaps at this later recension—he defines a naval supremacy as the very foundation of our national existence. For he appends the significant insinuation 'if we have of late suffered usurpation of other methods...it is time now to restore the sea to its right'.

Regarded as a contribution to the importunate question of naval reform, the tract is very inadequate, both in form and contents. It treats of one aspect only, that of naval *command*. But if wanting in the weight, and formal perfection, of his more celebrated tracts, there is none perhaps which displays to fuller advantage—especially in the more generalized passages which we assign to the later revision—the philosophic breadth and scientific acumen of his political outlook. Political dogma he repudiates: '*Circumstances*', he persists, '*must come in, and are to be made a part of the matter of which we are to judge; positive decisions are always dangerous, more especially in politics.*' In accordance with this fundamental method of political induction, the questions immediately at issue in naval circles are referred to their true place as a detail of the national economy. The peculiarities of the English Constitution become, therefore, the theme of the essayist; who develops with admirable insight the central principle that forms of government are essentially a natural product, the expression of national character and national circumstance; and that while they necessarily presuppose the existence of a political ideal, their excellence consists less in approximation to a theoretic model of perfection, than in their suitability to the actual stage of development attained by the people in question. The logical superiority of the Republican conception cannot, he maintains, invalidate the conclusion, that a limited monarchy, modified as circumstances may require, is the only form of government appropriate to the English people. From this premise he deduces the further necessity of leavening the Naval Service with equal proportions of competent gentlemen commanders and of officers risen from the ranks; though he does not conceal his own conviction that, where other qualifications are equal, men accord the more willing obedience to superior social position.

To this, the last year of his life, we may also conjecturally assign some revision of those *Memoirs* of which Pope's subsequent action so unjustifiably deprived the world; and with even greater probability the arrangement, at least, of that remarkable series of maxims, suggested no doubt by those *Maximes* of M. de la Rochefoucauld, of which the first edition had appeared thirty years earlier, and the most recent in 1693.

Lord Halifax, of course, cannot boast of 'plus d'esprit' than his celebrated predecessor; but he certainly excels in breadth and variety of experience, and in 'wit' of the English breed; i.e. in quaint, vivid, allusive idiosyncracies of expression, and in the shrewd common sense, which is the fruit not of theory but of observation. One would give a good many of the stabs which M. de la Rochefoucauld's keen scalpel—penetrating rather than discriminating—deals at 'self-love', for the sound and balanced conclusion of his successor: 'That self-love rightly defined is far from being a fault; a man that loveth himself rightly will do everything else right.' The bitter denunciation of party spirit, the keen disquisitions on the contrasting issues of prerogative and political liberty, show Halifax a 'Trimmer' to the last. And in the acute observation that in organization, rather than in numbers, lies the true secret of strength he anticipates much that the twentieth century has learnt, to its weal and bale. The bitterness of personal experience is latent in the chapters on envy and malice; in the rather pathetic exclamation that those alone are the happiest whose convictions coincide with those of the majority; and in the lament that the building up of a family, and of a house of cards, are comparable.

About this time, too, we find him studying the *Life of Bishop Williams*, which had appeared during the preceding year. His marginal notes, which have been preserved, embody severe strictures, not only on the subservient prelate-statesman himself, but also upon the Government of those earlier Stuarts, to whose interests his own family had been so ardently devoted.

And to this summer belongs the last letter of Lord Halifax which we have been able to trace. It is addressed to Robert Harley, his interest in whom we have already noted, and whose family were rather puritanically inclined. It was written on 26 August, and runs as follows:

Sunday morning

I hope you will not think it a profane proposal to know whether after you have had your spiritual meal this morning, you will for digestion take the air to Acton; if you do not reject the offer, the method I propose is, that you would call upon me at one of the clock, when a cup of chocolate shall be ready for you, after which, if we can gather a peach and perhaps a bunch of grapes, it may so whet your stomach, that it will not take exception against the un-noblemanlike supper you are to expect from, etc.

For Halifax himself, meanwhile, this summer had been a time of renewed family misfortunes. The death of his widowed daughter-in-law, Esther Lady Eland, had been followed by that of her sister-in-law, the wife of his sole remaining son. Neither left an heir; and the fears he had once expressed, lest his line should become extinct, thus threatened to be realized, as in the event they were.

We now enter upon the Session which was to see the end of his own career. The three measures, so much contested already, were once more revived. The *Treason Bill* fell through, as before, owing to the perennial dispute over the Lord Steward's Court; Lord Halifax having protested against a Government-sponsored vote that the operation of the Bill, if passed, should be postponed for three years.

The *Place Bill* was defeated in the Commons, while the *Triennial Bill* passed both Houses. That Lord Halifax approved both Bills is certain, though there is a curious divergency of evidence as to his action *re* the clause, which extended the extreme life of the existing Parliament till November 1696. The Bill was notoriously popular, and on 22 December William created a favourable impression by at length conceding the Royal Assent.

It is probable that Halifax anticipated the eventual fact that William preferred to vindicate his own prerogative by dissolving *before* the appointed time. For, during the next three months, Lord Halifax must have composed the *Cautions* to Parliamentary electors, which appeared anonymously a few months after his death, were included in his *Miscellanies*, and were to be several times reprinted during the eighteenth century.

Some of his counsels, one is glad to believe, have somewhat lost their point; and the witty denunciation of incompetent dandies, notorious drunkards, provincial tyrants, absentee representatives, and persons backed by Court influence, point on the whole to an obsolete stage in political development. The war has brought us indeed a large contingent of military members; but permanent officials cannot invade the precincts at Westminster, and whatever criticisms may be passed upon our modern representatives, they are at any rate free from the stigma of pecuniary corruption. The candidates whose 'stake in the country', as far as concerns their constituents, is confined by popular idiom to the limits of a carpet-bag, remain, on the other hand, a familiar political feature; while lawyers, even practising lawyers, still pervade the assembly from whose benches the fiat of Halifax so ruthlessly tends to exclude them. Unscrupulous canvassers, restless busybodies, club-room wise-acres are still with us; nor can we boast an immunity from solemn inveterate bores. Spendthrifts and possibly misers (the former rather than the latter) are no doubt still represented by Parliamentary returns; while the extent to which personal poverty may impair the independence of legislators is a controversy still debated, with respect to the payment of members. But these more general reflections, though very vivacious and amusing, and illustrative in the highest degree of post-Revolution society, are less interesting in the present connection than the sections which tend to elucidate the actual standpoint of the writer. We detect no Jacobite leanings, and indeed by this time even informers had grown tired of attributing Jacobite sentiments to one by now fully identified with the Revolution settlement.* 'Pretenders to exorbitant merit in the late Revolution' are, indeed, exhaustively satirised, but with the distinct admission that their services had proved beneficial. The pamphlet is obviously written in the spirit of Parliamentary opposition; but the incisive reference to pseudo-patriots whose Parliamentary virtue is a form of political coquetry, the laudatory allusions to the 'Place' and 'Triennial' Bills are compatible with an entire repudiation of party spirit and party ties. For Whig as well as Tory, the zealots of political warfare, the 'Trimmer' to the last reserves the vials of his scorn; it is to the

* See the author's *Life and Works of Halifax*, II, 186.

attitude of the ideal patriot, pledged only to the common weal, that the veteran statesman would recall his readers.

One bitter personal allusion in the pamphlet, easily identified by contemporaries, and by those who have followed us so far, had a tragic sequel. There are, says Halifax, 'some splenetic gentlemen, who confine their favourable opinion within so narrow a compass that they will not allow it to any man that was not hanged in the late reigns; now by that rule one might expect they should rescue themselves from the disadvantage of being now alive; and by abdicating a world so little worthy of them, get a great name to themselves, with the general satisfaction of all those they would leave behind them.' This reference (only too obvious) to his old enemy, Hampden the Younger, must have been poignantly recalled by some; when, at the general election which followed the death of Lord Halifax, John Hampden, rejected by his native constituency of Buckinghamshire, committed suicide.

Finally, he recommends his readers emphatically to fix their choice on true 'Englishmen'; but, sarcastic to the last, he appends the rider: 'I will not undertake that they are easy to be found.'

With these words conclude, not only a brilliant little tract, but also the literary career of Halifax himself. His political activity was to end only with his life, but a few weeks later.

Early in 1694/5 he appears to have supported his old friend Lord Nottingham—who had now formally seceded to the ranks of the Opposition—in a vigorous attempt to secure what we should to-day describe as a vote of censure on the Government. In the course of debates on the state of the nation, Lord Nottingham seems to have made a violent speech, in which he animadverted on the management of the navy, the state of the coinage, the latest pretended conspiracy, and the creation of the Bank. The last named was defended by Godolphin, as a pecuniary bulwark to the Government, who thus exposed himself to a 'malicious' retort from Lord Halifax. Possibly this may have involved a reference to the large grants received by Portland, which Halifax is said to have censured.[32] The onslaught failed; and when towards the end of March, while the Session was still in progress, Lord Nottingham went down to Exton, political disappointment was freely ascribed as the cause. The step, however, had been for some time pressed on him by Lord Halifax, for family reasons of his own.

The anxiety of Halifax for the perpetuation of his race had led him to hasten, with what would nowadays be considered very indecent haste, the remarriage of his son. Within only a few weeks of Lady Eland's death, gossip had been busy with the choice of her successor. A union was almost at once suggested between Lord Eland and her cousin Lady Mary Finch, Lord Nottingham's eldest daughter, and like her cousin a considerable heiress. By February the engagement was public. The marriage was, however, delayed, as Lord Nottingham insisted on a wedding at Exton. But Queen Mary had died in December; and so dilatory had been the Committee of Council appointed to take charge of her funeral, that the House of Lords had been forced to take charge of the proceedings, and had appointed Lords Halifax and Nottingham as its representatives. This naturally detained them in town and Lord Halifax chafed in vain. An early date in April was, however, at length settled. Lord Eland left London, but his father, possibly kept back by political engagements, did not accompany him.

On 30 March, accordingly, Lord Halifax attended as usual—though as the event proved, for the last time—the debates in which he had borne for twenty-eight years so conspicuous a part.

On the following day, a Sunday, he seemed unusually well, declared to his friends that he had not felt better for years; and at supper, as a contemporary notes, 'eat (*sic*) very plentifully of a roasted pullet, which his lady thought not to be roasted enough, and desired him not to eat of it, but could not prevail; he declaring he liked it very well, and having a good appetite and digestion it would not hurt him. But in the night he was taken very ill and vomited much'. The violence of the spasms aggravated the condition of a neglected rupture, and his state became extremely critical; but so great was his solicitude for the completion of his son's marriage, that he countermanded a summons to Lord Eland 'lest the festivities should be disturbed'. The marriage was accordingly solemnized on 2 April; and Lord Nottingham on the following day wrote his congratulations to the Marquis in a charming letter, which probably never reached him. For at the moment it was written the state of the Marquis had become desperate; and an express having been at length dispatched to Exton, Lord Halifax prepared for the end.

Cunningham—who always displays a relentless antipathy to Burnet[33]—declared that Halifax expressly refused the professional services of the Bishop 'lest he should triumph over him after his death'; by claiming the credit of a conversion, as he had done in the case of Lord Rochester. Be that as it may, it is clear that at the express desire of the dying man, Dr Birch was summoned. The choice seems a natural one. Not only was Dr Birch chaplain to the House of Commons, but he had been appointed in 1692 by the Bishop of London to the rectorship of St James's, Piccadilly, the parish church of St James's Square. The Crown, however—some say from political reasons—had claimed the patronage; and the dispute had been decided in January 1694/5 against Dr Birch.

'When', says Burnet, in his contemporary record, possibly on Dr Birch's authority, 'he was warned that his condition was hopeless, he showed a great firmness of mind and composed himself to die with a calm that had much of a true philosopher in it. He professed himself to be a sincere Christian, and expressed great resentment [sense] of many former parts of his life, with settled resolutions of becoming quite another man, if God should have raised him up.' Even more impressive is the very obvious reference in a letter of Burnet dated some two years later: 'I have known some who have delighted mightily in the writing of paradoxes and for that reason passed as Atheists, who yet I am sure were not so, as appeared at their deaths.' He requested, says a letter in the Hatton correspondence, the administration of the Communion, and on 4 April received that sacrament 'very devoutly' and with 'great humility and submission'; expressing 'with great Christian piety' resignation 'to the Will of Heaven'.

At the same time being, as he himself informs us, 'though weak in body yet of perfect memory and understanding, praised be God for it', he secured, by codicil to his will, annuities to his servants, and small legacies to the poor of the parish, to the Charterhouse, of which he was a Governor, and to the French Protestant refugees.

About five o'clock the next afternoon, Lord Eland arrived post haste from Exton. By that time his father was speechless, and it was thought knew nobody. But as soon as Lord Eland came to the bedside, though he could not speak, he reached out his arms and embraced him. An hour later, at six o'clock on the evening of Friday, 5 April 1695, Lord Halifax breathed his last. He had attained his sixty-first year.

The suddenness of his death gave rise in certain quarters to an extraordinary rumour, that his death had been hastened by poison, in revenge of his Parliamentary opposition.

He was buried by his express desire and without ostentation in Westminster Abbey, then the usual place of interment for dwellers in St James's Square.

His wife—the 'dear wife' of his last will—survived him for thirty-two years. She died 1 October 1727, at the age of eighty-six, and was buried, by her express wish, at the side of her 'dear Lord'. Dr Maty, the family biographer—and eulogist—of the Stanhope race said that hers was the best influence under which her orphan grandson, the celebrated Earl of Chesterfield, ever passed. The latter himself always remembered seeing the old Dukes of Leeds and Montague at her house, the daily amicable resort of these old enemies.

On the first marriage of William, Lord Eland, the Rufford estates had been settled, in default of direct heirs, on the Saviles of Lupset. By an earlier codicil to his will, Halifax had left to a young 'godson', George Savile, representative of that House, the sum of £1000 towards the expenses of his education, expressly that he might be better qualified for his inheritance, should he succeed to the family baronetcy and estates.

The second Marquis also dying without male issue, the young man did so succeed, and became ancestor of Sir George, the well-known eighteenth-century reformer. Through his sister the estates passed to the Earl of Scarborough whose descendants assumed the additional name of Savile; and it is from the name of Savile that the Rufford estates have but now passed away.

Lord Halifax has been generally regarded as having left an illegitimate son. Henry Carey, the poet, grandfather of Edmund Kean, claims to have received a pension from the Savile family, and always declared himself the son of the 'Marquis of Halifax'. But Carey, eighteen years after the death of his reputed father, described himself as still 'very young,' a phrase which then bore a less extended significance than at present. Moreover, it was, in fact, the *second* and last Marquis who by a deathbed codicil to his will, charged his estate with an annuity of fifty-five pounds, to be disposed 'as I have directed by word of mouth'. We may therefore conclude that there has been a mistake as to the generation concerned, and that the testator was acknowledging a moral responsibility of his own, or more probably, of a brother.

And now, to conclude, how shall we sum up the character and intellect of the great man, whose career we have so far followed?

That he was a great man, even his contemporaries—few of whom attempted to understand, and many of whom cordially disliked, him—would have universally allowed. That he was a man of marked individuality, all would have conceded. That he was a man in many respects in advance of his time, it was left to the nineteenth-century to discover; and we can even maintain with Dr Garnett that as a statesman he would have found himself most at his ease in the days of Queen Victoria. For thus he would have certainly escaped many of the pitfalls by which, during his brief terms of office, he was persistently thwarted; and would have found, from some quarters and on some questions, sympathy with not a few points of view which, to the men of his own day, appeared fantastic.

He believed for instance in compulsory education at the public cost. He advocated religious toleration; though, under existing conditions, he saw in the political pretensions of Rome, grave reason for restriction. He perceived that Ireland had grievances, which called for redress. His colonial policy, could he have urged it a century later, might have spared us the breach with America. In our own day he would have championed a sane Imperialism; visualizing, as he did, our nation as rooted in the sea and sending forth its branches to both the Indies. Admittedly, most Englishmen of his time (the Stuart princes not excepted) were at one as to the necessity for a powerful navy; but no man in his day so insistently stressed the importance of sea power. Moreover, and in another direction, he was undoubtedly prophetic. He clearly foresaw the enormous powers, for good or evil, which inhere in political organization, as contrasted with mere numerical superiority.

He was, in fact, as regards the age in which he lived, remarkably unconventional. We have noted the variety of strains which contributed to his character. Quite as important were those circumstances of his youth which must have fostered, and indeed forced, a premature development of self-confidence and originality. He had known while yet a boy the miseries of civil war, and the trials of exile; and had learnt in more than one European environment to form his unfettered judgments of men and things, rather than of books. He had spent but a few months at an English grammar school; and only two references in his works show traces of a classical education. A brief interlude at a French university may account for a fluent French style and a passion for Montaigne, besides giving to his English prose a touch of ease and lightness rare in his own day.

Nor was he either in temperament or taste characteristically insular. Suave rather than hearty, caustic rather than morose, and not altogether free from an occasional tinge of affectation, no one ever less resembled the typical John Bull. A certain delicacy of constitution may explain for us the country gentleman who abjured field sports, rarely if ever mounted a horse, went to Newmarket as to penance, and comparatively early abandoned his ancestral seat for a villa at Acton; but even more remarkable is the entire absence in his writings of any allusion whatever to English Literature, the English version of the Bible alone excepted.

Yet, strange as it must appear, this was the man, of whom it can be said, that no one ever showed himself more passionately attached to the land of his birth; no one ever entertained a clearer sense of the national character, interests, and destiny; no one ever evinced a stronger infusion of that saving common-sense which is the heritage of the race.

His outlook, however, though wide, was in one direction restricted. From the hour—or perhaps even before the hour—that he entered the House of Lords, to the moment when he passed its doors, three days before his death, his time and attention were devoted to politics. And in politics it was the great trends and issues alone which really attracted him. Though a master of Parliamentary forms he had none of Shaftesbury's keen interest and undoubted talent for the day by day minutiae of departmental work; and seems indeed on some occasions to have been regrettably careless in matters of detail. It was when confronted with questions of principle that he was in his element.

As regards his own career, if he effected few things of moment, if he was greater in opposition than in office, the times in which he lived offer a sufficient explanation. For under the two last Stuarts, and again under the quasi-Stuart William III, no great and honest minister could hope for a prolonged tenure of power. The French and Roman proclivities of the first two, and the natural and deeply rooted Dutch prepossessions of the third, together with the rancorous party feuds of 1689–95, forbade it. Only one minister—the subtle 'knave' Sunderland—retained office for long periods under all three. Indeed, none of the later Stuarts was ever restrained, save by force or subtlety, from going his own way; and reason, rather than driving force or intrigue, was the appropriate weapon of Halifax.

So it was only in opposition, or when circumstances for a brief period gave him a free hand, that Halifax rose to his height; and then it may have become his magnificent fate to have twice saved his country from the ravages of civil war.

His own general policy, whether in office or in opposition, was simple and consistent. His first object was always to secure these islands and their dependencies from foreign interference, dynastic or ecclesiastical. With this end in view he necessarily worked for a balance of power on the neighbouring Continent; for only by an overgrown, aggressive, and predatory power can our national interests be threatened.

At home he was equally concerned to preserve, in the interest of the average citizen, our Laws, our Liberties, and our Unity as a nation. This, in his eyes, demanded a Balance of Power as between Executive and Legislature, between Crown and Parliament; and it was his object so to 'trim' the barque of State as to keep her on an even keel. With this object it was necessary for him to throw his own weight now on one side, now on another.

He does not, however, seem to have realized how little such a course of procedure could have been understood by the rank and file of politicians; or what bitterness can be excited by manœuvres which, to the purely party mind, seem born either of personal ambition, mere intrigue, or rank apostasy.

Perhaps—though the House of Lords was his most appropriate ultimate sphere—he would have profited by a longer initial experience in the more numerous and popular assembly. He might there have got into closer touch with public opinion in all parts of the Kingdom; and have become more intimately known, through their representatives, to electors all over the country. For public men had not then the opportunities they now have for explaining themselves to the world; and his pamphlets, being all anonymous, could recommend his policies but not his person. More House of Commons experience in earlier life might also have taught him that public ridicule is the last thing the average Englishman forgives; and have induced him to curb that exquisite sense of the ludicrous, from which nothing was safe; neither the faith in whose essence he sincerely believed, nor the enemies it was his interest to conciliate.

In his private life he seems to have lived up to the requirements of his own religious ideal, whatever may have been its exact form. An affectionate husband, an admirable brother, a careful and anxious if not conspicuously successful father; a staunch friend, and (in general) a placable enemy; a kind and considerate employer, just and equal in all his dealings—he seems to have been free from all the grosser vices of his time, and in fact to have been 'temperate in all things'. Perhaps therefore even the most rigidly orthodox would acknowledge, that despite the flippant excesses of an ungovernably sarcastic tongue, our statesman, through life, at least did justly, loved mercy, and—in his heart of hearts—walked humbly with his God.

Of his Works, to which this volume should be only an Introduction, enough has been said by the way; and if it leads some to the perusal or reperusal of these masterpieces, it will have served the writer's purpose. And perhaps none of us would be the worse for being reminded—by one who so successfully 'turned to scorn the falsehood of extremes'—that 'circumstances are to come in and are to be made a part of the matter of which we are to judge; positive* decisions are always dangerous, more especially in politics.'

* I.e. theoretic.

Notes and References

(*See* PREFACE)

ıge 7, *note* 1:
For all this, see Miss Phare, *Review of English Studies*, IX, 62.

p. 13, *n*. 2:
For letters of Lady Chicheley, see Lady Newton's *Lyme Letters*, and *House of Lyme*. For other references to her, consult *Life and Works of the First Marquis of Halifax*, index.

p. 13, *n*. 3:
At p. 57, vol. I, of *Life and Works of the First Marquis of Halifax* there is a list of Savile properties with figures appended; conjecturally interpreted by the present writer in terms of acres, roods and perches. These Mr C. N. Clarke suggests should be replaced by '*£. s. d.*'

p. 23, *n*. 4:
These allusions may refer to his reckless passion for Lady Northumberland.

p. 28, *n*. 5:
See Harris, *Life of Sandwich*, II, 230–1.

p. 33, *n*. 6:
For all this consult Hartmann's *Clifford*; Miss Brown's *Shaftesbury*; and Miss Barbour's *Arlington*, pp. 154, 157 and 261; also Hartmann's *Charles II and Madame*, especially p. 342.

p. 44, *n*. 7:
'An appeal from the private Cabal at Whitehall', etc. Presumably written by Pierre du Moulin, who had been working in Arlington's office, and was at this time probably Secretary to the Prince of Orange. See Miss Browne's *Shaftesbury*; and Miss Barbour's *Arlington*, pp. 201, 205.

p. 46, *n*. 8:
See Miss Browne's *Shaftesbury* for reference to a letter, signed by all three ambassadors, before leaving the Continent; and seen by her at Record Office (State Papers, Holland).

p. 46, *n*. 9:
Klopp, *Fall des Hauses Stuart*, II, 71, 408.

p. 81, *n*. 10:
This poem is by Marvell, and contains satirical allusions to both the Coventry's.

p. 100, *n*. 11:
Published in *Camden Miscellany*, vol. XV.

p. 112, *n.* 12:

The present writer's attention was drawn to this publication by Mrs Robertson-Glasgow, now owner of the pictures mentioned on p. 3 of this work.

p. 116, *n.* 13:

Bodleian Library Carte MS. 77, pp. 649–51. Published by Mr de Beer in the *Bulletin of the Institute of Historical Research*, xx (1946), 22–37.

p. 118, *n.* 14:

See *p.* 116, *n.* 13.

p. 132, *n.* 15:

A conjectural but obviously correct emendation of the 'N. Chevins' in Cooper's *Savile Correspondence*. William Chiffinch was the page of the back-stairs at whose house Charles II held private and convivial interviews. See Scott's *Peveril of the Peak*.

p. 175, *n.* 16:

The episode of the 'Quo Warranto' writs is perhaps the most obscure in the history of Halifax. Mr de Beer (and through him, Professor Thomson) has been good enough to contribute to the substance of the following summary.

It seems established: (1) that the legal validity or invalidity of the warrants, and consequently of their passing the Seal has never been decided. (2) That the exact terms of the revised Charters have not been studied. (3) That no allusion to the matter occurs in the published works or known letters of Halifax. (4) That all the reported allusions of Halifax to the subject are ambiguous; excepting the one printed on our p. 175. But this comes to us from the *Diary of Reresby*; and the expression 'do well' may be the diarist's. Of what Halifax said to Charles II, we know nothing.

Finally, it would be interesting to make a complete study of the effect which these 'regulations' may have had on the composition of James II's complacent Parliament of 1685.

p. 202, *n.* 17:

It must be remembered in considering the action of Halifax during the earlier 'Popish Plot' revelations, that strong suspicion centred upon Somerset House, the residence of Queen Catherine. Mr Pollock, in his *Popish Plot* (1903), argues that these suspicions were not without foundation, and thinks it possible that Sir Edmundberry Godfrey was actually murdered there, though not by the unfortunate men who were executed for the crime; and of course, without the connivance of the Queen. Moreover, before 1679 or 1680, it is unlikely that Halifax had any personal acquaintance with Queen Catherine.

p. 233, *n.* 18:
See Klopp, III, 205–6, 240, 280.

p. 236, *n.* 19:
I.e., the great victory of the Emperor over the Turks. (See Klopp *in loco*).

p. 239, *n.* 20:
Mr Hugh Macdonald has seen a copy of the pirated version in the British Museum.

p. 240, *n.* 21:
Klopp, III, 205–6, 231, 284, 285.

p. 250, *n.* 22:
See Klopp, IV, 9, 10 for the preparations against invasion actually made.

p. 251, *n.* 23:
There was published in Edinburgh in 1706 a condensed version ingeniously adapted to the 'Equivalents' offered Scotland in return, for the Union. It then appeared under the name of Halifax.

p. 256, *n.* 24:
See Klopp, IV, 175–6, 228, 248. He quotes C. de Cavelli.

p. 257, *n.* 25:
Cunningham, Alexander, *History of Great Britain*, I, 86–7.

p. 263, *n.* 26:
For the rest of the page, see *Hist. MSS. Comm.* VIII, p. 555.

p. 265, *n.* 27:
See Klopp, IV, 278.

p. 265, *n.* 28:
See Klopp, IV, 280, 288.

p. 271, *n.* 29:
See Klopp, IV, 293, from Campana de Cavelli.

p. 285, *n.* 30:
James, afterwards third Lord Talbot de Malahide, the present writer's great-grandfather, was introduced, while in Italy during the first quarter of the nineteenth century, to the Countess of Albany. She pointed to a cabinet in her sitting-room and said: 'Papers in that cabinet could ruin half the great families in England.'

p. 326, *n.* 31:
For further details see 'Sidelights on Catherine of Braganza' by the present author, *Longman's Magazine*, March, 1899.

p. 334, *n.* 32:
Cunningham, I, 146.

p. 335, *n.* 33:
Cunningham, I, 146.

INDEX